# DYNAMIC ECONOMICS

# DYNAMIC ECONOMICS

## Optimization by the Lagrange Method

GREGORY C. CHOW

New York Oxford
Oxford University Press
1997

Oxford University Press

Oxford New York
Athens Auckland Bangkok Bogota Bombay Buenos Aires
Calcutta Cape Town Dar es Salaam Delhi Florence Hong Kong
Istanbul Karachi Kuala Lumpur Madras Madrid Melbourne
Mexico City Nairobi Paris Singapore Taipei Tokyo Toronto

and associated companies in
Berlin Ibadan



Published by Oxford University Press, Inc.
198 Madison Avenue, New York, New York 10016



Library of Congress Cataloging-in-Publication Data
Chow, Gregory C., 1929–
Dynamic economics: optimization by the Lagrange method / by Gregory C. Chow.
p. cm.
Includes bibliographical references and index.
ISBN 0-19-510192-8
1. Mathematical optimization. 2. Multipliers (Mathematical analysis) 3. Equilibrium (Economics) 4. Statics and dynamics (Social sciences) 5. Economic development. I. Title.
HB143.7.C46 1997 96-25957
330'.01'51—dc20

9 8 7 6 5 4 3 2

Printed in the United Sates of America
on acid-free paper

*To Paula*

# Preface

Classical economic ideas, beginning with those recorded in Adam Smith's *Wealth of Nations* (1776), have been refined, improved, and challenged. Two main ideas are that individuals pursue self-interests (or maximize utility and profits in a "rational" manner) and that markets can coordinate individual self-interests for the common good (or achieve a competitive equilibrium which is Pareto optimal) without government intervention. Observing the poverty of British workers in the 19th century, Karl Marx rejected these ideas. Witnessing the Great Depression in the 1930s Keynes wrote the *General Theory* (1936) and started a revolution against classical economics. Later the ideas of classical economics have been recovering from the Keynesian attack, to a large extent through the efforts of University of Chicago economists, beginning with Milton Freidman in the 1950s. Thus, the two main ideas of classical economics, the rationality of economic agents and the efficiency of markets, have gone through refinement and challenge. This book reports on the development of the economic ideas of self-interest and market equilibrium from the 1960s to the 1990s.

As the subtitle indicates, dynamic economic behavior is explained by assuming rationality of economic agents who optimize. Much of the book presents models in which markets are both clear and efficient. Both ideas are opposed to the main ideas of Keynes' *General Theory*. When I studied dynamic economics in the early 1970s, the idea of using optimization as the basis of dynamic economics was not as widely accepted as it is today. [See my *Analysis and Control of Dynamic Economic Systems* (1975, p. 22).] Today, some leading economists—including Robert Solow, who is the father of modern growth theory—do not believe that optimization together with market equilibrium is necessarily the way to model economic behavior. [See Solow's article "Perspective on Growth Theory," *Journal of Economic Perspectives* (1994, pp. 45–54) and his recent book *A Critical Essay on Modern Macroeconomic Theory* (MIT Press, 1995), coauthored with Frank Hahn.] Without taking a stand, I present in this book the optimization framework for dynamic economics so that readers can understand the approach and use it as they see fit.

Once optimization is selected as the main theme for dynamic economics, there is a choice of the method of dynamic optimization. In this book, the choice is clear. It is the method of Lagrange multipliers rather than dynamic programming. From the methodological point of view, much of this book contains applications of the method of Lagrange multipliers to modeling dynamic economic behavior. As a by-product, it will convince most readers that this method is easier and more efficient than dynamic programming. Being able to economize on the tool, the reader can understand the substance of dynamic economics better.

When I first worked on dynamic optimization as it is applied to macroeconomic policy (*Journal of Money, Credit and Banking*, 1970, pp. 291–302), I used the method of Lagrange multipliers. The Lagrange method and dynamic programming were presented in my 1975 book in chapters 7 and 8, respectively. I applied the method in special cases, mainly in the case of a quadratic objective function and a linear dynamic model. Not until 1991, did I discover that, for the general case, the Lagrange method can and should (for most applications) replace dynamic programming, as I wrote in *Economic Modelling* (January, 1992) and *Journal of Economic Dynamics and Control* (July, 1993). In the last three years, in research and teaching, I found the Lagrange method so much more convenient to use that I decided to record my experience in this book and share it with interested readers.

Dynamic economics has experienced rapid growth in the last three decades. This book provides a unified and simple treatment of the subject using dynamic optimization as the main theme and using the method of Lagrange multipliers to solve dynamic optimization problems. That economic agents try to maximize an objective function subject to resource constraints is a fundamental tenet of economic theory. This tenet is adopted to explain economic behavior at one instance of time and the evolution of economic behavior through time. The use of the Lagrange method allows the author to treat different topics in economics, including economic growth, macroeconomics, microeconomics, finance, and dynamic games. It also allows the treatment to be presented in an elementary level that makes the text accessible to first-year graduate students.

This book is written as a reference or a supplementary text for first-year graduate courses in macroeconomics (by using chapters 2, 3, 4, and 5), microeconomics (by using chapters 2 and 3, section 5.6, and chapters 6 and 8), mathematics for economists, and finance (by using chapters 2, 7, 8, and 9). It could be used as a text for a graduate course or an advanced undergraduate course on dynamic economics. It can also be used by researchers who would like to learn dynamic economics without the requirement of advanced mathematics. Because dynamic optimization or optimal control is a set of tools useful in operations research, engineering, and other applied fields, students and researchers in these other areas may also benefit from reading this book.

As human knowledge accumulates, the education process becomes more efficient. Holders of bachelor's and doctoral degrees today know much more than their counterparts three decades ago. For more knowledge to be acquired in the same interval of time, university education has to be and has become more efficient. Efficiency is achieved by presenting once difficult and advanced concepts in easier and more elementary forms. The writing of this book illustrates the simplification of knowledge in the study of economics.

Like many other fields of knowledge, dynamic economics is a field that has gone through a rapid development in the last three decades. Many ideas and concepts were discovered using advanced and difficult mathematical tools. As these ideas become better understood, they can be presented in a more elementary and simple fashion. A solid background in intermediate-level economics, in multivariate calculus, and in mathematical statistics is sufficient for reading most of this book. Of course, presenting the subject in an elementary fashion may sacrifice mathematical rigor and leaves some fundamental theorems unproved, as in the case of teaching calculus to beginning students. The gain is that the tools so presented can be more easily understood and hence more readily applied to solve economic problems. Most of this book should be accessible to first-year graduate students and a small fraction of advanced undergraduate students. It is hoped that a future edition of this book that incorporates further improvements in exposition should be accessible to a larger fraction of undergraduates.

Besides being elementary, this book teaches by using examples. Rather than introducing concepts in general forms, it begins by using the concepts and tools to solve simple problems. After learning the methods through examples, the reader is encouraged to apply them to solve other problems provided at the end of each chapter. Human beings learn by examples encountered in their daily experience. After they learn from particular examples, they generalize and summarize their experience in the form of general propositions. This process of learning and generalizing occurs not only in scientific inference through induction, but also in the discovery of mathematical theorems through deduction. Mathematicians have confirmed that, while they state their results in general theorems, they have often discovered them by encountering and thinking through simple examples in special cases. By introducing examples before stating general results, this book allows the reader to go through a common learning process. Some might argue that stating a general theorem first, before illustrating it by examples, is a more efficient way of teaching, even if it is not the way that the theorem was first discovered. It certainly is a more efficient way of presenting results in mathematics, but it may or may not be a more efficient way of teaching a subject. The author is not opposed to the other style of presentation, but merely makes a case for his own style and recognizes that both have merits. A list of mathematical statements is provided at the end of the book for lease of reference.

Teaching by using examples applies also to the discussion of substantive economics, in addition to the discussion of analytical techniques. The subject matter of each chapter is presented by discussing theories and models proposed by different authors, in addition to stating general approaches to the subject. Readers may learn to formulate their own theories and solve new problems in dynamic economics by studying how others have done so. Readers are encouraged to learn by using the techniques and formulations presented and illustrated here.

I acknowledge the congenial intellectual atmosphere provided at the Economics Department of Princeton University under the able chairmanship of Stephen Goldfeld and Harvey Rosen, which made the writing this book possible. Many students have worked through drafts of various chapters and helped me understand the subject and improve the writing. Colleagues and friends who have commented on and contributed ideas to this book include, among others, Andrew Abel, Dilip Abreu, Giuseppe Bertola, Alberto Bisin, Claudia Choi, Avinash Dixit, Y. K. Kwan, Robin Lumsdaine, Richard Quandt, Mark Watson, Harald Uhlig, and Dahai Yu. To all of them, I express my sincere thanks. Thanks also to Cynthia Cohen, who has typed drafts of the manuscript with efficiency and cheer.

*Princeton, New Jersey*
*February, 1996*

G. C. C.

# Contents

# DYNAMIC ECONOMICS

## CHAPTER ONE

# Introduction

## 1.1 Dynamic Economics and Optimization

Dynamic economics is concerned with explaining economic behavior through time. Because economic behavior of individuals and enterprises always occurs through time, should all of economics be dynamic economics? No, because of the power of abstraction in scientific theorizing. Of course, all behavior occurs through time. Yet, without explicitly taking into account the temporal aspects of behavior, economists are able to explain a great deal of economic behavior. For example, static demand theory implies that if the price goes up, the quantity demanded goes down. The price and quantity referred to are supposed to be observed in the same time period. The price is the price on a certain Wednesday, and the quantity is the amount purchased on that same Wednesday. The term *dynamic economics* is used because there was a long period in its development when much of economic theorizing ignored the dynamic aspects of economic behavior and failed to explain the time paths of economic variables. Built on the method of comparative statics, economic theory explains only the directions of change of economic variables resulting from a change in the parameters, but it does not date the changes at each instance of time. Dynamic economics can explain the time paths of economic variables.

How do economists explain the time paths of economic variables? At an early stage of the development of dynamic economics in the 1950s and 1960s, a significant portion of dynamic theories is ad hoc. Starting with a static theory explaining a variable $y$ by a variable $x$, delayed effects of $x$ can be introduced by using distributed lags to obtain a dynamic theory. For example if $y_t$ at time $t$ is assumed to equal $\beta x + \gamma y_{t-1}$, the time path $y_t$ for $t = 1, 2, \ldots$ is determined once the initial value $y_0$ and the time path $x_t$ for $t = 1, 2, \ldots$ are given. Baumol (1951) is a good exposition of dynamic economics as it was known at the time, as is Allen (1956), which appeared a few years later. Many of the models introduced are based on ad hoc assumptions. The main tool of analysis was difference equations. The building of dynamic econometric models from the 1950s to the 1970s was also characterized by the introduction of ad hoc assumptions concerning the lagged effects of economic variables. Distributed lags were estimated from the data empirically without much guidance from economic theory. Not until the late 1970s did economists begin to adopt, as a general principle, the method of economic theorizing based on maximizing behavior in the study of dynamic economic phenomena in the same way that the method had been applied in the formulation of static theories.

My opinion concerning the role of optimization in dynamic economic theory in the early 1970s was as follows (Chow, 1975, p. 20):

> From the practical point of view we have dynamic macroeconomic models that are built from a combination of theory (of whatever kind) and statistical measurement, and these econometric models deserve to be studied by the methods of dynamics described. Furthermore, we introduce methods of optimization over time for the purpose of improving the dynamic performance of an economy—methods that will be useful for those theorists who wish to derive dynamic economic theories from optimization over time and presumably under uncertainty. There is no need to entertain the question whether the basis of static economics under certainty, namely maximizing behavior, should always be extended to the study of dynamic behavior over time under uncertainty. Possibly, or possibly not, maximizing behavior is a better approximation to human situations in which time and uncertainty are less relevant.

An important concept in economics, perhaps the most important, is optimization. Because economics deals with the optimum allocation of resources to achieve a given objective, economic agents are assumed to maximize an objective function subject to resource constraints. In dynamic economics, the choice is among the use of resources in different time periods. Maximizing a multiperiod objective function of variables in many periods, subject to budget and resource constraints on these variables through time, constitutes a basic method for theorizing in dynamic economics.

In this book, I use dynamic optimization as a unifying theme to study some important problems in dynamic economics, just as constrained maximization has served as a unifying theme for much of static economics since the publication of Hicks (1939) and Samuelson (1948). The topics to be studied include economic growth, theories of market equilibrium, business cycles, dynamic games, models in finance, models of investment, and numerical methods of dynamic optimization. Because these topics are studied from one unifying point of view, the coverage of each topic is selective and not complete. Nevertheless, the use of dynamic optimization as a unifying theme enables an understanding of the important elements of each topic and the relationship among different topics. Another objective of this book is to provide an elementary exposition of dynamic economics and to make the topics covered more easily accessible. Drawing from a variety of sources, some of which are difficult to read, the exposition provided facilitates understanding these topics. A final objective is to introduce the Lagrange method for dynamic optimization under uncertainty as an alternative and a supplement to dynamic programming. In the middle 1990s, researchers and teachers have been trained to use dynamic programming and will continue to use it for some time because they are familiar with it. However, in this book, I will demonstrate that for most applications the Lagrange method is analytically simpler and numerically more accurate. The Lagrange method suggested here is essentially a generalization of Pontryagin's maximum principle to the case of uncertainty in which the dynamic model in the optimization problem is stochastic. To solve dynamic optimization problems under certainty, students and researchers have found Pontryagin's maximum principle useful and often more convenient than dynamic programming. For similar reasons, which are partly stated in section 1.2, students and researchers should also find the Lagrange method useful and often more convenient than dynamic programming in solving many dynamic optimization problems under uncertainty.

Dynamic economics experienced rapid growth in the 1960s and 1970s. The growth was partly stimulated by the analysis of dynamic econometric models and the use of these models for policy analysis. Chow (1975) reports on some of the work done since the 1960s, and on the analysis and formulation of optimum policies based on dynamic econometric models. The method of dynamic programming advanced by Bellman (1957) has been a main tool for optimization over time under uncertainty. In addition, since the early 1970s, the use of optimal control techniques for the formulation and analysis of macroeconomic policy and for the characterization of macroeconometric models has been an important activity in applied economics.

In the middle 1970s, in academic circles, doubts were expressed on such uses of optimal control methods by some critics, notably Lucas (1976). Following the early ideas of Marschak (1953), Lucas points out that if government policy changes, rational economic agents will take that change into account and make corresponding changes in their own decision rules that are behavioral equations of econometric models. Hence, an econometrician cannot assume that the equations of the econometric models are fixed when assisting the government in designing an optimal decision rule. Applied economists continued to use econometric models for policy analysis, believing that the changes in the parameters of the behavioral equations of econometric models alluded to by Lucas are too small or too slow in practice to seriously affect the usefulness of optimal control calculations using econometric models. Lucas is correct in principle, but how relevant or how frequently is his point encountered in practice?

Sims (1980, pp. 12–13) answers this question by stating that Lucas' point is rarely relevant because, in practice, econometricians seldom assist the government in changing a policy rule or regime. A policy rule can be expressed in the form of a reaction function. For example, a reaction function may specify a monetary policy variable as a function of observed states of the economy including, for example, real output, inflation rate, and unemployment rate. Sims observes that such policy rules or reaction functions are seldom changed. Otherwise, econometric models estimated by using data that span several decades without structural breaks cannot be useful. In performing optimal control exercises using an existing econometric model, an econometrician merely assists the government in implementing an existing policy rule and not a change in the policy rule. In other words, a reaction function is a means by which econometricians describe government behavior, just as a demand function is a means for describing consumer behavior. To derive a reaction function or a demand function, the economist assumes that the government or the consumer is implicitly performing some maximization exercises; the former maximizes a social objective function, and the latter maximizes a utility function. The econometricians are assisting the government in computing its existing reaction function and not, in most econometric policy exercises, in designing a new reaction function or policy regime. The application of optimal control techniques for government policy analysis is like the application of mathematical programming and other techniques taught in business schools to assist firms to maximize profits. While the debate on the usefulness and limitations of macroeconometric models in policy analysis goes on in academic circles, practitioners continue to use such models and optimal control methods, partly to understand the dynamic characteristics of the econometric models used and partly to assist the government in implementing a given policy regime.

Econometric models are defined as "structural" if the parameters do not change when a policy regime changes. Such a definition of structural parameters underlied the research of the members of the Cowles Commission at the University of Chicago when they proposed simultaneous structural equations in econometrics, as aptly pointed out by Marschak (1953). Some economists later believed that simultaneous equations models built by profitmaking model builders are not structural in the sense of being invariant after policy regime shifts. If a regime shift does occur (though rarely), to build models with invariant structural parameters, one should start from a model of optimizing behavior on the part of economic agents who are assumed to solve a dynamic optimization problem under uncertainty. The parameters of the optimization problem are the structural parameters. Once these structural parameters are known, the behavioral equations of economic agents, or the reduced-form equations of the model, can be derived by using dynamic optimization techniques. When government decision rules change, because the rules are part of the environment facing the optimizing agents, the behavioral equations of the agents will also change. The new behavioral equations can be rederived by solving the dynamic optimization problem by using the new government decision rules as part of the environment. Hence, in addition to macroeconomic policy analysis from the viewpoint of the government under a fixed regime, dynamic optimization techniques can be used to study the behavior of nongovernment economic agents, which are assumed to optimize, over time, under uncertainty and to evaluate the economic effects of government policy changes viewed as changes in regimes. Dynamic programming and optimal control methods remain an indispensable tool of dynamic economics in either case. The former case assumes that the government optimizes and the latter assumes that the nongovernment economic agents optimize.

A theme of this book is that as long as optimization remains a key concept in economics, the method of Lagrange multipliers is a convenient tool to use. Dynamic optimization can be viewed as a constrained maximization problem. The tool to solve this problem is the method of Lagrange multipliers; the same tool used in static economics as treated by Hicks (1939) and Samuelson (1948). In this book, I examine many dynamic economic problems by using the method of Lagrange multipliers. The reader will be able to learn the Lagrange method and to use it in future research. Each of the following sections introduces or summarizes the contents of one chapter of this book.

## 1.2 Methods of Dynamic Optimization

Consider a Robinson Crusoe economy in which the economic agent is assumed to live only two periods. Capital stock $x_1$ at the beginning of period 1 is given. The economic agent derives utility in period $t$ equal to a differentiable function $r(x_t, u_t)$, where $x_t$ is the quantity of capital stock and $u_t$ is the quantity of consumption at period $t$. As a special case, $x_t$ may not enter the utility function, but in general a capital good, such as an apple tree, may provide shade and a nice view besides yielding apples for consumption. Capital stock evolves through time according to

$$x_{t+1} = f(x_t, u_t) = \mathrm{A}x_t^{\alpha} - u_t$$

if one assumes that output (including depreciated capital stock from the previous period) is produced by a Cobb-Douglas production function $\mathrm{A}x_t^{\alpha}$, given one unit of labor, and can be used either for consumption $u_t$ or as future capital stock $x_{t+1}$. The economic agent's problem is to maximize

$$r(x_1, u_1) + \beta r(x_2, u_2)$$

in which $\beta$ is a subjective discount factor by choosing the optimum amounts of consumption $u_1$ and $u_2$ for the two periods. As $u_t$ is subject to the control of the agent, it is called a *control variable*; $x_t$ is called a *state variable*, the dynamic evolution of which has to be specified in an optimization problem.

Assume that both $r$ and $f$ are differentiable and concave (i.e., having negative second partial derivatives) and that the solution is an interior solution. By the method of *dynamic programming*, one begins by solving the problem for the last period and completes the following five steps.

*Step 1.* Maximize $\beta r(x_2, u_2)$ with respect to $u_2$ by differentiation and obtain an *optimum decision function* for $u_2$ as a function $g_2(x_2)$ of $x_2$.

$$\frac{\partial r(x_2, u_2)}{\partial u_2} = 0 \quad \Rightarrow \quad u_2 = g_2(x_2)$$

*Step 2.* Evaluate the *value function* $\mathrm{V}_2(x_2)$ for the second period by substituting the optimum decision function $g_2(x_2)$ for $u_2$ in the objective function in the problem of Step 1.

$$V_2(x_2) = r(x_2, g_2(x_2))$$

*Step 3*. Form an objective function for the 2-period problem of periods 1 and 2 by substituting $V_2(x_2)$ for $r(x_2, u_2)$.

$$r(x_1, u_1) + \beta r(x_2, u_2) = r(x_1, u_1) + \beta V_2(x_2)$$

*Step 4*. Using the dynamic model, substitute $f(x_1, u_1)$ for $x_2$ in the objective function in Step 3.

$$r(x_1, u_1) + \beta V_2(f(x_1, u_1))$$

*Step 5*. Maximize the objective function of Step 4 with respect to $u_1$ by differentiation and obtain an optimum decision function for $u_1$ as a function of $x_1$.

$$\frac{\partial r(x_1, u_1)}{\partial u_1} + \beta \frac{\partial f(x_1, u_1)}{\partial u_1} \cdot \frac{\partial V_2}{\partial x_2} = 0 \quad \Rightarrow \quad u_1 = g_1(x_1)$$

When $g_1(x_1)$ is substituted for $u_1$ in the above expression, the result is the value function $V_1(x_1)$ for period 1. The result can be summarized by the following *Bellman equation*

$$V_1(x_1) = \max_{u_1}\{r(x_1, u_1) + \beta V_2(x_2)\}$$

For problems involving more than 2 periods, the subscript 1 above is replaced by $t$ and the subscript 2 by $t + 1$. If the value function $V_t(x_t)$ converges to some function $V(x_t)$ after solving the problem backward in time for many periods starting from the last period T, the subscripts $t$ and $t + 1$ of $V_t$ and $V_{t+1}$ can be dropped. When the value function reaches a *steady state* the *Bellman equation* becomes

$$V(x_t) = \max_{u_t}\{r(x_t, u_t) + \beta V(x_{t+1})\}$$

Solving this functional equation for $V(\cdot)$ yields the solution for the dynamic optimization problem.

By the method of Lagrange multipliers, one forms a Lagrangean expression by using the constraint of the dynamic model and by treating $x_1$ as given.

$$\mathcal{L} = r(x_1, u_1) + \beta r(x_2, u_2) - \beta\lambda_2(x_2 - f(x_1, u_1))$$

Setting to zero the derivatives with respect to $u_2$, $u_1$, and $x_2$ one obtains three first-order conditions

$$\frac{\partial \mathcal{L}}{\partial u_2} = \beta \frac{\partial r(x_2, u_2)}{\partial u_2} = 0$$

$$\frac{\partial \mathcal{L}}{\partial u_1} = \frac{\partial r(x_1, u_1)}{\partial u_1} + \beta \frac{\partial f(x_1, u_1)}{\partial u_1} \lambda_2 = 0$$

$$\frac{\partial \mathscr{L}}{\partial x_2} = \beta \frac{\partial r(x_2, u_2)}{\partial x_2} - \beta\lambda_2 = 0$$

which can be solved for $u_1$, $u_2$, and $\lambda_2$.

To compare the two methods, note that the first condition of the Lagrange method is identical with the condition from maximizing $\beta r(x_2, u_2)$ in Step 1 using dynamic programming. The second condition is also identical with the condition from maximizing $r(x_1, u_1) + \beta V_2(x_2)$ with respect to $u_1$ in Step 5 of dynamic programming, provided that $\lambda_2 = \partial V_2(x_2)/\partial x_2$. The difference is that the Lagrange method uses the third first-order condition to obtain $\lambda_2$ and avoids Steps 2, 3, and 4 of dynamic programming. If we consider

$$r(x_1, u_1) + \beta V_2(x_2)$$

as a function of two variables $u_1$ and $x_2$, subject to the constraint $x_2 = f(x_1, u_1)$, the Lagrange method introduces the constraint by using the multiplier $\lambda_2$, whereas dynamic programming substitutes $f(x_1, u_1)$ for $x_2$ in the value function $V_2(x_2)$. The Bellman equation fails to exploit an important first-order condition: $\partial\mathscr{L}/\partial x_2 = 0$. It is important to note that by either method, there is no need to know the value function $V_2(x_2)$. By dynamic programming, Step 5 requires only $\partial V_2/\partial x_2$ and not $V_2$ itself. Thus, trying to obtain the value function either analytically or numerically in Step 2 and to set up the objective function in Steps 3 and 4, as is done in practice when dynamic programming is used, amounts to finding a function and introducing steps that are unnecessary for obtaining the optimum. It is sometimes claimed that *backward induction* (solving a dynamic optimization problem backward in time) is a virtue of dynamic programming. The preceding example illustrates that backward induction is also applied in the Lagrange method, because the optimum control function for $u_2$ must be obtained first. Backward induction has nothing to do with keeping the value function. This is true for decision problems of one person or several persons, the latter case being demonstrated in section 6.4, equations (6.33) and (6.34).

Knowledge of the value function may have other uses than for deriving an optimum decision function. Some of its uses are discussed in this book. However, for solving the dynamic optimization problem knowledge of the Lagrange multiplier, or the Lagrange function, is necessary. One must find the Lagrange function to exploit all the first-order conditions for optimality by either method of dynamic programming or Lagrange multipliers. Hence, one's effort should be concentrated on obtaining the Lagrange function rather than the value function. There are circumstances in which the value function is easy to obtain by solving the Bellman equation. Under these circumstances one should, by all means, obtain the value function. To find the necessary Lagrange function, one simply differentiates the value function. In almost all economic applications that I have encountered, including those discussed in this book, the value function is more difficult, or at least not easier, to find than the Lagrange function. Hence, it is more efficient to seek the Lagrange function directly by the Lagrange method. I have applied the Lagrange method to solve a number of problems that were originally solved by dynamic programming. Notable examples showing the efficiency of the Lagrange method are contained in sections 3.1, 3.2, 4.1, 4.4, 6.2, and 7.5. Possible computational advantages of the Lagrange method are discussed in sections 2.4, 7.4, and chapter 9.

The Lagrange method is easier, because the value function demands and contains more information than is required. Given the value function, one can always find its derivatives, but more work is often required to obtain the value function itself from its derivatives, and such work is unnecessary. In the univariate case when the state variable $x_t$ is a scalar, often, the derivative of the value function is simpler than the value function itself. For example, if the value function is quadratic, the Lagrange function is linear. Even if the derivative is not simpler, one still needs the Lagrange function to solve the optimization problem using first-order conditions. In the multivariate case where $x_t$ is a vector, often the derivatives of the value function with respect to only a subset of but not all components of $x_t$ are required. This is the case when the dynamic evolution of some components of the vector of state variables $x_t$ does not depend on the vector of control variables $u_t$. The Lagrange multipliers are introduced only for those state variables that are constrained by the control variables. Notable examples are given in sections 3.1 and 3.2. In these cases, because the value function contains much more knowledge than required, it is likely to be more difficult to obtain than a subset of its partial derivatives. After the optimization problem is solved by the Lagrange method, the value function can be obtained by integrating the Lagrange functions or by substituting the optimum control function into the dynamic model to evaluate the objective function. These advantages of the Lagrange method remain valid for an optimization problem involving a stochastic model for the evolution of $x_t$, in both discrete and continuous time. In the stochastic case, the objective function is a mathematical expectation and, using the Lagrange method, one simply differentiates the Lagrange expression on the right side of the expectation operator. Optimization in discrete time and in continuous time is discussed in chapters 2 and 7, respectively.

In chapter 2, I explain both methods of dynamic optimization in discrete time more fully, provide a numerical method for solving the first-order conditions derived from the Lagrange method, discuss sufficient conditions for optimum, and relate the Lagrange method to well-known results on optimization in economics.

## 1.3 Economic Growth

A key problem of allocation of resources over time is the choice between current consumption and future consumption. By reducing current consumption, more resource is made available to augment the capital stock that can be used to produce consumption goods in the future. This statement is illustrated by the relationship discussed in section 1.2, namely

$$k_{t+1} = k_t^{\alpha} z_t - c_t \tag{1.1}$$

where in a one-good economy $k_t$ is the quantity of capital stock at the beginning of period $t$, $c_t$ is consumption in period $t$, and output (inclusive of depreciated capital input) is produced by the Cobb-Douglas production function, $k_t^\alpha z_t$ by using one unit of labor. $z_t$ is a measure of technology in period $t$ and is assumed to be given. For simplicity, the quantity of labor is assumed constant through time. Given the initial capital stock $k_0$, let the objective be to maximize the time-separable utility function for T + 1 periods

$$\sum_{t=0}^{\mathrm{T}} \beta^t \ln c_t$$

in which $\beta < 1$ denotes a subjective discount factor. The control variable is $c_t$, and the state variable is $k_t$.

Intertemporal choice can be understood by solving the above dynamic optimization problem. By using the method of Lagrange multipliers, we form the Lagrange expression

$$\mathscr{L} = \sum_{t=0}^{\mathrm{T}} \left\{ \beta^t \ln c_t - \beta^{t+1}\lambda_{t+1}\left(k_{t+1} - k_t^\alpha z_t + c_t\right)\right\} \tag{1.2}$$

As a matter of notation, the subscript of the Lagrange multiplier $\lambda_{t+1}$ matches that of the state variable $k_{t+1}$, which is subject to the dynamic constraint. $\beta^{t+1}$ is introduced so that $\lambda_{t+1}$ can be interpreted as the marginal contribution of $k_{t+1}$ to total multiperiod utility evaluated at period $t + 1$; $\lambda_{t+1}$ has to be discounted by $\beta^{t+1}$ to obtain the marginal contribution of $k_{t+1}$ valued at time 0. Without this factor $\beta^{t+1}$, $\lambda_{t+1}$ would mean the marginal contribution valued at time 0. Differentiating $\mathscr{L}$ with respect to $c_t$ and $k_t$ provides two first-order conditions

$$\beta^{-t}\frac{\partial \mathscr{L}}{\partial c_t} = c_t^{-1} - \beta\lambda_{t+1} = 0 \qquad t = 0,\ 1, \ldots,\ \mathrm{T} \tag{1.3}$$

$$\beta^{-t}\frac{\partial \mathscr{L}}{\partial k_t} = -\lambda_t + \beta\lambda_{t+1}\alpha k_t^{\alpha-1} z_t = 0 \qquad t = 1,\ 2, \ldots,\ \mathrm{T} \tag{1.4}$$

which can be solved for $c_t$ and $\lambda_t$, given equation (1.1).

Equations (1.3) and (1.4) can be solved backward in time, starting from the last period T. Because $k_{\mathrm{T}+1}$ provides no utility by assumption, it should be set equal to zero. To maximize utility in period T, consumption $c_T$ should equal the entire output $k_{\mathrm{T}}^\alpha z_{\mathrm{T}}$. Using $c_{\mathrm{T}}^{-1} = k_{\mathrm{T}}^{-\alpha} z_{\mathrm{T}}^{-1}$ to substitute for $\beta\lambda_{\mathrm{T}+1}$ in (1.4) gives $\lambda_{\mathrm{T}} = \alpha k_{\mathrm{T}}^{-1}$. For period T − 1, substitute for $\lambda_{\mathrm{T}}$ in (1.3) and use (1.1),

$$c_{\mathrm{T-1}}^{-1} = \beta\lambda_{\mathrm{T}} = \beta\alpha k_{\mathrm{T}}^{-1} = \beta\alpha\left(k_{\mathrm{T-1}}^\alpha z_{\mathrm{T-1}} - c_{\mathrm{T-1}}\right)^{-1}$$

yielding

$$c_{\mathrm{T-1}} = \left(1 + \beta\alpha\right)^{-1} k_{\mathrm{T-1}}^\alpha z_{\mathrm{T-1}}$$

Substituting for $\beta\lambda_{\mathrm{T}}$ in (1.4) gives

$$\lambda_{\mathrm{T-1}} = \left(1 + \beta\alpha\right)k_{\mathrm{T-1}}^{-\alpha} z_{\mathrm{T-1}}^{-1} \cdot \alpha k_{\mathrm{T-1}}^{\alpha-1} z_{\mathrm{T-1}} = \left(1 + \beta\alpha\right)\alpha k_{\mathrm{T-1}}^{-1}.$$

For period T − 2, substitute for $\lambda_{\mathrm{T-1}}$ in (1.3) and use (1.1),

$$c_{T-2}^{-1} = \beta\lambda_{T-1} = \beta\alpha(1+\beta\alpha)\left(k_{T-2}^{\alpha} z_{T-2} - c_{T-2}\right)^{-1}$$

yielding

$$c_{T-2} = \left[1+\beta\alpha(1+\beta\alpha)\right]^{-1} k_{T-2}^{\alpha} z_{T-2}.$$

Substituting for $\beta\lambda_{T-1}$ in (1.4) gives

$$\lambda_{T-2} = \left[1+\beta\alpha(1+\beta\alpha)\right]\alpha k_{T-2}^{-1}.$$

Continuation of this process backward in time yields, for large $T - t = \tau$

$$c_{\tau} = \left[1+\beta\alpha+(\beta\alpha)^2+\ldots\right]^{-1} k_{\tau}^{\alpha} z_{\tau} = (1-\beta\alpha) k_{\tau}^{\alpha} z_{\tau}$$

$$\lambda_{\tau} = \left[1+\beta\alpha+(\beta\alpha)^2+\ldots\right]\alpha k_{\tau}^{-1} = (1-\beta\alpha)^{-1}\alpha k_{\tau}^{-1}$$

The optimum consumption decision is to consume a fraction $(1 - \beta\alpha)$ of output $k_{\tau}^{\alpha} z_{\tau}$. This fraction increases if the discount factor $\beta$ decreases, making future consumption less desirable as compared with present consumption.

Chapter 3 begins with this simple optimum-growth model, except for treating the technology variable $z_t$ as a random variable. The objective function is the mathematical expectation of the objective function of the deterministic problem just described. Section 3.2 generalizes to a multisector model with N goods with the output of the $i$th good produced by a Cobb-Douglas production function

$$y_{i,t+1} = z_{i,t+1} \prod_{j=1}^{N} x_{ij,t}^{a_{ij}} \qquad i = 1, \ldots, N$$

in which $x_{ij,t}$ denotes the quantity of good $j$ used as input to produce good $i$, and $z_{i,t+1}$ is the random technology shock in the production of good $i$. The utility in each period is a weighted sum $\Sigma_{i=1}^{N} \theta_i \ln c_{it}$ of the logarithms of consumption $c_{it}$, with the weight $\theta_i$ equal to zero if the $i$th good cannot be used for consumption, and with leisure possibly included as a consumption good and labor possibly included as an input.

The role of human capital as a productive factor in economic growth is studied in section 3.3, following Becker, Murphy, and Tamura (1990). The role of technology conceived as a set of designs or patents in economic growth is studied in section 3.4 following Romer (1990). The role of research and development (R&D) in economic growth as studied by Stokey (1995) is summarized in section 3.5.

## 1.4 Theories of Market Equilibrium

Chapter 4 owes a great deal to Stokey and Lucas (1989). In fact, except for sections 4.4 and 4.6, it is an exposition of the most important economic applications contained in that book. Section 4.4 is based on a 1988 *Econometrica* article by the same authors. Section 4.6 is a general equilibrium analysis of a multisector model similar to the model of section 3.2 using the same method as explained in section 4.5 for a one-sector model. The origin of this chapter may be of some interest. After I discovered the Lagrange method to be applicable to dynamic optimization problems under uncertainty in general in 1991, and not only to special cases including the linear-quadratic control problem as expounded in Chow (1970), Chow (1975), and several articles in between, I wanted to find out how general and how convenient the method is. What better way was there to find out than to go through Stokey and Lucas (1989)? I therefore offered to teach a second year graduate course at Princeton, in part to go over that book. As I explained dynamic programming and went over economic applications in the book, I was also explaining the Lagrange method and using it to solve the same problems. The notes for that course at Princeton form the basis of an early draft of chapters 2 and 4.

Section 4.1 is an exposition of a well-known article by Lucas on the pricing of assets. Although it does not cover many of the fine points in the original article, it reaches the essential result in a very brief and simple way and may therefore be useful to graduate students and researchers who wish to understand the basic ideas and results for the purpose of application. I can say about the same thing concerning the other sections of chapter 4. They are simple expositions that use the Lagrange method. Understanding the simple exposition is sufficient to master the topic for the purpose of doing applied research on similar topics in the future. The exposition of Chapter 4, and, in fact, of most of the rest of this book, makes the subject of dynamic economics accessible to a wide class of students of economics.

## 1.5 Business Cycles

The approach to business cycle research presented in Chapter 5 is based on the notion that the market is always in equilibrium. The approach is sometimes called real business cycles to emphasize the importance of the real or technology side of the problem, and sometimes called equilibrium business cycles to indicate that the models are general equilibrium models derived from dynamic optimization on the part of economic agents. As such, the topic of Chapter 5 is a natural follow-up of the topics of Chapter 4 on equilibrium models.

After setting the stage in section 5.1, I present a discussion of real business cycles by using the multisector growth model of Radner as presented in section 3.2. That this model is relevant to business cycles was pointed out by Long and Plosser (1983). In section 5.3, I discuss an application of the dynamic optimization framework to explaining economic fluctuations in China as generated by political events. This section not only shows the wide applicability of the method, but also serves as an introduction to the base-line business cycle model for the US economy summarized in section 5.4. Section 5.4 also suggests that standard econometric methods of estimation and hypothesis testing should be applied to the study of real business cycles in addition to the method of calibration. It demonstrates this point by applying standard econometric methods as compared with calibration to the base-line RBC model. Sections

5.5 and 5.6 report on two more models. One is an extension of the baseline model to improve the explanation of labor market fluctuations. The other is based on oligopoly pricing rather than on perfectly competitive product markets as postulated in previous models. Oligopoly pricing is explained by dynamic game theory. Therefore, section 5.6 can serve as an introduction to chapter 6 on dynamic games as well. In the last section of chapter 5 I survey briefly the role of models based on dynamic optimization for markets in equilibrium in business cycle research.

## 1.6 Dynamic Games

Although section 5.7 can serve as an introduction to the topic of dynamic games, another introduction is provided in section 6.1. It is followed by an application of dynamic games to study the pricing behavior of two duopolists that have very loyal customers that will not switch suppliers once they have selected one of the two suppliers. The solution is worked out explicitly, because the relevant demand and cost functions are specified in explicit parametric forms. The method of Lagrange multipliers is used to derive the optimal pricing rules for the duopolists. Section 6.3 is a characterization of market equilibrium in terms of the important concept of subgame perfect Nash equilibrium. A Nash equilibrium is a set of strategies of all players such that, given the strategies of all other players, no player can improve his or her expected utility by changing his or her strategy. A Nash equilibrium is subgame perfect if, for any subgame of a dynamic game that begins at any time $t$, no player can be better off by changing his strategy. The characterization given in section 6.3 is due to Dilip Abreu, who uses the most severe punishment, which is itself an equilibrium path, to deter possible deviation by a player from an equilibrium path in any subgame of an infinitely repeated game. Such a game need not specify a dynamic model for the evolution of the state variables that are relevant for the decision making of each player. When such a dynamic model as imbedded in a standard optimal control problem is formulated in a dynamic game, the strategy of each player in each period can be defined as a reaction function of the state variables. Section 6.4 gives a characterization of subgame perfect Nash equilibrium in terms of reaction functions for dynamic games in which the dynamic evolution of state variables is explicitly specified.

The terms *subgame perfection*, *time consistency*, and *credible policy* are different names for the same idea. I have defined a subgame perfect Nash equilibrium. A solution to an optimum strategy by a player, usually a decision maker such as the government, is time consistent if at any time of play in the future, there is no incentive for the government-player to deviate from the strategy. This is the case if and only if the strategy is a subgame perfect strategy. Such a strategy or policy is credible, because the other player or the public will believe that it will be carried out, given that the government will have nothing to gain by deviating from it at any time in the future. Section 6.5 is a study of credible government policies including an application of restrictive monetary policy to control inflation, with and without introducing state variables in the model. Section 6.6 is a study of credible policies of taxation to redistribute income. Although the treatment of dynamic games in chapter 6 is far from complete, it introduces the reader to some of the most important concepts and tools and illustrates them with interesting applications.

## 1.7 Models in Finance

Like chapter 6, chapter 7 introduces the reader to some of the most important concepts and tools in the field of finance together with important applications without treating the subject exhaustively. I first introduce the subject of dynamic optimization when the dynamic model for the state variables is formulated in continuous time in the form of a system of stochastic differential equations. Dynamic optimization that uses such a model was once considered a difficult subject. In fact, as shown in sections 7.1 to 7.3, the subject is fairly easy. If one understands dynamic optimization for stochastic models in discrete time, one can easily understand the same for models in continuous time. A stochastic differential equation is written with $dx$ rather than $x(t+1)$ as the left-hand side variable. All that one has to know is that $dx$ stands for $x(t + dt) - x(t)$ for a very small time interval $dt$. Accordingly, whenever one sees $dx$ one can write it as $x(t+dt) - x(t)$ and treat the resulting equation as an equation in discrete time. Another thing to remember is that the random residual in a stochastic differential equation is written as $dv$, which equals $v(t + dt) - v(t)$. $v(t)$ is a Brownian motion, also called a Wiener process. The increment $v(t + dt) - v(t)$ is normally distributed with mean zero and variance proportional to $dt$. The last fact is easy to understand and is important. It is true, because the successive increments are assumed to be normal and statistically independent. Statistical independence implies that if $dt$ is three units, the variance is three times the variance for $dt$ equal to one unit, because the variance of the sum $v(t+3) - v(t)$ is the sum of the variances for $v(t+1) - v(t)$, $v(t+2) - v(t+1)$, and $v(t + 3) - v(t + 2)$. In other words, the variance of $v(t + dt) - v(t)$ is proportional to the time interval $dt$, and hence the standard deviation of $dv$ is proportional to the square root of $dt$. The ratio $dv/dt$ is of order $1/\sqrt{dt}$ that approaches infinity as $dt$ approaches zero. Thus, the derivative $dv/dt$ does not exist. Write the left-hand side of a stochastic differential equations as $dx$ rather than $dx/dt$ as in the case of a nonstochastic differential equation. To evaluate the stochastic differential $dy$, given a stochastic differential equation for $dx$ when $y$ is a differentiable function of $x$, apply Ito's lemma or Ito's differentiation rule. That is the only formula that one needs in solving dynamic optimization problems in continuous time that involves stochastic differential equations.

Section 7.2 presents the method of dynamic programming for dynamic models written in the form of stochastic differential equations, and section 7.3 applies the method of Lagrange multipliers to solve the same dynamic optimization problem. Section 7.4 provides a numerical method to solve such dynamic optimization problems. The method of dynamic programming was first applied to solve portfolio selection problems in continuous time by

Robert Merton. Sections 7.5 and 7.6 are presentations of two of his classic papers written in the early 1970s. The well-known and useful formula on the pricing of options first introduced by Fisher Black and Myron Scholes is derived and discussed in section 7.7. The remaining two sections of chapter 7 borrow from a recent Princeton University Ph.D. thesis by Chunsheng Zhou. As the titles suggest, the first incorporates noise in the supply of assets whereas in the early Merton models supply was regarded as fixed. The second postulates two groups of consumer-investors, with one group possessing less information about the state variables used to determine the underlying values of the assets. These two ideas are among the most important new developments in asset pricing after the original works of Merton. In the second model, the uninformed investors have to estimate the unobserved state variables using the Kalman filter. Section 7.9a, which is a part of section 7.9, derives and explains the Kalman filter in continuous time as it is applied to solve the problem of asset pricing that is discussed in section 7.9. The exposition is self-contained and similar to the author's exposition of the Kalman filter in discrete time in Chow (1975).

## 1.8 Models of Investment

Chapter 8 borrows first from the work of Dixit and Pindyck (1994), who study investment by allowing for the possibility that an investment project is indivisible and, once taken, is irreversible. They formulate investment decisions in continuous time and solve the problem by finding the critical time at which the decision to undertake an indivisible project should take place. They solve the optimum waiting time problem by dynamic programming. As the reader can anticipate, this problem is solved in Chapter 8 by the method of Lagrange multipliers also. Section 8.1 discusses some basic cases of investment decisions when the control variable is a 0–1 variable, taking the value zero at time $t$ if the investment project is not taken at $t$ and taking the value 1 if the investment project is undertaken at time $t$. Section 8.2 is an investment model in continuous time proposed by Andrew Abel in the early 1980s and solved by dynamic programming. My exposition solves it by the Lagrange method. Section 8.3 summarizes a paper by Andrew Abel and Janice Eberly on gradual capacity expansion with adjustment costs.

One important characteristic of the models discussed so far is the use of a discrete control variable. Similar solution methods that use Lagrange multipliers can be applied to solve decision problems involving discrete control variables but formulated in discrete time. Two such problems are presented and solved in sections 8.4 and 8.5. The former is due to John Rust (1987 and 1994) and is concerned with the decision as to when to replace a piece of indivisible capital, as in the example, when to replace a bus engine when both the engine and the bus get old. The latter is due to Lumsdaine, Stock, and Wise (1992) and is concerned with when to retire a piece of human capital—in other words, when a person should retire from the work force given his or her wages if he or she did not retire and the persion benefits should he or she decide to retire. The models selected are subjects of current research. To provide a perspective of the rich literature on investment without going into detailed discussions, which are readily available in other references, I try to point out in section 8.6 the relation of the models included in Chapter 8 and some of the other literature on investment.

## 1.9 Numerical Methods for Solving First-Order Conditions in Dynamic Optimization Problems

Chapter 9 begins by pointing out the vast literature on numerical solution to dynamic optimization problems based on dynamic programming. Much of this literature involves the value function in the Bellman equation. Because the Lagrange method is based on the first-order conditions for the control function and the Lagrange function, I concentrate on the numerical solution of the first-order conditions. After an introduction in Section 9.1, I discuss the important topic of change of variables in section 9.2. The reader should note that, for the same economic problem formulated in a dynamic optimization framework, there are alternative ways to select state and control variables and, accordingly, the first order conditions can be written in terms of alternative variables. The former point is illustrated in a simple one-sector model of economic growth in which one can freely choose consumption, investment, or the capital stock of the following period as the control variable. Given aggregate output, consumption is determined once investment is decided. Given initial capital stock, the capital stock of the next period implies a definite amount of investment. The second point is based on the simple fact that, because the first-order conditions are functional equations in the control function $u(x)$ and the Lagrange function $\lambda(x)$, if we change the state variables from $x$ to $y$ given $x = x(y)$, the new functions will be $u(x(y))$ and $\lambda(x(y))$. The change of variables has at least two important applications. First, if the dynamic model has a unit root, as in the case in which the log of total factor productivity $z$ in an aggregate Cobb-Douglas production function follows a random walk, changing the variable $z_t$ to $z_t/z_{t-1}$ would eliminate the stochastic trend in the model provided that other state variables such as capital stock $k$ are also changed to $k_t/z_{t-1}$, etc. This change of variables will make an originally nonstationary model stationary in terms of the new variables. Second, often taking logarithms will make the residuals of the dynamic model more nearly homoskedastic. Section 9.2 provides examples of useful transformations of variables.

After detrending by division by $z_{t-1}$ as suggested above, and taking logarithms of the detrended variables, one may wish to linearize the first-order conditions in terms of the log detrended variables. This can be achieved by taking first-order Taylor expansion of the first-order conditions in terms of the log detrended variables about the steady-state values of the deterministic version of the optimal control problem. Specifically, first solve the first-order conditions after getting rid of the expectations signs (to convert to the deterministic version of the original problem) and the time subscripts (to obtain the steady-state values). The resulting first-order conditions become a set of algebraic equations in the steady-state values of control variables and the Lagrange multipliers. In addition, the dynamic equations for the state variables, with the random term and the time subscripts omitted, become algebraic equations for the steady-state values of the state variables. About these steady-state values, take a first-order Taylor expansion of the first-order conditions to obtain a linear system of equations in the log detrended variables as an approximation to the first-order conditions. These linear equations can be solved to obtain optimal linear control functions in the log detrended variables. All of this sounds tedious. However, there is a short cut to do all the algebra and calculus involved without even knowing how to take derivatives. This is done by applying one simple algebraic formula suggested by Harald Uhlig, which equates the log detrended variables measured as deviations from the steady-state values to the original variables; the formula already incorporates a first-order Taylor expansion. By knowing this formula alone and by using only algebraic substitutions, one can perform the log linearization of the first-order conditions in detrended variables. Section 9.3 discusses this shortcut.

Section 9.4 presents some methods to speed up the numerical solution of the matrix Riccati equations. These equations are solved in order to obtain the matrix coefficients of linear optimal control functions when the objective function is quadratic. Section 9.5 explains how to obtain linear optimal functions by solving the log linearized first-order conditions by using the method of undetermined coefficients. To take advantage of the Lagrange method for solving dynamic optimization problems, I suggest approximating the Lagrange function by a quadratic function of the state variables. This would improve on the approximation by a linear function as is commonly done. A linear approximation for the Lagrange function is equivalent to a quadratic approximation of the value function. A quadratic approximation of the Lagrange function is equivalent to a cubic approximation to the value function, which is difficult to achieve if one tries to solve the Bellman equation. Sections 9.6 and 9.7 provide, respectively, an algorithm to calculate the matrix parameters of the quadratic approximations to the Lagrange function in discrete time and in continuous time. Section 9.8 presents the Galerkin method, which provides higher-order approximations to the control and Lagrange functions when the number of state variables is small. More computational experience is desired. To conclude the introduction of chapter 9, note that this chapter should be regarded as an initial exploration of the subject of numerical solution of dynamic optimization problems based on the Lagrange method. A theoretical discussion of dynamic programming using the Bellman equation is only the beginning of the discussion of numerical methods. Similarly, a theoretical discussion of the Lagrange method that uses the corresponding first-order conditions is only the beginning of the study of numerical solutions. In the same vein, it is hoped that the economic analyses based on the Lagrange method presented in this book will serve as a beginning of more fruitful analyses of dynamic economic problems.

## CHAPTER TWO

# Dynamic Optimization in Discrete Time

## 2.1 The Method of Lagrange Multipliers by an Example

Much of dynamic economics is concerned with maximizing a time separable objective function subject to a set of equations that describe the dynamic evolution of the state variables $x_t$. To illustrate, consider the problem of maximizing the objective function for three periods ($t = 0, 1, 2$)

$$\sum_{t=0}^{2} \beta^t r(x_t, u_t) \tag{2.1}$$

subject to the dynamic equation

$$x_{t+1} = f(x_t, u_t) + \varepsilon_{t+1}. \tag{2.2}$$

Here, $\beta$ is the discount factor; $r(x_t, u_t)$ is the return for period $t$, which may depend on the p-component vector $x_t$ of state variables and the q-component vector $u_t$ of control variables to be set by the decision maker; $f$ is a p-component vector function, and $\varepsilon_{t+1}$ is a vector of random shocks. To treat a deterministic optimization problem first, temporarily regard $\varepsilon_{t+1}$ as a vector of constants known to the decision maker at time $t$. Assume the functions $r$ and $f$ to be differentiable and concave. The three-period problem is to maximize the objective function (2.1) with respect to $u_0$, $u_1$, and $u_2$ subject to the constraint (2.2).

It is natural and easy to solve this problem by the method of Lagrange multipliers. Introduce the $p \times 1$ vectors $\lambda_1$ and $\lambda_2$ of Lagrange multipliers and form the Lagrangean expression

$$\mathcal{L} = \{ r(x_0, u_0) + \beta r(x_1, u_1) + \beta^2 r(x_2, u_2)$$
$$- \beta \lambda_1' [x_1 - f(x_0, u_0) - \varepsilon_1] - \beta^2 \lambda_2' [x_2 - f(x_1, u_1) - \varepsilon_2] \}$$

treating $x_0$ as given and the variables $u_0$, $u_1$, $u_2$, $x_1$, and $x_2$ as unknowns but subject to the two constraints on $x_1$ and $x_2$, as given by equation (2.2). Differentiate $\mathscr{L}$ with respect to each $u_t$ and each $x_t$, which yields

$$\beta^{-2}\frac{\partial \mathscr{L}}{\partial u_2} = \frac{\partial}{\partial u_2} r(x_2,\, u_2) = 0 \tag{2.3}$$

$$\beta^{-1}\frac{\partial \mathscr{L}}{\partial u_1} = \frac{\partial}{\partial u_1} r(x_1,\, u_1) + \beta\frac{\partial}{\partial u_1} f'(x_1,\, u_1)\lambda_2 = 0 \tag{2.4}$$

$$\frac{\partial \mathscr{L}}{\partial u_0} = \frac{\partial}{\partial u_0} r(x_0,\, u_0) + \beta\frac{\partial}{\partial u_0} f'(x_0,\, u_0)\lambda_1 = 0 \tag{2.5}$$

$$\beta^{-2}\frac{\partial \mathscr{L}}{\partial x_2} = \frac{\partial}{\partial x_2} r(x_2,\, u_2) - \lambda_2 = 0 \tag{2.6}$$

$$\beta^{-1}\frac{\partial \mathscr{L}}{\partial x_1} = -\lambda_1 + \frac{\partial}{\partial x_1} r(x_1,\, u_1) + \beta\frac{\partial}{\partial x_1} f'(x_1,\, u_1)\lambda_2 = 0 \tag{2.7}$$

The above equations can be solved backward in time using *backward induction*. The solution of equation (2.3) gives an optimal feedback control function $u_2 = g_2(x_2)$, provided that the solution is an interior solution. Equation (2.6), together with the solution $u_2 = g_2(x_2)$, gives $\lambda_2(x_2) = \partial r(x_2, g_2(x_2))/\partial x_2$. Having obtained $u_2$ and $\lambda_2$, solve equation (2.4) for $u_1(x_1)$ and equation (2.7) for $\lambda_1(x_1)$. Finally, $u_0(x_0)$ is obtained from equation (2.5).

## 2.2 The Method of Dynamic Programming by an Example

The method of dynamic programming as suggested by Bellman (1957) can also be used to solve this problem. By this method, also solve first the problem of the last period 2. Maximizing $r(x_2, u_2)$ with respect to $u_2$ yields an optimal feedback control function $u_2 = g_2(x_2)$. When this maximizing value is substituted in the return function for period 2, we obtain the value function

$$V_2(x_2) = r(x_2,\, g(x_2))$$

which depends on the state $x_2$ at the beginning of period 2. The next step is to solve the problem for both periods 2 and 1. Having obtained the optimal control function $u_2 = g(x_2)$ and the value function $V_2(x_2)$, the problem is to find

$$V_1(x_1) = \max_{u_1}\{r(x_1,\, u_1) + \beta V_2(x_2)\} \tag{2.8}$$

In this two-period problem, because the optimal $u_2$ is already determined, the only control variable remaining is $u_1$. At the beginning of period 1, the economic agent maximizes the sum of the two terms inside the curly brackets in (2.8) with respect to $u_1$ to obtain an optimal control function $u_1 = g_1(x_1)$. Specifically, assuming differentiable $r$ and $V_2$ and an interior solution, set to zero the vector of derivatives of the expression in curly brackets in (2.8) with respect to $u_1$

$$\frac{\partial\{\;\}}{\partial u_1} = \frac{\partial}{\partial u_1} r(x_1, u_1) + \beta \frac{\partial}{\partial u_1} f'(x_1, u_1) \frac{\partial}{\partial x_2} V_2(x_2) = 0 \tag{2.9}$$

in which $\partial f'(x_1, u_1)/\partial u_1$ or $\partial x_2'/\partial u_1$ is a $q \times p$ matrix of partial derivatives of the row vector $x_2' = f'(x_1, u_1) + \varepsilon_2'$ with respect to the column vector $u_1$, and $\partial V_2(x_2)/\partial x_2$ is the $p \times 1$ vector of derivatives of $V_2(x_2)$ with respect to $x_2$. Solving (2.9) for $u_1$ yields the optimal control function $u_1 = g_1(x_1)$. When the optimal $u_1$ is substituted into the two-period objective function, the result is the value function for period 1

$$V_1(x_1) = r(x_1, g_1(x_1)) + \beta V_2(f(x_1, g(x_1)) + \varepsilon_2) \tag{2.10}$$

Note that $V_1(x_1)$ is the value of the objective function from period 1 onward, assuming all control variables from period 1 onward, namely $u_1$ and $u_2$, to be optimal. Thus, one problem that involves two vector variables $u_1$ and $u_2$ is reduced to two problems, each of which involves only one variable. Instead of finding $u_1$ and $u_2$ simultaneously, first find $u_2$, and then, having found $u_2$, find $u_1$. Having found $u_2$ and $u_1$ and knowing $V_1(x_1)$, the next step would be to solve the three-period problem by finding $u_0$ only. That is, find

$$V_0(x_0) = \max_{u_0}\{r(x_0, u_0) + \beta V_1(x_1)\}$$

To generalize, at each period, take $x_t$ as given and, having found all future control $u_{t+1}, u_{t+2}, \ldots$ and obtained $V_{t+1}(x_{t+1})$, solve

$$V_t(x_t) = \max_{u_t}\{r(x_t, u_t) + \beta V_{t+1}(x_{t+1})\} \tag{2.11}$$

Equation (2.11) is known as the Bellman equation. By the principle of optimality, this solution method, which uses the Bellman equation for each period and begins from the last period, gives the optimal solution for all periods. The argument is that, whatever the initial state $x_t$ for each period is, the solution $u_t = g_t(x_t)$ so obtained is optimal, because all future policies $u_{t+1}$, $u_{t+2}, \ldots$ have been found to be optimal whatever their respective initial states $x_{t+1}, x_{t+2}, \ldots$ shall be. As a historical note to explain *dynamic programming* and the *principle of optimality*, I first met Richard Bellman in the summer of 1956 when I participated in teaching a summer course on operations research at MIT organized by Philip Morse. Bellman from Princeton was invited to lecture on dynamic programming. He said in a lecture that the term was chosen to sell the method because both "dynamic" and "programming" are attractive and sellable words, with linear programming gaining popularity during that period. The reader may infer the motivation for coining the term *principle of optimality*.

To contrast the two methods, given $V_2(x_2)$ dynamic programming recommends solving a pair of equations (2.9) and (2.10) for $u_1 = g_1(x_1)$ and $V_1(x_1)$. Given $\lambda_2(x_2)$, the method of Lagrange multipliers consists of solving a pair of equations (2.4) and (2.7) for $g_1(x_1)$ and $\lambda_1(x_1)$. Because (2.9) is the same as

(2.4), the choice is between (2.10) and (2.7). Equation (2.7) could be obtained by differentiating (2.10) with respect to $x_1$. To obtain the optimal control $u_1 = g_1(x_1)$, (2.7) is preferable because by both methods knowledge of $V_2$ is unnecessary in obtaining $g_1(x_1)$ from (2.9) but $\partial V_2/\partial x_2$ or $\lambda_2$ is required. For each period $t$, to seek the value function $V_{t+1}$, either analytically or numerically, and then differentiate it to find the optimal $u_t$ is an uneconomical method, as I pointed out in section 1.2. After the optimization problem is solved by the Lagrange method, one can obtain the value function by substituting the optimal control function into the dynamic model to evaluate the objective function or by integrating the Lagrange function.

## 2.3 Solution of a Standard Dynamic Optimization Problem

A standard dynamic optimization problem is

$$\max_{\{u_t\}_{t=0}^{\infty}} E_0\left[\sum_{t=0}^{\infty} \beta^t r(x_t, u_t)\right], \tag{2.12}$$

subject to

$$x_{t+1} = f(x_t, u_t) + \varepsilon_{t+1}, \tag{2.13}$$

in which $E_0$ is expectation given information at time 0, and $\varepsilon_{t+1}$ is an independent and identically distributed (i.i.d.) random vector with mean zero and covariance matrix $\Sigma$. As in section 2.1, this problem is solved by introducing the $p \times 1$ vector $\lambda_t$ of Lagrange multipliers and setting to zero the derivatives of the Lagrangean expression

$$\mathscr{L} = E_0\left[\sum_{t=0}^{\infty}\left\{\beta^t r(x_t, u_t) - \beta^{t+1}\lambda'_{t+1}\left[x_{t+1} - f(x_t, u_t) - \varepsilon_{t+1}\right]\right\}\right], \tag{2.14}$$

with respect to $u_t$ ($t = 0, 1 \ldots$) and $x_t$ ($t = 1, 2 \ldots$). The first-order conditions analogous to (2.4) and (2.7) are

$$\frac{\partial}{\partial u_t} r(x_t, u_t) + \beta \frac{\partial}{\partial u_t} f'(x_t, u_t) E_t \lambda_{t+1} = 0, \tag{2.15}$$

$$\lambda_t = \frac{\partial}{\partial x_t} r(x_t, u_t) + \beta \frac{\partial}{\partial x_t} f'(x_t, u_t) E_t \lambda_{t+1}. \tag{2.16}$$

To justify this method of solution, four observations can be made. First, if the problem were nonstochastic, that is, if $E_0$ were absent and $\varepsilon_{t+1}$ were constants, the use of Lagrange multipliers is justified because variables in different time periods are simply treated as different variables, and the constraint $x_{t+1} - f(x_t, u_t) - \varepsilon_{t+1} = 0$ for each period requires a separate (vector) multiplier $\beta^{t+1}\lambda_{t+1}$. The factor $\beta^{t+1}$ is used to discount the marginal value $\lambda_{t+1}$ of $x_{t+1}$ dated at $t + 1$. Second, if the problem were stochastic but unconstrained, the procedure is also justified, because the expectation to be maximized is a function of the variables $u_t$, $x_t$, and $\lambda_t$, and first-order conditions can be obtained by differentiation with respect to these variables, with the order of differentiation and taking expectation interchanged under suitable regularity conditions. Third, the method of Lagrange multipliers is to convert a constrained maximization problem to an unconstrained one by introducing the additional variables $\lambda_t$ as is done above. Fourth, note that the problem is not to choose $u_0$, $u_1 \ldots$ all at once in an open-loop policy, but to choose $u_t$ sequentially given the information $x_t$ at time $t$ in a closed-loop policy. Because $x_t$ is in the information set when $u_t$ is to be determined, the expectations in equations (2.15) and (2.16) for the determination of $u_t$ and $\lambda_t$ at period $t$ are $E_t$ and not $E_0$. As in section 2.1, I suggest using equation (2.16) instead of the Bellman equation (2.11), with $E_t$ inserted before $V_{t+1}$, to obtain the optimal control function $u_t = g_t(x_t)$. In the next section, I present a well-known numerical method to solve (2.15) and (2.16) for a pair of functions $u_t = g(x_t)$ and $\lambda_t = \lambda(x_t)$ when the functions $g$ and $\lambda$ are time invariant in an infinite horizon dynamic optimization problem.

## 2.4 Numerical Solution by Linear Approximations for λ and *g*

To solve the first-order conditions (2.15) and (2.16) for $u$ and $\lambda$, one can approximate the function $\lambda(x)$ by a linear function

$$\lambda(x) = Hx + h \tag{2.17}$$

One can also approximate $\partial r/\partial x$, $\partial r/\partial u$, and $f$ by linear functions

$$\frac{\partial}{\partial x} r(x, u) = K_{11}x + K_{12}u + k_1 \tag{2.18}$$

$$\frac{\partial}{\partial u} r(x, u) = K_{21}x + K_{22}u + k_2 \tag{2.19}$$

$$f(x, u) = Ax + Cu + b \tag{2.20}$$

The linear functions are obtained by first-order Taylor expansion about some $(\bar{x}, \bar{u})$. The values $(\bar{x}, \bar{u})$ might be the sample means of the state and control variables in an econometric application. They may be the steady-state values of these variables under optimal control for the nonstochastic version of the optimal problem obtained by setting $\varepsilon_t = 0$. These values are obtained by solving equations (2.13), (2.15), and (2.16) as algebraic equations for $x$, $u$ and $\lambda$ omitting all time subscripts and the expectation sign (see problem 5).

In the first step of the solution procedure, the right-hand sides of (2.19) for $\partial r/\partial u$ and of $\lambda_{t+1} = Hx_{t+1} + h$ are substituted into (2.15) to yield

$$\partial r/\partial u + \beta C' E_t \lambda_{t+1} = K_{22}u + K_{21}x + k_2 + \beta C'H(Ax + Cu + b) + \beta C'h = 0. \tag{2.21}$$

Solving (2.21) for $u$ gives $u = Gx + g$, in which

$$G = -(K_{22} + \beta C'HC)^{-1}(K_{21} + \beta C'HA), \tag{2.22}$$

$$g = -(K_{22} + \beta C'HC)^{-1}[k_2 + \beta C'(Hb + h)]. \tag{2.23}$$

In the next step, observe

$$\begin{aligned} E_t\lambda_{t+1} &= H(Ax + Cu + b) + h \\ &= H[(A + CG)x + Cg + b] + h, \end{aligned} \tag{2.24}$$

which is linear in $x$. Substituting (2.24) for $E_t\lambda_{t+1}$ and (2.18) for $\partial r/\partial x$ in (2.16),

$$\lambda_t = \lambda(x) = Hx + h = K_{11}x + K_{12}(Gx + g) + k_1 + \beta A'\{H[(A + CG)x + Cg + b] + h\}.$$

Equating coefficients on both sides gives

$$H = K_{11} + K_{12}G + \beta A'H(A + CG), \tag{2.25}$$

$$h = (K_{12} + \beta A'HC)g + k_1 + \beta A'(Hb + h). \tag{2.26}$$

Equations (2.22) and (2.25) are used to solve for G and H. Given H and G, (2.23) and (2.26) are used to solve for $g$ and $h$. Equations (2.22) and (2.25) can be combined to yield the following equation in H alone:

$$H = K_{11} + \beta A'HA - (K_{12} + \beta A'HC)(K_{22} + \beta C'HC)^{-1}(K_{21} + \beta C'HA). \tag{2.27}$$

Equation (2.27) is known as the matrix Riccati equation. It can be solved iteratively. Given H, one can find G by using (2.22).

The method just described is an example of the *method of undetermined coefficients*. To solve two functional equations (2.15) and (2.16) for $u = g(x)$ and $\lambda = \lambda(x)$, assume both to be linear with coefficients (G, $g$, H, $h$). Substitute the linear functions into the equations. Equate the coefficients on both sides to solve for the unknown coefficients. The above method yields the same answer as given by the solution to the well-known linear quadratic optimal control problem. The latter problem assumes the function $f$ to be linear and the function $r$ to be quadratic and, hence, $\partial r/\partial x$ and $\partial r/\partial u$ to be linear. Under these assumptions the optimal control function $g$ and the Lagrange function $\lambda$ will be linear, and the value function V will be quadratic. When $f$ is nonlinear and $r$ is not quadratic, one may linearize $f$, $\partial r/\partial x$, and $\partial r/\partial u$ about a certain point $(\bar{x}, \bar{u})$ and solve equations (2.22), (2.23), (2.25), and (2.26) to find a linear control function $Gx + g$ together with a linear Lagrange function $\lambda = Hx + h$.

The first-order conditions (2.15) and (2.16) may have no solution when linear approximations are used for $\lambda$ and $g$. Assuming that solutions for linear $\lambda$ and $g$ exist and that (2.27) can be solved for H and, hence, (2.22) can be solved for G, one finds an approximately optimum control function $u = g + Gx$. If a time-invariant linear control function $g + Gx$ is found, the steady-state value for $x$, if it exists, can be found by solving

$$x = f(x,\ g + Gx)$$

Note that a time-invariant optimal control function does not necessarily produce a steady state for $x_t$, depending on the dynamic model specified by $f(x, u)$. For example, if there are two explosive roots in the $2 \times 2$ matrix A in a linear $f$,

$$x_{t+1} = Ax_t + Cu_t$$
$$= \begin{bmatrix} 1.1 & 0 \\ 0 & 1.2 \end{bmatrix} \begin{bmatrix} x_{1t} \\ x_{2t} \end{bmatrix} + \begin{bmatrix} 1 \\ 1 \end{bmatrix} u_t$$

and if

$$K_{11} = \begin{bmatrix} -1 & 0 \\ 0 & -1 \end{bmatrix}, \quad K_{12} = K_{21}' = \begin{bmatrix} 0 \\ 0 \end{bmatrix}, \quad K_{22} = -1$$

H can be found by solving (2.27) and hence G by solving (2.22). However $x_t$ will not converge to a steady-state value as $t$ increases. (See problem 6.) The state variable $x_t$ will reach a steady-state $\bar{x}$ if and only if the matrix A + CG in the dynamic equation for $x_t$ under optimum control, namely in the equation

$$x_{t+1} = Ax_t + C(Gx_t + g) = (A + CG)x_t + Cg,$$

has both characteristic roots (or eigenvalues) ($\mu_1$, $\mu_2$) smaller than unity in absolute value. That is, $x_t$ will reach a steady state $\bar{x}$ if and only if both roots $\mu_1$ and $\mu_2$ of the determinantal equation

$$\left| (A + CG) - \mu I \right| = 0$$

are smaller than unity in absolute value (see problem 9).

In this connection, it is important to point out that even if the state vector $x_t$ explodes under optimal control, one can still use the first-order conditions derived by the Lagrange method to find an optimal control function. If the return function $r$ is increasing in $x$, $r$ itself increases without bound, and the value function can approach infinity. Yet, the Lagrange method yields an optimum control function. This is another point suggesting that one should not use the value function, but only its derivatives $\lambda$, in deriving an optimum control rule. Even if the expectation of the sum of all discounted future utilities as given by the value function is infinity, one can still decide whether the current policy is optimum. Using an optimum policy, starting from any period $t$, one obtains a highest possible expected sum of discounted utilities from period $t$ to period $T = t + k$ for any positive integer $k$.

## 2.5 Sufficient Conditions for a Globally Optimal Solution

Equations (2.15) and (2.16) are first-order necessary conditions for the optimal control function $u = g(x)$ and the associated Lagrange function $\lambda(x)$ to satisfy. It is important to explore a set of sufficient conditions for the solution to be globally optimal. In other words, when will the function $\mathscr{L}$ defined by (2.14) achieve a global maximum? We answer this question in three stages. First consider the nonstochastic version of this problem with the expectation signs in (2.14), (2.15), and (2.16) omitted and provide a set of sufficient conditions for a local maximum. Second, the stochastic version is considered. Third, sufficient conditions for a global maximum are given.

To consider the deterministic case, define

$$\mathcal{L}_t(x_t, u_t, x_{t+1}) \equiv \beta^t r(x_t, u_t) - \beta^{t+1}\lambda'_{t+1}\left[x_{t+1} - f(x_t, u_t)\right] \tag{2.28}$$

Using this definition, rewrite the Lagrangean and the optimization problem as: given $x_0$

$$\max_{\{u_t, x_{t+1}\}_{t=0}^{\infty}} \mathcal{L} = \sum_{t=0}^{\infty} \mathcal{L}_t(x_t, u_t, x_{t+1}) \tag{2.29}$$

The first-order conditions (2.15) and (2.16) can be obtained by maximizing $\mathcal{L}_t + \beta\mathcal{L}_{t+1}$ with respect to $u_t$ and $x_{t+1}$, treating $x_t$, $u_{t+1}$, and $x_{t+2}$ as given. Thus,

$$\max_{u_t, x_{t+1}} \beta^{-t}(\mathcal{L}_t + \beta\mathcal{L}_{t+1}) = r(x_t, u_t) - \beta\lambda'_{t+1}\left[x_{t+1} - f(x_t, u_t)\right]$$

$$+ \beta r(x_{t+1}, u_{t+1}) - \beta^2\lambda'_{t+2}\left[x_{t+2} - f(x_{t+1}, u_{t+1})\right]. \tag{2.30}$$

Differentiating (2.30) yields the deterministic version of (2.15) and (2.16), namely

$$\frac{\partial}{\partial u_t}\beta^{-t}(\mathcal{L}_t + \beta\mathcal{L}_{t+1}) = \frac{\partial}{\partial u_t} r(x_t, u_t) + \beta\frac{\partial}{\partial u_t} f'(x_t, u_t)\lambda_{t+1} = 0 \tag{2.31}$$

$$\frac{\partial}{\partial x_{t+1}}\beta^{-t}(\mathcal{L}_t + \beta\mathcal{L}_{t+1}) = -\beta\lambda_{t+1} + \beta\frac{\partial}{\partial x_{t+1}} r(x_{t+1}, u_{t+1})$$

$$+ \beta^2\frac{\partial}{\partial x_{t+1}} f'(x_{t+1}, u_{t+1})\lambda_{t+2} = 0 \tag{2.32}$$

Let $\{u_t^*, x_{t+1}^*\}$, $t = 0, 1, \ldots$ satisfy the first-order conditions (2.31) and (2.32). The task is to find a set of sufficient conditions to guarantee that the function $\mathcal{L}$ defined by (2.29) evaluated at $\{u_t^*, x_{t+1}^*\}$, $t = 0, 1, \ldots$ which satisfy (2.31) and (2.32) will attain a value larger than or equal to the value of $\mathcal{L}$ evaluated at any $\{u_t, x_{t+1}\}$ in the neighborhood of $\{u_t^*, x_{t+1}^*\}$, for $t = 0, 1, \ldots$ This would guarantee that $\{u_t^*, x_{t+1}^*\}$ is a local maximum.

Following standard treatment of sufficient conditions for a maximum as in Courant (1936, vol. II, pp. 204–208), consider a point $(u_t^* + h_t, x_{t+1}^* + k_{t+1})$ for sufficiently small values of vectors $h_t$ and $k_{t+1}$ and expand the difference D between $\mathcal{L}$ evaluated at $(u_t^* + h_t, x_{t+1}^* + k_{t+1})$, $t = 0, 1, \ldots$ and $\mathcal{L}$ evaluated at $(u_t^*, x_{t+1}^*)$ by a second-order Taylor series with the remainder of the third order. The difference D is

$$\mathrm{D} = \sum_{t=0}^{\infty} \mathcal{L}_t(x_t^* + k_t, u_t^* + h_t, x_{t+1}^* + k_{t+1}) - \sum_{t=0}^{\infty} \mathcal{L}_t(x_t^*, u_t^*, x_{t+1}^*)$$

$$= \frac{1}{2}\sum_{t=0}^{\infty}\left\{\begin{bmatrix} h'_t & k'_{t+1} \end{bmatrix} \frac{\partial^2(\mathcal{L}_t + \beta\mathcal{L}_{t+1})}{\partial\begin{bmatrix} u_t \\ x_{t+1} \end{bmatrix}\partial\begin{bmatrix} u'_t & x'_{t+1} \end{bmatrix}} \begin{bmatrix} h_t \\ k_{t+1} \end{bmatrix} + \delta_t\rho_t^2\right\} \tag{2.33}$$

in which, by virtue of the first-order conditions (2.31) and (2.32), the first-order terms of the expansion vanish, and $\delta_t$ tends to zero with $\rho_t$, $\rho_t^2$ being equal to $h_t'h_t + k_{t+1}'k_{t+1}$. A sufficient condition for the point $(u_t^*, x_{t+1}^*)$ to be a maximum is that the following matrix of second partials of $\mathcal{L}_t + \beta\mathcal{L}_{t+1}$:

$$\beta^t \begin{bmatrix} \frac{\partial^2 r(x_t, u_t)}{\partial u_t \partial u_t'} + \beta \sum_{i=1}^{\rho} \frac{\partial^2 f_i(x_t, u_t)}{\partial u_t \partial u_t'} \lambda_i(x_{t+1}) & 0 \\ 0 & \beta \frac{\partial^2 r(x_{t+1}, u_{t+1})}{\partial x_{t+1} \partial x_{t+1}'} + \beta^2 \sum_{i=1}^{\rho} \frac{\partial^2 f_i(x_{t+1}, u_{t+1})}{\partial x_{t+1} \partial x_{t+1}'} \lambda_i(x_{t+2}) \end{bmatrix} \tag{2.34}$$

be negative definite. Hence, provided that $\lambda(x)$ is positive (a statement to be proved at the end of section 2.6), a sufficient condition for the solution satisfying the first-order conditions (2.31) and (2.32) to give a maximum is that both $r(x, u)$ and $f(x, u)$ are concave in $x$ and $u$, which will guarantee that all the second partials in (2.34) are negative. A function $r(x, u)$ is concave in $x$ if for any two points $x^a$ and $x^b$ and for $\theta \in [0, 1]$,

$$r\left(\theta x^b + (1-\theta)x^a, u\right) \geq \theta r\left(x^b, u\right) + (1-\theta) r\left(x^a, u\right) \tag{2.35}$$

that is, the chord joining any two points $(x^a, r(x^a, u))$ and $(x^b, r(x^b, u))$ on the graph $(x, r(x, u))$ lies below the graph. If in addition $r$ is differentiable, its second partials must be negative.

The above sufficient condition remains valid in the stochastic case when a random vector $\varepsilon_{t+1}$ is added to $f(x_t, u_t)$. In the above derivation, $E_t$ should be inserted before $\mathcal{L}_t$ in (2.29) and in (2.30), and before $\lambda_{t+1}$ in (2.31), and $E_{t+1}$ should be inserted before $\lambda_{t+2}$ in (2.32). Hence, (2.31) and (2.32) would be the same as equations (2.15) and (2.16) in section 2.3. $E_t$ should be inserted before $\lambda_i(x_{t+1})$ and $E_{t+1}$ before $\lambda_i(x_{t+2})$ in (2.34). Therefore, the above sufficient condition remains valid. If, instead of an additive $\varepsilon_{t+1}$, $f(x_t, u_t, \varepsilon_{t+1})$ is specified, $E_t$ and $E_{t+1}$ should be inserted immediately after the summation signs in (2.34). With $E_t$ and $E_{t+1}$ so inserted in (2.34), observe that, given positive $\lambda(x)$, the concavity of $r$ and $f$ in both $x$ and $u$ is still sufficient for a maximum. For the maximum to be global, the concavity of $r$ and $f$ in both $x$ and $u$ also suffices because it guarantees that both nonzero terms of (2.34), with $E_t$ and $E_{t+1}$ inserted as described above, are always negative. A concave function can have only one maximum.

Finally, note that the above proof does not assume $\mathcal{L}$ of (2.29) to be finite. Because the argument is presented for $u_t^*$ and $x_{t+1}^*$ for any $t$, this policy achieves a higher value of $\mathcal{L}_t$ for any $t$ than any other policy. In other words, even if total expected discounted returns for all future periods are infinite, the policy yielding $u_t^*$ and $x_{t+1}^*$ by the first-order conditions (2.31) and (2.32), or (2.15) and (2.16) for the stochastic version, will give a higher return than an alternative policy for any period $t$, provided that $r$ and $f$ are concave in both $x$ and $u$.

## 2.6 Relations to Known Results on Optimization

Section 2.3 specifies a standard (though by no means most general) dynamic optimization problem and provides a set of first-order necessary conditions for an optimum solution. Section 2.5 provides a set of sufficient conditions for optimum. To the extent that the standard dynamic optimization problem in section 2.3 was viewed as a constrained maximization problem to be solved by the classic method of Lagrange multipliers, the results on sufficiency in section 2.5 are not new because such constrained maximization problems have been extensively studied. It is a virtue of the Lagrange method for dynamic optimization that well-known results on constrained maximization can be utilized. Dynamic optimization in economics can follow the tradition of constrained maximization as expounded by Hicks (1939), Samuelson (1948), and the literature on mathematical programming related to the Kuhn-Tucker theorem and as expounded by Dorfman, Samuelson and Solow (1958); Henderson and Quandt (1980); Chiang (1984); Intriligator (1971); Dixit (1990); and others. The following discussion draws mainly on the excellent exposition of Dixit (1990).

For each period $t$, take $x_t$ as given and try to maximize $\mathcal{L}_t + \beta\mathcal{L}_{t+1}$ as given in (2.30) with respect to $u_t$ and $x_{t+1}$. Rewrite $\mathcal{L}_t + \beta\mathcal{L}_{t+1}$, omitting $\lambda'_{t+2}x_{t+2}$, as

$$r(x_t, u_t)+\beta r(x_{t+1}, u_{t+1})+\beta^2\lambda'_{t+2}f(x_{t+1}, u_{t+1})-\beta\lambda'_{t+1}[x_{t+1}-f(x_t, u_t)]$$
$$= F(u_t, x_{t+1})-\lambda' G(u_t, x_{t+1}) \quad (2.36)$$

in which we have defined the sum of the first three terms as $F(u_t, x_{t+1})$, $\beta\lambda_{t+1}$ as $\lambda$, and $x_{t+1} - f(x_t, u_t)$ as $G(u_t, x_{t+1})$. Take as given not only $x_t$, but $u_{t+1}$ and $x_{t+2}$, because these are the variables for the following period and the optimality conditions are considered one period at a time. Rewriting the problem for period $t$ as in (2.36) allows one to draw on the results contained in Dixit (1990).

Chapter 7 of Dixit (1990, p. 87) treats the problem of *concave programming*: the maximization of $F(x)$ subject to a vector constraint $G(x) \leq c$, where F is differentiable and concave, and each component constraint function $G^i$ is differentiable and convex. The Lagrangean of this problem is

$$L(x, \lambda) = F(x) + \lambda'[c - G(x)] \quad (2.37)$$

For the dynamic optimization problem, the vector $x$ consists of $u_t$ and $x_{t+1}$ in (2.36), and the constant $c$ is zero. The assumption of G being differentiable and convex is equivalent to $f(x_t, u_t)$ being differentiable and concave in $u_t$, because $G = x_{t+1} - f(x_t, u_t)$. These are precisely the assumptions used in section 2.5 to prove sufficiency. A basic theorem of concave programming is stated in Dixit (p. 95) as

NECESSARY CONDITIONS OF CONCAVE PROGRAMMING

*Suppose that F is a concave function and G is a vector convex function, and that there exists an $x^0$ satisfying each element of $G(x^0) < c$. If $\bar{x}$ maximizes $F(x)$ subject*

*to $G(x) \leqslant c$, there is a row vector $\lambda$, such that (i) $\bar{x}$ maximizes $F(x) - \lambda G(x)$ without any constraints, and (ii) $\lambda \geqslant 0$, $G(\bar{x}) \leqslant c$ with complementary slackness. This means that if $G^i(x_i) = c_i$, the corresponding $\lambda_i > 0$; if $G^i(x_i) < c_i$, the corresponding $\lambda_i = 0$.*

This theorem applies to optimization problems that are more general than the formulation of sections 2.3 and 2.5 in two respects. First, it allows for inequality constraints that contain the equality constraints as a special case. In future applications, I will also deal with inequality constraints, as in sections 4.2 and 7.2, for example. Second, this theorem does not require F and G to have derivatives. If the functions are differentiable, Dixit (p. 95) gives the first-order necessary conditions for maximization as

$$F_x(\bar{x}) - \lambda G_x(\bar{x}) = L_x(\bar{x}, \lambda) = 0$$

that are identical to the equations (2.31) and (2.32). This is the necessary condition of Lagrange's Theorem with Inequality Constraints.

Dixit (p. 97) gives the following theorem on sufficient conditions.

SUFFICIENT CONDITIONS FOR CONCAVE PROGRAMMING

*If $\bar{x}$ and $\lambda$ are such that (i) $\bar{x}$ maximizes $F(x) - \lambda G(x)$ without any constraints, and (ii) $\lambda \geqslant 0$, $G(\bar{x}) \leqslant c$ with complementary slackness, then $\bar{x}$ maximizes $F(x)$ subject to $G(x) \leqslant c$.*

*If $(F - \lambda G)$ is concave (for which it suffices to have F concave and G convex), then the preceding equation implies (i) above.*

Note that no constraint qualification appears in the sufficient conditions; it pertains to the validity of the necessary conditions. Moreover, note that the sufficient conditions of F being concave and G being convex are equivalent to the sufficient conditions of concave $r$ and concave $f$ as applied in section 2.5.

Based on the work of Arrow and Enthoven (1961), Dixit (1990, p. 97) further discusses quasi-concave programming in which F is merely quasi-concave, and each component constraint function in G is quasi-convex. F is quasi-concave if, for any two points $x^a$ and $x^b$ and for $\theta \in [0, 1]$

$$G\left(\theta x^b + (1-\theta)x^a\right) \geqslant \max\left(G(x^a),\ G(x^b)\right) \qquad (2.38)$$

Under the weaker assumptions of quasi-concavity and quasi-convexity, the necessary conditions remain essentially the same, and the sufficient conditions are similar to the ones for concave programming, but only if some further technical conditions are specified.

It should also be pointed out that the solution of the deterministic version of the standard dynamic optimization problem of section 2.3 is known and is closely related to the solution by Pontryagin's maximum principle. For an exposition of this principle, the reader may refer to sections 3.5 and 7.4, Dixit (1990, p. 147), and Intriligator (1971). The novelty of section 2.3 is the discovery that the same ideas apply to the stochastic version as well, essentially with the conditional expectation $E_t$ added in appropriate places and by assuming sufficient regularity conditions to justify differentiation on the right of $E_t$, or under the corresponding integral defining $E_t$. Thus, the literature on the maximum principle can also be drawn upon, as well as the literature on concave programming.

In this section, I have tried to point out that by viewing dynamic optimization as a constrained maximization problem, I can utilize the results of constrained maximization that are well-known in the literature on dynamic economics. In chapter 7 and sections 3.4 and 8.1 to 8.3, I study dynamic optimization in continuous time as a constrained maximization problem and solve the problem by the method of Lagrange multipliers as a generalization of Pontryagin's maximum principle.

## Problems

1. Consider the optimal growth model

$$\max \sum_{t=0}^{\infty} \beta^t \ln(c_t)$$

subject to $$k_{t+1} = k_t^{\alpha} - c_t.$$

This is an example of the problem of equations (2.1)–(2.2) if we define $c_t$ as the control variable $u_t$ and $k_t$ as the state variable $x_t$. Then $r(x_t, u_t) = \ln(u_t)$ and $f(x_t, u_t) = x_t^{\alpha} - u_t$.

   (a) Define $k_{t+1}$ as the control variable $u_t$ and $k_t$ as the state variable $x_t$. Specify $r(x_t, u_t)$ and $f(x_t, u_t)$.
   (b) Define $\ln k_{t+1} = u_t$ and $\ln k_t = x_t$. Specify $r(x_t, u_t)$ and $f(x_t, u_t)$.

2. Using dynamic programming, find the optimal control rule and the value function for
   (a) Problem 1(a).
   (b) Problem 1(b).

3. Using the Lagrange method, find the optimal control rule and the Lagrange function for
   (a) Problem 1(a).
   (b) Problem 1(b).

4. Consider the optimal growth model

$$\max \sum_{t=0}^{\infty} \beta^t \ln(c_t)$$

subject to

$$k_{t+1} = k_t + q_t - c_t$$

$$q_t = A_t k_t^{(1-\alpha)}$$

$$\ln A_{t+1} = \gamma + \ln A_t + \varepsilon_{t+1}$$

(a) Define the control variable $u_t = c_t$ and the state variables $x_t = (\ln A_t, k_t)$. What are $r(x_t, u_t)$ and $f(x_t, u_t)$ in the standard optimum control problem?
(b) Define $u_t = k_{t+1}$ and $x_t = (\ln A_t, k_t)$. Specify $r(x_t, u_t)$ and $f(x_t, u_t)$.
(c) Define $u_t = \ln k_{t+1}$, and $x_t = (\ln A_t, k_t)$. Specify $r(x_t, u_t)$ and $f(x_t, u_t)$.

5. Explain how to solve the nonstochastic optimal control problem associated with equations (2.12) and (2.13) when $\varepsilon_t = 0$ for all $t$. Under what circumstances will the optimal path $(x_t, u_t)$ reach a steady-state $(\bar{x}, \bar{u})$? How do you find the steady-state $(\bar{x}, \bar{u})$?

6. For the numerical example with $f$, $\partial r/\partial x$, and $\partial r/\partial u$ given at the end of section 2.4, find H, G, $h$, and $g$ of the linear Lagrange function and control function. Specify the dynamic equation for $x_t$ under optimal control. Explain why $x_t$ does or does not reach a steady state $\bar{x}$ as $t$ increases. How do you characterize the condition for $x_t$ to reach a steady-state $\bar{x}$?

7. Using the method of section 2.4, state an algorithm to find an approximately optimal linear decision rule for

   (a) Problem 4(a).
   (b) Problem 4(b).
   (c) Problem 4(c).

8. Consider the same problem as in problem 4. Define $\ln z_t = \ln A_t/\alpha$. Let $u_t = \ln(k_{t+1}/z_t)$ and $x_t = [\ln(z_t/z_{t-1}), \ln(k_t/z_{t-1})]$.

   (a) Specify $r(x_t, u_t)$ and $f(x_t, u_t)$.
   (b) Using the method of section 2.4, state an algorithm to find an approximately optimal linear decision rule.

9. Assuming $A + CG$ to be $2 \times 2$, show that $x_t$ satisfying the difference equation $x_t = (A + CG)x_{t-1} + Cg$ will reach a steady rate if and only if the two roots of the determinantal equation $|(A + CG) - \mu I| = 0$ are smaller than one in absolute value. [This important theorem can be found in any standard text on difference equations, including Chow (1975).]

# Economic Growth

## 3.1 The Brock-Mirman Growth Model

Consider a very simple optimal growth model

$$\max_{\{c_t\}} \sum_{t=0}^{\infty} E_t \beta^t \ln c_t \tag{3.1}$$

subject to

$$k_{t+1} = k_t^{\alpha} z_t - c_t \tag{3.2}$$

in which consumption $c_t$ is the control variable, and capital stock $k_t$ and random shock $z_t$ are state variables. By using dynamic programming, set up the Bellman equation

$$V(x_t) = \max_{u_t} \{ r(x_t, u_t) + \beta E_t V(x_{t+1}) \} \tag{3.3}$$

for this problem and solve for the value function. Assuming, in favor of Bellman, that I conjecture correctly that the value function takes the form

$$V(k_t, z_t) = a + b \ln k_t + c \ln z_t, \tag{3.4}$$

where $a$, $b$, and $c$ are three parameters to be determined. Evaluating $V_{t+1} = V(k_{t+1}, z_{t+1})$ by using the dynamic constraint and taking its conditional expectation $E_t$ give

$$V(k_{t+1}, z_{t+1}) = a + b \ln(k_t^{\alpha} z_t - c_t) + c \ln z_{t+1}$$

$$E_t V(k_{t+1}, z_{t+1}) = a + b \ln(k_t^{\alpha} z_t - c_t) + c E_t \ln z_{t+1},$$

where $E_t \ln z_{t+1}$ is assumed to be zero. Maximizing the expression in curly brackets in (3.3) by differentiation with respect to $c_t$, one obtains

$$\frac{\partial\{\quad\}}{\partial c_t} = c_t^{-1} - \beta b (k_t^{\alpha} z_t - c_t)^{-1} = 0$$

yielding the optimal control function

$$c_t = \left(1+\beta b\right)^{-1} k_t^{\alpha} z_t.$$

Substituting this optimal $c_t$ into the expression in curly brackets, one obtains

$$\max_{c_t}\{\quad\} = -\ln\left(1+\beta b\right) + \beta a + \beta b \ln\left(\frac{\beta b}{1+\beta b}\right) + \alpha\left(1+\beta b\right)\ln k_t + \left(1+\beta b\right)\ln z_t, \tag{3.5}$$

which, by the Bellman equation (3.3), equals the value function (3.4). By equating coefficients of (3.4) and (3.5), one solves for the unknown parameters of the value function and obtains, after some algebraic manipulations,

$$\begin{aligned} \mathrm{a} &= \left[1-\beta\right]^{-1}\left[\ln\left(1-\alpha\beta\right) + \beta\alpha\left(1-\alpha\beta\right)^{-1}\ln\left(\alpha\beta\right)\right] \\ \mathrm{b} &= \alpha\left(1-\alpha\beta\right)^{-1} \\ \mathrm{c} &= \left(1-\alpha\beta\right)^{-1}. \end{aligned} \tag{3.6}$$

The method of Lagrange multipliers is simpler than dynamic programming because it does not seek the value function. By this method, solve the first-order conditions given by (2.15) and (2.16) of chapter 2, or

$$c_t^{-1} - \beta E_t \lambda_{t+1} = 0 \tag{3.7}$$

$$\lambda_t = \beta\alpha k_t^{\alpha-1} z_t E_t \lambda_{t+1} \tag{3.8}$$

If the time horizon is $T$ and $k_{T+1} = 0$, the optimal $c_T$ is $k_T^{\alpha} z_T$, which suggests the function $c_t = d k_t^{\alpha} z_t$, $d$ being a parameter to be determined. By using this conjecture for $c_t$ and combining conditions (3.7) and (3.8), one obtains $\lambda_t = d^{-1}\alpha k_t^{-1}$. By using this to evaluate $\lambda_{t+1} = d^{-1}\alpha(k_t^{\alpha} z_t - d k_t^{\alpha} z_t)^{-1}$ on the right side of (3.8) and equating coefficients on both sides of equation (3.8), one obtains $d = 1 - \alpha\beta$. Thus, easily obtained are the optimal control function for $c_t$ and the Lagrangean function $\lambda_t$, namely,

$$\begin{aligned} c_t &= \left(1-\alpha\beta\right) k_t^{\alpha} z_t \\ \lambda_t &= \left(1-\alpha\beta\right)^{-1} \alpha k_t^{-1}. \end{aligned} \tag{3.9}$$

Only one unknown parameter $d = 1 - \alpha\beta$ is required, rather than three in the case of solving the Bellman equation (3.3). Note that $\lambda_t = \partial \mathrm{V}/\partial k_t$.

This example demonstrates that, as pointed out in sections 1.2 and 2.2, to obtain the optimal control function, it is unnecessary to seek the value function, because the first-order condition (3.7) involves only $\lambda_{t+1} = \partial \mathrm{V}(x_{t+1})/\partial x_{t+1}$ and not $\mathrm{V}(x_{t+1})$ itself. The method of Lagrange multipliers is simpler in this example also because only the partial derivative of V with respect to the state variable $k_t$ subject to constraint is required.

## 3.2 A Multisector Growth Model

The model of section 3.1 can be generalized into a model with N goods. Each good may be a consumption good $c_{it}$, an input $x_{ki,t}$, which is used for production of output $Y_{kt}$ at time $t$, or may serve both purposes. The problem is

$$\max_{\{x_{ij,t}\}} \sum_{t=0}^{\infty} E_t \beta^t \sum_{i=1}^{N} \theta_i \ln c_{it} \tag{3.10}$$

subject to the constraints of the Cobb-Douglas production functions with technology shocks $z_{i,t+1}$.

$$Y_{i,t+1} = z_{i,t+1} \prod_{j=1}^{N} x_{ij,t}^{a_{ij}} \qquad i = 1, \ldots, N \tag{3.11}$$

and the budget constraints

$$Y_{it} = c_{it} + \sum_{k=1}^{N} x_{ki,t} \qquad i = 1, \ldots, N \tag{3.12}$$

The state variables are $(Y_{it}, z_{it})$ $(i = 1, \ldots, N)$ and the control variables are $x_{ij,t}$ $(i,j = 1, \ldots, N)$. Equation (3.12) can be used to substitute for $c_{it}$ in the objective function.

This problem was solved by Radner (1966) by dynamic programming and was discussed by Long and Plosser (1983). To solve this problem, introduce the Lagrange multipliers $\lambda_{i,t+1}$ for the constraints (3.11) and form the Lagrange expression

$$\mathcal{L} = \sum_{t=1}^{\infty} E_t \left\{ \beta^t \sum_{i=1}^{N} \theta_i \ln\left( Y_{it} - \sum_{k=1}^{N} x_{ki,t} \right) - \beta^{t+1} \sum_{i=1}^{N} \lambda_{i,t+1} \left( Y_{i,t+1} - z_{i,t+1} \prod_{j=1}^{N} x_{ij,t}^{a_{ij}} \right) \right\}. \tag{3.13}$$

If the $i$th good is not a consumption good $\theta_i = 0$. If the $j$th good is not an input for production, $a_{ij} = 0$ for all $i$. The first-order conditions are

$$\beta^{-t} \frac{\partial \mathcal{L}}{\partial x_{ij,t}} = -\left( Y_{jt} - \sum_{k=1}^{N} x_{kj,t} \right)^{-1} \theta_j + \beta a_{ij} \left( \prod_{j=1}^{N} x_{ij,t}^{a_{ij}} \right) \left( x_{ij,t} \right)^{-1} E_t z_{i,t+1} \lambda_{i,t+1} = 0$$

$$i, j = 1, \ldots, N \tag{3.14}$$

$$\beta^{-t} \frac{\partial \mathcal{L}}{\partial Y_{it}} = \left( Y_{it} - \sum_{k=1}^{N} x_{ki,t} \right)^{-1} \theta_i - \lambda_{it} = 0 \qquad i = 1, \ldots, N \tag{3.15}$$

Combining (3.15) with (3.14), one finds an equation for $\lambda_{jt}$:

$$\lambda_{jt} = \beta a_{ij} \left( \prod_{k=1}^{N} x_{ik,t}^{a_{ik}} \right) x_{ij,t}^{-1} E_t z_{i,t+1} \lambda_{i,t+1}$$

If one follows the solution given by equation (3.9) for the one-sector model, one may conjecture

$$\lambda_{jt} = \gamma_j Y_{jt}^{-1} \tag{3.16}$$

for a parameter $\gamma_j$ yet to be determined. This equation implies, using the production function (3.11) for $Y_{i,t+1}$,

$$\gamma_j Y_{jt}^{-1} = \beta a_{ij}\left(\prod_{k=1}^{N} x_{ik,t}^{a_{ik}}\right) x_{ij,t}^{-1} E_t z_{i,t+1} \gamma_i z_{i,t+1}^{-1}\left(\prod_{k=1}^{N} x_{ik,t}^{a_{ik}}\right)^{-1}$$
$$= \beta a_{ij} x_{ij,t}^{-1} \gamma_i. \qquad i = 1, \ldots, N$$

Solving the optimal control function for $x_{ij,t}$, one obtains

$$x_{ij,t} = \gamma_j^{-1} \beta \gamma_i a_{ij} Y_{jt}. \tag{3.17}$$

Substituting this solution for $x_{kj,t}$ in (3.15) yields

$$\left(Y_{jt} - \gamma_j^{-1} \beta Y_{jt} \sum_{k=1}^{N} \gamma_k a_{kj}\right)^{-1} \theta_j = \lambda_{jt} = \gamma_j Y_{jt}^{-1} \quad k = 1, \ldots, N$$

and a system of N linear equations for the unknowns $\gamma_j$,

$$\gamma_j - \beta \sum_{k=1}^{N} a_{kj} \gamma_k = \theta_j \qquad j = 1, \ldots, N$$

Letting $\gamma' = (\gamma_1, \ldots, \gamma_N)$, $\theta' = (\theta_1, \ldots, \theta_N)$ and $A = (a_{ij})$, one can write this system of equations as

$$[I - \beta A']\gamma = \theta \tag{3.18}$$

With the parameter vector $\gamma$ given by (3.18), the Lagrange multipliers $\lambda_{jt}$ and the optimal control functions for $x_{ij,t}$ are given by (3.16) and (3.17), respectively. This solution appears to be simplier than the solution by dynamic programming provided by Radner (1966) and cited in Long and Plosser (1983).

The model presented above is a slightly simplified version of the model discussed in Radner (1966) and Long and Plosser (1983). The original version has leisure $W_t$ in the utility function and labor $L_t$ in the production functions, but the utility function and the production functions have the same forms as above, except with one additional variable introduced. Specifically, the utility function is

$$u(c_t, W_t) = \theta_0 \ln W_t + \sum_{i=1}^{N} \theta_i \ln c_{it} \tag{3.19}$$

and the production functions are

$$Y_{i,t+1} = z_{i,t+1} L_{it}^{b_i} \prod_{j=1}^{N} x_{ijt}^{a_{ij}}. \qquad i = 1, \ldots, N \tag{3.20}$$

Besides the budget constraints (3.12), there is a constraint on total time H

$$W_t + \sum_{i=1}^{N} L_{it} = H. \tag{3.21}$$

It is suggested as an exercise (see problem 4) to set up the Lagrangean expression corresponding to (3.13) for this slightly more general problem and to derive the first-order conditions corresponding to (3.14), (3.15), and (3.16). The solution of the first-order conditions would yield the following decision functions, with $(\gamma_1, \ldots, \gamma_N)$ defined by (3.18)

$$c_{it} = (\theta_i/\gamma_i)Y_{it} \tag{3.22}$$

$$W_t = \theta_0\left(\theta_0 + \beta\sum_{i=1}^{N}\gamma_i b_i\right)^{-1} H \tag{3.23}$$

$$x_{ij,t} = (\beta\gamma_i a_{ij}/\gamma_j)Y_{jt} \tag{3.24}$$

$$L_{it} = \beta\gamma_i b_i\left(\theta_0 + \beta\sum_{j=1}^{N}\gamma_j b_j\right)^{-1} H. \tag{3.25}$$

Note that by (3.22), consumption $c_{it}$ of the $i$th good is proportional to output $Y_{it}$. By (3.23), leisure is proportional to total time H. Input $x_{ij}$ of the $j$th good in producing good $i$ is proportional to the quantity of output $Y_{jt}$. Labor $L_{it}$ employed in producing the $i$th good is proportional to total time $H_t$. As in the case of the one-sector growth model of section 3.1, although the random shocks $z_{it}$ are state variables and are therefore variables in the value function, these variables do not have Lagrange multipliers associated with them, because their dynamic evolution is independent of the control variables, and no constraints need to be introduced for them. They are also absent from the optimal decision functions (3.22)–(3.25). If dynamic programming is used to solve this problem as in Radner (1966), the Bellman Equation is

$$V(Y_t,\ z_t) = \max\{u(c_t,\ W_t) + \beta E_t V(Y_{t+1},\ z_{t+1})\}$$

and the solution is

$$V(Y_t,\ z_t) = \sum_{i=1}^{N}\gamma_i \ln Y_{it} + J(z_t) + \text{constant}$$

in which

$$J(z_t) = \beta E\left[\sum_{i=1}^{N}\gamma_i \ln z_{i,t+1} + J(z_{t+1})\middle|z_t\right].$$

If total time H is fixed, by (3.25) labor input $L_{it}$ in producing each good $i$ is fixed; a production function with constant return to scale (or homogeneous of degree one) in all inputs including labor, such as production function (3.20) with $b_i + \sum_{j=1}^{N} a_{ij} = 1$, will exhibit diminishing marginal product for each physical input as its quantity increases. As the economy accumulates physical capital per consumer-worker, output of each good per consumer-worker will increase but less than proportionally. For example, if the economy maintains a 4 percent annual increase in physical capital per consumer-worker, with

$\sum_{j=1}^{N} a_{ij} = 0.4$ and $b_i = 0.6$, output per consumer-worker will increase by only $0.4 \times 4$ or 1.6 percent per year. Empirically, however, for the United States and many other developed western economies, the ratio of output per person and physical capital stock per person remained fairly constant for decades and did not decrease as the model of this section would predict. One explanation is the increase in technology as measured by $z_{it}$ in equation (3.20), also termed the Solow residual in view of the classical work of Robert Solow (1957) on economic growth in which such a phenomenon was pointed out.

Much of the literature on economic growth is devoted to the explanation of the Solow residual, or technological change in the framework of a neoclassical production function, such as (3.20) with constant return to scale in labor and physical inputs. One important explanation is investment in human capital, making one laborer in 1990 more productive than one laborer in 1960, as the former has more human capital invested through more education and on-the-job training. If investment in human capital is itself determined endogenously by the worker-consumer's dynamic optimization behavior, it is an endogenous growth theory. Examples of endogenous growth models are given in sections 3.3, 3.4, and 3.5.

## 3.3 A Growth Model Based on Human Capital and Fertility

In economic development of nations, a key question is why some countries remain stagnant for a long time, and others, having achieved development, continue to grow. The model of Becker, Murphy, and Tamura (1990), henceforth BMT, has attempted to answer this question. The model is capable of producing a stationary state with no growth and a state of continued growth, with approximately constant rates of growth in the important variables. The key idea is that a more developed country has more knowledge and skill, or human capital, imbedded in its people. Economic development is measured by the amount of human capital per working person $H_t$ in the population. The growth of $H_t$ is the result of conscious choice of an adult parent to devote effort $h_t$, using ones own capital $H_t$, to educate each child to yield per capita human capital $H_{t+1}$ for the next generation, while devoting effort $l_t$ to produce $c_t$ unit of consumption good for ones own consumption and $fn_t$ units of consumption good to feed $n_t$ children. In the simplest version of the model, physical capital is assumed constant and thus ignored. Every person in the economy is assumed to be identical and live for two periods, childhood and adulthood. As a child the person invests in H. At the beginning of adulthood, the person chooses the number $n$ of children and works T hours as an adult. To rear each child, $v$ hours and $f$ units of consumption good have to be spent. Each child is endowed with $H^0$ units of human capital at birth.

Human capital can be used to produce $c_t$ units of consumption good for ones own consumption and $fn_t$ units to feed $n_t$ children per adult parent, according to the production function

$$c_t + fn_t = Dl_t(dH^0 + H_t) \tag{3.26}$$

in which D measures productivity, $l$ is the time spent by each adult producing consumer goods, and $d$ is the rate of productivity of $H^0$ as compared with $H_t$. Human capital per worker is produced according to the production function

$$H_{t+1} = Ah_t(bH^0 + H_t)^\beta \tag{3.27}$$

in which $h_t$ is the time spent educating children. Total time T per adult can be used to produce consumption good and to rear $n$ children according to the time constraint

$$T = l_t + n_t(v + h_t) \tag{3.28}$$

Parents are assumed to maximize the utility function

$$V_t = u(c_t) + a(n_t)n_t V_{t+1} \tag{3.29}$$

that depends on the parent's own consumption $c_t$ and the utility per child $V_{t+1}$ in the future, times the number of children $n_t$ and a factor $a(n_t)$ to discount the utility per child from the viewpoint of the parent. The control variables are $c_t$, $l_t$, $h_t$, and $n_t$. The state variable is $H_t$. Note that $h_t$ hours are spent to produce human capital $H_{t+1}$ for the next period according to the dynamic equation (3.27). Human capital $H_t$ is combined with $l_t$ hours of labor to produce consumption good $c_t$ for the parent's own consumption and for the consumption of $n_t$ children, according to (3.26).

Using the production function (3.26) to eliminate $c_t$ and the time constraint (3.28) to eliminate $l_t$, one is left with only two control variables, $n_t$ and $h_t$. These two control variables serve to emphasize the decisions on the number of children and on the number of hours spent to educate them, which are important topics of BMT. By using (3.26) and (3.28), write $c_t$ as

$$c_t = Dl_t(dH^0 + H_t) - fn_t = D[T - n_t(v + h_t)](dH^0 + H_t) - fn_t. \tag{3.30}$$

Substituting (3.30) for $c_t$ in the objective function (3.29), treat the objective function (3.29) for a parent of period $t$ as a function of the state variable $H_t$ and the two control variables $n_t$ and $h_t$. This objective function differs from the standard infinite-period time-separable objective function. If one tries to convert (3.29) to an infinite-period objective function by repeated substitutions, one obtains

$$V_t = u(c_t) + a(n_t)n_t\{u(c_{t+1}) + a(n_{t+1})n_{t+1}[u(c_{t+2}) + \ldots\}$$

and finds that the control variable $n_t$ affects all future utilities as a multiplicative factor of $u(c_{t+1})$, $u(c_{t+2})$, ... Therefore, retain the objective function (3.29) and note that $V_{t+1}$ is obtained by the parent of period $t + 1$, who will solve the same optimization problem. If the Lagrange multiplier $\lambda_{t+1}$ of the dynamic constraint for $H_{t+1}$ is the marginal utility of per-worker capital $H_{t+1}$ to a parent in period $t + 1$ (currently a child of a parent in period $t$), it must be discounted by $a(n_t)n_t$ to yield marginal utility for the maximizing parent in period $t$. These remarks justify the following Lagrangean for the dynamic optimization problem of an adult parent in period $t$ and its associated first-order conditions.

$$\mathscr{L} = u\left(D\left[T - n_t(v + h_t)\right](dH^0 + H_t) - fn_t\right) + a(n_t)n_t V_{t+1}$$
$$-\lambda_t\left[H_t - Ah_{t-1}(bH^0 + H_{t-1})^{\beta}\right] - a(n_t)n_t\lambda_{t+1}\left[H_{t+1} - Ah_t(bH^0 + H_t)^{\beta}\right] \quad (3.31)$$

$$\frac{\partial\mathscr{L}}{\partial n_t} = u'(c_t)\left[-D(v + h_t)(dH^0 + H_t) - f\right] + \left[a'(n_t)n_t + a(n_t)\right]V_{t+1} = 0 \quad (3.32)$$

$$\frac{\partial\mathscr{L}}{\partial h_t} = u'(c_t)\left[-Dn_t(dH^0 + H_t)\right] + a(n_t)n_t A(bH^0 + H_t)^{\beta}\lambda_{t+1} \leqslant 0 \quad (3.33)$$

$$\frac{\partial\mathscr{L}}{\partial H_t} = -\lambda_t + u'(c_t)D\left[T - n_t(v + h_t)\right] + a(n_t)n_t Ah_t\beta(bH^0 + H_t)^{\beta-1}\lambda_{t+1} \leqslant 0 \quad (3.34)$$

The equality sign holds in (3.33) when $h_t > 0$ and in (3.34) when $H_t > 0$; the sign < holds when the variable is zero. Postpone the solution of (3.32) for $n_t$. Treating $n_t$ as given temporarily, solve the two first-order conditions (3.33) and (3.34) for the control variable $h_t$ and the Lagrange multiplier $\lambda_t$. By using (3.33) to substitute for the term involving $\lambda_{t+1}$ in (3.34), one obtains

$$\lambda_t \geqslant u'(c_t)\left\{D\left[T - n_t(v + h_t)\right] + Dn_t(dH^0 + H_t)h_t\beta(bH^0 + H_t)^{-1}\right\}. \quad (3.35)$$

By using the assumptions introduced by BMT (p. S20) that $\beta = 1$ and $d = b = 1$, one can simplify (3.35) to

$$\lambda_t \geqslant u'(c_t)D\left[T - vn_t\right] \quad (3.36)$$

By using (3.36) to replace $\lambda_{t+1}$ in (3.33), one obtains

$$u'(c_t) \geqslant a(n_t)A\left[T - vn_{t+1}\right]u'(c_{t+1}) \quad (3.37)$$

BMT treat a special case of the utility function (3.29) by assuming (p. S21)

$$a(n) = \alpha n^{-\varepsilon}, \quad u(c) = c^{\sigma}/\sigma \quad (3.38)$$

in which $0 \leqslant \varepsilon < 1$ and $0 < \sigma < 1$, $\alpha$ is the degree of pure altruism on the part of the parents (when $n = 1$), and $\varepsilon$ is the constant elasticity of altruism per child as their number increases. Given (3.38), equation (3.37) implies,

$$\frac{u'(c_t)}{a(n_t)u'(c_{t+1})} = \alpha^{-1}n_t^{\varepsilon}\left(\frac{c_{t+1}}{c_t}\right)^{1-\sigma} \geqslant A(T - vn_{t+1}) = A(l_{t+1} + h_{t+1}n_{t+1}), \quad (3.39)$$

which is the result contained in equations (9) and (10) of BMT (p. S21), derived by dynamic programming. In equilibrium, the rate of substitution between the marginal utilities of per capita consumptions $c_t$ and $c_{t+1}$ in periods $t$ and $t + 1$ given on the left-hand side of (3.39) must be greater than or equal to

$R_{ht} = 1 + r_{ht}$, in which $r_{ht}$ is the rate of return on investment in human capital with equality holding when investment is positive. According to the right-hand side of (3.39), the latter depends on the productivity A in the human capital accumulation equation (3.27) to produce $H_{t+1}$ and on the productivity of per-worker $H_{t+1}$, which in turn depends on $l_{t+1}$ by equation (3.26), $h_{t+1}$ by equation (3.27), and the number of children $n_{t+1}$.

Birth rate or fertility $n_t$ can be determined by equation (3.32). Under assumptions $d = b = \beta = D = 1$ and (3.38), equation (3.32) can be written as

$$u'(c_t)\left[(v + h_t)(H^0 + H_t) + f\right] = \alpha(1 - \varepsilon)n_t^{-\varepsilon}V_{t+1} \tag{3.40}$$

Under the same assumptions, equation (3.33) can be written as

$$u'(c_t) \geqslant A\alpha n_t^{-\varepsilon}\lambda_{t+1}. \tag{3.41}$$

These two first-order conditions will determine $n_t$ and $h_t$.

A main motivation of this study is to use investment in human capital $H_t$ per worker to explain two important facts about fertility $n_t$ in economic growth. First, in some less developed countries, effort $h_t$ in investment in human capital per child is small and human capital remains very low. There is no development. Second, in an advanced stage of development, $H_t$ continues to growth, fertility $n_t$ remains roughly constant, and the effort $h_t$ to educate each child is large. This model has an equilibrium at $H_t = 0$, which can be obtained by solving (3.40) and (3.41). Noting $\lambda_{t+1} = \partial V_{t+1}/\partial H_{t+1}$, differentiate (3.40) with respect to $H_{t+1}$, after replacing $(H^0 + H_t)$ on the left-hand side by $A^{-1}h_t^{-1}H_{t+1}$ to obtain

$$u'(c_t)(v + h_t)A^{-1}h_t^{-1} = \alpha(1 - \varepsilon)n_t^{-\varepsilon}\lambda_{t+1} \tag{3.42}$$

Substituting (3.41) for $u'(c_t)$ in (3.42) gives

$$(v + h_t) \geqslant (1 - \varepsilon)h_t$$

Because equality holds for $h_t = -v/\varepsilon$, the solution for the optimum is a corner solution with $h_t = 0$ for all $t$. Given $h_t = 0$ and $H_t = 0$, there are only two control variables $c_t$ and $n_t$ for the parent to choose. These variables are subject to the constraint (3.30), rewritten as

$$c_t = \left[T - vn_t\right]H^0 - fn_t = TH^0 - (vH^0 + f)n_t. \tag{3.43}$$

The objective function (3.29), with $V_t(H_t) = V(0) = V_{t+1}(H_{t+1}) \equiv V$, can be solved for V to yield

$$V = \frac{u(c_t)}{1 - a(n_t)n_t} = \frac{c_t^\sigma}{\sigma(1 - \alpha n_t^{1-\varepsilon})} \tag{3.44}$$

By using (3.44) for $V_{t+1}$ and (3.43) for $c_t$ in (3.40), one derives the following equation to determine fertility $n_t$ in this no-growth equilibrium:

$$c_t^{\sigma-1}\left[vH^0 + f\right] = \alpha(1 - \varepsilon)n_t^{-\varepsilon}\frac{c_t^\sigma}{\sigma(1 - \alpha n_t^{1-\varepsilon})}$$

or

$$\left(v\mathrm{H}^0 + f\right)\sigma n_t^{\varepsilon} + \alpha\left(1 - \varepsilon - \sigma\right)\left(v\mathrm{H}^0 + f\right)n_t - \alpha\left(1 - \varepsilon\right)\mathrm{TH}^0 = 0. \qquad (3.45)$$

Besides this equilibrium with no growth, there is another equilibrium with constant rates of growth in per capita human capital $\mathrm{H}_t$ and in consumption $c_t$, with fertility $n_t$ and effort to invest $h_t$ constant. A country would need some exogenous technological shock to get to a state with high $\mathrm{H}_t$. Given a high $\mathrm{H}_t$, this equilibrium can be obtained by solving equations (3.40) and (3.41). The ratio of (3.41) to (3.40) is

$$\frac{\mathrm{A}\lambda_{t+1}}{\left(1-\varepsilon\right)\mathrm{V}_{t+1}} = \frac{1}{\left(v+h_t\right)\left(\mathrm{H}^0+\mathrm{H}_t\right)+f} = \frac{\mathrm{A}h_t}{\mathrm{H}_{t+1}\left[\left(v+h_t\right)+f\mathrm{A}\,h_t/\mathrm{H}_{t+1}\right]}$$

Noting $\lambda_{t+1} = d\mathrm{V}_{t+1}/\partial\mathrm{H}_{t+1}$ and denoting $d\log\mathrm{V}_{t+1}/d\log\mathrm{H}_{t+1}$ or $\lambda_{t+1}\mathrm{H}_{t+1}/\mathrm{V}_{t+1}$ by $\sigma_{t+1}$, write the preceding equation as

$$\sigma_{t+1}\left[v + h_t + f\mathrm{A}h_t/\mathrm{H}_{t+1}\right] = \left(1-\varepsilon\right)h_t$$

When $\mathrm{H}_{t+1}$ is large compared with $f\mathrm{A}h_t$, use the approximation

$$\sigma_{t+1}\left(v+h_t\right) \doteq \left(1-\varepsilon\right)h_t. \qquad (3.46)$$

In an equilibrium with $h_t$ equal to a constant $h^*$, equation (3.46) implies that $\sigma_t = d\log\mathrm{V}_t/d\log\mathrm{H}_t$ is a constant $\sigma$. If the growth rate of consumption is defined by $g^*$ and (3.30) is used for consumption, then

$$1+g^* = \frac{c_{t+1}}{c_t} = \frac{\mathrm{H}^0+\mathrm{H}_{t+1} - fn^*l}{\mathrm{H}^0+\mathrm{H}_t - fn^*l} \simeq \frac{\mathrm{H}^0+\mathrm{H}_{t+1}}{\mathrm{H}^0+\mathrm{H}_t}, \qquad (3.47)$$

which is approximately equal to the growth rate of per capita human capital $\mathrm{H}^0 + \mathrm{H}_t$ if $fn^*/l$ is small compared with $\mathrm{H}^0 + \mathrm{H}_t$.

By (3.27), one has

$$\frac{\mathrm{H}^0+\mathrm{H}_{t+1}}{\mathrm{H}^0+\mathrm{H}_t} = \mathrm{A}h^* + \frac{\mathrm{H}^0}{\mathrm{H}^0+\mathrm{H}_t} \simeq \mathrm{A}h^*$$

if $\mathrm{H}^0$ is small compared with $\mathrm{H}^0 + \mathrm{H}_t$. Then, obtain by this relation and (3.47)

$$h^* = \left(1+g^*\right)/\mathrm{A} \qquad (3.48)$$

Substituting (3.48) for $h_t$ in (3.46) yields

$$1+g^* = \frac{\sigma v\mathrm{A}}{1-\varepsilon-\sigma} \qquad (3.49)$$

and

$$h^* = \frac{\sigma v}{1-\varepsilon-\sigma} \qquad (3.50)$$

The constant fertility rate $n^*$ can be obtained from (3.39) or

$$n^{*\varepsilon}\left(1+g^*\right)^{1-\sigma} = \alpha\mathrm{A}\left(\mathrm{T}-vn^*\right) \qquad (3.51)$$

Equations (3.47), (3.49), (3.50), and (3.51) characterize a developed economy with constant rates of growth in per capita consumption $c_t$ and per capita human capital $H^0 + H_t$, and fertility $n_t$ and effort $h_t$ in educating the young are constant. The above discussion gives the key elements of the role of human capital formation in development. Physical capital can be incorporated as has been done in BMT.

## 3.4 Technology and Economic Growth

Although the model of section 3.3 treats an increase in human capital as an increase in skill and knowledge imbedded in humans, Roemer (1990) identifies technology $A_t$ as knowledge in the economy not necessarily imbedded in people, as measured by the number of designs in an economy, and attempts to explain the change in technology. In place of equation (3.27) to explain the accumulation of human capital $H_t$, the following equation explains the accumulation of the stock of designs or the advance in technology from time $t$ to time $t + dt$:

$$A(t+dt) - A(t) = \delta H_A(t)A(t)dt \tag{3.52}$$

in which $H_A(t)$ is the quantity of human capital devoted to the production of technology. The notation of (3.52) facilitates modeling in continuous time. If we divide both sides of (3.52) by $dt$ and take the limit as $dt \to 0$, the left-hand side is the time derivative $\dot{A}(t) = dA/dt$, and a differential equation results. The notation of (3.52) allows one to use the Lagrange method of optimization for discrete time. Although there are four factors of production, labor L and human capital H are assumed to be fixed. Only (physical) capital K and technology A vary over time to emphasize the change in technology in the development process.

There are three productive sectors in the economy. First, the production of technology or the number of designs $A(t)$ is given by (3.52). Second, an intermediate-goods sector uses $A(t)$ and forgone output to produce a large number of producer durables $x(1)$, $x(2)$, . . . Third, a final-good sector uses labor L, human capital H, and $x(1)$, $x(2)$, . . . , to produce final output Y, which can be used for consumption or as new capital. The production function for final output is

$$Y(H_Y, L, x) = H_Y^\alpha L^\beta \sum_{i=1}^{\infty} x(i)^{1-\alpha-\beta} \tag{3.53}$$

The representative firm in the final output sector will demand the quantities $x(i)$ of all inputs to maximize its profit

$$\sum_{i=1}^{\infty}\left[H_Y^\alpha L^\beta x(i)^{1-\alpha-\beta} - p(i)x(i)\right]$$

Differentiation with respect to each $x(i)$ yields an inverse demand function for input $x(i)$:

$$p(i) = (1 - \alpha - \beta) H_Y^{\alpha} L^{\beta} x(i)^{-\alpha-\beta} \tag{3.54}$$

In the intermediate-goods sector, firm $i$ producing intermediate good $x(i)$ under monopolistic competition tries to maximize its profit $\pi(i)$. Each firm $i$ is assumed to use one design $i$ for which it has paid a fixed cost. The maximum profit of firm $i$ is

$$\begin{aligned}\pi(i) &= \max_{x(i)} \left[ p(i)x(i) - r\eta x(i) \right] \\ &= \max_{x(i)} \left[ (1 - \alpha - \beta) H_Y^{\alpha} L^{\beta} x(i)^{1-\alpha-\beta} - r\eta x(i) \right]\end{aligned} \tag{3.55}$$

in which $x(i)$ units of intermediate goods require $\eta x(i)$ units of final output (with unit price) to produce at a total interest cost of $r\eta x(i)$. The resulting price $\bar{p}(i)$ satisfies

$$\bar{p}(i) = r\eta / (1 - \alpha - \beta) \tag{3.56}$$

and maximum profit satisfies

$$\pi(i) = (\alpha + \beta)\bar{p}(i)\bar{x}(i) \tag{3.57}$$

in which $\bar{x}(i)$ is the profit-maximizing output of firm $i$ given by (3.54) and (3.56), namely

$$\bar{x}(i) = \left( H_Y^{\alpha} L^{\beta} \right)^{1/(\alpha+\beta)} (r\eta)^{-1/(\alpha+\beta)} \tag{3.58}$$

A potential firm deciding whether to enter the intermediate-goods sector by buying a new design costing $P_A$ will equate the discounted value of its future profits $\pi(\tau)$ with $P_A$, namely

$$\int_t^{\infty} e^{-\int_t^{\tau} r(s)ds} \pi(\tau) d\tau = P_A(t). \tag{3.59}$$

If $P_A$ is constant in equilibrium, as it is shown below, differentiating (3.59) with respect to $t$ yields

$$\pi(t) - r(t) \int_t^{\infty} e^{-\int_t^{\tau} r(s)ds} \pi(\tau) d\tau = 0$$

which together with equation (3.59) implies

$$\pi(t) = r(t) P_A \tag{3.60}$$

Thus, each firm that invests in a new design to enter the intermediate-goods sector must earn sufficient profit to cover the interest cost of the initial investment.

In the final-good sector, demand for aggregate consumption C is determined by identical consumers maximizing utility

$$\int_0^{\infty} e^{-\rho t} U(C) dt; \quad U(C) = \frac{C^{1-\sigma} - 1}{1 - \sigma} \quad \sigma \in [0, \infty] \tag{3.61}$$

The consumers supply a fixed quantity L of labor to the final-good sector. They divide a fixed quantity H of human capital between $H_Y$ to supply to firms producing the final good and $H_A$ to firms doing research to produce a technology A. They own the firms producing intermediate goods and receive the net revenues of these firms as dividends. Firms producing the final good own no assets and have zero profits under perfect competition.

Because L and H are fixed, the growth of this economy depends on the growth of capital K and technology A. Study the equilibrium of this economy by first treating K and A as given and then explaining their growth. A is the number of existing designs or the number of existing firms producing intermediate goods. Firm $i$ requires $\eta x(i)$ units of capital to produce $x(i)$ units of its intermediate good. Each firm $i$ faces the same demand function (3.54) and solves the same profit maximization problem (3.55), thus producing equal quantity of output $x(i) = \bar{x}$. As in equilibrium total supply K of capital stock equals total demand $\eta A\bar{x}$ by A intermediate-goods firms, output $\bar{x} = K/(\eta A)$ of each firm is determined once K and A are given. Total final output Y of the economy is also determined by equation (3.53) as

$$Y(H_Y, L, x) = H_Y^{\alpha}L^{\beta}A\bar{x}^{1-\alpha-\beta} = H_Y^{\alpha}L^{\beta}A\left(\frac{K}{\eta A}\right)^{1-\alpha-\beta}$$

$$= (H_Y A)^{\alpha}(LA)^{\beta}K^{1-\alpha-\beta}\eta^{\alpha+\beta-1}, \tag{3.62}$$

which is a constant-returns Cobb-Douglas production function with physical capital K, technology-augmented labor LA and technology-augmented human capital $H_Y A$ as inputs.

Given K, A, and $\bar{x}$, if $r$ were known, equations (3.54), (3.57), (3.58), and (3.60) of the intermediate-goods sector will determine $\bar{p}$, $\pi$, $H_Y$ and $P_A$ respectively, yielding

$$P_A = \pi/r = (\alpha+\beta)\bar{p}\bar{x}/r = (\alpha+\beta)(1-\alpha-\beta)H_Y^{\alpha}L^{\beta}\bar{x}^{1-\alpha-\beta}/r \tag{3.63}$$

Because human capital engaged in producing research must receive the same wage as in producing final output, equating the respective values of marginal product $P_A\delta A$ given by equation (3.52) and $\alpha Y/H_Y$ given by (3.62) yields

$$w_A = P_A\delta A = \alpha H_Y^{\alpha-1}L^{\beta}A\bar{x}^{1-\alpha-\beta} \tag{3.64}$$

Substituting (3.63) for $P_A$ in (3.64), we can solve for $H_Y$:

$$H_Y = \frac{\alpha r}{\delta(\alpha+\beta)(1-\alpha-\beta)} \tag{3.65}$$

Equation (3.65) states that as $r$ increases, price $P_A$ of designs decreases, lowering the value of marginal product of human capital in research and inducing more human capital in producing final output. The effect of $r$ on the rate of growth $g = \delta H_A$ for the stock of technology A given by equation (3.52) is

$$g = \delta H_A = \delta H - \delta H_Y = \delta H - \frac{\alpha r}{(\alpha+\beta)(1-\alpha-\beta)} \equiv \delta H - \Lambda r. \tag{3.66}$$

With $r$ given, $K = \bar{x}\eta A$ is proportional to A and hence K will grow at the same rate $g$ as A. Equation (3.62) ensures that Y will also grow at the same rate as A. Because the ratio of consumption to final output Y

$$\frac{C}{Y} = \frac{Y - \dot{K}}{Y} = 1 - \frac{\dot{K}}{K} \cdot \frac{K}{Y}$$

is constant when $\dot{K}/K$ and K/Y are both constant, consumption C will also grow at the same rate as Y and A. Thus if $r$ is given, A, K, Y, and C will all grow at the rate $g$ given by (3.66).

To determine $r$, appeal to the consumers maximizing discounted life-time utility given by (3.61). When the rate of interest is $r$ optimum intertemporal substitution implies

$$u'(C(t)) = e^{-\rho dt} e^{r dt} u'(C(t+dt)),$$

because one dollar spent for consumption at $t$ should yield the same marginal utility as $e^{rdt}$ dollars spent for consumption at $t + dt$, the latter discounted by time preference $e^{-\rho dt}$. By using the utility function given in (3.61), one has $u'(C) = C^{-\sigma}$ and

$$C(t)^{-\sigma} = e^{(r-\rho)dt} C(t+dt)^{-\sigma}$$

or

$$C(t+dt) = e^{[(r-\rho)/\sigma]dt} C(t).$$

the optimum rate of consumption growth $(r - \rho)/\sigma$ can be equated to the rate of growth $g$, giving $r = \sigma g + \rho$. Combining this result with (3.66) provides a solution for the rate of growth $g$:

$$g = \frac{\delta H - \Lambda\rho}{\sigma\Lambda + 1}, \quad \Lambda = \frac{\alpha}{(\alpha+\beta)(1-\alpha-\beta)} \tag{3.67}$$

Because human capital is employed to produce designs each of which is used by an intermediate-good firm to make monopolistic profit, the quantity $H_A$ employed is smaller than optimum. If the intermediate-good firms were more competitive, there would be more of them demanding more technology. Compare the above (monopolistically competitive) market solution with the solution of a social planner maximizing life-time utility on behalf of the consumers subject to the resource constraints (3.52) for the accumulation of A, (3.53) for Y and

$$K(t+dt) - K(t) = [Y(t) - C(Y)]dt \tag{3.68}$$

for the accumulation of K. The planner has an advantage over monopolistic firms producing intermediate goods. Without making monopolistic profit by restricting output to $\bar{x}(i)$ given by (3.58), the planner can produce output $x(i)$ directly using $\eta x(i)$ units of capital and one design and produce aggregate final good Y by the production function (3.62). The state variables are K and A. The control variables are C and $H_A = H - H_Y$. With Y given by (3.62), the Lagrangean is (argument $t$ omitted when understood)

$$\mathcal{L} = \int_0^\infty \{ e^{-\rho t}(1-\sigma)^{-1} C^{1-\sigma} dt - e^{-\rho(t+dt)} \lambda_1(t+dt)[K(t+dt) - K(t) - (Y - C)dt]$$
$$-e^{-\rho(t+dt)}\lambda_2(t+dt)[A(t+dt) - A(t) - \delta H_A A dt]\}. \quad (3.69)$$

If one denotes the derivatives of Y with respect of $H_A$, K and A by $Y_{HA}$, $Y_K$ and $Y_A$, the first-order conditions are

$$e^{-\rho t}\frac{\partial \mathcal{L}}{\partial C} = C^{-\sigma} dt - e^{-\rho dt}\lambda_1(t+dt)dt = 0 \quad (3.70)$$

$$e^{-\rho t}\frac{\partial \mathcal{L}}{\partial H_A} = e^{-\rho dt} Y_{HA}\lambda_1(t+dt)dt + e^{-\rho dt}\delta A \lambda_2(t+dt)dt = 0 \quad (3.71)$$

$$e^{-\rho t}\frac{\partial \mathcal{L}}{\partial K} = -\lambda_1(t) + e^{-\rho dt}[1 + Y_K dt]\lambda_1(t+dt) = 0 \quad (3.72)$$

$$e^{-\rho t}\frac{\partial \mathcal{L}}{\partial A} = -\lambda_2(t) + e^{-\rho dt}[1 + \delta H_A dt]\lambda_2(t+dt) + e^{-\rho dt} Y_A \lambda_1(t+dt)dt = 0. \quad (3.73)$$

By equation (3.70), $C^{-\sigma} = e^{-\rho dt}\lambda_1(t + dt)$. When this equation is evaluated at $dt = 0$, $C^{-\sigma} = \lambda_1$, equating $\lambda_1$ to the marginal utility of consumption. Equations (3.71) and (3.73) will determine the rate of growth of $\lambda_2$. By equation (3.71),

$$\lambda_1(t+dt) = -\delta A \lambda_2(t+dt)/Y_{HA}$$

When this is substituted for $\lambda_1(t + dt)$, equation (3.73) becomes

$$\lambda_2(t) = e^{-\rho dt}\lambda_2(t+dt) + e^{-\rho dt}[\delta H_A - Y_A \delta A / Y_{HA}]\lambda_2(t+dt)dt$$

Evaluating $Y_A = (\alpha + \beta)Y/A$ and $Y_{HA} = -\alpha Y/(H - H_A)$ by (3.63), the term in square brackets equals

$$\delta[H_A + (\alpha+\beta)(H - H_A)/\alpha] = \delta[(\alpha+\beta)H/\alpha - \beta H_A/\alpha]$$

and the dynamics of $\lambda_2(t)$ is given by

$$\lambda_2(t+dt) = e^{\rho dt}\lambda_2(t) - \delta[(\alpha+\beta)H/\alpha - \beta H_A/\alpha]\lambda_2(t+dt)dt$$

Writing $e^{\rho dt} = 1 + \rho dt + o(dt)$, dividing through by $dt$, and taking the limit of $(\lambda_2(t + dt) - \lambda_2(t))/dt$ as $dt < 0$, one has

$$\dot{\lambda}_2 = \frac{d\lambda_2}{dt} = \lambda_2\{\rho - \delta[(\alpha+\beta)H/\alpha - \beta H_A/\alpha]\} \quad (3.74)$$

The term in curly brackets is the proportional rate of growth of $\lambda_2$.

In an equilibrium with balanced growth, $\dot{\lambda}_1/\lambda_1$ equals $\dot{\lambda}_2/\lambda_2$ and $\dot{C}/C$ equals $\dot{A}/A$. Because $\dot{\lambda}_1/\lambda_1 = -\sigma(\dot{C}/C)$ by equation (3.70) and $\dot{A}/A = \delta H_A$ by equation (3.52), one obtains

$$\dot{\lambda}_1/\lambda_1 = -\sigma\delta H_A = \dot{\lambda}_2/\lambda_2 = \rho - \delta\left[(\alpha+\beta)H/\alpha - \beta H_A/\alpha\right]. \tag{3.75}$$

Solving (3.75) for $H_A$ and using $g = \delta H_A$, we obtain the rate of balanced growth of the economy under optimal social planning:

$$g^* = \frac{\delta H - \theta\rho}{\sigma\theta + (1-\theta)}, \quad \theta = \frac{\alpha}{\alpha+\beta}. \tag{3.76}$$

The market solution of $g$ given by equation (3.67) is smaller than $g^*$ given by (3.76). First, the numerator of g is smaller as $\Lambda$ is larger than $\theta$, $\Lambda$ being equal to $\theta$ times the markup $1/(1 - \alpha - \beta)$ from the monopoly sector. Second, the denominator of $g$ is larger as $\Lambda$ is larger than $\theta$.

The Lagrange method of solving the social planner's optimization problem in continuous time given by equations (3.69) through (3.73) is equivalent to applying Pontryagin's maximum principle. It is generalized to optimization problems with stochastic models in continuous time in section 7.3.

### 3.5 Research and Development and Economic Growth

To study the effect of technological innovations on economic growth, Stokey (1995) formulates the following model. Let $n_t$ denote the highest level of technology available at time $t$. All levels of technology available are denoted by $n_t$, $n_t - 1, \ldots$, which are combined respectively with labor quantities $x_{0t}$, $x_{1t}, \ldots$, in production. Let $U(n, x)$ denote the consumer's utility if $n$ is the highest technology used in production together with $x = (x_0, x_1, \ldots)$ units of labor, the only factor of production in the economy, because the vector $(n, x)$ determines the vector of outputs uniquely. The utility function is assumed to be

$$U(n, x) = \left\{\left[\gamma^n u(x)\right]^{1-\sigma} - 1\right\}\Big/(1-\sigma), \quad \sigma > 0, \quad \gamma > 1. \tag{3.77}$$

Let L be the inelastic supply of labor per capita in each period. Let $\theta(z)$, $0 \leqslant z \leqslant L$, be the probability of making a discovery if $z$ is the quantity of labor per capita devoted to R & D. Assume that $\theta$ is strictly increasing at $z$ if $\theta(z) < 1$, weakly concave, and once continuously differentiable, with $\theta(0) \geqslant 0$ and $\theta(L) \leqslant 1$. The parametric form to be used for computation is $\theta(z) = \theta z^{\xi}$, $\theta > 0$ and $0 < \xi \leqslant 1$. Let

$$f(l) = \max_x u(x) \quad s.t. \quad \sum_{i=0}^{\infty} x_i \leqslant l$$

be the indirect utility function of labor. Because $u$ is assumed to be homogeneous of degree one, one has $f(l) = al$.

To find the optimum path of the quantity $z$ of labor devoted to R & D, form the Lagrangean expression

$$\mathcal{L}=\sum_{t=0}^{\infty}\mathrm{E}_t\left\{\beta^t(1-\sigma)^{-1}\left[\left(\gamma^{n_t}a(\mathrm{L}-z_t)\right)^{1-\sigma}-1\right]-\beta^{t+1}\lambda_{t+1}\left[n_{t+1}-n_t-\varepsilon_{t+1}\right]\right\} \tag{3.78}$$

The first part is utility in period $t$, which depends on the highest level of technology $n_t$ and the amount of labor $\mathrm{L}-z$ devoted to producing consumer goods rather than R & D. The second part is a constraint on the increase in $n_t$, which is random, with the increment $\varepsilon_{t+1}$ equal to 1 with probability $\theta(z)$ and equal to zero with probability $1-\theta(z)$. This formulation of technological innovations to move up the level of technology is due to Grossman and Helpman (1991a,b). The control variable is $z_t$ and the state variable is $n_t$.

The first-order conditions are, with $t$ subscripts of $z$ and $n$ omitted when understood,

$$\beta^{-t}\frac{\partial\mathcal{L}}{\partial z_t}=-\left[\gamma^n a(\mathrm{L}-z)\right]^{-\sigma}\gamma^n a+\beta\theta'(z)\lambda(n+1)=0 \tag{3.79}$$

$$\begin{aligned}\beta^{-t}\frac{\Delta\mathcal{L}}{\Delta n_t}&=\left[\gamma^n a(L-z)\right]^{1-\sigma}\left(1-\gamma^{\sigma-1}\right)/(1-\sigma)-\lambda(n)\\&\quad+\beta\theta(z)\lambda(n+1)+\beta\left(1-\theta(z)\right)\lambda(n)=0\end{aligned} \tag{3.80}$$

In the last part of (3.79), $E_t\lambda_{t+1}\varepsilon_{t+1}=\theta(z)\lambda(n+1)$ is used. One takes the difference $\mathcal{L}(n_t)-\mathcal{L}(n_t-1)$ in (3.80) with respect to $n_t$, because it is an integer. The last two terms of (3.80) result from evaluating $\beta E_t\lambda_{t+1}$. Equations (3.79) and (3.80) can be solved for the optimum $z(n)$ and $\lambda(n)$.

Using (3.79) to substitute for $\lambda(n+1)$ in (3.80) and solving the resulting equation for $\lambda(n)$, one obtains

$$\lambda(n)=\left[\gamma^n a(L-z)\right]^{1-\sigma}\left[\left(1-\lambda^{\sigma-1}\right)/(1-\sigma)+(L-z)^{-1}\theta/\theta'\right]\Big/\left[1-\beta+\beta\theta\right]$$

implying, for a constant $z$, which is the stationary solution of the optimization problem,

$$\lambda(n+1)=\left[\gamma^n a(L-z)\right]^{1-\sigma}\left[\left(1-\gamma^{\sigma-1}\right)/(1-\sigma)+\gamma^{1-\sigma}(L-z)^{-1}\theta/\theta'\right]\frac{1+\rho}{\rho+\theta}$$

Substituting the above expressions for $\lambda(n+1)$ in (3.79), and defining $g=(\gamma^{1-\sigma}-1)/(1-\sigma)$, one obtains the following equation for $z$,

$$\theta'(z)(L-z)=\rho/g-\theta(z)(1-\sigma) \tag{3.81}$$

which determines the optimum quantity $z$ of labor per capita to be devoted to R & D, given the parameters $\beta$, $\sigma$, $\gamma$ (of the objective function) and L and the function $\theta$. Using (3.81) one can show (see problem 7) that an increase in $\beta$, an increase in $1/\sigma$, an increase $\gamma$, or an increase in L will raise the optimum amount of labor devoted to research and development.

Stokey (1995) studies competition among producers in the goods market to determine relative prices of goods, their quantities, and profits in each period; shows the determination of the rate of interest by the allocation of consumer expenditures over time; and derives, through free entry into R & D, the equilibrium condition that the probability of successful innovation times its value must equal to the cost of carrying out R & D. This work extends the work of Grossman and Helpman (1991a,b). The reader is referred to these interesting references.

## Problems

1. Solve the problem of equations (3.1) and (3.2) with a finite horizon T by using dynamic programming and by beginning with the problem for the last period T.
2. Solve the problem of equations (3.1) and (3.2) with a finite horizon T using the Lagrange method and beginning with the problem for the last period T.
3. Derive equations (3.22) to (3.25) by dynamic programming.
4. Derive equations (3.22) to (3.25) by the Lagrange method.
5. Ehrlich and Lui (1992) on corruption and economic growth extend the model of section 3.3 by introducing political capital $Q_t$ which can be produced by effort $q_t$ according to the equation

$$Q_{t+1} = B(\lambda\bar{H} + Q_t)q_t$$

Consumption $c_t$ depends not only on output $y_t$ but also on the net income generated by the consumer's own political capital $Q_t$ as compared with the economy's average stock of political capital $Q_t^*$ (taken as given by the consumer) thus,

$$c_t = \left[1 + \theta \ln\left(Q_t / Q_t^*\right)\right] y_t = \left[1 + \theta \ln\left(Q_t / Q_t^*\right)\right]\left(\bar{H} + H_t\right)\left(1 - h_t - q_t\right)$$

The control variables are $h_t$ and $q_t$. The state variables are $H_t$ and $Q_t$ with $H_t$ given by

$$H_{t+1} = A\left(\bar{H} + H_t\right)h_t$$

By using the Lagrange method, derive for an individual with political capital $Q_t$ equal to $Q_t^*$:

$$\left(c_{t+1}/c_t\right)^{\sigma} = \beta A\left(1 - q_{t+1}\right) \equiv \beta R_h$$

$$\left(c_{t+1}/c_t\right)^{\sigma} = \beta\left(\theta M_t + N_t\right) \equiv \beta R_q$$

where

$$\left(c_{t+1}/c_t\right) = \left[\left(\bar{H} + H_{t+1}\right)\left(1 - h_{t+1} - q_{t+1}\right)\right] \Big/ \left[\left(\bar{H} + H_t\right)\left(1 - h_t - q_t\right)\right]$$

$$M_t = \left[\left(\bar{H} + H_{t+1}\right)\left(1 - h_{t+1} - q_{t+1}\right)\right] \Big/ \left[q_t\left(\bar{H} + H_t\right)\right]$$

$$N_t = \left[\left(\overline{H} + H_{t+1}\right) q_{t+1} Q_{t+1}\right] / \left[\left(\overline{H} + H_t\right) q_t \left(\overline{H} + Q_{t+1}\right)\right]$$

6. Solve the social planner's problem of equation (3.69) and derive equation (3.74) by Pontryagin's maximum principle.
7. Using (3.81) show that an increase in β, an increase in 1/σ, an increase γ, or an increase in L will raise the optimum amount of labor denoted to R & D.

## CHAPTER FOUR

# Theories of Market Equilibrium

## 4.1 Asset Prices of an Exchange Economy

A simple and basic model of equilibrium in economics consists of a demand function and a supply function. These two functions jointly determine the price and output of a commodity. If the quantity of supply is fixed and given, the demand function evaluated at the fixed supply determines price, as in the following model of an exchange economy of Lucas (1978).

In this exchange economy, there exists only one consumer good (e.g., apples). The good is produced by $k$ firms (e.g., farms), each using one type of capital good or asset (e.g., apple tree). Each firm is owned by the consumers. The $i$th firm has $x_{it}$ units of capital assets. The units of the assets of each firm are so defined that there is one asset per consumer. Each unit of the assets of the $i$th firm yields a random $z_{it}$ units of the consumer good in period $t$. In other words, each share of the stock of the $i$th firm yields a random $z_{it}$ units of dividends in period $t$. Let the vectors $x_t$ and $z_t$ denote $(x_{1t}, \ldots, x_{kt})'$ and $(z_{1t}, \ldots, z_{kt})'$, respectively. Let $p(z_t)$ denote the vector $(p_1(z_t), \ldots, p_k(z_t))$ of the prices of the $k$ assets (shares of the $k$ firms). The prices are functions of the dividends of all firms. The problem is to find the price functions $p(z_t)$. To solve this problem, first find the demand functions for the $k$ assets, and then equate the demands with the fixed supplies of these assets.

The representative consumer in this economy is assumed to maximize expected discounted utility $U(c_t)$ of consumption subject to the budget constraint for period $t$

$$c_t + p'(z_t)x_{t+1} = \left[z_t + p(z_t)\right]'x_t. \tag{4.1}$$

The right-hand side of (4.1) gives the total revenue available to the consumer who owns the vector $x_t$ of assets of the $k$ firms, as these assets yield dividends $z_t$ and can be sold at post-dividend prices $p(z_t)$. The left-hand side of (4.1) is the total expenditures for consumption and for keeping $x_{t+1}$ units of assets at the beginning of period $t + 1$.

To set up the consumer's dynamic optimization program, let $y_t = x_t - x_{t+1}$ be the vector of net dissavings of the $k$ assets; $y_t$ is a vector of control variables to be determined by the representative consumer. By using this definition of $y_t$, solve (4.1) for $c_t$ and substitute the result in the utility function $U(c_t)$. The constrained maximization problem facing the consumer can be solved by using the Lagrangean expression

$$\mathcal{L} = E\sum_{t=0}^{\infty}\left\{\beta^t U\left(z_t' x_t + p'(z_t) y_t\right) - \beta^{t+1}\lambda_{t+1}'\left(x_{t+1} - x_t + y_t\right)\right\}$$

from which are derived the first-order conditions

$$\beta^{-t}\frac{\partial \mathcal{L}}{\partial y_t} = U'\left(z_t' x_t + p'(z_t) y_t\right)\cdot p(z_t) - \beta E_t \lambda_{t+1} = 0 \tag{4.2}$$

$$\beta^{-t}\frac{\partial \mathcal{L}}{\partial x_t} = -\lambda_t + U'\left(z_t' x_t + p'(z_t) y_t\right) z_t + \beta E_t \lambda_{t+1} = 0 \tag{4.3}$$

Equations (4.2) and (4.3) imply

$$\lambda_t = U'\left(z_t' x_t + p'(z_t) y_t\right)\left[z_t + p(z_t)\right] \tag{4.4}$$

In equilibrium, $y_t = 0$ and $x_t = \underline{1} = (1, \ldots, 1)$, with each consumer owning one unit of assets in each of $k$ firms. Combining equations (4.2) and (4.4) yields the following equation to determine the pricing function $p(z_t)$ given by Stokey and Lucas (1989, p. 303):

$$U'\left(z_t' \cdot \underline{1}\right)\cdot p(z_t) = \beta E_t U'\left(z_{t+1}' \cdot \underline{1}\right)\left[z_{t+1} + p(z_{t+1})\right]. \tag{4.5}$$

Equation (4.5) is a vector equation that consists of $k$ components. It has nice economic interpretations. The arguments $z_t' \cdot \underline{1}$ and $z_{t+1}' \cdot \underline{1}$ in the (marginal) utility functions on both sides of equation (4.5) imply that at each period all the incomes from dividends are consumed. The prices $p(z_t)$ in equilibrium must be such that if one sells one share of any firm $i$ at $p_i(z_t)$ and uses the proceeds for consumption at period $t$, the marginal utility so obtained (left side of the equation) must be equal to the discounted (by $\beta$) expected utility at period $t + 1$ of spending the proceeds from keeping the share until period $t + 1$, which provides $z_{i,t+1}$ units of dividends and can be sold at price $p_i(z_{t+1})$ (right side of the equation). Dividing both sides of equation (4.5) by $U'(z_t' \cdot \underline{1}) = U'(c_t')$, one has an equation for the (vector) price function $p(z_t)$.

To illustrate the use of equation (4.5), let there be only one kind of capital assets or $k = 1$. Let $U(c_t) = \ln c_t$. Equation (4.5) implies

$$p(z_t) = \beta z_t E_t\left\{z_{t+1}^{-1}\left[z_{t+1} + p(z_{t+1})\right]\right\} = \beta z_t\left\{1 + E_t\left[p(z_{t+1})/z_{t+1}\right]\right\}.$$

If the price function is conjectured to be $p(z_t) = \alpha z_t$, for some parameter $\alpha$ yet to be determined, one has

$$\alpha z_t = \beta z_t\{1 + \alpha\}$$

Equating coefficients on both sides gives $\alpha = \beta/(1-\beta)$. Thus, the price of the capital asset is proportional to the dividend $z_t$, the factor of proportionality being $\beta/(1-\beta)$, with $\beta$ denoting the discount factor.

Another example is given by Sargent (1987, p. 107). Let $k = 2$ and $s_t = z_{1t} + z_{2t}$ be the sum of dividend incomes from both assets. The vector price function is

$$\begin{bmatrix} p_1(z_t) \\ p_2(z_t) \end{bmatrix} = \beta s_t \mathrm{E}_t \left\{ s_{t+1}^{-1} \begin{bmatrix} z_{1,t+1} + p_1(z_{t+1}) \\ z_{2,t+1} + p_2(z_{t+1}) \end{bmatrix} \right\}$$

Let $p_1(z_t) = \phi_{1t} s_t$ and $p_2(z_t) = \phi_{2t} s_t$, with functions $\phi_{1t}$ and $\phi_{2t}$ yet to be determined. The dividends from the two capital assets are assumed to be random, being respectively

$$z_{1t} = \frac{1}{2}(1-\varepsilon_t)s_t; \quad z_{2t} = \frac{1}{2}(1+\varepsilon_t)s_t$$

in which $\varepsilon_t$ is assumed to have martingale property $\mathrm{E}_t\varepsilon_{t+1} = \rho\varepsilon_t$, with $|\rho| < 1$, implying $\mathrm{E}_t\varepsilon_{t+j} = \rho^j\varepsilon_t$. The equation for $p_1(z_t)$ yields

$$\phi_{1t} = \beta\left[\mathrm{E}_t(z_{1,t+1}/s_{t+1}) + \mathrm{E}_t\phi_{1,t+1}\right]$$

Solving this difference equation for $\phi_{1t}$ forward by repeated substitutions for future $\mathrm{E}_t(z_{1,t+1}/s_{t+1})$ gives

$$\begin{aligned}
\phi_{1t} &= \beta\mathrm{E}_t(z_{1,t+1}/s_{t+1}) + \beta\mathrm{E}_t\beta\mathrm{E}_{t+1}(z_{1,t+2}/s_{t+2}) + \cdots \\
&= \sum_{j=1}^{\infty}\beta^j\mathrm{E}_t(z_{1t+j}/s_{t+j}) = \sum_{j=1}^{\infty}\beta^j\mathrm{E}_t\left[\frac{1}{2}(1-\varepsilon_{t+j})\right] \\
&= \frac{1}{2}\sum_{j=1}^{\infty}\beta^j(1-\rho^j\varepsilon_t) = \frac{1}{2}\left[\frac{\beta}{1-\beta} - \frac{\beta\rho}{1-\beta\rho}\varepsilon_t\right]
\end{aligned}$$

Similarly,

$$\phi_{2t} = \frac{1}{2}\left[\frac{\beta}{1-\beta} + \frac{\beta\rho}{1-\beta\rho}\varepsilon_t\right]$$

Thus, the coefficients of the price functions $p_i(z_t) = \phi_{it}(z_{1t} + z_{2t})$, $i = 1, 2$, are determined.

### 4.2 Equilibrium in a Pure Currency Economy

A demand function for assets together with a fixed supply of assets can determine the prices of assets. Similarly a demand function for money and a given supply of money determine the price level. Let an economy consist of a large number of households. A household starts the day with money holding $m_t$ and uses money to buy consumption goods $c_t$. After the purchase of $c_t$, the household produces and sells $y$ units of consumption goods for money that can be used to buy consumption goods in the next period. Money holding evolves according to

$$m_{t+1} = m_t - c_t + y,$$

while the cash constraint $m_t - c_t \geqslant 0$ prevails. These yield two constraints in the household's dynamic optimization problem. The Lagrangean expression is

$$\mathcal{L} = \sum_t \mathrm{E}_t\left\{\beta^t u(c_t,\ z_t) - \beta^{t+1}\lambda_{t+1}(m_{t+1} - m_t + c_t - y) + \beta^t \mu_t (m_t - c_t)\right\}$$

The state variables are $m_t$ and the random shock $z_t$ to preference. The control variable is $c_t$. In each period, a multiplier $\mu_t$ is introduced for the nonnegativity constraint $m_t - c_t \geqslant 0$.

To deal with nonnegativity constraints, apply the Kuhn-Tucker Theorem, which is summarized in Dixit (1990, pp. 181–182) as follows:

KUHN-TUCKER THEOREM

*To maximize a scalar function $F(x)$ with respect to an $m \times 1$ vector $x$ subject to the inequality constraints $k_i - G_i(x) \geqslant 0$ and $x_i \geqslant 0$, form the expression*

$$L(x,\ \mu) = F(x) + \mu'[k - G(x)].$$

*A set of necessary conditions for maximum is*

$$\partial L/\partial x_i = 0 \text{ for } x_i > 0; \quad \partial L/\partial x_i < 0 \text{ for } x_i = 0$$
$$\partial L/\partial \mu_i = k_i - G_i(x) = 0 \text{ for } \mu_i > 0; \quad \partial L/\partial \mu_i = k_i - G_i(x) > 0 \text{ for } \mu_i = 0. \tag{4.6}$$

The intuition for these conditions is as follows. When $x_i > 0$, an interior solution requires $\partial L/\partial x_i$ be zero. When $x_i$ hits the boundary 0, the derivative of L must be negative; otherwise L can be increased by increasing $x_i$. Similarly, when the Lagrange multiplier $\mu_i > 0$, the corresponding constraint is an equality $k_i - G_i(x) = 0$. When $k_i - G_i(x) > 0$, there is no equality constraint, and the multiplier $\mu_i$ should be zero.

The first-order conditions obtained by differentiating the Lagrangean expression associated with the household's dynamic optimization problem are

$$\beta^{-t}\frac{\partial \mathcal{L}}{\partial c_t} = \frac{\partial}{\partial c_t}u(c_t,\ z_t) - \mu_t - \beta \mathrm{E}_t \lambda_{t+1} = 0 \text{ for } c_t > 0$$
$$< 0 \text{ for } c_t = 0 \tag{4.7}$$

$$\beta^{-t}\frac{\partial \mathcal{L}}{\partial m_t} = -\lambda_t + \mu_t + \beta \mathrm{E}_t \lambda_{t+1} = 0 \tag{4.8}$$

Consider two cases:

Case A. The equality constraint $m_t - c_t = 0$ is not binding, that is, $m_t - c_t > 0$, and there is money left over for the next period $t + 1$. In this case, the multiplier $\mu_t = 0$.

Case B. The money constraint is binding, i.e., $c_t = m_t$, and all of $m_t$ is used to buy consumer goods. In Case B, $\mu_t > 0$.

Assume the utility function to be $u = z_t c_t$. In Case A, equations (4.7) and (4.8) become

$$z_t - \beta E_t \lambda_{t+1} = 0 \text{ for } c_t > 0$$

$$\lambda_t = \beta E_t \lambda_{t+1}$$

For $c_t > 0$ (and $c_t < m_t$), these two equations imply

$$\lambda_t = z_t = \beta E_t \lambda_{t+1} = \beta E_t z_{t+1} \equiv \xi \text{ (a constant)}.$$

Because $\lambda = \partial V/\partial m = \xi$, where V is the value function, for some constant A,

$$V = \xi m + A$$

If the random shock $z_t$ turns out to be smaller than the constant $\xi \equiv \beta E_t z_{t+1}$, one cannot satisfy the first first-order condition by equating $\partial\mu/\partial c_t$ or $z_t$ to $\xi$, because $\partial u/\partial c_t$ is too small. Hence, when $z_t < \beta E_t \lambda_{t+1}$, $c_t = 0$.

In Case B, $\mu_t > 0$ and the money constraint is binding or $c_t = m_t$. Therefore, given the utility function $u = z_t c_t$, either the taste shock $z_t$ is small (less than $\beta E_t z_{t+1}$, $\equiv \xi$), leading to zero consumption in period $t$, or $c_t = m_t$, with the household spending the money available for consumption in period $t$.

Let the probability distribution of $z_t$ be such that prob($z_t \geqslant \xi$) = $\alpha$ and prob( ($z_t < \xi$) = $(1 - \alpha)$. With probabiliy $\alpha$, $c_t = m_t$ and $m_{t+1} = y$. With probability $1 - \alpha$, $c_t = 0$, and $m_{t+1} = m_t + y$. One can easily find the probability distribution of the demand for money $m_t$ in equilibrium. Let $\pi_i$ = prob($m = iy$).

$$\pi_1 = P(m = y) = \alpha.$$

$$\pi_2 = P(m = 2y) = P(m_t = y) \cdot P(m_{t+1} = m_t + y) = \alpha(1 - \alpha).$$

$$\pi_3 = P(m_t = 2y) \cdot P(m_{t+1} = m_t + y) = \alpha(1 - \alpha)^2.$$

$$\pi_i = \alpha(1 - \alpha)^{i-1}.$$

If the supply of money is held constant, say equal to $3y + \varepsilon$, when the demand for money is larger than the fixed supply, the unit price of output $y$ will go down, so that the money value of $y$ decreases to equate the demand and supply of money. The problem of this section is solved in Stokey and Lucas (1989, section 13.5) by using dynamic programming.

### 4.3 A Pure Credit Economy with Linear Utility

Another model, discussed in Stokey and Lucas (1989, section 13.7), introduces random taste shock $z_t$ in determining asset prices, rather than random productivity stock $z_t$ as in section 4.1. A representative consumer in the economy is assumed to own $w_t$ shares of capital assets at time $t$, with each share yielding a fixed income of $y$ per period. With $c_t$ denoting consumption and $q$ denoting the (constant) price of one share of the assets, the consumer's budget constraint is

$$qw_{t+1} + c_t = (y+q)w_t$$

which is similar to equation (4.1) in section 4.1. The Lagrangean for the consumer's dynamic optimization problem is

$$\mathcal{L} = \sum_{t=0}^{\infty} \mathrm{E}_t\left\{\beta^t u(c_t) - \beta^{t+1}\lambda_{t+1}\left[w_{t+1} - (1+y/q)w_t + c_t/q\right]\right\}$$

yielding first-order conditions

$$\beta^{-t}\frac{\partial\mathcal{L}}{\partial c_t} = u'(c_t) - \beta q^{-1}\mathrm{E}_t\lambda_{t+1} = 0$$

$$\beta^{-t}\frac{\partial\mathcal{L}}{\partial w_t} = -\lambda_t + (1+y/q)\beta\mathrm{E}_t\lambda_{t+1} = 0$$

If $u = z_t c_t$, where $z_t$ is a random taste shock as in section 4.2, $u'(c_t) = z_t$, and these first-order conditions imply

$$z_t = \beta q^{-1}\mathrm{E}_t\lambda_{t+1}$$

and

$$\lambda_t = (1+y/q)qz_t = (q+y)z_t$$

From these equations we obtain

$$z_t = \beta q^{-1}\mathrm{E}_t(q+y)z_{t+1} = \beta(1+y/q)\mathrm{E}_t z_{t+1} \tag{4.9}$$

Let $z_t$ be independent and identically distributed. Let the asset price $q$ be such that $z_t > \beta(1 + y/q)\mathrm{E}_t z_{t+1}$ with probability 0.6. With probability 0.6, the marginal utility of consumption $z_t$ is larger than the right-hand side of the first-order condition (4.9), and the consumer will consume as much as possible subject to the budget constraint. He or she will set $c_t = (y + q)w_t$ and $w_{t+1} = 0$. With probability 0.4, $z_t \leqslant \beta(1 + y/q)\mathrm{E}_t z_{t+1}$, and he or she will set $c_t = 0$ and $w_{t+1} = (1+y/q)w_t$. Let $\pi_i = \mathrm{P}[w_t = (1 + y/q)^{i-1}y]$ for $i \geqslant 1$. One finds the following probability distribution of the demand for assets

$$\pi_0 = \mathrm{P}(w_t = 0) = 0.6$$

$$\pi_1 = \mathrm{P}(w_t = y)$$

$$\pi_2 = \mathrm{P}\left[w_t = (1+y/q)y\right] = 0.4\pi_1$$

$$\pi_3 = \mathrm{P}\left[w_t = (1+y/q)^2 y\right] = 0.4^2\pi_1$$

Because

$$1=\sum_{i=0}^{\infty}\pi_i=0.6+\pi_1\left(1+0.4+0.4^2+\ldots\right)=0.6+\pi_1/0.6$$

we find $\pi_1 = 0.24$. The mean of this distribution is

$$\sum_{i=1}^{\infty}\pi_i\left(1+y/q\right)^{i-1}y=y\sum_{i=1}^{\infty}\pi_1\left[0.4\left(1+y/q\right)\right]^{i-1}$$

Let the stochastic process for the taste shock $z_t$ be such that $E_t z_{t+1} = \theta z_t$. The equilibrium condition (4.9) gives $\beta(1 + y/q)\theta = 1$, which can be used to solve for the price $q$ of the stock, given $\beta$, $y$, and $\theta$. If $\beta\theta = 1$, $q$ will be infinity. For $q$ to be finite, $\beta\theta$ has to be smaller than 1. To illustrate, let $\beta\theta = 1/1.05$, so that $(1 + y/q) = 1.05$, and $q = 20y$.

## 4.4 Money and Interest in a Cash-In-Advance Economy

To continue the discussion of the demand for money when money is required to purchase consumption goods as assumed in section 4.2, consider the model of Lucas and Stokey (1987). In the model there are two types of consumer goods: $c_{1t}$ is the quantity of cash goods, which can be purchased only by cash or is subject to a cash-in-advance constraint; $c_{2t}$ is the quantity of credit goods, which can be paid by credit, to be settled by cash at the beginning of period $t + 1$. Income $y(s)$ of the consumer in each period is subject to a vector $s$ of random shocks. The government determines the rate of growth $g(s)$ of money supply through a lump-sum transfer for each consumer as a function of the shocks. Both $y(s)$ and $g(s)$ are given exogenously. If $\hat{m}_{t-1}$ is per capita money stock at the end of period $t - 1$, each consumer receives at the end of period $t - 1$ a money transfer from the government equal to $[g(s_{t-1}) - 1]\hat{m}_{t-1}$. Per capita money stock $\hat{m}_t$ is normalized to unity in each period, so that $m_t$ for each consumer is his or her money balance relative to per capita money balance in the economy.

There are two constraints for the representative consumer. The first is the budget constraint. Given initial money stock $m_t$ (again relative to the economy's per capita money stock $\hat{m}_t = 1$ and after government money transfer of period $t - 1$), the end-of-period money balance $x_{3t}$ (prior to government money transfer of period $t$) must satisfy

$$x_{3t}=m_t+p(s_t)\left(y(s_t)-c_{1t}-c_{2t}\right)$$

in which $p(s_t)$ is the price function taken as given by the consumer, but to be determined by the model in equilibrium. Because $m_{t+1}$, again relative to the next period's per capita money stock $g(s_{t+1})\hat{m}_t = g(s_{t+1})$, consists of $x_{3t}$, and government money transfer $[g(s_{t+1}) - 1]\hat{m}_t = g(s_{t+1}) - 1$, the following is the equation for the dynamic evolution of $m_t$:

$$\begin{aligned}m_{t+1}&=\left[x_{3t}+g(s_{t+1})-1\right]/g(s_{t+1})\\&=g(s_{t+1})^{-1}\left[m_t+p(s_t)\left(y(s_t)-c_{1t}-c_{2t}\right)+g(s_{t+1})-1\right].\end{aligned}$$

The second constraint is the finance constraint or the cash-in-advance constraint

$$m_t - p(s_t)c_{1t} \geqslant 0$$

in which both $m_t$ and $p(s_t)$ are expressed as ratios to the current period's per capita money supply.

The Lagrangean for the representative consumer's infinite-horizon optimization problem is

$$\mathcal{L} = \sum_{t=0}^{\infty} \mathrm{E}_t \Big\{ \beta^t u(c_{1t}, c_{2t}) - \beta^{t+1}\lambda_{t+1}\Big[ m_{t+1} - g(s_{t+1})^{-1}\big[m_t + p(s_t)(y(s_t) - c_{1t} - c_{2t}) + g(s_{t+1}) - 1\big]\Big] + \beta^t \mu_t \big[m_t - p(s_t)c_{1t}\big]\Big\}$$

The state variables are $s_t$ and $m_t$. The control variables are $c_{1t}$ and $c_{2t}$. The first-order conditions are:

$$\beta^{-t}\frac{\partial \mathcal{L}}{\partial c_{1t}} = \frac{\partial}{\partial c_{1t}} u(c_{1t}, c_{2t}) - p(s_t)\mu_t - \beta p(s_t)\mathrm{E}_t g(s_{t+1})^{-1} \cdot \lambda_{t+1} = 0 \qquad (4.10)$$

$$\beta^{-t}\frac{\partial \mathcal{L}}{\partial c_{2t}} = \frac{\partial}{\partial c_{2t}} u(c_{1t}, c_{2t}) - \beta p(s_t)\mathrm{E}_t g(s_{t+1})^{-1} \cdot \lambda_{t+1} = 0 \qquad (4.11)$$

$$\beta^{-t}\frac{\partial \mathcal{L}}{\partial m_t} = -\lambda_t + \mu_t + \beta \mathrm{E}_t g(s_{t+1})^{-1} \cdot \lambda_{t+1} = 0 \qquad (4.12)$$

There are two cases:

Case A. $m_t - p(\mathrm{s})c_{1t} > 0$ and the cash-in-advance constraint is not binding.
Case B. $p(\mathrm{s})c_{1t} = m_t$ and the cash-in-advance constraint is binding.

In Case A, $\mu_t = 0$. In Case B, $\mu_t > 0$.

A stationary equilibrium of this economy consists of a price function $p(s)$, a Lagrange function $\lambda(m, s)$ and the associated policy functions $c_1 = c_1(m, s)$ and $c_2(m, s)$, which satisfy (4.10), (4.11), and (4.12), and for $m_{t+1} = m_t = \hat{m}_t = 1$ the policy functions satisfy $c_1(1, s) + c_2(1, s) = y(s)$, all $s$. This market clearing equation, and equations (4.10), (4.11), and (4.12) provide 4 equations to determine the functions $c_1(1, s)$, $c_2(1, s)$, $\lambda(1, s)$, and $p(s)$ in Case A ($\mu_t = 0$), or the functions $c_2(1, s)$, $\lambda(1, s)$ $p(s)$ and $\mu$ in Case B ($\mu > 0$ and $c_1 = m_t/p(s) = 1/p(s)$). Lucas and Stokey (1987, sections 3 and 4; 1992) and Hao (1992) study the existence and uniqueness of the functions satisfying these equations. Lucas and Stokey (1987, section 5) also extend this model to include other securities than money as follows.

Let securities trading at time $t$ occur at the beginning of period $t$, before $s_t$ is known, but after some signal $z_t$ is announced and after money injections take place. The information available to consumers at the time of securities trading in period $t$ consists of $s_{t-1}$ and $z_t$ with the conditional distribution $p(z_t|s_t)$ assumed to be known. Let only one security be traded, and let one unit of this security pay $b(s_t, z_{t+1})$ dollars at the beginning of the next period if this period's shock is $s_t$ and next period's signal is $z_{t+1}$. The problem is to determine the price function $q(s_{t-1}, z_t)$ for this security. The first step is to solve the consumer's optimization problem to determine the optimal decision functions for $c_{1t}$, $c_{2t}$, and security purchase $d_t$, given this price function.

Let $m_t$ denote money holding at the beginning of period $t$, after the last period's purchase $d_{t-1}$ of securities has yielded payment of $b(s_{t-1}, z_t)$ per unit and after the government has injected money $g(s_t) - 1$ into the system. Presumably, the government observes $s_t$ to inject money $g(s_t) - 1$, while the consumer only observes $z_t$ and not $s_t$. Because the quantity $g(s_t)$ is known to the consumer at the time of security trading, write $g(s_t)$ as $\hat{g}(z_t)$. The amount of money $m_t$ can be used to pay for $d_t$ units of security at price $q(s_{t-1}, z_t)$ and for cash good $c_{1t}$, both subject to the finance constraint.

$$m_t - q(s_{t-1}, z_t)d_t - p(s_t)c_{1t} \geqslant 0 \tag{4.13}$$

The end-of-period money balance $x_{3t}$, prior to government money transfer $g(s_{t+1}) - 1$ and payments from security $b(s_{t-1}, z_t)d_t$, satisfies the budget constraint

$$x_{3t} = m_t + p(s_t)\left(y(s_t) - c_{1t} - c_{2t}\right) - q(s_{t-1}, z_t)d_t.$$

Because $m_{t+1}$, relative to next period's per capita money stock $g(s_{t+1})$, consists of $x_{3t}$, government transfer $g(s_{t+1}) - 1$ and payment from security $b(s_{t-1}, z_t)d_t$, the equation for the dynamic evolution of $m_t$ is

$$\begin{aligned} m_{t+1} &= \left[x_{3t} + b(s_{t-1}, z_t)d_t + g(s_{t+1}) - 1\right]/g(s_{t+1}) \\ &= g(s_{t+1})^{-1}\left[m_t + p(s_t)\left(y(s_t) - c_{1t} - c_{2t}\right) - q(s_{t-1}, z_t)d_t + b(s_{t-1}, z_t)d_t + g(s_{t+1}) - 1\right] \end{aligned}$$

These statements explain the two constraints in the Lagrangean for the consumer's dynamic optimization problem:

$$\begin{aligned} \mathcal{L} = \sum_{t=0}^{\infty} \mathrm{E}_t \Big\{ \beta^t u(c_{1t}, c_{2t}) - \beta^{t+1}\lambda_{t+1}\Big[ m_{t+1} - g(s_{t+1})^{-1}\Big[m_t + p(s_t)\left(y(s_t) - c_{1t} - c_{2t}\right) \\ - q(s_{t-1}, z_t)d_t + b(s_t, z_{t+1})d_t + g(z_{t+1}) - 1\Big]\Big] + \mu_t\left[m_t - q(s_{t-1}, z_t)d_t - p(s_t)c_{1t}\right]\Big\} \end{aligned}$$

$\mathrm{E}_t$ denotes conditional expectation given information $m_t$, $s_{t-1}$, and $z_t$. The first constraint, with multiplier $\lambda_{t+1}$, specifies the dynamic evolution of the representative consumer's money stock. The second constraint, with multiplier $\mu_t$, is the cash-in-advance constraint in the purchases $d_t$ of securities and $c_{1t}$ of cash goods. If the nonnegativity constraint $m_t \geqslant qd_t + pc_{1t}$ is binding, $\mu_t$ is positive; otherwise $\mu_t = 0$.

The first-order conditions are, given the information set $(m_t, s_{t-1}, z_t)$ but not $s_t$ at the beginning of period $t$,

$$\beta^{-t}\frac{\partial \mathcal{L}}{\partial c_{1t}} = \mathrm{E}_t\left[u_1(c_{1t}, c_{2t}) - \mu_t p(s_t) - \beta p(s_t) g(s_{t+1})^{-1}\lambda_{t+1}\right] = 0 \tag{4.14}$$

$$\beta^{-t}\frac{\partial \mathcal{L}}{\partial c_{2t}} = \mathrm{E}_t\left[u_2(c_{1t}, c_{2t}) - \beta p(s_t) g(s_{t+1})^{-1} \lambda_{t+1}\right] = 0 \tag{4.15}$$

$$\beta^{-t}\frac{\partial \mathcal{L}}{\partial d_t} = -q(s_{t-1}, z_t)\mathrm{E}_t\mu_t - \beta\Big[q(s_{t-1}, z_t)\mathrm{E}_t g(s_{t+1})^{-1}\lambda_{t+1}$$
$$+\mathrm{E}_t b(s_t, z_{t+1}) g(s_{t+1})^{-1}\lambda_{t+1}\Big] = 0 \tag{4.16}$$

$$\beta^{-t}\frac{\partial \mathcal{L}}{\partial m_t} = -\mathrm{E}_t\lambda_t + \mathrm{E}_t\mu_t + \beta\mathrm{E}_t g(s_{t+1})^{-1}\lambda_{t+1} = 0 \tag{4.17}$$

in which $u_i$ denotes the derivative of $u(c_{1t}, c_{2t})$ with respect to its $i$th argument ($i = 1, 2$). Equations (4.14) and (4.15) are the same as the corresponding first-order conditions for the previous model before securities are introduced, except for the information set at the beginning of $t$, which excludes $s_t$ when the conditional expectation $E_t$ is defined. Because government money transfer $g(s_{t+1}) - 1$ at $t + 1$ occurs and is known before security trading when the consumer knows $z_{t+1}$ but not $s_{t+1}$, write $g(s_{t+1})$ as $\hat{g}(z_{t+1})$. For the consumer's optimization problem, the pricing functions $p$ and $q$ are treated as given; equations (4.13)–(4.17) determine $c_{1t}$, $c_{2t}$, $d_t$, $\lambda_t$, and $\mu_t$. In market equilibrium, $d_t = 0$, $c_{1t} + c_{2t} = y(s_t)$, and the same five equations (with $m = 1$) determine the pricing functions $p$ and $q$ as well.

In the case of a one-period bond to be redeemed at one unit (or any fixed number of units) of currency, i.e., $b(s_t, z_{t+1}) = 1$, the first-order conditions can be simplified. Equation (4.16) yields

$$q(s_{t-1}, z_t) = \beta\mathrm{E}_t g(s_{t+1})^{-1}\lambda_{t+1} \Big/ \mathrm{E}_t\left(\mu_t + \beta g(s_{t+1})^{-1}\lambda_{t+1}\right) \tag{4.18}$$

Equation (4.14) implies, at time $t+$ when $s_t$ is known,

$$u_1(c_{1t}, c_{2t})/p(s_t) = \mathrm{E}_{t+}\left[\mu_t + \beta g(s_{t+1})^{-1}\lambda_{t+1}\right]$$

or, at time $t$ before $s_t$ is observed,

$$\mathrm{E}_t\left[u_1(c_{1t}, c_{2t})/p(s_t)\right] = \mathrm{E}_t\left(\mu_t + \beta g(s_{t+1})^{-1}\lambda_{t+1}\right)$$

Similarly equation (4.15) implies

$$\mathrm{E}_t\left[u_2(c_{1t}, c_{2t})/p(s_t)\right] = \beta\mathrm{E}_t g(s_{t+1})^{-1}\lambda_{t+1}$$

Substituting these expressions into (4.18) gives

$$q(s_{t-1}, z_t) = \mathrm{E}_t\left[u_2(c_{1t}, c_{2t})/p(s_t)\right] \Big/ \mathrm{E}_t\left[u_1(c_{1t}, c_{2t})/p(s_t)\right] \tag{4.19}$$

The price of a security which promises to pay one dollar in period $t + 1$ equals, at the beginning of time $t$ and before $s_t$ is observed, the ratio of the expected marginal utility of spending a dollar on the credit good to the expected marginal utility of spending a dollar on the cash good. The latter expected marginal utility is higher. In comparison with the former expected marginal utility, it shows the relative value of having money now (which is required for the purchase of the cash good) as compared with having credit (which suffices to purchase credit good). If the signal $z_t$ suffices to ascertain $s_t$ exactly, drop the conditional expectation operators $E_t$ in equations (4.14)–(4.19) that are placed before the functions $\lambda_t$, $\mu_t$, and $p$, because $s_t$ becomes given information once $z_t$ is known.

Stokey and Lucas (1987, pp. 508–510) provide three examples. Example 1 is a deterministic model with endowment $y$ and the rate of money growth $g$ being assumed to be constants. Use equations (4.13)–(4.17) and the market equilibrium conditions $y_t = c_{1t} + c_{2t}$ and $d_t = 0$ to find $q$ and $p$. The functions $c_1$, $c_2$, $d$, $\lambda$, and $\mu$ have arguments $m = 1$ and $s$. To determine $c_{1t}$ and $c_{2t}$ use equations (4.14), (4.15), and (4.17), namely,

$$u_1(c_{1t}, c_{2t}) = p(s_t)[\mu_t + \beta E_t g^{-1}\lambda_{t+1}]$$

$$u_2(c_{1t}, c_{2t}) = p(s_t) \cdot \beta E_t g^{-1}\lambda_{t+1}$$

$$\lambda_t = \mu_t + \beta E_t g^{-1}\lambda_{t+1}$$

implying

$$\frac{u_1(c_{1t}, c_{2t})}{u_2(c_{1t}, c_{2t})} = \frac{\lambda_t}{\lambda_t - \mu_t}.$$

$\lambda_t$ is the marginal utility of having an additional dollar, according to the dynamic constraint for $m_{t+1}$; it is the partial derivative of the Lagrangean function $\mathcal{L}$ (or the value function if one follows the terminology of Bellman) with respect to $m_t$. This dollar can be spent on the cash good $c_{1t}$, yielding marginal utility $u_1$. The marginal utility of consuming the credit good $c_{2t}$ is lower, because a dollar of credit is worth less than a dollar of money.

The multiplier $\mu_t$ is positive if the cash-in-advance constraint is binding, which yields

$$m_t = qd_t + pc_{1t} = pc_{1t}$$

Once $c_{1t}$ and $c_{2t}$ are determined by equating marginal utilities, the price level is determined by the above equation or $p = m_t/c_{1t}$. Assume that $m_t$ grows at the rate $g$. If $c_{1t}$ were constant, the price level $p$ would also grow at the rate $g$ as $m_t$ does, obeying the quantity theory of money. However, as Milton Friedman (1969) points out, if $g < 1$, the stock of money is decreasing and the price level $p$ is also decreasing, which provides a positive yield to holding money. Keeping a dollar bill until the next period, rather than spending it today on cash good, would enable a consumer to buy more of the same good in the next period, but the marginal utility of consuming the cash good in the next period has to be discounted by the factor $\beta$ of the multiperiod utility function. If $g = \beta$, there is no gain nor loss by keeping the dollar bill rather than spending it on the cash good today. If $g < \beta$, the growth in purchasing power of the dollar bill makes it worthwhile to save it until the next period and not worthwhile to spend it on the cash good today. No money will be spent on the cash good. The cash-in-advance constraint is not binding and $\mu_t = 0$. For the cash-in-advance constraint to be binding, or for $\mu_t$ to be positive, assume $g > \beta$, yielding $m_t = pc_{1t}$. For $c_{1t}$ to be constant and $y = c_{1t} + c_{2t}$ to be constant with $g < 1$, one needs the ratio $u_1/u_2$ or the ratio $\lambda_t/(\lambda_t - \mu_t)$ to be constant. This will happen if $\lambda$ and $\mu$ are constants. For constant $\lambda$ and $\mu$, and for $s_t$ to be a constant in a deterministic model, (4.17) becomes

$$\lambda = \mu + \beta g^{-1}\lambda$$

and one obtains the price $q$ for a one-period bond yielding $b = 1$ dollar from equation (4.19)

$$q = u_2/u_1 = (\lambda - \mu)/\lambda = \beta g^{-1}\lambda/\lambda = \beta/g$$

As $c_{1t}$ and $c_{2t}$ are constant through time, and the price level $p = m_t/c_1$ is proportional to the money stock, the inflation rate $\pi$ satisfies $1 + \pi = g$, and the pricing function $q$ for the one-period bond is $\beta/(1 + \pi)$. As the inflation rate or the money growth rate increases, the price of a bond falls. Because $q$ is related to the nominal rate of interest $r$ by $q = 1/(1 + r)$, the rate of interest has two components in this model. The real component depends on the discount factor $\beta$, and the nominal component depends on the rate of inflation $\pi$.

It is interesting to compare the solution method of this section with the method of dynamic programming used by Lucas and Stokey (LS) (1987). For the first model with only a cash-in-advance constraint but not the finance constraint (4.13), LS use three control variables $x_1 = c_1$, $x_2 = c_2$, and $x_3$ = end-of-period money balance prior to government injection of money. Only two control variables $c_1$ and $c_2$ are used here, after $x_3$ is incorporated in the dynamic constraint for $m_{t+1}$. The first-order conditions (4.10), (4.11), and (4.12) are respectively their (2.7), (2.8), and (2.9)–(2.11). Their equation (2.10) defines $v(s)$. [Note that, to distinguish between equations from LS and my equations, I have set equation numbers for their equations on the left.]

(2.10) $$v(s) = \beta E_t g(s_{t+1})^{-1} \lambda_{t+1}$$

Given their (2.10), their equation (2.11) is our equation (4.12):

(2.11) $$F_m(1, s) = \lambda(1, s_t) = w(s) + v(s) \equiv \mu_t + \beta E_t g(s_{t+1})^{-1} \cdot \lambda_{t+1}$$

in which $F(m, s)$ is the value function, our $\lambda$ is $\partial F/\partial m$, $\lambda_t = \lambda(m_t, s_t)$, and $w = \mu$. Combining their (2.10) and (2.11) yields their (2.12):

(2.12) $$v(s) = \beta E_t g(s_{t+1})^{-1}\left[w(s_{t+1}) + v(s_{t+1})\right].$$

We do not work with the function $v(s)$, but with the function $\lambda(1, s)$ instead.

To study the existence and uniqueness of solutions to the system of five equations (2.7), (2.8), (2.12),

(2.6) $$c_1(s) + c_2(s) = y(s)$$

and

(2.9) $$p(s)c_1(s) - 1 \leq 0, \text{ with equality if } \mu = w(s) > 0$$

for the five functions $c_1(s)$, $c_2(s)$, $v(s)$, $p(s)$, and $w(s)$ in general equilibrium, LS use (2.8) to eliminate $p = u_2/v$ and (2.6) to eliminate $c_2 = y - c_1$, writing (2.7) as

$$w = v\left[\frac{u_1(c_1,\ y-c_1)}{u_2(c_1,\ y-c_1)}\right] \tag{3.1}$$

and (2.9) as

$$u_2(c_1,\ y-c_1)c_1 \leqslant v \tag{3.2}$$

Equations (3.1), (3.2), and (2.12) for $v(s)$, $w(s)$, and $c_1(s)$ are finally reduced to one equation for $v(s)$:

$$v(s) = \beta \mathrm{E}_t g(s_{t+1})^{-1} h(v(s_{t+1}),\ y(s_{t+1})), \tag{3.7}$$

in which the function $h(v, y)$ is defined by their (3.6a) and (3.6b). Much effort is devoted to proving existence and uniqueness of solution to equation (3.7).

It appears convenient to study the five equations, with my equation (4.12) replacing their (2.12), for the five unknown functions with $\lambda$ replacing $v$. I will study the existence and uniqueness of solutions to (4.10), (4.11), (4.12), the cash-in-advance constraint, and $y = c_1 + c_2$ for the functions $c_1$, $c_2$, $\lambda$, $\mu$, and $p$ given $m = 1$ in general equilibrium. To do so, I first use the cash-in-advance constraint to find $p = m/c_1 = 1/c_1$. Multiplying equations (4.10) and (4.11), respectively, by $c_1$ gives

$$c_1 u_1(c_1,\ y-c_1) - \mu - \beta \mathrm{E}_t g(s_{t+1})^{-1}\lambda_{t+1} = 0 \tag{4.20}$$

$$c_1 u_2(c_1,\ y-c_1) - \beta \mathrm{E}_t g(s_{t+1})^{-1}\lambda_{t+1} = 0 \tag{4.21}$$

Substituting (4.20) for $\mu$ in (4.12) yields

$$\lambda(1,\ s) = c_1 u_1(c_1,\ y-c_1) \tag{4.22}$$

Equations (4.21) and (4.22) are two functional equations for $\lambda(1,s)$ and $c_1(1,s)$. Combining these two equations and denoting $c_1(1, s)$ by $c(s)$ yield

$$c(s) = u_2^{-1}(c(s),\ y(s)-c(s))\beta \int_s g(s')^{-1} c(s')u_1(c(s'),$$
$$y(s)-c(s))\pi(s,\ ds') \equiv \mathrm{T}c(s) \tag{4.23}$$

I will state a set of sufficient assumptions under which solution of (4.23) for $c(s)$ exists and is unique. Given $c(s)$, one can obtain $\lambda(1, s)$ by (4.22), $c_2 = y - c_1$, and $p = 1/c_1$. I modify assumptions A1 to A3 of LS by dropping the stationarity of the transition function in A1 and the boundedness of the utility function in A2, while replacing the assumption A2 by A2′ (see Hao (1992) for work required to construct the set $\mathrm{D} \subset \mathrm{R}_{++}$, to avoid the solution $c(s) = 0$):

*A1′. Let s and s′ be points in a metric space S. The transition function $\pi(s, s')$ from $s_t = s$ to $s_{t+1} = s'$ has the Feller property, i.e., for any bounded,* *continuous function $f: S \to \boldsymbol{R}$, the function $\int f(s')\pi(s, ds')$ is bounded and continuous in* s.

*A2′. u: (a) $R^2_+ \to R$ is continuously differentiable, strictly increasing, strictly concave. (b) For any function c with image in $D \subset \boldsymbol{R}_{++}$, D being closed and convex, the functions u, y and g are such that the function G defined by (4.26) is also in D. (c) For $u_I$ and $u_{II}$ denoting the first and second derivative of u with respect to the first argument,*

$$-2 < \frac{cu_{II}(c,\ y-c)}{u_I(c,\ y-c)}.$$

*A3. $y: S \to R_+$ and $g: S \to R_+$ are continuous functions, and both are bounded away from zero.*

To prove the existence and uniqueness of the solution to the functional equation (4.23), Lemma 17.2 of Stokey and Lucas (1989, p. 511) will be applied. Consider the functional equation

$$f(s) = (Tf)(s) \equiv \int G[s,\ s',\ f(s')]\pi(s,\ ds') \tag{4.24}$$

LEMMA: *(1) Let $F \subset C(s)$ be the space of bounded continuous strictly positive functions $f: s \to D$ with the sup norm, $D \subset \boldsymbol{R}_{++}$ being closed and convex. (2) Let $G: S \times S \times D \to D$ be a positive, continuously differentiable function on D for each $(s, s') \in S \times S$. (3) Let $\pi(s, s')$ have the Feller property. (4) Assume that there exists some $0 \leqslant \theta < 1$ such that, with $G_3$ denoting derivative of G with respect to the third argument,*

$$\left|\frac{yG_3(s,\ s',\ y)}{G(s,\ s',\ y)}\right| \leqslant \theta,\ all\ (s,\ s',\ y) \in S \times S \times D \tag{4.25}$$

*Then the operator* T *on* F *defined by (4.24) has a unique fixed point* f*.

THEOREM 4.4

*Given assumptions A1′, A2′, and A3, the functional equation (4.23) has a unique solution.*

PROOF: Equation (4.23) is a special case of equation (4.24) with $c(s) \equiv f(s)$ and

$$G[s,\ s',\ f(s')] = \frac{\beta c(s')u_1(c(s'),\ y(s') - c(s'))}{u_2(c(s),\ y(s) - c(s)) \cdot g(s')} \tag{4.26}$$

$$G_3[s,\ s',\ f(s')] = \frac{\beta[u_1(c(s'),\ y(s') - c(s')) + c(s')u_{11}(c(s'),\ y(s') - c(s'))]}{u_2(c(s),\ y(s) - c(s)) \cdot g(s')}$$

implying

$$\frac{c(s')G_3(s, s', f(s'))}{G(s, s', f(s'))} = 1 + \frac{c(s')u_{11}(c(s'), y(s') - c(s'))}{u_1(c(s'), y(s') - c(s'))} < 1$$

where the second partial $u_{11}$ of the utility function is negative by assumption A2′(a). The last expression is larger than –1 by assumption A2′(c). Thus the assumption (4) of the Lemma is satisfied. Assumption A2′(b) implies assumption (2) of the Lemma. Hence the functional equation (4.23) has a unique solution.

In the preceding proof, I have avoided the restrictive assumption that the value function is bounded. When the optimum is achieved, the value function $F(m, s)$ may be infinite. Yet, $\lambda(m, s) = \partial F/\partial m$ is finite. Provided that $u(c_1, c_2)$ and $m_t + p(s_t)(y(s_t) - c_{1t} - c_{2t})$ are both concave, the first-order conditions obtained by the Lagrange method yield a maximum to the dynamic optimization problem. Thus, even if $F(m, s)$ may be infinite, the solution gives the maximum expected discounted utility for any finite number of periods beginning with the initial state $(m, s)$ in any period $t$. I have also avoided the assumption that $u$ is bounded.

For the model incorporating the finance constraint (4.13), LS use five control variables, $x_1 = c_1$, $x_2 = c_2$, $x_3$ = end-of-period cash holdings before government money injection and payoff from bonds purchased at the beginning of period $t$, $x_4 = d_t$, and $x_5 = m - q(s_{t-1}, z_t)d_t$ or money holding after bond purchase that is available to buy cash goods. The exposition of this section uses only three control varilables, $c_1$, $c_2$, and $d$. It adds their constraints (5.1) and (5.2) to yield my finance constraint (4.13). Add their constraints (5.1) and (5.3) to get an equation for $x_3$, which is used to get my dynamic equations for $m_{t+1}$. Thus, my model that uses the finance constraint and the dynamic constraint for $m_t$ no longer requires variables $x_3$ and $x_5$. Their equations (5.6) and (5.9) define $v(s)$ and $\lambda$.

$$(5.6) \qquad v(s) = \beta E_{z'}\left[F_m(1, s, z')\frac{1}{\hat{g}(z')}\middle|s\right] = \beta E_t\lambda(1, s_t, z_{t+1})\hat{g}(z_{t+1})^{-1}$$

Their equations (5.7) and (5.8) correspond to equations (4.15) and (4.16), respectively. Combining (5.6) and (5.8), they obtain a functional equation (5.10) for $v(s)$, which involves $w(s) = \mu(s)$, which is the same as their (2.12). Again, I do not work with the function $v(s)$, but with $\lambda$ instead.

To complete the comparison, consider their Example 3. Let

$$u(c_1, c_2) = \alpha\ln(c_1) + (1-\alpha)\ln(c_2)$$

Equation (4.23) implies

$$c_1 = \frac{(y - c_1)}{(1-\alpha)}\alpha\beta E_t g(s_{t+1})^{-1}$$

so that

$$c_1(s) = y(s)\alpha\beta E_t g(s_{t+1})^{-1} \Big/ \left[1 - \alpha + \alpha\beta E_t g(s_{t+1})^{-1}\right]$$

$$c_2(s) = y(s) - c_1(s) = y(s)(1-\alpha) \Big/ \left[1 - \alpha + \alpha\beta E_t g(s_{t+1})^{-1}\right]$$

Equation (4.19) gives the price of a one-period bond, when $s_t = z_t$, to be

$$q(s) = E_t\left[(1-\alpha)c_2(s)^{-1} \cdot c_1(s)\right] \Big/ E_t\left[\alpha c_1(s)^{-1} \cdot c_1(s)\right]$$
$$= \beta E_t g(s_{t+1})^{-1}.$$

The same solution as in LS (p. 510) is obtained without using the function $v(s)$.

This section has demonstrated the convenience to bypass the value function and to concentrate on the control function by using the Lagrange method in solving dynamic optimization problems under uncertainty.

## 4.5 A One-Sector Model of General Equilibrium

The previous sections give examples of equilibrium theory for particular markets based on dynamic optimization behavior. I now set out a framework for general equilibrium theory as expounded by Stokey and Lucas (1989). I begin by considering a one-sector growth model (section 16.1, p. 476). In the economy, there is only one good used for consumption and as capital. One consumer owns one firm. Consumers and firms determine (1) the dynamics of capital formation and (2) the real rate of interest through a capital accumulation function of the firm and an asset accumulation or a consumption function of the representative consumer. In equilibrium, four functions are determined: (1) $k_{t+1} = g(k_t)$, the growth equation for economy-wide capital $k_t$ per firm or per consumer; (2) $q(k_t)$, the price at time $t$ of a claim to one unit of consumption or capital good available in period $t + 1$, analogous to the pricing of a one-period bond paying one dollar in the next period of the last section; (3) capital accumulation function for the firm $z_{t+1} = h(k_t, z_t)$, with $z_t$ denoting the capital stock of the firm, while $k_t$ denotes the per capita or the per firm capital stock of the economy; (4) an asset accumulation function $a_{t+1} = \omega(k_t, a_t)$ of the representative consumer, with $a_t$ denoting the value of her asset. When the representative firm and the representative consumer maximize over time, they take as given the price $q(k_t)$ of the next period's capital. In equilibrium, the first-order conditions of their dynamic optimization calculations determine the growth process of the economy and the price of next period's capital.

In each period, the entire output of the firm is given by

$$f(z_t) = F(z_t, 1) + (1-\delta)z_t,$$

in which F is the production function with a fixed input that is set equal to one unit, and $\delta$ is the rate of depreciation. $f(z_t) - z_{t+1} = y_t$ is the amount of output available for distribution to the consumer-owner as a dividend, after leaving $z_{t+1}$ units as capital for the following period. The firm is assumed to maximize the sum of discounted dividends from all future periods subject to the constraint of the capital accumulation process. The Lagrangean and the associated first-order conditions are:

$$\mathcal{L} = \sum_{t=0}^{\infty} \left\{ p_t y_t - p_{t+1} \lambda_{t+1} \left[ z_{t+1} - f(z_t) + y_t \right] \right\} \tag{4.27}$$

$$p_t^{-1} \frac{\partial \mathcal{L}}{\partial y_t} = 1 - \left( p_{t+1} / p_t \right) \lambda_{t+1} = 0 \tag{4.28}$$

$$p_t^{-1} \frac{\partial \mathcal{L}}{\partial z_t} = -\lambda_t + f'(z_t)\left( p_{t+1} / p_t \right) \lambda_{t+1} = 0 \tag{4.29}$$

If $p_t$ is the period-zero price of one unit of dividend to be paid out $t$ periods later, and $q(k_s) = 1/(1 + r_s)$ is the price at time $s$ of one unit of consumer good to be paid in period $s + 1$, $r_s$ being the rate of interest in period $s$, one has

$$p_t = \prod_{s=0}^{t-1} q(k_s) = \prod_{s=0}^{t-1} \left( \frac{1}{1 + r_s} \right) \quad (t = 1, 2, \ldots)$$

with $p_0 = 1$, $p_1 = q(k_0)$, $p_2 = q(k_0) \cdot q(k_1)$, and $q(k_t) = p_{t+1}/p_t$. The preceding equation gives a familiar relation between the long-term discount factor $p_t$ and the short-term or one-period rates of interest $r_s$. First-order conditions (4.28) and (4.29) imply

$$\lambda_t = f'(z_t)$$

and

$$\lambda_{t+1} = p_t / p_{t+1} = q(k_t)^{-1} = f'(z_{t+1}) \tag{4.30}$$

Solving (4.30) for $z_{t+1}$, obtain the capital accumulation function of the firm

$$z_{t+1} = h(k_t), \tag{4.31}$$

which is a function of the economy-wide capital stock $k_t$ alone, as $k_t$ suffices to determine the marginal rate of return to the firm's capital. Equation (4.30) states that the marginal product of next-period's capital $f'(z_{t+1})$ should be equal to the inverse of the discount factor $q(k_t)^{-1}$.

As an example of the firm's optimization problem, let the output function be $f(z) = z^\alpha$. Given $q(k_t)^{-1}$, use this function and (4.30) to obtain

$$f'(z_{t+1}) = \alpha z_{t+1}^{\alpha-1} = q(k_t)^{-1},$$

which yields the following function for the firm's capital accumulation

$$z_{t+1} = \left[ \alpha q(k_t) \right]^{1/(1-\alpha)} = h(k_t)$$

and the firm's dividend

$$y_t = f(z_t) - z_{t+1} = z_t^{\alpha} - \left[\alpha q(k_t)\right]^{1/(1-\alpha)} = y(k_t, z_t).$$

Also, by (4.28) and (4.29),

$$\lambda_{zt} = f'(z_t) = \alpha z_t^{\alpha-1}$$

where $\lambda_{zt}$ is used to distinguish between the Lagrange multipliers for the firm's and the consumer's optimization problems.

To solve the representative consumer's problem, assume that he or she owns assets $a_t$ and consumes $c_t$ at period $t$, leaving the amount $q(k_t)a_{t+1}$ of assets for the next period, $q(k_t)$ being the discount factor as discussed in the previous paragraph. The Lagrangean and the first-order conditions for his or her dynamic optimization problem are

$$\mathcal{L} - \sum_{t=0}^{\infty}\left\{\beta^t u(c_t) - \beta^{t+1}\lambda_{t+1}\left[a_{t+1} - (a_t - c_t)/q(k_t)\right]\right\} \tag{4.32}$$

$$\beta^{-t}\frac{\partial \mathcal{L}}{\partial c_t} = u'(c_t) - \beta q(k_t)^{-1}\lambda_{t+1} = 0 \tag{4.33}$$

$$\beta^{-t}\frac{\partial \mathcal{L}}{\partial a_t} = -\lambda_t + \beta q(k_t)^{-1}\lambda_{t+1} = 0 \tag{4.34}$$

Equations (4.33) and (4.26) imply $\lambda_t = u'(c_t)$, $\lambda_t$ being the marginal utility of assets. When $u'(c_t)$ is substituted for $\lambda_t$ in (4.26), one obtains

$$u'(c_t) = \beta q(k_t)^{-1} u'(c_{t+1}) \tag{4.35}$$

which is a familiar first-order condition (see section 4.1). This condition states that one unit of consumption good can be used for current consumption to yield marginal utility $u'(c_t)$ or to yield $q(k_t)^{-1}$ units of consumption good in period $t+1$, yielding marginal utility $q(k_t)^{-1}u'(c_{t+1})$, which has to be discounted by $\beta$. Given the utility function $u$ and the discount function $q(k_t)$, equation (4.35) can explain $c_{t+1}$ as a function of $c_t$ and hence the evolution of $c_t$.

To illustrate the solution of the consumer's optimization problem, let $u(c) = \ln c$. Equations (4.33) and (4.34) provide two equations for the functions $c$ and $\lambda$, provided that $q(k_t)$ is known. Conjecture the consumption function to be $\gamma q(k_t)^{\delta}a_t$, for some parameters $\gamma$ and $\delta$ yet to be determined. This method of solving functional equations assumes particular functional forms for the unknown functions and then uses the functional equations (4.33) and (4.34) to find the parameters. An example is given in section 2.4, in which I assume the optimal control function to be linear. In chapter 9, I discuss methods to solve numerically for the control function and Lagrange function. Given this functional form for $c$ and $u(c) = \ln c$, equations (4.33) and (4.34) imply

$$\lambda_t = u'(c_t) = \gamma^{-1}q(k_t)^{-\delta}a_t^{-1} = \beta q(k_t)^{-1}\gamma^{-1}q(k_{t+1})^{-\delta}a_{t+1}^{-1}$$

Because

$$a_{t+1} = q(k_t)^{-1}[a_t - c_t] = q(k_t)^{-1}\left[1 - \gamma q(k_t)^{\delta}\right]a_t$$

substitute the right-hand side for $a_{t+1}$ in the equation above to obtain

$$q(k_t)^{-\delta} a_t^{-1} = \beta q(k_{t+1})^{-\delta}\left[1 - \gamma q(k_t)^{\delta}\right]^{-1} a_t^{-1}$$

or

$$q(k_t)^{-\delta} = \beta q(k_{t+1})^{-\delta}\left[1 - \gamma q(k_t)^{\delta}\right]^{-1}.$$

The last equation can hold only if $\delta = 0$, in which case $1 = \beta[1 - \gamma]^{-1}$ or $\gamma = 1 - \beta$. We have thus obtained the consumption function

$$c_t = \gamma q(k_t)^{\delta} a_t = (1 - \beta)a_t \tag{4.36}$$

Once $c_t$ is found, one has

$$\lambda_t = u'(c_t) = c_t^{-1} = (1 - \beta)^{-1} a_t^{-1} \tag{4.37}$$

and

$$a_{t+1} = q(k_t)^{-1}[a_t - c_t] = \beta q(k_t)^{-1} a_t \tag{4.38}$$

Equations (4.36) and (4.38) illustrate that, once $q(k_t)$ is given, the first-order conditions of the consumer's dynamic optimization problem yield a consumption function and a function for the evolution of $a_t$, to be written respectively as

$$c_t = c(k_t,\ a_t); \quad a_{t+1} = \omega(k_t,\ a_t) \tag{4.39}$$

Having solved both the representative firm's and the representative consumer's optimization problems, one can define a competitive equilibrium for the economy following the lines of Stokey and Lucas (1989, p. 478). Note, however, that in the following definition, dynamic programming and the associated Bellman equations for the value functions of the firm and of the consumer are not employed. A competitive equilibrium consists of six functions:

1. $k_{t+1} = g(k_t)$ for the growth of per firm or per consumer capital stock of the economy;
2. $q(k_t)$, current price of one unit of next-period's consumption good or capital good, equal to $1/(1 + r_t)$ where $r_t$ is the rate of interest;
3. $\lambda_{zt} = \lambda_z(k_t,\ z_t)$, the Lagrange function for the firm's optimization problem;
4. $z_{t+1} = h(k_t,\ z_t)$, the firm's capital accumulation equation, or equivalently $y_t = y(k_t,\ z_t) = f(z_t) - h(k_t,\ z_t)$, the firm's dividend equation;
5. $\lambda_{at} = \lambda_a(k_t,\ a_t)$, the Lagrange function for the consumer's optimization problem; and

6. $c_t = c(k_t, a_t)$, the consumption function, or equivalently $a_{t+1} = \omega(k_t, a_t)$, the consumer's asset accumulation equation,

such that

(1) the functions $\lambda_z$ and $y$ (or $h$) satisfy equations (4.30) and (4.31);
(2) the functions $\lambda_a$ and $c$ (or $\omega$) satisfy equations (4.33) and (4.34);
(3) $k_{t+1} = h(k_t, k_t) \equiv g(k_t)$ since in equilibrium $z_t = k_t$;
(4) $c_t = y_t$, or consumption equals the amount of dividend distributed by the firm. This equation also means that the savings of the consumer equal the capital accumulation of the firm that he or she owns, because the asset accumulation of the consumer for the next period is net of current consumption, and the capital stock of the firm for the next period is net of the output of current consumer good distributed as dividend. When the market is in equilibrium, the current price $q(k_t) = 1/(1 + r_t)$ of next-period's good, or the rate of interest $r_t$ must equate the consumer's savings with the firm's capital accumulation.

Note that in the formulation of Stokey and Lucas (1989, pp. 478–480), the corresponding value functions instead of the Lagrangean functions $\lambda_z$ and $\lambda_a$ are used in (1) and (2); (4) is replaced by

$$\text{(R4)} \qquad a_{t+1} = \omega(k_t, a_t) = \omega(k_t, \psi(k_t, k_t)) = \psi(k_{t+1}, k_{t+1}) = \psi[g(k_t), g(k_t)]$$

in which the value of the firm $\psi(k_t, k_t)$ equals the value of the consumer-owner's asset $a_t$ with $\psi(k_t, z_t)$ defined by the following Bellman's equation for the firm

$$\psi(k_t, z_t) = \max_{0 \le z_{t+1} \le f(z_t)} \{f(z_t) - z_{t+1} + q(k_t)\psi(k_{t+1}, z_{t+1})\} \tag{4.40}$$

in which $k_{t+1} = g(k_t)$. I have solved the firm's optimization problem by using first-order conditions (4.28) and (4.29).

To illustrate the solution of general equilibrium by an example, let $f(z) = z^\alpha$ and $u(c) = \ln c$. From the firm's optimization, I have found the firm's capital accumulation equation and by the market equilibrium condition $z_t = k_t$, I have

$$k_{t+1} = z_{t+1} = [\alpha q(k_t)]^{1/(1-\alpha)} = g(k_t) \tag{4.41}$$

To find the current price $q(k_t)$ of next period's good, use the consumer's optimization condition (4.35)

$$u'(c_t) = \beta q(k_t)^{-1} u'(c_{t+1})$$

together with the market clearing conditions $c_t = y_t$ and the optimal dividend

$$y_t = f(z_t) - z_{t+1} = z_t^\alpha - [\alpha q(k_t)]^{1/(1-\alpha)}$$

Given $u'(c) = c^{-1} = y^{-1}$, these conditions imply

$$y_{t+1} = z_{t+1}^\alpha - [\alpha q(k_{t+1})]^{1/(1-\alpha)} = \beta q(k_t)^{-1}\{z_t^\alpha - [\alpha q(k_t)]^{1/(1-\alpha)}\}$$

Omitting the subscript $t$ and substituting $(\alpha q)^{1/(1-\alpha)}$ for $z_{t+1}$ and for $k_{t+1}$, we have

$$q\left\{(\alpha q)^{\alpha/(1-\alpha)} - \left[\alpha q\left(\left[\alpha q\right]^{1/(1-\alpha)}\right)\right]^{1/(1-\alpha)}\right\} = \beta\left\{k^{\alpha} - (\alpha q)^{1/(1-\alpha)}\right\}$$

One can easily check that the function

$$q(k) = \alpha^{-\alpha}\beta^{(1-\alpha)}k^{\alpha(1-\alpha)}$$

satisfies the above equation. We have thus found the pricing function $q(k)$ and, hence, the economy-wide capital accumulation equation

$$k_{t+1} = \left[\alpha q\right]^{1/(1-\alpha)} = \alpha\beta k_t^{\alpha}$$

Thus, through the firm's optimal capital accumulation and dividend (or current output) decisions and the consumer's optimal asset accumulation and consumption decisions, the economy's rate of interest and its capital accumulation process are determined in the framework of general equilibrium.

The preceding example illustrates a basic theorem in welfare economies, namely, that a competitive equilibrium solution is Pareto optimal. If there were a central planner making the decisions on capital accumulation and consumption for the economy by taking the preferences of the representative consumer into account, he or she would maximize the sum of discounted utilities subject to the capital accumulation constraint. The Lagrangean is

$$\mathcal{L} = \sum_{t=0}^{\infty}\left[\beta^t u(c_t) - \beta^{t+1}\lambda_{t+1}\left(k_{t+1} - f(k_t) + c_t\right)\right]$$

with $\partial\mathcal{L}/\partial c_t = 0$ and $\partial\mathcal{L}/\partial k_t = 0$ as first-order conditions. Given $u(c) = \ln c$ and $f(k) = k^{\alpha}$, I have found in section 3.1 that the optimal consumption and capital accumulation plans are respectively

$$c_t = (1 - \alpha\beta)k_t^{\alpha}$$

$$k_{t+1} = k_t^{\alpha} - c_t = \alpha\beta k_t^{\alpha}$$

which agree with the market equilibrium solution just given.

## 4.6 Equilibrium of a Multisector Model

To generalize the discussion of section 4.5 to a multisector economy, consider a model more general than the one treated in section 3.2. There are N goods. Good $j$ may be a consumption good $c_{jt}$, an input $x_{ij,t}$ used for production of output $Y_{i,t+1}$ at time $t+1$, or serve both purposes. Output $Y_{i,t+1}$ is produced by a production function

$$Y_{i,t+1} = \phi_i\left(x_{i1,t}, \ldots, x_{iN,t}, z_{i,t+1}\right) \quad i = 1, \ldots, N \tag{4.42}$$

which has equation (3.11) as a special case, with $z_{i,t+1}$ denoting a random shock in the production of $Y_{i,t+1}$.

I put more details in this model than I did in section 3.2 by distinguishing between consumption goods and producer goods, and between durables and nondurables. Let the first M goods (M < N) be consumption goods, the first $m(m < \mathrm{M})$ be nondurable consumption goods, and the remaining $\mathrm{M} - m$ be consumer durables. Goods $\mathrm{M} + 1, \ldots, \mathrm{M} + n$ are nondurable producer goods (materials in production), and goods $\mathrm{M} + n + 1, \ldots, \mathrm{N}$ are capital goods. The representative consumer's utility $u$ is a function of $(c_{1t}, \ldots, c_{\mathrm{M}t})$ with $c_{it} = \mathrm{Y}_{it}$ $(i = 1, \ldots, m)$, $\mathrm{Y}_{it}$ being the output of the $i$th consumer good at time $t$, and $c_{it} = x_{it}$ $(i = m + 1, \ldots, \mathrm{M})$, $x_{it}$ being the stock of the $i$th durable good, obeying $x_{it} = \mathrm{Y}_{it} + (1 - \delta_i)x_{i,t-1}$, $\delta_i$ being the rate of depreciation. Input $x_{it}$ in the economy's production function equals $\mathrm{Y}_{it}$ $(i = \mathrm{M} + 1, \ldots, \mathrm{M} + n)$ when the $i$th input is nondurable, and $x_{it} = \mathrm{Y}_{it} + (1 - \delta_i)x_{i,t-1}$ $(i = \mathrm{M} + n + 1, \ldots, \mathrm{N})$ when it is a durable good. If $\mathrm{Y}_{it}$ is the quantity of output of a consumption good, it is either consumed, being equal to $c_{it}$ $(i = 1, \ldots, m)$, or added to the existing depreciated stock of the durable good for consumption $(i = m + 1, \ldots, \mathrm{M})$ in the quantity of $c_{it} = x_{it} = \mathrm{Y}_{it} + (1 - \delta_i)x_{i,t-1}$.

In equation (3.12) of section 3.2, I used the identity

$$\mathrm{Y}_{it} = c_{it} + \sum_{k=1}^{\mathrm{N}} x_{ki,t}, \tag{4.43}$$

which states that output $\mathrm{Y}_{it}$ can be used either for consumption or as an input in the production of good $k$ $(k = 1, \ldots, \mathrm{N})$. If the $i$th good is a nondurable consumption good $(i = 1, \ldots, m)$, equation (4.43) is still valid with $\mathrm{Y}_{it} = c_{it}$ and $x_{ki} = 0$ $(k = 1, \ldots, \mathrm{N})$, because the $i$th good is not an input. If the $i$th good is a durable consumption good $(i = m + 1, \ldots, \mathrm{M})$, $x_{ki} = 0$ $(k = 1, \ldots, \mathrm{N})$, but $c_{it} = \mathrm{Y}_{it} + (1 - \delta_i)x_{i,t-1} = x_{it}$, $x_{it}$ being the total stock of this durable good. If the $i$th good is a nondurable producer good $(i = \mathrm{M} + 1, \ldots, \mathrm{M} + n)$, the equation (4.43) is valid with $c_{it} = 0$ and $\mathrm{Y}_{it} = \Sigma_{k=1}^{\mathrm{N}} x_{ki,t}$. If the $i$th good is a capital good, $c_{it} = 0$ and $x_{it} = \Sigma_{k=1}^{\mathrm{N}} x_{ki,t} = \mathrm{Y}_{it} + (1 - \delta_i)x_{i,t-1}$, with the stock $x_{it}$ divided among the production of N goods. The equation (4.43) is valid if I redefine the function $\mathrm{Y}_{it}^* = \phi_i^*(x_{\mathrm{M}+1,t-1}, \ldots, x_{\mathrm{N},t-1}) = x_{it}$ to include not only net output $\mathrm{Y}_{it}$ but depreciated old stock $(1 - \delta_i)x_{i,t-1}$. For notational simplicity and to preserve equation (4.43), it behooves me to redefine $\mathrm{Y}_{it}$ and $\phi_i$ to be inclusive of depreciated old capital stock. For expositional convenience, rule out the existence of consumer durables by letting $m = \mathrm{M}$, so that equations (4.42) and (4.43) remain valid, with $\mathrm{Y}_{i,t+1}$ and $\phi_i$ in (4.42) denoting output inclusive of depreciated old capital stock for $i = \mathrm{M} + n + 1, \ldots, \mathrm{N}$. The reader may wish to include consumer durables in the model as an exercise (see problem 4).

If a social planner is to solve the economy's optimization problem given utility function $u(c_{1t}, \ldots, c_{\mathrm{M}t})$, the state variables at time $t$ are $x_{\mathrm{M}+1,t-1}, \ldots, x_{\mathrm{N},t-1}$, and the control variables are $\mathrm{Y}_{1t} = c_{1t}, \ldots, \mathrm{Y}_{\mathrm{M}t} = c_{\mathrm{M}t}$, and $x_{ki,t}$ $(i = \mathrm{M} + 1, \ldots, \mathrm{N}; k = 1, \ldots, \mathrm{N})$. In other words, given the initial stocks of materials and capital $x_{k,t}$ $(k = \mathrm{M} + 1, \ldots, \mathrm{N})$, the social planner tries to maximize expected sum of discounted utilities of future consumption (per capita) by assigning in each period $x_{ik,t}$ units of each input $k$ for the production of goods $i$ $(i = 1, \ldots, \mathrm{N})$ in the next period, which can be used for consumption or as future inputs. Use $x_{it}$ $(i = 1, \ldots, \mathrm{M})$ instead of $c_{it}$ to denote outputs of consumption goods, and $x_{it}$ ($i$ = M + 1, . . . , N) instead of $Y_{it}$ to denote outputs of producer goods. Given $x_{M+1,0}, \ldots, x_{N,0}$, the Lagrangean and the first-order conditions are

$$\mathscr{L} = \sum_{t=0}^{\infty} E_t \left\{ \beta^{t+1} u\left(x_{1,t+1}, \ldots, x_{M,t+1}\right) + \beta^t \sum_{k=M+1}^{N} \mu_{kt} \left( x_{kt} - \sum_{i=1}^{N} x_{ik,t} \right) \right.$$
$$\left. -\beta^{t+1} \sum_{i=1}^{N} \lambda_{i,t+1} \left[ x_{i,t+1} - \phi_i\left(x_{i,M+1t}, \ldots, x_{i,N,t}, z_{i,t+1}\right)\right] \right\} \qquad (4.44)$$

$$\beta^{-t} \frac{\partial \mathscr{L}}{\partial x_{ikt}} = -\mu_{kt} + \beta E_t \phi_{ikt} \lambda_{i,t+1} = 0 \qquad k = M+1, \ldots, N; \text{ all } i; \ t = 0, 1, \ldots \qquad (4.45)$$

$$\beta^{-t} \frac{\partial \mathscr{L}}{\partial x_{it}} = u_{it} - \lambda_{it} = 0 \qquad i = 1, \ldots, M; \ t = 1, 2, \ldots \qquad (4.46)$$

$$\beta^{-t} \frac{\partial \mathscr{L}}{\partial x_{kt}} = \mu_{kt} - \lambda_{kt} = 0 \qquad k = M+1, \ldots, N; \ t = 1, 2, \ldots \qquad (4.47)$$

in which $\phi_{ikt}$ denotes the partial derivative of $\phi_i$ with respect to its $k$th argument evaluated at values as of period $t$, and $u_{it}$ denotes the partial derivative of $u$ with respect to its $i$th argument evaluated at values as of time $t$. The control variables are $x_{ikt}$ ($k$ = M + 1, . . . , N for producer goods). The system of equations (4.45), (4.46), and (4.47), together with the constraints in (4.44) with multipliers $\mu_{kt}$ and $\lambda_{it}$ provide sufficient equations to solve for the same number of unknowns $x_{ikt}$ ($k$ = M + 1, . . . , N; $i$ = 1, . . . , N), $x_{it}$ ($i$ = 1, . . . , M), $x_{kt}$ ($k$ = M + 1, . . . , N), $\mu_{kt}$ ($k$ = M + 1, . . . , N), and $\lambda_{it}$ ($i$ = 1, . . . , N).

By (4.46), $\lambda_{it}$ is the marginal utility of the $i$th consumption good ($i$ = 1, . . . , M). By (4.45) and (4.47), inputs are employed in such a way that the marginal value of the $k$th producer good (either material input or service from a capital good) at time $t$ should equal the discounted expectation of the value of its marginal product $\phi_{ikt}\lambda_{i,t+1}$ in producing any good $i$ ($i$ = 1, . . . , N) in the next period. If good $i$ is a consumption good, combining (4.45) and (4.46) yields

$$\mu_{kt} = \beta E_t \phi_{ikt} u_{i,t+1} \qquad (4.48)$$

which states that the marginal value of the $k$th producer good at time $t$ should equal the discounted expectation of its marginal product $\phi_{ikt}$ in producing good $i$ times the latter's marginal utility $u_{i,t+1}$ in the next period. If good $i$ is a producer good, combining (4.45) and (4.47) yields

$$\mu_{kt} = \beta E_t \phi_{ikt} \mu_{i,t+1} \qquad (4.49)$$

which states that the marginal value of the $k$th producer good at time $t$ should equal the discounted expectation of its marginal product $\phi_{ikt}$ in producing good $i$ times the latter's marginal value $\mu_{i,t+1}$ in the next period. Equations (4.48) and (4.49) provide optimality conditions for the tradeoff between using resources in period $t$ and $t$ + 1.

The optimal control problem as I have just formulated and solved is somewhat different from the standard form as treated in section 2.3 in which the dynamic evolution of the state variables is given by equation (2.13)

$$x_{t+1} = f(x_t, u_t) + \varepsilon_{t+1} \tag{2.13}$$

Here, N state variables are $x_{it}$, which evolve according to

$$x_{i,t+1} = \phi_i(x_{i,M+1,t}, \ldots, x_{i,N,t}, z_{i,t+1}) \qquad i = 1, \ldots, N \tag{4.50}$$

First, in section 2.3, I introduced an additive random disturbance $\varepsilon_{t+1}$ for convenience of exposition. I could have written the right-hand side of (2.13) as $f(x_t, u_t, \varepsilon_{t+1})$ and changed equations (2.15) and (2.16) by placing the expectation sign $E_t$ just after $\beta$, that is, by writing instead

$$\beta E_t \frac{\partial}{\partial u_t} f'(x_t, u_t, \varepsilon_{t+1})\lambda_{t+1},$$

which might make numerical solution more difficult. To make the two dynamic models comparable, denote the control variables $x_{ikt}$ by $u_{ikt}$, so that the right-hand side of (2.13) becomes $f(u_t, \varepsilon_{t+1})$. The main difference is that I now introduce a set of constraints between the state and control variables in the form

$$x_{kt} = \sum_{i=1}^{N} u_{ikt} \qquad k = M+1, \ldots, N$$

Thus, instead of having equation (2.13) to describe the dynamics of the state variables, I have a pair of equations

$$x_{t+1} = f(u_t, \varepsilon_{t+1}) \tag{4.50a}$$

$$h(u_t) = x_{2t} \tag{4.50b}$$

in which $x_{2t}$ is a subvector of the state variables $x_t$, and $h$ is a vector function (in this example linear). This example shows the versatility of the method of Lagrange multipliers.

Having solved the central planner's optimization problem, I turn to a market solution to determine the prices. As in the previous section, let the representative consumer own N firms, with the $i$th firm producing $Y_{i,t+1} = x_{i,t+1}$ by using technology $\phi_i$ given by (4.42). The $i$th firm tries to maximize the expected present value of its future net revenues $p_{it}x_{it} - \Sigma_k p_{kt}x_{ikt}$ by choosing the quantities of inputs $x_{ikt}$ ($k = M + 1, \ldots, N$) subject to the constraint (4.42), in which $p_{it}$ denotes the period-zero price (or rental) of the $i$th good to be delivered at time $t$. The $i$th firm's Lagrangean and first-order conditions corresponding to (4.45) and (4.47) are

$$\mathcal{L} = \sum_{t=0}^{\infty} E_t \left\{ p_{i,t+1}x_{i,t+1} - \sum_{k=M+1}^{N} p_{k,t+1}x_{ik,t+1} - \lambda_{i,t+1}\left[x_{i,t+1} - \phi_i(x_{i,M+1,t}, \ldots, x_{iNt}, z_{i,t+1})\right]\right\}$$

$$\frac{\partial \mathcal{L}}{\partial x_{ikt}} = -p_{kt} + \mathrm{E}_t \phi_{ikt} \lambda_{i,t+1} = 0 \quad k = \mathrm{M}+1, \ldots, \mathrm{N} \tag{4.52}$$

$$\frac{\partial \mathcal{L}}{\partial x_{it}} = p_{it} - \lambda_{it} = 0 \tag{4.53}$$

implying

$$p_{kt} = \mathrm{E}_t \phi_{ikt} p_{i,t+1} \qquad k = \mathrm{M}+1, \ldots, \mathrm{N} \tag{4.54}$$

Equation (4.54) states that the firm producing good $i$ will pay for its $k$th input at a price $p_{kt}$ equal to the expected value of its marginal product to be completed in the next period. The firm's optimization could be solved by replacing $x_{it+1}$ in (4.51) by $\phi_{it}$ without using the Lagrange multiplier $\lambda_{i,t+1}$. Using the multiplier makes it convenient to compare with the model of section 3.2 (which generalizes the classic one-sector model of section 3.1) and to compare the market equilibrium solution with the central planners's solution in this section.

For arithmetical convenience, assume that there are 100 identical consumers and there are 100 identical firms producing each product $i$, so that one consumer owns one firm in each industry producing product $i$. Each consumer receives the net revenue $p_{it}x_{it} - \Sigma_{k=\mathrm{M}+1}^{\mathrm{N}} p_{kt}x_{ik,t}$ of one firm in each industry $i$. In addition, the consumer is assumed to own the initial material or capital stock $x_{it}$ ($i = \mathrm{M} + 1, \ldots, \mathrm{N}$) used in production for which he or she receives price or rental totaling $\Sigma_{i=\mathrm{M}+1}^{\mathrm{N}} p_{it}x_{it}$. The sum of these two sources of incomes is $\Sigma_{i=1}^{\mathrm{N}} p_{it}x_{it}$, using $\Sigma_{i=1}^{\mathrm{N}} x_{ikt} = x_{kt}$. Given the expected net revenues from N firms in N industries and from rental of capital goods in all future periods, the consumer is assumed to maximize discounted life-time utility with respect to his or her consumption $c_{it}$ of M goods in all future periods subject to a life-time total wealth constraint. The Lagrangean and the associated first-order conditions are

$$\mathcal{L} = \sum_{t=1}^{\infty} \mathrm{E}_t \left\{ \beta^t u\left(c_{1t}, \ldots, c_{\mathrm{M}t}\right) + \lambda \left[ \sum_{i=1}^{\mathrm{N}} p_{it}x_{it} - \sum_{i=1}^{\mathrm{M}} p_{it}c_{it} \right] \right\} \tag{4.55}$$

$$\frac{\partial \mathcal{L}}{\partial c_{it}} = \beta^t u_{it} - p_{it}\lambda = 0 \qquad i = 1, \ldots, \mathrm{M} \tag{4.56}$$

$\lambda$ is the marginal utility of wealth. By the first-order condition (4.56), the period-zero price $p_{it}$ of the $i$th consumption good delivered in period $t$ equals the discounted marginal utility $\beta^t u_{it}/\lambda$ of one unit of wealth spent on consuming the $i$th consumption good in period $t$.

To consider general equilibrium of this economy, observe that all prices $p_{it}$ ($i = 1, \ldots, \mathrm{N}$) are treated as given when the firms and the consumers make their decisions. Given the prices, equation (4.52) for firms in all industry $i$ ($i = 1, \ldots, \mathrm{N}$) determines the quantities of all inputs $x_{ikt}$ ($k = \mathrm{M} + 1, \ldots, \mathrm{N}$) to be employed. Given the production functions $\phi_i$, the outputs or supplies of all consumer goods and stocks of producer goods of the next period will be determined. Given the prices, equation (4.56) determines the demand $c_{it}$ ($i$ = 1, . . . , M) for the consumer goods. In equilibrium, demand $c_{it}$ equals supply $x_{it}$, thus giving M conditions to determine the prices $p_{it}$ ($i = 1, \ldots, M$) of consumer goods for each period $t$. After each firm $i$ decides on its inputs $x_{ikt}$, the demand $x_{kt} = \Sigma_{i=1}^{N} x_{ikt}$ for each input $k$ ($k = M + 1, \ldots, N$) is determined. Equating the demand with available supply, which was produced in the previous period, one determines the prices $p_{kt}$ ($k = M + 1, \ldots, N$) of all producer goods. In addition, (4.54) gives the relationship between period-zero prices (or present values) of producer goods in different periods, and thus the rates of interest for the capital goods. Because I lack one equation to determine the marginal utility $\lambda$ of wealth, I need to assign one good in period 1 (or an arbitrary period $t$) as the numeraire with its price being utility. It is well known that considerations of tastes and technology can determine real outputs and relative prices (over time in this case), but not absolute prices.

I leave it as an exercise to show that the real outputs over time in this economy are the same under the guidance of a central planner or under the general equilibrium of a decentralized market economy with firms and consumers making their own decisions to maximize expected net revenues or expected discounted life-time utility (see problem 5). Such a demonstration is not difficult, because the first-order conditions derived by the method of Lagrange multipliers in the two cases can be easily compared.

## 4.7 Equilibrium of a One-sector Model with Tax Distortion

Following Stokey and Lucas (1989, section 18.1), a tax is introduced on consumers' income from capital in the one-sector economy of section 4.5. Based on dynamic optimization behavior, an equilibrium is sought for such an economy. This one-sector economy is assumed to have many consumers with identical preferences. The economy's production function is $f(k_t)$, in which $k_t$ denotes per capita capital stock. The economy's capital accumulation function is $k_{t+1} = g(k_t)$, and hence per capita consumption is $f(k_t) - k_{t+1}$ or $f(k_t) - g(k_t)$. Each consumer will solve his or her dynamic optimization problem assuming that all other consumers will follow the capital accumulation rule $k_{t+1} = g(k_t)$. His or her own capital is denoted by $x_t$. His or her wage income is output minus payment to capital in the economy, of $f(k_t) - k_t f'(k_t)$. His or her income from capital is $x_t f'(k_t)$.

To introduce a tax into this economy, assume that income from capital is taxed at a rate $\theta$, with proceeds returned to each consumer as a lump-sum subsidy $\theta k_t f'(k_t)$. A consumer with capital $x_t$ will have after-tax income plus the lump-sum subsidy equal to

$$f(k_t) - k_t f'(k_t) + (1-\theta)x_t f'(k_t) + \theta k_t f'(k_t) = f(k_t) + (1-\theta)(x_t - k_t) f'(k_t)$$

Maximizing the discounted sum of life-time utilities, the consumer's dynamic optimization problem will have the following Lagrangean and associated first-order conditions

$$\mathcal{L} = \sum_t \beta^t \Big\{ u(c_t) - \beta\lambda_{t+1}\big[x_{t+1} - f(k_t) - (1-\theta)(x_t - k_t)f'(k_t) + c_t\big]\Big\} \quad (4.57)$$

$$\beta^t \frac{\partial \mathcal{L}}{\partial c_t} = u'(c_t) - \beta\lambda_{t+1} = 0 \quad (4.58)$$

$$\beta^t \frac{\partial \mathcal{L}}{\partial x_t} = -\lambda_t + \beta(1-\theta)f'(k_t)\lambda_{t+1} = 0 \quad (4.59)$$

Given the economy's per capita capital stock $k_t$, equations (4.58) and (4.59) determine the consumption function $c_t = \mathrm{C}(x_t, k_t)$ and the Lagrangean function $\lambda_t = \lambda(x_t, k_t)$ for the consumer provided that these functions are time-invariant. His or her capital accumulation equation is

$$x_{t+1} = f(k_t) + (1-\theta)(x_t - k_t)f'(k_t) - \mathrm{C}(x_t,\, k_t) \equiv \mathrm{H}(x_t,\, k_t;\, h)$$

Here, I define the consumer's capital accumulation function by H, the last argument $h$ being the economy's capital accumulation function $k_{t+1} = h(k_t)$, without which the dynamic evolution of $k_t$ and hence of $x_t$ cannot be ascertained. Use the functions H and $h$, rather than G and $g$, to denote the capital accumulation functions for the consumer and for the economy, respectively, to distinguish the equilibrium with tax distortion from the one without distortion.

Stokey and Lucas (1989, section 18.1) define an equilibrium by an aggregate capital accumulation function $h$ for the economy and an optimal capital accumulation function for the individual consumer such that $\mathrm{H}(k, k; h) = h(k)$. When each individual consumer holds the economy's per capita capital stock, his or her capital stock $x_{t+1}$ for the next period should be the same as the economy's $k_{t+1}$, and the economy's capital accumulation function $h$ is obtained from aggregating the individual's functions with $x_t = k_t$. Alternatively, one can define an equilibrium by an aggregate consumption function $c$ for the economy and an optimal consumption $\mathrm{C}(x_t, k_t)$ for the individual consumer such that $\mathrm{C}(k_t, k_t) = c(k_t)$. The functions $\mathrm{C}(x_t, k_t)$ and $\lambda(x_t, k_t)$ are obtained by solving equations (4.58) and (4.59) as previously pointed out. $k_t$ is taken as given in the solution. To specify the dynamic evolution of $k_t$ in equilibrium, use

$$k_{t+1} = f(k_t) - c(k_t) = f(k_t) - \mathrm{C}(k_t,\, k_t)$$

To illustrate the dynamic equilibrium of this one-sector tax-distorted economy, assume $u(c) = \ln c$ and $f(k) = k^\alpha$. Given $k$, solve (4.58) and (4.59) for the function $\mathrm{C}(x, k)$ and $\lambda(x, k)$. In this example equations (4.58) and (4.59) become

$$c_t^{-1} - \beta\lambda_{t+1} = 0$$

$$\lambda_t = \beta\alpha k_t^{\alpha-1}(1-\theta)\lambda_{t+1}$$

When $x_t = k_t$, the evolution of $k_t$ based on the constraint of equation (4.57) is given by

$$k_{t+1} = f(k_t) - c_t = k_t^{\alpha} - c_t$$

Recalling the one-sector optimal growth model of section 3.1, observe that the first-order conditions above are algebraically the same as those given by equations (3.7) and (3.8), except with the expectation $E_t$ now omitted and $z_t$ replaced by $(1 - \theta)$. The solution borrowed from equation (3.9) is

$$c_t = (1 - \alpha\beta)(1 - \theta)k_t^{\alpha}$$

$$\lambda_t = (1 - \alpha\beta)^{-1} \alpha k_t^{-1}$$

From the consumption functions, we find the capital accumulation function to be

$$k_{t+1} = k_t^{\alpha} - c_t = (\alpha\beta\theta - \alpha\beta - \theta)k_t^{\alpha}$$

Note that in this tax-distorted economy, the first-order conditions (4.58) and (4.59) do not depend on the state variable $x_t$ for two reasons. First, in the dynamic constraint of (4.57) for $x_{t+1}$, $x_t$ appears linearly on the right-hand side and thus the first-order condition (4.59) obtained by differentiating with respect of $x_t$ is not a function of $x_t$, but only of $k_t$. Second, given the equilibrium condition $x_t = k_t$, the dynamic evolution of $k_t$ is $k_{t+1} = f(k_t) - c_t$. Hence $x_t$ disappears as a state variable when (4.58) and (4.59) are solved. As a simple exercise to generalize this example to the stochastic case with random shock $z_t$ in the production function, see problem 8.

## Problems

1. Given the production technology $f(z) = z^{\alpha}$ and the utility function $u(c) = \ln c$, and given $k_{t+1} = \alpha\beta k_t^{\alpha}$ and $q(k_t) = \alpha^{-\alpha}\beta^{(1-\alpha)}k_t^{\alpha(1-\alpha)}$, use equation (4.40) to find the value function $\psi(k_t, z_t)$ for the firm. Hint: Let $\psi = bk_t^{\alpha} + az_t^{\alpha}$ for parameters $a$ and $b$ yet to be determined.
2. For the same technology and utility as in the preceding problem, and given $z_{t+1} = [\alpha q(k_t)]^{1/(1-\alpha)} = h(k_t, z_t)$, $a_{t+1} = \beta q(k_t)^{-1}a_t$ and $q(k_t)$ given in the preceding problem, prove conditions (4) and (R4) of competitive equilibrium as stated at the end of section 4.5.
3. If the one-good economy of section 4.5 is modified to make a capital good (apple tree) as input physically different from the consumption good (apples), how should the optimization problem for the firm and the analysis of competitive equilibrium be changed to take account of this difference?
4. Solve the central planner's optimization problem of section 4.6 by introducing consumer durables in the model as good $i$, $i = m + 1, \ldots, M$, while goods 1 to $m$ are nondurable consumer goods.
5. Show that the real inputs and outputs of all industries over time for the multisector economy of section 4.6 are the same under the guidance of a

completely knowledgeable central planner as under a decentralized market economy as specified in that section.

6. Add labor inputs $L_{it}$ ($i = 1, \ldots, N$) into the model of section 4.6 in a manner analogous to the treatment in section 3.2 following equations (3.19). Formulate and solve the central planner's problem.

7. Add labor inputs as in problem 6. Provide a market equilibrium solution to this multisector economy.

8. Find the general equilibrium solution of the one-sector economy with tax distortion of section 4.7 by specifying the production function to be $f(k_t, z_t)$, $z_t$ being a random shock on technology. How would equations (4.58) and (4.59) be affected? If $u(c) = \ln c$ and $f(k, z) = zk^{\alpha}$, find the economy-wide consumption function and capital accumulation equation. Compare them with the solution in the deterministic case and comment on the similarities and differences.

# Business Cycles

## 5.1 Keynes and the Classics

The title of this section is borrowed from a well-known article of Hicks (1937), which attempted to give an exposition of Keynes' *General Theory* (1936). Observing the Great Depression in the United States in the early 1930s, Keynes thought that full-employment equilibrium could sometimes fail to be attained by the institutions of a market economy. His influential book has guided research in economic fluctuations since the 1940s. The classical ideas in economics, as taught at the University of Chicago since at least the time of Henry Simon and Frank Knight in the early 1930s, consist of two key words: competitive equilibrium. By competitive, one can mean perfectly competitive or monopolistically (or imperfectly) competitive. In a class on the history of economic thought given in the academic year 1951–1952, Knight said that when Chamberlin (1933) had first appeared, he had thought that the contribution was important, but with more deliberation, he later thought Chamberlin's book on monopolistic competition was merely a footnote to Marshall (1920). When Milton Friedman, a student of Frank Knight, taught price theory in the autumn quarter of 1951, Marshall's *Principles of Economics* was still the main text. Friedman remarked in class, "Marshall is still the best text even though some newer expositions have appeared." There is no question that the word competitive means mainly "perfectly competitive" rather than "monopolistically competitive" to the classical economists in Chicago.

The second difference between the classics and the Keynesians, or between Chicago and Cambridge, Mass., is that the word "equilibrium" is more relevant than "disequilibrium." Keynes' idea of wage rigidity suggests that the market consisting of demand for and supply of labor might not be in equilibrium, with wage frequently adjusting to guarantee full employment. The observation of mass unemployment in the early 1930s in the United States has led Keynes and others following him to believe that perhaps the labor market is not always near its equilibrium point. Furthermore, the rate of interest is determined by liquidity preference in the short-run and cannot serve to equate desired saving with desired investment. The latter is based on entrepreneurs' expectations and need not equal desired saving, which depends mainly on current income as does aggregate consumption according to the Keynesian consumption function. Therefore models based on market equilibrium may not be able to explain short-run fluctuations in employment and output.

Most economists would grant that the discussion of market equilibrium in a dynamic setting as presented in chapter 4 is interesting economics belonging to microeconomic theory, growth theory, and general equilibrium theory. They differ as to the applicability of such models to explain economic fluctuations. Those doing research on real business cycles, the subject of this chapter, believe that it is worthwhile to try to confront such competitive equilibrium dynamic theories with macroeconomic data and to find out how well they succeed in explaining the data, or by how much they fail to explain the data. Such models are discussed in sections 5.2 through 5.6. In section 5.7, an equilibrium model based on monopolistic competition is presented.

## 5.2 Dynamic Properties of a Multisector Model with Technology Shocks

When a multisector optimal growth model with technology shocks was presented in section 3.2, it was pointed out at the end of the section that such models cannot explain observed technological progress except by assuming that the technology shocks have positive trends. Empirical researchers using such models often assume that the multiplicative shock $z_{it}$ to the production function of product $i$ obeys

$$\log z_{it} = \log z_{i,t-1} + \gamma + \varepsilon_{it} \tag{5.1}$$

in which $\varepsilon_{it}$ is assumed to be serially independent and identically distributed. The time series $\log z_{it}$ specified above is said to be a random walk with drift $\gamma$. When the constant term $\gamma$ is zero, it is simply called a random walk. If instead we were to specify that $\log z_{it}$ follows a deterministic trend

$$\log z_{it} = \alpha + \gamma t$$

by taking the difference between $\log z_{it}$ and $\log z_{i,t-1}$, we would find

$$\log z_{it} = \log z_{i,t-1} + \gamma$$

The time series $\log z_{it}$ specified by equation (5.1), or as a random walk with drift, is therefore sometimes said to have a stochastic trend. By specifying a stochastic trend for the logarithm of the multiplicative technology shock $z_{it}$ in the production function for product $i$, one can explain technological progress statistically (though not theoretically without introducing some endogenous growth process as in sections 3.3 through 3.5). The question in this chapter is, how well can such models explain statistically the cyclical properties of economic time series?

To begin to answer this question, examine how the decision or control variables including consumption $c_{it}$, leisure $W_t$, demand $x_{ijt}$ for input $j$ in the production of good $i$, and labor input $L_{it}$ in producing good $i$ behave, given the parameters $\theta_i$ of the utility function, $a_{ij}$ in the production functions, and the derived parameters $\gamma_i$ from the former parameters through equation (3.18). Equation (3.22) states that $c_{it}$ equals $(\theta_i/\gamma_i)Y_{it}$, and equation (3.24) states that $x_{ij,t} = (\beta\gamma_i a_{ji}/\gamma_j)Y_{jt}$, $\beta$ being the discount factor. Thus, consumption of good $i$ is proportional to the output $Y_{it}$ of good $i$, and so is the demand for good $i$ in the production of good $k$. Equations (3.23) and (3.25) state that leisure $W_t$ and labor input $L_{it}$ used in producing good $i$ are both given fractions of total hours H. If random shock $z_{it}$ is introduced in the production of $Y_{it}$, output of each good $i$ is subject to this shock. Consumption $c_{it}$ of each good $i$ and the use of good $i$ as input $x_{ki,t}$ in the production of good $k$ will be affected proportionally, because both are given fractions of $Y_{it}$. Because H is fixed, and leisure $W_t$ and labor input $L_{it}$ are both given fractions of H, they will not be affected by the random shock $z_{it}$. Thus, the Cobb-Douglas utility and production functions impose very restrictive behavior on $c_{it}$, $x_{kit}$, $W_t$, and $L_{it}$ if the only shock is a multiplicative shock $z_{it}$ in the production of output $Y_{it}$.

The above dynamic characteristics of the economic variables generated by this multisector model are examined by Long and Plosser (1983) who emphasize the implied comovements of economic variables:

> If the output of commodity $i$ is unexpectedly high at time $t$ [due to a stochastic shock on the production function], then inputs of commodity $i$ in all of its productive employments will also be unexpectedly high at time $t$. Assuming that the commodity has at least several alternative employments, this not only propagates the output shock forward in time, it also spread the future effects of the shock across sectors of the economy. At the most simplistic level of analysis, this is the primary explanation of persistence and comovement in the consumption, input, and output time series in our example. (p. 49)

Long and Plosser (1983) also examine the dynamic properties of price, wage rates, and interest rates. Prices and wages are studied by using the partial derivatives of the value function with respect to the state variables output $Y_{it}$ and leisure $W_t$. Using the Lagrange method to solve the dynamic optimization problem for the central planner (or equivalently for the market economy), one can obtain prices and wages by the Lagrange multipliers themselves. The rate of interest is found as the ratio of prices of goods in $t$ and $t + 1$, as discussed in section 4.4, 4.5, and 4.6. As the optimal decision functions for the control variables $c_{it}$, $x_{kit}$, and $L_{it}$ are linear in the logarithms of the state variables $Y_{it}$ and $z_{it}$, with a Cobb-Douglas production function explaining the output $Y_{i,t+1}$ by the inputs at time $t$, Long and Plosser could write down a system of first-order linear stochastic difference equations in the logarithms of the variables and study their cyclical properties.

Real business cycle models based mainly on the multisector model of section 3.2 rely on technology shocks in the production function and the substitution of work and leisure over time to explain economic fluctuations. Modern

Keynesians question the ability of these two basic mechanisms to do so satisfactorily (see the discussions of Plosser (1989) and Mankiw (1989), the former representing an RBC viewpoint, and the latter a new Keynesian viewpoint). As pointed out in section 5.1, Keynes did not, and the modern Keynesians do not, believe that an equilibrium theory with full employment of resources always prevailing can explain observed economic fluctuations. For example, Mankiw (1989, p. 85) questions whether most recessions can be associated with some exogenous deterioration in the economy's productive capabilities. Although the model of section 3.2 may be able to explain the simultaneous comovements of macroeconomic variables to some extent, it might be inadequate in explaining the lead-lag relationships among economic variables. On the other hand, such lead-lag relations appear to be well captured, through spectral analysis, by a simple linear multiplier-accelerator liquidity-preference model consisting of an aggregate consumption function, two aggregate investment functions based on the investment accelerator, and a liquidity-preference relation. See Chow and Levitan (1969), Chow (1975, chapter 5), and Chow (1993b). The key question is whether the dynamic characteristics of the major macroeconomic variables through business cycles can be adequately explained by models of optimizing agents in equilibrium. Research is still being carried out to answer this question. No consensus of opinion has been reached by the economics profession. The remainder of this chapter summarizes the results of some recent studies, with the purpose of throwing some light on this question.

## 5.3 Estimating Economic Effects of Political Events in China

Dynamic optimization models are useful not only for studying economic fluctuations in developed economies, but also for studying economic changes in developing countries. To illustrate, I provide a one-sector model to study economic changes in China and to measure the economic effects of political movements, including the Great Leap Forward and the Cultural Revolution. This section serves as an introduction to sections 5.4 and 5.5. It draws from Kwan and Chow (1996).

The Chinese economy is modeled as if there were central planners who maximize, at any initial year zero,

$$\sum_{t=0}^{\infty} \mathrm{E}_t \beta^t \ln c_t \tag{5.2}$$

in which $c_t$ stands for per capita consumption, subject to the constraint on the evolution of per capita capital stock $k_t$

$$k_{t+1} = k_t + \mathrm{A}_t k_t^{(1-\alpha)} - c_t \tag{5.3}$$

in which net output per capita $\mathrm{A}_t k_t^{(1-\alpha)}$ is produced by a Cobb-Douglas production function, and net investment per capita equals net output minus consumption. Let $z_t = \mathrm{A}_t^{1/\alpha}$ and

$$\ln z_{t+1} = \ln z_t + \mu + \varepsilon_{t+1} \tag{5.4}$$

Per capita consumption or investment is determined by the social planners solving the dynamic optimization problem. One might object that this model is too simple, but it is useful in providing a crude answer to the question: If the Great Leap had not occurred, what would per capita output in 1992 be as compared with actual output? (By the way, the answer is, Twice as large.)

To arrive at this answer, estimate the optimization model by using annual Chinese data from 1952 to 1993. The model consists of the random walk equation for $\ln z$ and an equation for $\ln k_{t+1}$ derived from solving the dynamic optimization problem. Because the variables are nonstationary, first detrend by dividing by $z_t$, yielding $\bar{k}_{t+1} = k_{t+1}/z_t$, $\bar{z}_t = z_t/z_{t-1}$ and $\bar{c}_t = c_t/z_t$. The model in terms of the detrended variables consists of

$$\ln \bar{z}_t = \mu + \varepsilon_t \tag{5.5}$$

$$\ln \bar{k}_{t+1} = g + G_1 \ln \bar{z}_t + G_2 \ln \bar{k}_t + e_t \tag{5.6}$$

with $\ln \bar{k}_{t+1}$ as the control variable, and $\ln \bar{z}_t$ and $\ln \bar{k}_t$ as two state variables. The coefficients ($g$, $G_1$, $G_2$) are derived from optimization, given the structural parameters $\alpha$, $\beta$, and $\gamma = \alpha\mu$. The residual $e_t$ is added to the optimal control equation for $\ln \bar{k}_{t+1}$ to account for the fact that the simple model cannot explain the actual data on $\ln \bar{k}_{t+1}$ completely. Given the structural parameters, and time-series data on per capita output $q_t$ and per capita capital stock $k_t$, we can construct $z_t$ by solving $q_t = z_t^{\alpha} k_t^{(1-\alpha)}$ and derive the coefficients ($g$, $G_1$, $G_2$) and hence the residuals $\varepsilon_t$ and $e_t$ in the above statistical model. Assuming ($\varepsilon_t$, $e_t$) to be jointly normal, we can evaluate the likelihood function and maximize it with respect to the parameters $\alpha$, $\beta$, $\gamma$ and $\mu$.

The results are, with standard errors in parentheses,

$$\left(\hat{\alpha}, \hat{\beta}, \hat{\gamma}\right) = \left[0.7495\,(0.0108),\ 0.9999\,(0.0001),\ 0.0218\,(0.0025)\right]$$

The labor exponent 0.7495 in the Cobb-Douglas production function is reasonable. The large $\hat{\beta} = 0.9999$ shows that the Chinese planners place great weight on future consumption as compared with current consumption, thus devoting a large fraction of output to investment, which is in the neighborhood of 0.35 for most years from 1952 to 1993. The annual labor augmented technological progress of 2 percent is reasonable if I include the years 1979–1993 after the economic reform. In Chow (1993c), a Cobb-Douglas production function with constant total factor productivity was shown to fit China data from 1952 to 1980, excluding certain abnormal years, but total factor productivity increased substantially after 1980. The current production function incorporates a random total factor productivity and fits the data well enough for the entire sample from 1952 to 1993 to be included in estimating the parameters.

Figure 5.1 shows the estimated residual $\hat{\varepsilon}_t$ in the log productivity equation. The impacts of the Great Leap and the Cultural Revolution on this residual is obvious. To estimate the economic effects of the Great Leap, smooth out the residuals $\hat{\varepsilon}_t$ and $\hat{e}_t$ in the Great Leap period and simulate the model using the

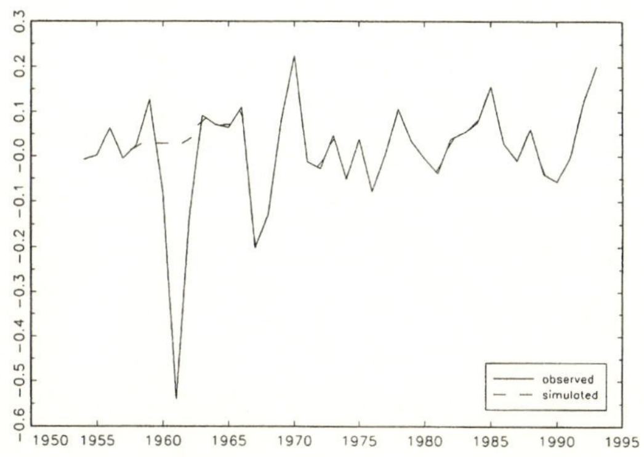


FIGURE. 5.1 Observed and simulated residual ε

smoothed residuals. The result is a factor of 2.0 in per capita output in 1992 using the residuals free of the effects of the Great Leap, and a factor of 1.2 using the residuals free of the effects of the Cultural Revolution. The latter estimate appears reasonable, because this estimate is concerned only with measured physical output and not with emotional sufferings.

## 5.4 Estimating and Testing a Base-line Real Business Cycle Model

Returning to the study of economic fluctuations in the United States, I present in this section a base-line real business cycle model discussed in King, Plosser, and Rebelo (1988a,b). The model is slightly more complicated than the one presented in section 5.3, having another control variable, the number of working hours per capita $u_{2t}$, in addition to investment $u_{1t}$. The representative economic agent is assumed to maximize

$$E\sum_{t=0}^{\infty} E_t\beta^t\left[\ln c_t + \theta\ln\left(1-u_{2t}\right)\right] \tag{5.7}$$

subject to the constraint on the evolution of capital stock $s_{2t}$,

$$s_{2,t+1} = \left(1-\delta\right)s_{2,t} + u_{1t} \tag{5.8}$$

Given a Cobb-Douglas production function for per capita output, per capita consumption is

$$c_t = s_{2t}^{1-\alpha}\left(z_t u_{2t}\right)^{\alpha} - u_{1t} \tag{5.9}$$

in which the first state variable $s_{1t} = \ln z_t$ follows a random walk with drift $\gamma$.

$$s_{1,t+1} = \gamma + s_{1,t} + \varepsilon_{t+1} \tag{5.10}$$

Maximizing the objective function subject to the constraint on $s_{2,t+1}$ with respect to investment $u_{1t}$ and hours $u_{2t}$ gives two linear optimal control equations to which we add residuals $e_{1t}$ and $e_{2t}$ respectively, as was done in section 5.3 for the control variable $\ln k_{t+1}$. These two equations can be combined with the random walk equation for $s_{1,t+1}$ to form a system of three simultaneous equations to be estimated by the method of maximum likelihood. The material in this section is taken from Chow and Kwan (1997).

Before estimation, it is desirable to detrend the state variables and the first control variable investment to make the dynamic model stationary. While the old state variables are $s_1 = \ln z$ and $s_2$ = capital stock $k$, the new state variables are $s_1 = \ln(z/z_{-1}) \equiv \ln \bar{z}$ and $s_2 = \ln(k/z_{-1}) = \ln \bar{k}$. The new control variables are $u_1 = \ln(\text{investment}/z) = \ln \bar{i}$ and $u_2$ = per capita hours worked, the same as before. Approximate the first-order conditions in the new variables $s_1, s_2, u_1, u_2$, and $\lambda_2$ (multiplier for the evolution of $\bar{k}_t$) by linear functions. The techniques for detrending and expressing the first-order conditions as linear functions of log detrended variables are found in sections 9.2–9.4.

I use CITIBASE quarterly data for the US from 1947.1 to 1993.4 in estimation; all monetary figures are in constant 1987 dollars. Consumption is defined as expenditures on nondurables plus services (CITIBASE variables GCNQ + GCSQ). Investment is nonresidential private investment plus expenditures on consumer durables (CITIBASE variables GINQ + GCDQ). Output is the sum of consumption and investment by definition. Capital stock is the sum of nonresidential private capital and durable goods owned by consumers as reported in the *Survey of Current Business* (August 1994, p. 62), loglinearly interpolated to quarterly frequency from the annual series. Labor input is defined as the ratio of total man-hours employed per week (CITIBASE variable LHOURS) to a weekly endowment of 112 hours, converted to quarterly frequency by three-month averaging the monthly series. These figures are divided by population, which is the number of persons over 16 years old (also loglinearly interpolated from annual to quarterly frequency). I report the results from estimating the system (5.11) of three simultaneous equations consisting of equation (5.10) and two optimal control functions for $u_{1t}$ and $u_{2t}$ (the state variable $s_{2t}$ being treated as exogenous) by the method of maximum likelihood, assuming that the residuals are trivariate normal.

The parameters to be estimated are $\alpha$, $\beta$, $\gamma$, $\delta$, and $\theta$, representing, respectively, the labor exponent of the Cobb-Douglas production function, the discount factor of the utility function, the drift in the random walk model for log productivity, the rate of depreciation of the capital accumulation equation, and the weight of log leisure relative to log consumption in the utility function, besides the covariance matrix of the residuals. Given the parameter values, dynamic optimization is used to derive the coefficients ($g$ G) of the two behavioral equations for investment (log detrended) and labor hours. These two equations are combined with the random walk equation for $\ln z$ to form three simultaneous equations, which are the log detrended version of equation (5.8). The log likelihood function for these simultaneous equations is maximized with respect to the parameters to form the estimates.

Using a standard simultaneous-equations notation, rewrite the log detrended version of (5.10) together with two optimal control equations for $u_1 = \ln \bar{i}$ and $u_2$ = per capita hours.

$$\mathrm{B}y_t + \Gamma x_t = e_t, \tag{5.11}$$

in which $y_t = (s_{1t}, u_{1t}, u_{2t})$, and $x_t$ is a column vector consisting of $s_{2t}$ and 1, and

$$\mathrm{B} = \begin{bmatrix} 1 & 0 & 0 \\ -g_{11} & 1 & 0 \\ -g_{21} & 0 & 1 \end{bmatrix}, \quad \Gamma = \begin{bmatrix} 0 & -\gamma \\ -g_{12} & -g_1 \\ -g_{22} & -g_2 \end{bmatrix}, \quad e_t = \begin{bmatrix} \varepsilon_t \\ e_{1t} \\ e_{2t} \end{bmatrix} \tag{5.12}$$

$n$ observations of (5.11) can be written as

$$\mathrm{BY}' + \Gamma \mathrm{X}' = \mathrm{E}'$$

in which Y′ is $3 \times n$, X′ is $2 \times n$ and E′ is $3 \times n$.

Notice that $y_t$ involves $\ln z_t$, which is constructed from the data ($\ln q_t$, $\ln k_t$, $\ln n_t$) through the production function, conditional on parameter $\alpha$. Because $\alpha$ is an unknown parameter to be estimated, I have to allow for the Jacobian in writing down the likelihood function. It is not hard to check that the Jacobian of the transformation from $y_t$ to ($\ln q_t$, $\ln k_t$, $\ln n_t$) is $1/\alpha$. Assuming normal and serially uncorrelated $e_t$ with covariance matrix $\Sigma$, the concentrated log-likelihood function (see Chow, 1983, pp. 170–171) is

$$\operatorname{Log} \mathrm{L} = \text{const} + n \log |\mathrm{B}| - \frac{n}{2} \log \left| \hat{\Sigma} \right| - n \ln \alpha \tag{5.13}$$

in which

$$\hat{\Sigma} = n^{-1} (\mathrm{BY}' + \Gamma \mathrm{X}')(\mathrm{YB}' + \mathrm{X}\Gamma') \tag{5.14}$$

To obtain maximum likelihood estimates of the five structural parameters by iterations, each iteration takes three steps: (a) given initial values of the parameters, compute G and $g$ by a dynamic optimization algorithm (chapter 2): (b) evaluate log L using (5.13) and the results of step (a); and (c) apply a maximization algorithm to revise the initial values of the parameters.

I will first present the estimates of the five structural parameters of the dynamic optimization model and the associated test for the specification of the model. I will then report (1) the restricted reduced form where the coefficients ($g$, G) are derived from the deep structural parameters of the dynamic optimization model; (2) the unrestricted reduced form in which the coefficients in ($g$, G) are estimated freely without derivation from dynamic optimization; (3) unrestricted reduced form with one lagged dependent variable in each equation; and (4) unrestricted reduced form with other lagged variables. A main purpose of introducing lagged dependent variables is to show how poorly the baseline RBC model formulated by dynamic optimization fits the data. The defects of the model revealed by standard estimation and testing methods are not revealed by the method of calibration.

Because the determinant of the B matrix is one, maximum likelihood estimation of the reduced form can be efficiently performed by iterative, seemingly unrelated regressions (ISUR) together with a line-search algorithm, rather than searching all parameters simultaneously by using a standard hill-climbing algorithm. Conditional on $\alpha$, the log likelihood in (5.13) can be obtained by ISUR. Then, the optimal $\alpha$ is found by a line-search algorithm in the interval between zero and one.

Maximum likelihood estimates of the five structural parameters of the model are given below with standard errors in parentheses:

$$\underset{(0.0017)}{\alpha = 0.7791} \qquad \underset{(0.00001)}{\beta = 0.9999} \qquad \underset{(0.0006)}{\gamma = 0.0041} \qquad \underset{(0.0600)}{\delta = 0.3950} \qquad \underset{(1.060)}{\theta = 3.1384}$$

The covariance matrix of the estimated parameters is computed by inverting the Hessian. The estimated values of the five parameters are all reasonable except for the quarterly rate of depreciation of the private nonresidential stock, which is too high. A high $\delta$ means that the capital accumulation equation (5.8) in the model does not fit the data. The reason for the poor fit is that, although in theory, capital of the next period equals depreciated capital stock from the current period plus gross investment, such a concept of gross investment does not correspond to gross investment data; recorded gross investment contributes not only to the capital stock of the next quarter, but also to capital stocks of several more quarters that follow. Regressing capital of the next period on current capital stock and recorded gross investment yields a coefficient of less than unity for the investment variable and a coefficient exceeding (1–0.39) for current capital stock. Forcing the coefficient of recorded investment to be unity by equation (5.8) reduces the coefficient of current capital stock or increases the estimate of the depreciation rate. In any case, using a standard econometric method to estimate the depreciation rate of the model reveals a weakness of the capital accumulation equation not noticed by calibration.

Table 5.1 presents estimates of the parameters of several versions of equation (5.11). The first two columns are restricted reduced form, referring to the fact that the parameters ($g$, G) in (5.11) are derived from the structural optimization model with the five structural parameters either (a) specified *a priori* as in model calibration, or (b) estimated by the method of maximum likelihood reported above. In other words, the five structural parameters imply through optimization the restricted reduced form parameters given in columns (a) and (b) in Table 5.1. The calibrated parameters are chosen to be $(\alpha, \beta, \gamma, \delta, \theta) = (0.58, 0.988, 0.004, 0.025, 3.2431)$, a set of values standard in the calibration literature as in Plosser (1989) and Watson (1993), among numerous others. Columns (c)–(e) are unrestricted reduced form, which refers to the estimation of (5.11) as a system of three simultaneous equations without regard to the derivation from the structural optimization model.

Comparing the two restricted reduced forms, calibration gives a log likelihood of 1373.52, and estimation gives 1980.94. The likelihood ratio statistic registers a value of –2 times (1373.52–1980.94), implying a critical value far exceeding any reasonable level of significance for a Chi-square distribution

TABLE 5.1 Restricted versus unrestricted reduced form (Standard errors in parentheses.)

| | Restricted reduced form | | Unrestricted reduced form | | |
|---|---|---|---|---|---|
| | (a) | (b) | (c) | (d) | (e) |
| **eq 1:** $\ln \bar{z}_t$ | | | | | |
| **constant** | 0.004 | 0.0041 | 0.0037 | 0.0045 | 0.0039 |
| | | (0.0006) | (0.0009) | (0.0006) | (0.0008) |
| **DW** | 2.082 | 2.24 | 2.15 | 2.288 | 2.211 |
| **eq 2:** $\ln \bar{i}_t$ | | | | | |
| **constant** | –1.9767 | –2.7839 | –2.0131 | –0.0178 | –0.0210 |
| | | | (0.0331) | (0.0412) | (0.0635) |
| $\ln \bar{z}_t$ | –0.3502 | –0.1441 | –1.0896 | 0.2536 | 0.4992 |
| | | | (0.3813) | (0.2047) | (0.1394) |
| $\ln \bar{k}_t$ | 0.3502 | 0.1441 | 0.8646 | 0.0106 | 5.5688 |
| | | | (0.0350) | (0.0244) | (1.5933) |
| $\ln \bar{i}_{t-1}$ | | | | 0.9900 | 1.1061 |
| | | | | (0.0167) | (0.0564) |
| $\ln \bar{i}_{t-2}$ | | | | | –0.1255 |
| | | | | | (0.0603) |
| $\ln \bar{z}_{t-1}$ | | | | | 5.7122 |
| | | | | | (1.5791) |
| $\ln \bar{z}_{t-2}$ | | | | | –4.6467 |
| | | | | | (1.5788) |
| $\ln \bar{k}_{t-1}$ | | | | | –10.5911 |
| | | | | | (2.9691) |
| $\ln \bar{k}_{t-2}$ | | | | | 5.0627 |
| | | | | | (1.5415) |
| **DW** | 0.05 | 0.052 | 0.206 | 1.438 | 2.007 |
| **eq 3:** $\ln n_t$ | | | | | |
| **constant** | –0.8750 | –1.7639 | –1.4842 | –0.0233 | –0.0235 |
| | | | (0.0162) | (0.0163) | (0.0222) |
| $\ln \bar{z}_t$ | 0.3001 | 0.1576 | –0.4276 | –0.4927 | –0.2266 |
| | | | (0.1869) | (0.0631) | (0.0530) |
| $\ln \bar{k}_t$ | –0.3001 | –0.1576 | 0.1203 | –0.0028 | 1.8632 |
| | | | (0.0172) | (0.0065) | (0.5971) |
| $\ln n_{t-1}$ | | | | 0.9859 | 1.0760 |
| | | | | (0.0108) | (0.0572) |
| $\ln n_{t-2}$ | | | | | –0.0953 |
| | | | | | (0.0561) |
| $\ln \bar{z}_{t-1}$ | | | | | 2.0053 |
| | | | | | (0.5874) |
| $\ln \bar{z}_{t-2}$ | | | | | –1.7581 |
| | | | | | (0.6040) |
| $\ln \bar{k}_{t-1}$ | | | | | –3.7773 |
| | | | | | (1.1504) |
| $\ln \bar{k}_{t-2}$ | | | | | 1.9211 |
| | | | | | (0.5912) |
| **DW** | 0.023 | 0.042 | 0.097 | 1.281 | 1.832 |
| $\alpha$ | 0.58 | 0.7791 | 0.6520 | 0.9698 | 0.7285 |
| **log likelihood** | 1373.52 | 1980.94 | 2078.64 | 2581.57 | 2602.58 |

with five degrees of freedom. The calibrated parameters are therefore seriously discordant with the data, even assuming that the structural model is correct. To assess the structural model, compare columns (b) and (c). It can be seen that the log likelihood of the structural model is 1980.94, and that of the unrestricted model is 2078.64. Twice the log likelihood ratio has a Chi-square distribution with two degrees of freedom under the null hypothesis that the specification of the optimization model is correct. Recall that the five structural parameters generate seven parameters $\gamma$ and ($g$ G) in equation (5.11). Hence, there are two restrictions imposed on the seven parameters by the structural model. The chi-square statistic is –2 times (1980.94–2078.64), so much larger than the critical value under any reasonable level of significance. Thus, the model is strongly rejected.

A person accepting the dynamic optimization rational expectation paradigm may defend the continued work on RBC models in the face of strong rejection by specification tests by saying that the model captures only a part of reality and that without a complete specification of the remaining part through the error term one cannot apply standard specification tests to test the model. Even before the tests one already knows that the model is misspecified in the sense of omitting important elements in the real world. This defense is not necessarily valid, because large variances of the error terms are consistent with a correct specification of the elements of reality included in the model. Of course, failure to model explicitly certain important elements of reality might lead to the rejection of a model for reasons other than the one stated above. I will not pursue this discussion further, because the main point of this section is to show how much more one can learn from standard econometric methods of estimation and testing than from calibration alone.

Continuing to apply standard econometric methodology, observe a very small Durbin-Watson (DW) statistic of 0.053 for the investment equation and of 0.042 for the labor supply equation. The DW statistic is used here as a descriptive static to show the high first-order serial correlation of the residuals, and hence that the two included explanatory variables in the investment and labor supply equations fail to explain the dynamics of these dependent variables. This point is missed in the practice of calibration. To show how much dynamics is missing in the model, I present the unrestricted reduced form in column (c) of Table 5.1. The DW statistics for the two equations increase to 0.206 and 0.097 respectively, suggesting that one can explain the dynamics of the data better by abandoning the restrictions imposed by the structural model. The next column (d) of Table 5.1 tells a more dramatic and revealing story. By adding the lagged dependent variable in each of the investment and labor supply equations, one finds that, in the investment equation, both current state variables become very insignificant, and, in the labor supply equation, only the log technology variable remains significant. This model with lagged dependent variables shows very clearly how much dynamics is missed by the baseline RBC model. The last column (e) of Table 5.1 reports unrestricted reduced form with other lagged variables. The DW statistic in each equation suggests that most of the positive serial correlation has been elimi-

TABLE 5.2 Calibrated structural model

| *Variables in log* | *Mean* | *Standard deviation* | Autocorrelation ρ(1) | ρ(2) | ρ(3) | *Correlation with output* | *Correlation with actual* |
|---|---|---|---|---|---|---|---|
| Panel A: Actual | | | | | | | |
| *output* | −1.2877 | 0.0744 | 0.9806 | 0.9646 | 0.9469 | 1.0000 | 1.0000 |
| *consumption* | −1.5540 | 0.0573 | 0.9718 | 0.9508 | 0.9258 | 0.9659 | 1.0000 |
| *investment* | −2.7451 | 0.1452 | 0.9753 | 0.9483 | 0.9210 | 0.9380 | 1.0000 |
| *hours* | −1.5986 | 0.0355 | 0.9523 | 0.8947 | 0.8297 | 0.6585 | 1.0000 |
| Panel B: Predicted | | | | | | | |
| *output* | −0.7152 | 0.0372 | 0.8757 | 0.8655 | 0.8307 | 1.0000 | 0.8917 |
| *consumption* | −0.9507 | 0.0345 | 0.7672 | 0.7729 | 0.7277 | 0.9892 | 0.7988 |
| *investment* | −2.2773 | 0.0524 | 0.9796 | 0.9602 | 0.9391 | 0.9319 | 0.9009 |
| *hours* | −0.6175 | 0.0449 | 0.9796 | 0.9602 | 0.9391 | −0.9319 | −0.4526 |

nated. The estimate 0.7285 for the labor exponent in the Cobb-Douglas production is now more reasonable than the estimate 0.9698 given in the previous model before lagged capital stock and lagged productivity are introduced.

Tables 5.2–5.6 compare model prediction with actual data in terms of the mean and standard deviation for each of the five cases in Table 5.1. The moments are computed for detrended output, consumption, investment, and hours worked (all in logarithm). Notice that the actual series are different for each case, because the detrending involves the log productivity series $\ln z$, which in turn depends on $\alpha$.

Comparing the first-, second-, and third-order autocorrelations of the actual and predicted series in Tables 5.2 and 5.3, the calibrated model appears to look better than the estimated structural model. However, in terms of the mean, the predicted series are much closer to the actual for the estimated model than for the calibrated model, thus producing a higher likelihood value. The predicted

TABLE 5.3 Estimated structural model

| *Variables in log* | *Mean* | *Standard deviation* | Autocorrelation ρ(1) | ρ(2) | ρ(3) | *Correlation with output* | *Correlation with actual* |
|---|---|---|---|---|---|---|---|
| Panel A: Actual | | | | | | | |
| *output* | −1.4769 | 0.0463 | 0.9729 | 0.9470 | 0.9178 | 1.0000 | 1.0000 |
| *consumption* | −1.7432 | 0.0320 | 0.9570 | 0.9280 | 0.8975 | 0.8720 | 1.0000 |
| *investment* | −2.9342 | 0.1183 | 0.9662 | 0.9261 | 0.8837 | 0.8943 | 1.0000 |
| *hours* | −1.5986 | 0.0355 | 0.9523 | 0.8947 | 0.8297 | 0.8807 | 1.0000 |
| Panel B: Predicted | | | | | | | |
| *output* | −1.4729 | 0.0139 | 0.4004 | 0.4691 | 0.4097 | 1.0000 | 0.5305 |
| *consumption* | −1.7366 | 0.0152 | 0.1301 | 0.2471 | 0.1743 | 0.9686 | 0.2358 |
| *investment* | −2.9349 | 0.0167 | 0.9804 | 0.9628 | 0.9436 | 0.6629 | 0.8425 |
| *hours* | −1.5987 | 0.0182 | 0.9804 | 0.9628 | 0.9436 | −0.6629 | −0.5138 |

TABLE 5.4 Unrestricted reduced form

| Variables in log | Mean | Standard deviation | Autocorrelation ρ(1) | ρ(2) | ρ(3) | Correlation with output | Correlation with actual |
|---|---|---|---|---|---|---|---|
| Panel A: Actual | | | | | | | |
| *output* | −1.3694 | 0.0614 | 0.9792 | 0.9619 | 0.9425 | 1.0000 | 1.0000 |
| *consumption* | −1.6358 | 0.0448 | 0.9682 | 0.9468 | 0.9216 | 0.9440 | 1.0000 |
| *investment* | −2.8268 | 0.1331 | 0.9722 | 0.9408 | 0.9084 | 0.9263 | 1.0000 |
| *hours* | −1.5986 | 0.0355 | 0.9523 | 0.8947 | 0.8297 | 0.7402 | 1.0000 |
| Panel B: Predicted | | | | | | | |
| *output* | −1.3657 | 0.0566 | 0.9652 | 0.9446 | 0.9211 | 1.0000 | 0.9229 |
| *consumption* | −1.6304 | 0.0392 | 0.8860 | 0.8733 | 0.8436 | 0.9843 | 0.8102 |
| *investment* | −2.8269 | 0.1171 | 0.9771 | 0.9595 | 0.9393 | 0.9811 | 0.8800 |
| *hours* | −1.5986 | 0.0173 | 0.9099 | 0.9093 | 0.8859 | 0.9257 | 0.4869 |

TABLE 5.5 Unrestricted reduced form with lagged dependent variables

| Variables in log | Mean | Standard deviation | Autocorrelation ρ(1) | ρ(2) | ρ(3) | Correlation with output | Correlation with actual |
|---|---|---|---|---|---|---|---|
| Panel A: Actual | | | | | | | |
| *output* | −1.5852 | 0.0362 | 0.9552 | 0.9022 | 0.8424 | 1.0000 | 1.0000 |
| *consumption* | −1.8515 | 0.0289 | 0.9462 | 0.8983 | 0.8531 | 0.7453 | 1.0000 |
| *investment* | −3.0426 | 0.1051 | 0.9570 | 0.9037 | 0.8458 | 0.7914 | 1.0000 |
| *hours* | −1.5986 | 0.0355 | 0.9523 | 0.8947 | 0.8297 | 0.9978 | 1.0000 |
| Panel B: Predicted | | | | | | | |
| *output* | −1.5807 | 0.0352 | 0.9238 | 0.8725 | 0.8151 | 1.0000 | 0.9441 |
| *consumption* | −1.8456 | 0.0299 | 0.8705 | 0.8445 | 0.8015 | 0.7387 | 0.9034 |
| *investment* | −3.0426 | 0.1029 | 0.9613 | 0.9064 | 0.8506 | 0.7557 | 0.9708 |
| *hours* | −1.5986 | 0.0352 | 0.9568 | 0.8977 | 0.8287 | 0.9667 | 0.9755 |

TABLE 5.6 Unrestricted reduced form with other lagged variables

| Variables in log | Mean | Standard deviation | Autocorrelation ρ(1) | ρ(2) | ρ(3) | Correlation with output | Correlation with actual |
|---|---|---|---|---|---|---|---|
| Panel A: Actual | | | | | | | |
| *output* | −1.4386 | 0.0513 | 0.9761 | 0.9547 | 0.9306 | 1.0000 | 1.0000 |
| *consumption* | −1.7049 | 0.0358 | 0.9621 | 0.9373 | 0.9099 | 0.9064 | 1.0000 |
| *investment* | −2.8960 | 0.1234 | 0.9686 | 0.9321 | 0.8938 | 0.9096 | 1.0000 |
| *hours* | −1.5986 | 0.0355 | 0.9523 | 0.8947 | 0.8297 | 0.8273 | 1.0000 |
| Panel B: Predicted | | | | | | | |
| *output* | −1.4346 | 0.0499 | 0.9486 | 0.9306 | 0.9007 | 1.0000 | 0.9698 |
| *consumption* | −1.6997 | 0.0354 | 0.8813 | 0.8662 | 0.8304 | 0.8917 | 0.9091 |
| *investment* | −2.8960 | 0.1220 | 0.9653 | 0.9256 | 0.8879 | 0.8953 | 0.9867 |
| *hours* | −1.5986 | 0.0350 | 0.9509 | 0.8887 | 0.8241 | 0.8058 | 0.9760 |

autocorrelations from the unrestricted reduced form, the unrestricted reduced form with lagged dependent variables, and the latter with other lagged variables continue to improve. Note that the negative correlation between hours and output (due to a positive correlation between leisure and output) in both the calibrated and the estimated structural models are very different from the actual positive correlation, showing convincingly a weakness of the baseline RBC model, as is well recognized. Examining the unrestricted reduced form as is done in standard econometric practice reveals the weakness of the RBC model, calibrated or estimated, when one compares the autocorrelations and correlations with output of the predicted and the actual. The correlations of hours with output are positive for the predicted data of the unrestricted reduced forms in Tables 5.4–5.6.

Comparing the actual growth rates of output and hours worked with the predicted values from the model concerned as is done in Plosser (1989) (charts not shown), the calibrated model does quite well for output growth, but misses some fluctuations in growth rates of hours worked, as is well known. The estimated version does about as well for output growth, but misses more fluctuations in the growth rates of hours worked. This shows that by concentrating on fitting particular characteristics of the data, a calibrated model could do better in fitting those characteristics than estimation. However, for fitting all important characteristics, one would do better by relying on standard econometric methodology that can reveal the weaknesses of a calibrated model and indicate what the better fitting models are. Charting the growth rates shows that the unrestricted reduced form improves on the restricted one by providing more fluctuations in the growth rate of hours worked, although it still does not fit as well as the calibrated model. By introducing lagged dependent variables into the unrestricted reduced form, one dramatically improves the fit for the growth rate of both output and hours worked. Furthermore, introducing other lagged variables improves the fit significantly as standard statistics provided in column (e) in Table 5.1 show. In this section it has been clearly demonstrated that standard econometric methods are much more powerful and revealing than calibration alone.

## 5.5 Real Business Cycles and Labor Market Fluctuations

A major objective of the study of Christiano and Eichenbaum (1992) reported in this section is to explain the correlation between labor hours and labor productivity (or real wage) through business cycles. According to a real business cycle (RBC) model driven by a productivity shock in the production function as discussed in the last section, a large shock raises both output $y_t$ and marginal product $(1 - \theta)y_t/n_t$ of labor hours $n_t$ employed, $(1 - \theta)$ being the exponent of labor input in a Cobb-Douglas production function. It shifts the demand curve for labor upward and leads to an increase in both hours and real wage. The model thus implies a positive correlation between labor hours and the marginal product of labor. On the other hand, according to Keynesian theory with a fixed demand curve for labor, the correlation between labor hours employed and real wage or marginal product of labor ought to be negative. The empirical correlation for the United States is near zero. To remedy this deficiency of RBC theory, consumption is divided into private consumption $c_t^p$, and government consumption $g_t$ and a stochastic shock is introduced into the evolution of $g_t$ to provide a second shock to the model. The second shock helps to lower the correlation between labor hours and marginal productivity of labor (or average productivity that is proportional to marginal productivity given a Cobb-Douglas production function).

Again appealing to the market equilibrium solution being the same as the social planner's solution, one can derive optimum decision functions for $c_t^p$ and $n_t$ by maximizing

$$E_0 \sum_{t=0}^{\infty} \beta^t \left\{ \ln\left(c_t^p + \alpha g_t\right) + \gamma V\left(N - n_t\right) \right\}, \tag{5.15}$$

in which the parameter $\alpha$ provides a weight for government consumption $g_t$ relative to private consumption $c_t^p$, N is the total number of hours available, and the function V can take two forms: (a) $\ln(N - n_t)$ and (b) $N - n_t$.

The constraints of this model include a Cobb-Douglas production function for per capita output $y_t$ subject to a stochastic shock $z_t$

$$y_t = k_t^{\theta}\left(z_t n_t\right)^{1-\theta} \tag{5.16}$$

$$z_t = z_{t-1} \exp\left(\varepsilon_t\right), \tag{5.17}$$

$\varepsilon_t$ being i.i.d. with mean $\varepsilon$ and standard deviation $\sigma_\varepsilon$. The evolution of per capita capital stock $k_t$ follows

$$k_{t+1} = \left(1 - \delta\right)k_t + y_t - c_t^p - g_t. \tag{5.18}$$

An equation for the evolution of $g_t$ is also exogenously given. One can treat $k_t$, $z_t$, and $g_t$ as state variables and $c_t$ and $n_t$ as control variables. Because the evolutions of $z_t$ and $g_t$ are not affected by the control variables, only one Lagrange multiplier $\lambda_t$ is needed to formulate the dynamic optimization problem using the Lagrangean

$$\begin{aligned} \mathcal{L} = \sum_{t=0}^{\infty} E_t \beta^t \Big\{ & \ln\left(c_t^p + \alpha g_t\right) + \gamma V\left(N - n_t\right) \\ & - \beta \lambda_{t+1}\left[k_{t+1} - \left(1-\delta\right)k_t - k_t^{\theta}\left(z_t n_t\right)^{1-\theta} + c_t^p + g_t\right]\Big\} \end{aligned} \tag{5.19}$$

First-order conditions can be obtained by differentiating $\mathcal{L}$ with respect to $c_t^p$, $n_t$, and $k_t$.

Christiano and Eichenbaum (1992) solve a dynamic optimization problem different from (5.19) in three respects. First, they use the constraint (5.18) to replace $c_t^p$ in the utility function and treat $k_{t+1}$ as a control variable instead of $c_t^p$. Second, they define new variables by dividing the variables $k_{t+1}$, $y_t$, $c_t$, and $g_t$ in the model by the stochastic trend $z_t$ to make the model stationary in the detrended variables. The detrended variables are

$$\bar{k}_{t+1} = k_{t+1}/z_t; \quad \bar{y}_t = y_t/z_t; \quad \bar{c}_t = c_t/z_t; \quad \bar{g}_t = g_t/z_t; \quad \bar{z}_t = z_t/z_{t-1} \qquad (5.20)$$

They specify the evolution of the detrended $\bar{g}_t$ by

$$\ln(\bar{g}_t) = (1-\rho)\ln(\bar{g}) + \rho\ln(\bar{g}_{t-1}) + \mu_t \qquad (5.21)$$

in which $\ln(\bar{g})$ is the mean of $\ln(\bar{g}_t)$, $|\rho| < 1$, and the random shock $\mu_t$ has standard deviation $\sigma_\mu$. Third, using the logarithms of the detrended variables (detrending $n_t$ not required), they approximate the utility function r in each period by a quadratic function of $\ln(\bar{k}_t)$, $\ln(\bar{g}_t)$, $\ln \bar{z}_t$, $\ln n_t$, and $\ln(\bar{k}_{t+1})$. The first three are the new state variables, and the last two are control variables. The quadratic approximation is obtained by substituting the detrended variables in, and performing a second-order Taylor expansion of the utility function

$$\ln(c_t^p + \alpha g_t) + \gamma V(N - n_t)$$
$$= \ln\left[(z_t n_t)^{(1-\theta)} k_t^\theta + (1-\delta)k_t - k_{t+1} + (\alpha - 1)g_t\right] + \gamma V(N - n_t) \qquad (5.22)$$

about the steady state $\ln(\bar{k}_t) = \ln(\bar{k}_{t+1}) = \ln \bar{k}$, $\ln \bar{g}_t = \ln \bar{g}$, $\ln \bar{z}_t = \varepsilon$, $\ln n_t = \ln n$ reached by the deterministic version of the model under optimum control. For a discussion of the change of variables and detrending, see section 9.2.

To describe the evolution of the detrended variables divide all terms of (5.18) by $z_t$ and use (5.16) for $y_t$.

$$\bar{k}_{t+1} = (1-\delta)\bar{k}_t(z_{t-1}/z_t) + n_t^{1-\theta}\bar{k}_t^\theta(z_{t-1}/z_t)^\theta - \bar{c}_t^p - \bar{g}_t \qquad (5.23)$$

There is no need to detrend the variable $n_t$. In terms of the detrended variables, the objective function becomes, using (5.17) for $z_t/z_{t+1}$,

$$E_0\sum_{t=0}^{\infty}\beta^t\left\{\ln(\bar{c}_t^p + \alpha\bar{g}_t) + \ln z_t + \gamma V(N - n_t)\right\} = E_0\sum_{t=0}^{\infty}\beta^t \ln z_t$$
$$+E_0\sum_{t=0}^{\infty}\beta^t\left\{\ln\left[n_t^{1-\theta}\bar{k}_t^\theta \exp(-\theta\varepsilon_t) + (1-\delta)\bar{k}_t\exp(-\varepsilon_t) - \bar{k}_{t+1} + (\alpha-1)\bar{g}_t\right] + \gamma V(N - n_t)\right\} \qquad (5.24)$$

If I set up a Lagrangean $\mathscr{L}$ similar to (5.19), methods of section 2.4 can be applied to solve this optimization problem numerically. The control variables are $\bar{c}_t \equiv \bar{c}_t^p + \alpha\bar{g}_t$ and $n_t$. The state variables are $\bar{k}_t$, $z_t$ and $\bar{g}_t$. The three first-order conditions are $\partial\mathscr{L}/\partial\bar{c}_t = 0$, $\partial\mathscr{L}/\partial n_t = 0$, and $\partial\mathscr{L}/\partial\bar{k}_t = 0$. Because the detrended variables are stationary, a steady state $\bar{c}$, n, and $\bar{k}$ can be found for the variables $\bar{c}_t$, $n_t$, and $\bar{k}_t$ in the deterministic version of the model when the stochastic terms $z_t/z_{t-1}$ and $\bar{g}_t$ in (5.23) equal to $\exp(\varepsilon)$ and $\bar{g}$, respectively. The steady-state values $\bar{c}$, $n$, and $\bar{k}$ can be obtained by solving the three first-order conditions and (5.23) for the four variables $\bar{c} = c_t$, $n = n_t$, $\lambda_t = \lambda_{t+1} = \lambda$, and $\bar{k} = \bar{k}_t = \bar{k}_{t+1}$.

If the rate of depreciation were equal to 1, $n_t$ were a constant and $\bar{g}_t$ were zero, the model would be reduced to the stochastic growth model of section 3.1, in which the optimal control function for consumption or for next-period capital stock is linear in the logarithms of consumption and capital stock. This suggests that perhaps using the logarithms of the detrended variables, as in Christiano and Eichenbaum (1992), may improve the linear approximations of the optimum control functions. This would require changing all variables to logarithms $\ln(\bar{k}_{t+1})$, $\ln(n_t)$, $\ln \bar{k}_t$, $\ln \bar{g}_t$, and $\ln(z_t/z_{t-1}) = \varepsilon_t$, and approximating the utility function in each period given in (5.24) by a quadratic function in the logarithms about their steady-state values $\ln \bar{k}$, $\ln n$, $\ln \bar{k}$, $\ln \bar{g}$, and $\varepsilon$, respectively. Applying linear-quadratic control theory (see sections 2.4, 9.3–9.5), one can derive optimal linear control functions for the control variables $\ln \bar{k}_{t+1}$ and $\ln n_t$

$$\ln \bar{k}_{t+1} = \ln \bar{k} + r_k \ln\left(\bar{k}_t/\bar{k}\right) + d_k \ln\left(\bar{g}_t/\bar{g}\right) + e_k\left(\varepsilon_t - \varepsilon\right) \tag{5.25}$$

$$\ln n_t = \ln n + r_n \ln\left(\bar{k}_t/\bar{k}\right) + d_n \ln\left(\bar{g}_t/\bar{g}\right) + e_n\left(\varepsilon_t - \varepsilon\right), \tag{5.26}$$

in which the six coefficients of the linear functions are derived from the structural parameters ($\alpha$, $\beta$, N, $\gamma$, $\delta$, $\theta$, $\rho$, $\bar{g}$, $\sigma_\mu$, $\varepsilon$, $\sigma_\varepsilon$) of the dynamic optimization problem.

Of particular interest is the coefficient $d_n$ that measures the effect of government consumption $\bar{g}_t$ on labor hours $n_t$, as the major objective of this study is to explain the fluctuations in $n_t$ in relation to average productivity $y_t/n_t$. If $\alpha = 1$, $\bar{g}_t$ no longer enters the utility function (5.24) and will have no effect on $\bar{k}_{t+1}$ and $n_t$, leaving $d_k = d_n = 0$. Output $y_t$ produced by $k_t$ and $n_t$ is not affected, and the model cannot reduce the correlation between $n_t$ and $y_t/n_t$. If $\alpha = 0$, the coefficient of $\bar{g}_t$ in (5.24) is –1. Government consumption takes away resources available for private consumption. An increase in $\bar{g}_t$ is equivalent to a reduction in output $y_t$ in the dynamic constraint (5.23). If $\bar{g}_t$ does not contribute to utility when private consumption $\bar{c}_t^p$ is reduced, the consumer will increase leisure and reduce working hours $n_t$. Thus, increases in $\bar{g}_t$ can lead to increases in $n_t$ and decreases in $y_t/n_t$, which contribute to a negative correlation between these variables to off-set the positive correlation due to the productivity shock.

The econometric methodology of this study differs from that of section 5.4. By the method of section 5.4, the optimum decision functions (5.25) and (5.26) are used to evaluate a likelihood function for different values of the structural parameters ($\alpha$, $\beta$, N, $\gamma$, . . .), and the likelihood function can be maximized with respect to these parameters. Testing hypotheses about the parameters can be performed by using likelihood ratio tests. In the study reported in this section, the generalized method of moments (GMM) is used to estimate the structural parameters as well as selected standard deviations, their ratios, and correlations of the variables. Important hypotheses are concerned with whether certain important ratios of standard deviations and the correlation between n and y/n generated by the model under optimal control (i.e., by the specified market economy in competitive equilibrium) are consistent with the data.

There are two sets of parameters describing the characteristics of the model. The first set

$$\Psi_1 = \{\delta,\ \theta,\ \gamma,\ \rho,\ \bar{g},\ \sigma_\mu,\ \varepsilon,\ \sigma_\varepsilon\} \tag{5.26}$$

consists of structural parameters to be estimated, and three other structural parameters are assumed known: N = 1,369 hours per quarter, $\beta = (1.03)^{-0.25}$, and $\alpha = 0$ or $\alpha = 1$. With $\sigma_x$ denoting standard deviation of x, corr denoting correlation and dk denoting investment, the second set is

$$\Psi_2 = \{\sigma_{c^P}/\sigma_y,\ \sigma_{dk}/\sigma_y,\ \sigma_n,\ \sigma_n/\sigma_{y/n},\ \sigma_g/\sigma_y,\ \text{corr}(y/n,\ n)\}. \tag{5.27}$$

If the numerical values of $\Psi_1$ are known, the model consisting of equations (5.16), (5.17), (5.21), (5.25), (5.26), and (5.23) can generate stochastic time paths for the variables $y_t$, $z_t$, $\bar{g}_t$, $\bar{k}_{t+1}$, $n_t$, and $\bar{c}_t^p$, respectively ($t = 0, 1, 2, \ldots$) given the initial capital stock $k_0$. From a large number of sample paths, one can compute the values of the parameters in the set $\Psi_2$. These values of the parameters in $\Psi_2$ can be compared with the values of the corresponding statistics estimated directly form U.S. data without using the model. If the two sets of values of $\Psi_2$ are close, the model is judged to be a good model. Of particular interest is the comparison of the two values of corr($y/n$, $n$), which motivates this study. GMM is used to estimate $\Psi_1$ and to test whether the values of parameters in $\Psi_2$ implied by the model are consistent with the observed values estimated directly from US data.

The eight parameters in $\Psi_1$, $\delta$, $\theta$, $\gamma$, $\varepsilon$, $\sigma_\varepsilon$, $\rho$, $\bar{g}$, and $\sigma_\mu$ are subject to the following eight moment restrictions, respectively

$$E\{\delta - [1 - (dk_t/k_t) - (k_{t+1}/k_t)]\} = 0$$
$$E\{\beta^{-1} - [\theta(y_{t+1}/k_{t+1}) + 1 - \delta]c_t/c_{t+1}\} = 0$$
$$E\{\gamma - (1-\theta)(y_t/n_t)/[c_t V'(N - n_t)]\} = 0$$
$$E[\Delta \ln(y_t) - \varepsilon] = 0$$
$$E[(\varepsilon_t - \varepsilon)^2 - \sigma_\varepsilon^2] = 0$$
$$E[\ln(\bar{g}_t) - (1-\rho)\ln(\bar{g}) - \rho\ln(\bar{g}_{t-1})] = 0$$
$$E[\ln(\bar{g}_t) - (1-\rho)\ln(\bar{g}) - \rho\ln(\bar{g}_{t-1})]\bar{g}_{t-1} = 0$$
$$E\{[\ln\bar{g}_t - (1-\rho)\ln\bar{g} - \rho\ln\bar{g}_{t-1}]^2 - \sigma_\mu^2\} = 0 \tag{5.28}$$

The first equation for $\delta$ is justified by the depreciation rate $\delta_t$, satisfying

$$k_{t+1} = (1 - \delta_t)k_t + dk_t$$

The second equation for $\theta$ is based on the intertemporal optimality condition for consumption derived by setting the derivatives of (5.19) with respect to $c_t = c_t^p + \alpha g_t$ and $k_t$ equal to zero and combining these two first-order conditions. The third equation for $n_t$ is derived by setting the derivative of (5.19) respect to $n_t$ equal to zero. The remaining five moment conditions define the parameters of the models (5.17) and (5.21). Let the eight equations of (5.28) be rewritten as

$$EH_{1t}(\Psi_1^0) = 0 \qquad \text{for all } t \geqslant 0, \tag{5.29}$$

in which $\Psi_1^0$ denotes the true values of the eight parameters, and $H_{1t}$ is the vector function with elements given by the left-hand side of (5.28).

The six parameters in $\Psi_2$ are subject to the following moment conditions for standard second-moment estimators, with all variables measured from their means,

$$E\left\{y_t^2(\sigma_x/\sigma_y)^2 - x_t^2\right\} = 0 \qquad \text{for } x_t = (c_t^p,\ dk_t,\ g_t)$$

$$E\left[n_t^2 - \sigma_n^2\right] = 0$$

$$E\left\{(y/n)_t^2(\sigma_n/\sigma_{y/n})^2 - n_t^2\right\} = 0$$

$$E\left\{\left[\sigma_n^2/(\sigma_n/\sigma_{y/n})\right]\text{corr}(y/n,\ n) - (y/n)_t n_t\right\} = 0. \tag{5.30}$$

These conditions are also written as a vector equation $EH_{2t}(\Psi_2^0) = 0$. Combining the two sets of moment conditions yields the following $14 \times 1$ vector equation

$$EH_t(\Psi^0) = E_t\begin{bmatrix} H_{1,t}(\Psi_1^0) \\ H_{2,t}(\Psi_2^0) \end{bmatrix} = 0 \qquad \text{for all } t > 0 \tag{5.31}$$

The sample analogue of the above expectations evaluated at $\Psi$ is

$$g_T(\Psi) = (1/T)\sum_{t=0}^{T} H_t(\Psi) \tag{5.32}$$

The estimator $\hat{\Psi}_T$ satisfying $g_T(\hat{\Psi}_T) = 0$ is consistent. Its covariance matrix can be consistently estimated by

$$D_T^{-1}S_T D_T'^{-1}/T; \qquad D_T = \frac{\partial g_T(\hat{\Psi}_T)}{\partial \Psi'}, \tag{5.33}$$

in which $S_T$ is a consistent estimator of the spectral density matrix of $H_t(\Psi_0)$ at frequency zero.

Next, test whether two important moments $[\text{corr}(y/n, n), \sigma_n/\sigma_{y/n}] = [f_1(\Psi_1), f_2(\Psi_1)]$, which are derived from the optimization model with parameter vector $\Psi_1$, are consistent with the corresponding two elements of $\Psi_2$, which can be estimated directly from the data without using the optimization model. The latter two elements of $\Psi_2$ can be written as $A\Psi_2$, in which A denotes a $2 \times 6$ matrix, with all zeros except two ones to select the two parameters in $\Psi_2$. The equality of these two sets of parameters is a restriction on $\Psi$, written as

$$\begin{bmatrix} f_1(\Psi_1) \\ f_2(\Psi_1) \end{bmatrix} - A\Psi_2 \equiv F(\Psi) = 0 \tag{5.34}$$

To test the null hypothesis $F(\Psi^0) = 0$, which is true if the optimization model is correctly specified, take a first-order Taylor expansion of $F(\hat{\Psi}_T)$ about the true parameter vector $\Psi^0$

$$F(\hat{\Psi}_T) = F(\Psi^0) + \left[\partial F(\Psi^0)/\partial \Psi'\right]\left[\hat{\Psi}_T - \Psi^0\right] \tag{5.35}$$

in which the matrix of derivatives $\partial F(\Psi^0)/\partial \Psi'$ is $2 \times 14$. The covariance matrix of $F(\hat{\Psi}_T)$ can be consistently estimated by $[\partial F(\hat{\Psi}_T)/\partial \Psi'] \mathrm{Cov}\hat{\Psi}_T [\partial F(\hat{\Psi}_T)/\partial \Psi']'$, $\mathrm{Cov}\hat{\Psi}_T$ being given by expression (5.33) before. One can form the statistic

$$F(\hat{\Psi}_T)\left[\mathrm{Cov}F(\hat{\Psi}_T)\right]^{-1} F(\hat{\Psi}_T)' \tag{5.36}$$

to test the null hypothesis that the RBC model is correctly specified as far as the two moments (corr($y/n$, $n$) and $\sigma_n/\sigma_{y/n}$ are concerned. Under the null hypothesis, this statistic is asymptotically distributed as a $\chi^2(2)$ random variable.

Data on $c_t^p$ refer to quarterly real expenditures on nondurable consumption goods plus services plus imputed services from the stock of consumer durables. Government consumption $g_t$ refers to real government purchases of goods and services minus real investment of government (federal, state, and local). Gross investment $dk_t$ is private-sector fixed investment plus government fixed investment plus real expenditures on consumer durables. $k_t$ measures the corresponding capital stock. Gross output $y_t$ equals $c_t^p$ plus $g_t$ plus $dk_t$ plus inventory investment. Two different measures of hours worked $n_t$ and output per hour ($y/n_t$) are used. The first measure of $n_t$ is based on household survey conducted by the U.S. Department of Labor; $y_t/n_t$ is the ratio of $y_t$ defined above to $n_t$. In the second, $n_t$ is per capita hours worked by wage and salary workers in private nongovernmental *establishments*, and $y_t/n_t$ is output per hour of all persons in the nonagricultural business sector, both also reported by the U.S. Department of Labor. The second are referred to as *establishment* data, and the first as *household* data. The sample period is 1955.3 to 1983.4.

By using the household data, corr(y/n, n) and $\sigma_n/\sigma_{y/n}$ in the parameter set $\psi$ are estimated by moment conditions (5.30) to be –0.20 (0.11) and 1.21 (0.11), respectively, standard errors in parentheses. The corresponding estimates of $f_1(\Psi_1)$ and $f_2(\Psi_1)$ based on the estimated structural parameters $\hat{\Psi}_1$ are reported below for RBC models with $\alpha = 1$ or $\alpha = 0$ and (a) $V(N - n_t) = \ln(N - n_t)$ or (b) $V(N - n_t) = N - n_t$.

| | $\alpha = 1$ | | $\alpha = 0$ | |
|---|---|---|---|---|
| | (a) $V(\cdot) = \ln(\cdot)$ | (b) $V = N - n_t$ | (a) $V(\cdot) = \ln(\cdot)$ | (b) $V = N - n_t$ |
| corr($y/n$, $n$) | 0.95 | 0.92 | 0.81 | 0.73 |
| | (0.014) | (0.022) | (0.058) | (0.074) |
| $\sigma_n/\sigma_{y/n}$ | 0.54 | 0.96 | 0.79 | 1.36 |
| | (0.01) | (0.03) | (0.07) | (0.14) |

All the corr/($y/n$, $n$) derived from the RBC model are much higher than the observed correlation. The utility function (b) $V(N - n_t) = N - n_t$ performs better. The introduction of government consumption $\alpha = 0$ performs better than $\alpha = 1$. The $\chi^2(2)$ statistics to test the hypothesis that these two moments based on $\Psi_1$ and $\Psi_2$ are the same turn out to be 168.84, 119.29, 62.18, and 41.46 respectively for the above four specifications, all leading to strongly rejecting the null hypothesis. When the establishment data are used, the two moments from $\Psi_2$ are estimated to be 0.16 (0.08) and 1.64 (0.16). From the structural parameters $\Psi_1$ with $\alpha = 0$ and $V = N - n_t$, they are estimated to be 0.575 (0.22) and 1.437 (0.19), much closer to the former estimates. The $\chi^2(2)$ statistic for testing the equality of these two sets is 3.48, not large enough to reject the null hypothesis at 15% level of significance.

## 5.6 Oligopolistic Pricing and Aggregate Demand

In the introduction to this chapter, I commented on one major difference between Chicago and Cambridge, Massachusetts, which manifests itself in the choice between perfectly competitive and imperfectly competitive equilibrium in business cycle research. A related difference in emphasis is between the relative effects of supply shocks and demand shocks on the level of economic activity. The baseline business cycle model discussed in section 5.4 emphasizes supply shocks that form a part of the production functions of firms. In this section, I present a model due to Rotemberg and Woodford (1992), which relies on oligopoly pricing and emphasizes the effects of demand shocks, suggesting that the effects of aggregate demand shocks are a consequence of imperfect competition. Demand shocks are represented by government military purchases in the empirical part of the analysis, which compares the effects derived from an imperfectly competitive model with those derived from a perfectly competitive model. Predictions from the model based on imperfect competition appears to be closer to empirical observations.

As usual, the economy consists of two sectors, firms and households. There is a large number I of industries, each consisting of $m$ firms producing close substitutes. $m$ is small, so that each industry is an oligopoly. Oligopolistic firms set their prices as $m$ players in an infinitely repeated game, given demands from the households. Firms in each oligopolistic industry maximize an expected sum of discounted profits as players in a repeated game to determine prices, or markups, given demand and production conditions. Individual households maximize the expected sum of discounted utilities by choosing consumption and working hours. In equilibrium, demand and supply of goods and labor are equated to determine eight endogenous variables: aggregate value added $Y_t$, capital stock $K_t$, hours worked $H_t^p$ in the private sector, wage $w_t$, markup $\mu_t$, expected sum of profits $X_t$, utility of wealth $\lambda_t$, and price $\rho_t$ of period-$t$ good in period $t$, given four exogenous stochastic processes: $\{G_t, H_t^g, z_t, N_t\}$ for government aggregate demand, hours worked in the government sector, technology shock, and population, respectively.

To begin modeling firm behavior, suitable assumptions are made, so that the demand function for the output $q_t^{ij}$ of firm $j$ in industry $i$ can be written as

$$q_t^{ij} = Q_t D^j\left(p_t^{i1}/p_t, \ldots, p_t^{im}/p_t\right) \tag{5.37}$$

$Q_t$ is the aggregate output, which is composed of outputs $x_t^i$ ($i = 1, \ldots, I$) from all I industries.

$$Q_t = f\left(x_t^1, \ldots, x_t^I\right); \qquad x_t^i = g\left(q_t^{i1}, \ldots, q_t^{im}\right) \tag{5.38}$$

Aggregations from firm outputs $q_t^{ij}$ to industry output $x_t^i$, and from industry output to economy output $Q_t$, are accomplished by the functions $g$ and $f$, respectively. If equilibrium in each industry $i$ is restricted to be symmetric, in the sense that all firms $j$ in the industry will adopt the same pricing strategy, an equilibrium price $p_t$ can be found by testing whether each firm $j$ can improve its profits in any period $t$ by setting a price $p_t^{ij}$ different from $p_t$, while other firms choose a uniform price $p_t$. The demand function $D^j$ is assumed to be the same for the industries.

Production function of each firm is assumed to be the same:

$$q_{it} = \min\left\{\left[F\left(K_t^{ij}, z_t H_t^{ij}\right) - \Phi z_t N_t\right] / \left(1 - s_m\right), \; M_t^{ij}/s_m\right\} \tag{5.39}$$

$K_t^{ij}$ is capital service; $H_t^{ij}$ is hours of labor and $M_t^{ij}$ is material inputs. $s_m$ is the share of material costs in the value of gross output. $N_t$ is population, assumed to grow exogenously. $z_t$ is a random shock to labor productivity. $\Phi z_t N_t$ represents fixed costs, which are affected by $z_t N_t$. Equation (5.39) determines output as the minimum of the amount that the firm could produce given its capital and labor inputs and the amount it could produce from a given amount of materials inputs, under the assumption of fixed input proportions in production. Inputs are purchased in competitive markets. In a symmetric equilibrium, each firm has the same output and the same capital and labor inputs. Therefore, in the aggregate, (5.39) implies

$$\left(1 - s_m\right) Q_t = F\left(K_t, z_t H_t^p\right) - \Phi z_t N_t; \qquad s_m Q_t = M_t \tag{5.40}$$

in which $K_t$ is the aggregate capital stock, $H_t^p$ is hours worked in private sector, and $M_t$ is total materials input. Given $Q_t$ and $K_t$, (5.40) can be interpreted as demand functions for labor hours and for material inputs. The number I of industries is large enough, so that no pricing and output decisions in any one industry can affect factor prices. Each firm has the same marginal cost, which (see problem 2) equals

$$\left(1 - s_m\right) w_t / \left[z_t F_H\left(K_t, z_t H_t^p\right)\right] + s_m p_t \tag{5.41}$$

$F_H$ is the partial derivative of F with respect to its second argument; $w_t$ is wage. Markup $\gamma_t$ is defined as the ratio of $p_t$ to marginal cost, that is,

$$\frac{1}{\gamma_t} = \frac{\left(1 - s_m\right) w_t}{z_t F_H\left(K_t, z_t H_t^p\right)} + s_m \tag{5.42}$$

For convenience, markup $\gamma_t^{ij}$ will replace price $p_t^{ij}$ as the control variable in discussing the decision of firm $j$ in industry $i$.

By using markup (the ratio of price to a uniform marginal cost) instead of price, one can rewrite the firm's demand function as

$$q_t^{ij} = Q_t D^j\left(\gamma_t^{i1}/\gamma_t, \ldots, \gamma_t^{im}/\gamma_t\right) \tag{5.43}$$

Firm $ij$ tries to maximize the expected value of its discounted profits

$$E_0 \sum_{t=0}^{\infty} \alpha^t \rho_t \left(\frac{\gamma_t^{ij} - 1}{\gamma_t}\right) q_t^{ij} \tag{5.44}$$

in which $\rho_t$ is the price of period-$t$ good in period $t$, so that the ratio $\rho_{t+k}/\rho_t$ can be used to discount period $t + k$ good in terms of period $t$ good in period $t$. Because $1/\gamma_t$ is the marginal cost in units of period $t$ good, $\gamma_t^{ij}/\gamma - 1/\gamma_t$ is profit per unit of output in period $t$ if firm $j$ charges markup $\gamma_t^{ij}/\gamma$. $\alpha$ is the probability that the game played by the $m$ firms in industry $i$ will continue for one more period; 1-$\alpha$ is the probability that the game ends, because the oligopoly is dissolved or the implicit agreement (guaranteeing industry equilibrium) has to be renegotiated.

Dynamic game theory (developed further in Chapter 6) is applied to determine an industry equilibrium. Consider a *repeated game* played by $m$ firms in each industry $i$ repeatedly for many periods. In each period $t$, there is a one-period *stage game* among $m$I firms. In the stage game, let

$$\pi\left(\gamma^i; \gamma\right) = \left(\gamma^i/\gamma - 1/\gamma\right) D^j\left(\gamma^i/\gamma, \ldots, \gamma^i/\gamma\right), \tag{5.45}$$

denote the period-$t$ profits per unit of aggregate demand Q received by each firm in industry $i$, assuming that each firm charges a common markup $\gamma^i$, but all firms in other industries charge $\gamma$. By denoting the markup of the $j$th firm by $\gamma^{ij} - \rho\gamma$, let

$$\pi^d\left(\gamma^i; \gamma\right) = \max_{\rho}\left(\rho - 1/\gamma\right) D^j\left(\gamma^i/\gamma, \ldots, \rho, \ldots, \gamma^i/\gamma\right) \tag{5.46}$$

be the maximum single-period profit per unit of aggregate output, which any firm $j$ in industry $i$ can obtain by deviating from the markup $\gamma^i$, while all other firms in industry $i$ charge $\gamma^i$, and all firms in other industries charge $\gamma$. The deviating firm $ij$ charges $\gamma^{ij} = \rho\gamma$; $\rho$ is $j$th argument of $D^j$.

First, assume that $\pi(\gamma^i; \gamma)$ is a unimodal function of $\gamma^i$, with maximum attained at $\gamma^i = \gamma^{iM}(\gamma)$. This is the profit-maximizing markup for all firms in industry $i$ when firms in all other industries choose $\gamma$. Industry $i$ is in a perfect collusion to maximize profits if all firms charge $\gamma^{iM}(\gamma)$. If all firms in the economy charge a markup $\gamma^M$, such that $\gamma^M = \gamma^{iM}(\gamma^M)$, the economy reaches a symmetric equilibrium with perfect collusion in each industry. Second, assume that $\pi(\gamma^i; \gamma) - \pi^d(\gamma^i; \gamma)$ is a unimodal function of $\gamma^i$, with zero as its maximum attained at $\gamma^i = \gamma^{iB}(\gamma)$. This means that if any firm in industry $i$ wishes to deviate from $\gamma^i$, its profit $\pi^d(\gamma^i; \gamma)$ cannot be larger than the profit $\pi(\gamma^i; \gamma)$ obtained by not deviating from $\gamma^i$, and hence that industry $i$ is in equilibrium with all firms in it charging $\gamma^{iB}(\gamma)$. Note that if $\pi(\gamma^i; \gamma)$ is negative, the profit $\pi^d(\gamma^i; \gamma)$ by deviating is higher than the profit $\pi(\gamma^{i}; \gamma)$ by not deviating and, thus, industry $i$ cannot be in equilibrium. The equilibrium markup $\gamma^{iB}(\gamma)$ charged by all firms in industry $i$ is a Bertrand equilibrium strategy (to be distinguished from a Cournot equilibrium strategy if the decision variable is quantity rather than price). This is a Nash equilibrium in the sense that if all other firms charge $\gamma^{iB}(\gamma)$, no firm can gain by deviating from it. If all firms in the economy charge a markup $\gamma^{B}$, such as $\gamma^{B} = \gamma^{iB}(\gamma^{B})$, the economy reaches a symmetric Bertrand equilibrium.

Symmetric equilibrium with perfect collusion in each industry $\gamma^{M}$ and symmetric Bertrand equilibrium $\gamma^{B}$ can be defined uniquely by assuming that, for any $\gamma \geqslant 1$, the profit of a potentially deviating firm $ij$

$$\left(\rho - \frac{1}{\gamma}\right) D^{j}\left(1, \ldots, \rho, \ldots, 1\right)$$

is a unimodal function of $\rho$. It is further assumed that the demand functions $D^{j}$ satisfy, denoting by $D^{j}_{k}$ its partial derivative with respect to the $k$th argument, (a) $D^{j}_{k}(\rho, \ldots, \rho) > 0$ for all $k \neq j$ and all $\rho > 0$, and (b)

$$\sum_{k} D^{j}_{k}\left(1, \ldots, 1\right) < -1$$

Part (a) asserts that when any other firm $k$ increases its markup, the demand for firm $j$'s product increases. Part (b) asserts that when all firms in industry $i$, including firm $j$ itself, increase their markups, the demand for $j$'s product decreases at a rate smaller than –1. This assumption guarantees that $1 < \gamma^{B} < \gamma^{M}$. Under these assumptions, the markup $\gamma^{M}$ in equilibrium with perfect collusion in each industry is obtained by maximizing the profit function (5.45) with respect to $\gamma^{i}$ and by using the equilibrium conditions $\gamma^{i} = \gamma^{M}$ and $\gamma^{i}/\gamma = 1$. By setting to zero the derivative of (5.45) with respect to $\gamma^{i}$ and by using the above two conditions to solve for $\gamma^{M}$, one obtains, recalling the normalization $D^{j}(1, \ldots, 1) = 1$,

$$\gamma^{M} = \sum_{k} D^{j}_{k}\left(1, \ldots, 1\right) \Big/ \left[1 + \sum_{k} D^{j}_{k}\left(1, \ldots, 1\right)\right].$$

Similarly, to find $\gamma^{B}$, set to zero the derivative of (5.46) with respect to $\rho = \gamma^{ij}/\gamma$ and use the equilibrium conditions $\gamma^{i} = \gamma^{B}$ and $\gamma^{i}/\gamma = 1$.

$$\gamma^{B} = D^{j}_{k}\left(1, \ldots, 1\right) \Big/ \left[1 + D^{j}_{k}\left(1, \ldots, 1\right)\right].$$

Now consider an infinitely repeated pricing game played by $m$ firms in each industry $i$. These firms take the stochastic process $(\gamma_{t})$ of the markup in other industries and the stochastic process $\{Q_{t}\}$ of aggregate demand as given, while determining their markups interactively. They also take as given the stochastic process $\{\rho_{t}\}$ for asset prices in different periods. In each period $t$ of the infinitely repeated game, the $m$ firms choose their markups $\gamma^{i1}_{t}, \ldots, \gamma^{im}_{t}$ simultaneously. In a symmetric equilibrium, all firms in industry $i$ choose $\gamma^{i}_{t}$. The expected value at $t$ of the sum of discounted profits for each firm in industry $i$ is

$$x_t^i = E_t\left\{\sum_{k=1}^{\infty}\alpha^k\left(\rho_{t+k}/\rho_t\right)\pi\left(\gamma_{t+k}^i;\ \gamma_{t+k}\right)Q_{t+k}\right\} \tag{5.47}$$

A key question is whether each firm in the industry will adhere to a symmetric equilibrium pricing (or markup) strategy, because it cannot gain more profits by deviating from it as deviation may lead to retaliations by other firms. In answering this question, it is convenient to assume perfect information for each firm. That is, when the $j$th firm chooses its markup $\gamma_t^{ij}$ in period $t$, it knows the stochastic process for the aggregate state variables $\{\rho_t\}$ and $\{Q_t\}$, as well as the strategies $\{\gamma_t^i\}$ of all other firms in industry $i$, and the historical realizations of these variables up to time $t$. If perfect information is not assumed, the solution of repeated games is more difficult as the process of learning by each firm has to be modeled (usually by Bayesian updating).

A subgame perfect Nash equilibrium (see also sections 6.3–6.5) is a set of strategies of the $m$ firms having the property that in each (repeated) subgame played at the beginning of any period $t$, no firm or player can improve its expected sum of discounted profits by deviating from the equilibrium strategies. Note that in the kind of repeated game discussed here, there are many subgame perfect Nash equilibria, even if $\gamma_t$ and $Q_t$ are fixed over time. Following Abreu (1986) and Rotemberg and Soloner (1986), choose the optimal symmetric (subgame) perfect equilibrium in which the expected sum of discounted profits for each firm is identical and is the highest among all subgame perfect equilibria, given the stochastic processes $\{\gamma_t, Q_t\}$. Refer to chapter 6, in which a particular duopoly pricing game is discussed in section 6.1 for which the subgame perfect equilibrium is unique. It is pointed out in section 6.4 that if each firm maximizes a multiperiod profit function, such as (5.47) in each period $t$, subject to a dynamic constraint on the state variables, one can apply the Lagrange method to obtain a unique subgame perfect Nash equilibrium, provided that the function $r(x_t, u_t)$ in the profit function and the function $f(x_t, u_t)$ in the dynamic equations for $x_{t+1} = f(x_t, u_t) + \varepsilon_{t+1}$ are both concave.

For the present model of oligopolistic pricing, assume that there is a markup $\bar{\gamma}$ smaller than one such that, when all firms in industry $i$ charge $\bar{\gamma}$, a deviating firm cannot sell positive quantities by charging any price in excess of marginal cost. In addition, the firms that charge $\bar{\gamma}$ cannot be hurt too badly, so that the threat of punishing the deviating firm is credible. The assumption is

$$\pi\left(\bar{\gamma},\ \gamma\right)Q_t + X_t^i \geqslant 0 \tag{5.48}$$

that is, firms that cut markup to $\bar{\gamma}$ can still obtain a nonnegative expected value for the sum of discounted profits. Therefore, in an optimal symmetric perfect equilibrium, a deviating firm earns a present discount value of zero after deviation. The opportunity cost of deviating is $X_t^i$. A firm in industry $i$ has an incentive to deviate in any period $t$ if the period-$t$ gain from deviating, namely $\pi^d(\gamma_t^i;\ \gamma_t)Q_t - \pi(\gamma_t^i;\ \gamma_t)$, $\pi^d$ and $\pi$ being defined by (5.45) and (5.46) respectively, exceeds $X_t^i$. Hence, a subgame perfect equilibrium exists if and only if

$$\pi^d\left(\gamma_t^i;\ \gamma_t\right)Q_t - \pi\left(\gamma_t^i;\ \gamma_t\right)Q_t \leqslant X_t^i \tag{5.49}$$

Compare equation (5.49) with equation (6.26) of chapter 6 for the condition to ensure a subgame perfect equilibrium for the strategy $\gamma_t^i$. $\gamma_t^i$ is chosen to maximize $\pi(\gamma_t^i; \gamma_t)$, subject to the incentive compatibility constraint (5.49), with $\gamma_t$, $Q_t$, and $X_t^i$ treated as given.

The equilibrium condition (5.49) implies that the optimum $\gamma_t^i$ is a function of $\gamma_t$ and the ratio $X_t^i/Q_t$. When $X_t^i/Q_t = 0$, $\pi^d(\gamma_t^i; \gamma_t) = \pi(\gamma_t^i; \gamma_t)$ and $\gamma_t^i = \gamma^{iB}(\gamma_t)$ is the solution. When $X_t^i/Q_t > 0$, $\gamma^{iB}(\gamma_t)$ still satisfies (5.49) but so do other values around $\gamma^{iB}(\gamma_t)$, because $\pi(\gamma^i; \gamma) - \pi^d(\gamma^i; \gamma)$ is assumed to be a unimodal function of $\gamma^i$. Because industry profits and the left-hand side of (5.49) are both strictly increasing in the industry markup $\gamma_t^i$ for values of the markup near $\gamma^{iB}(\gamma_t)$, for small enough positive values of $X_t^i/Q_t$, $\gamma_t^i$ is the largest value consistent with (5.49), and (5.49) must hold as an equality. As $X_t^i/Q_t$ increase further, (5.49) is consistent with a markup of $\gamma^{iM}(\gamma_t)$. Beyond that, $\gamma_t^i = \gamma^{iM}(\gamma_t)$ and (5.49) ceases to bind, with $X_t^i/Q_t$ having no effect no $\gamma_t^i$. To summarize, industry markup $\gamma_t^i$ equals $\gamma^{iB}(\gamma_t)$ for small values of the aggregate profit output ratio $X_t^i/Q_t$, increases with the ratio for larger values of the ratio and equals $\gamma^{iM}(\gamma_t)$ for even larger values of the ratio. If each industry sets prices in this way, in a symmetric equilibrium for the economy, $\gamma_t^i = \gamma_t$ and $X_t^i = X_t$ for all $i$. The common markup $\gamma_t$ is a function of $X_t/Q_t$. I have just shown that in each industry $i$, either $\gamma^{iB}(\gamma_t) \leqslant \gamma_t \leqslant \gamma^{iM}(\gamma_t)$, and (5.49) is an equality or $\gamma_t = \gamma^{iM}(\gamma_t)$, and (5.49) holds as an inequality. Thus, either $\gamma^B \leqslant \gamma_t \leqslant \gamma^M$ and $X_t/Q_t = \phi(\gamma_t)$ in which

$$\phi(\gamma) = \max_{\rho}\left(\frac{\rho\gamma - 1}{\gamma}\right)D^j\left(1,\ \ldots,\ \rho,\ \ldots,\ 1\right) - \left(\frac{\gamma - 1}{\gamma}\right)D\left(1,\ \ldots,\ 1\right)$$

or $\gamma_t = \gamma^M$ and $X_t/Q_t \geqslant \phi(\gamma_t)$. $\gamma_t$ can be written as

$$\gamma_t = \gamma\left(\frac{X_t}{Q_t}\right) = \min\left[\phi^{-1}\left(\frac{X_t}{Q_t}\right),\ \gamma^M\right] \tag{5.50}$$

To compare the properties of the model with GNP data, it is convenient to rewrite the function for markup and the other results, using value added GNP defined as $Y = Q_t - M_t$. The value added markup is the ratio of price to marginal cost of one unit of value added, that is,

$$\mu_t = \frac{\left(1 - s_M\right)\gamma_t}{1 - s_M\gamma_t} \tag{5.51}$$

The production function (5.39) and the equation relating wage to markup (5.42) can be rewritten as

$$Y_t = F\left(K_t,\ z_t,\ H_t^p\right) - \Phi z_t N_t \tag{5.52}$$

$$z_t F_H\left(K_t,\ z_t,\ H_t^p\right) = \mu_t w_t \tag{5.53}$$

The expected sum of profits equation (5.47), with (5.45) substituted for period-$t$ profit, becomes

$$X_t = E_t\left\{\sum_{j=1}^{\infty}\left(\frac{\alpha^j \rho_{t+j}}{\rho_t}\right)\left(\frac{\mu_{t+j}-1}{\mu_{t+j}}\right)Y_{t+j}\right\} \tag{5.54}$$

The markup equation (5.50) becomes

$$\mu_t = \mu\left(\frac{X_t}{Y_t}\right) \tag{5.55}$$

Equations (5.52)–(5.55) determine the processes ($\mu_t$, $X_t$, $H_t^p$, $Y_t$), given the processes $\{z_t, K_t, w_t, \rho_t\}$.

Next, consider the household sector, with the representative household maximizing

$$E_0\left\{\sum_{t=0}^{\infty}\beta^t N_t U(C_t/N_t,\ H_t/N_t)\right\} \tag{5.56}$$

The period-$t$ utility is a function of consumption per person in the family $C_t/N_t$ and hours worked per family member $H_t/N_t$, with $N_t$ denoting family size, or population size if the number of households is normalized to be one. Utility maximization yields the demand functions for consumption goods. The representative household is assumed to own the representative firm, the value of which is $X_t$. Thus, the budget constraint of the household is the dynamic constraint on wealth $X_t$.

$$X_{t+1} = X_t + w_t H_t - C_t$$

The Lagrangean for the household's optimization problem is

$$\mathcal{L} = \left\{\sum_{t=0}^{\infty}\beta^t E_t\{N_t U(C_t/N_t,\ H_t/N_t) - \beta\lambda_{t+1}[X_{t+1} - X_t - w_t H_t - C_t]\right\}$$

The first-order conditions $\partial\mathcal{L}/\partial(C_t/N_t) = 0$, $\partial\mathcal{L}/\partial(H_t/N_t) = 0$, and $\partial\mathcal{L}/\partial X_t = 0$ can be used to solve for the consumption function C, the hours of work function H, and the Lagrange function $\lambda$, which can be interpreted as the marginal utility of wealth. Given $\lambda_t$, the consumption function and the hours of work function can be written as

$$C_t/N_t = C(w_t,\ \lambda_t) \tag{5.57}$$

$$H_t/N_t = H(w_t,\ \lambda_t) \tag{5.58}$$

General equilibrium is obtained by equating the demand and supply of goods and hours. Assume that the government demands exogenously $G_t$ units of goods and $H_t^g$ units of hours. Then,

$$H_t^p + H_t^g = N_t H(w_t,\ \lambda_t) \tag{5.59}$$

$$K_{t+1} = (1-\delta)K_t + Y_t - N_t C - G_t. \tag{5.60}$$

Equations (5.57)–(5.60) provides four additional equations to determine four additional stochastic processes $\{\lambda_t, \rho_t, w_t, K_t\}$, in which $\rho_t = B^t\lambda_t$. The processes of $\{G_t, H_t^g, z_t, N_t\}$, are treated as exogenous.

The reader should refer to Rotemberg and Woodford (1992) for the use of the above imperfectly competitive equilibrium model in studying the effects of government policies in setting military expenditures $G_t$ and military employment $H_t^g$ on private value added, private hours worked, and real wage. It suffices to point out that, as in the study reported in section 5.5, the variables are first detrended to obtain a stationary model in the detrended variables, and the resulting equilibrium equations are log-linearized about the steady-state values of the deterministic version of the model. (See also sections 9.2 and 9.3 on detrending and log-linearization.) The dynamic responses of the three major economic variables in the log-linear model to changes in military purchases of goods and services and of labor hours are examined by these authors.

## 5.7 Research on Real Business Cycles

This chapter has presented the method and some examples of research on equilibrium business cycles. It is an introduction to the subject rather than a systematic treatise. Before closing, some comments on the state of current research are needed.

From the viewpoint of the evolution of economic science, or the refinement, improvement, and qualifications of the classical ideas of individuals pursuing self-interests and market clearing, the researchers on real business cycles have insisted on the assumptions of dynamic optimization on the part of economic agents and the market being always in equilibrium. The application of the method certainly is not confined to models that emphasize the supply side or technology shocks or even the real factors only. Aggregate demand and monetary factors can be incorporated into equilibrium models. The model discussed in section 5.6 in an example of incorporating aggregate demand in an oligopolistic competitive model. Furthermore, the term equilibrium can be broadly defined to include frictions, price rigidity, and time delays without insisting on market clearing in every instance of time. Keynes (1936) considers a model with wage rigidity as an equilibrium model. However, researchers of equilibrium business cycles insist that price rigidity and unemployment of resources be modeled as maximizing behavior, possibly under conditions of incomplete information. With incomplete information, economic agents are required to learn, and learning may be a time-consuming process. Hence, the theory of dynamic games under imperfect information is an important area of research (see chapter 6 and section 7.9 for an introduction to these ideas). Some current research along the directions indicated above can be found in Cooley (1995) and is surveyed in Stadler (1994). The pros and cons of real business cycle research are discussed in Summers (1986), Plosser (1989), Mankiw (1989), and Stadler (1994).

Since the early 1980s when the research on real business cycles started, it is fair to say that the simple models first introduced fail to explain important empirical facts about economic fluctuations, but the method of research has gained acceptance. Both of these facts are easy to understand. Economists have adhered to the idea of maximizing behavior for a long time, and there is no reason for them to abandon it. Hence, the popularity of the method. However, it has been difficult to formulate a simple model based on dynamic optimization on the part of several agents in each of many sectors that make decisions interactively on the basis of incomplete information. Hence the failure of the simple models proposed so far. Before succeeding in building a model based entirely on optimization and rational behavior, economists have been willing, and are perhaps wise, to combine optimization elements in some parts of a model with ad hoc assumptions on other parts, as long as the latter assumptions are stated explicitly. The revival of classical economics from the attack by Keynes (1936), as exemplified by the works of Modigliani and Blumberg (1954) and Friedman (1957) on the consumption function, alleged to be providing micro foundations for macroeconomics, is an effort to reduce ad hoc assumptions and expand the parts of the theory based on maximizing behavior. Later works by Lucas (1976), Kydland and Prescott (1982), Long and Plosser (1983), and researchers on real business cycles can be interpreted as a continuation of such efforts. In the future, it is safe to forecast that such efforts will continue. At the same time, economists not restricted by the methodology of dynamic optimization, rational expectations, and market equilibrium will continue to contribute to our understanding of economic growth and fluctuations.

Just insisting that behavioral equations or decision functions have to be derived by optimization over many periods is not sufficient to explain the phenomena of business cycles, as the analysis of the model in section 5.4 clearly demonstrates. A model based on optimization over an infinite time horizon subject to constraints on variables in different periods is better than a one- or two-period optimization model in explaining the intertemporal substitution of resources such as the long-run or equilibrium rate of saving and the rate of interest, but is not necessarily better in explaining cyclical fluctuations. In optimization models of both short and long horizons, cyclical fluctuations are generated by the propagation of random shocks. A slight improvement in a one-period optimization model in terms of the selection of explanatory variables for a given dependent variable, of a key equation in a system of simultaneous equations, or of the forms of distributed lags, could do much more in explaining business cycles than an extension to a multiperiod model. To put it differently, a slight oversimplification in a multiperiod optimization model in specifying a dynamic equation, such as a capital accumulation equation for $k_{t+1}$ with a constant depreciation rate (which does not fit the capital and investment data) or an autoregressive equation for a random shock, can make the explanation of business cycles worse than a corresponding one-period optimization model. To the extent that an economist is forced to simplify in a dynamic optimization model because of its mathematical complexity as compared with a one-period optimization model, he or she might do better in explaining short-run fluctuations by using a one- or two-period model for the propagation of random shocks and the introduction of distributed lags. Furthermore, by insisting on market clearing and rational expectation, and by ignoring imperfect information and myopic behavior, strict adherents of the infinite-horizon optimization framework might put themselves in a disadvantaged position in conducting business cycles research.

## Problems

1. For the RBC model of section 5.4 divide the control variable $c_t$ and the state variable $k_t$ by the technology shock to yield detrended variables $\bar{c}_t = c_t/z_t$ and $\bar{k}_t/z_{t-1}$. Use $\ln\bar{c}_t$ and $\ln n_t$ as new control variables. Use $\ln(z_t/z_{t-1})$ and $\ln\bar{k}_t$ as new state variables. Approximate $r$ by a quadratic function and $f$ by a linear function of these new variables about the steady state under optimal control for the deterministic model. Find the first-order conditions for the control functions and the Lagrangean function. Provide a numerical method for solving these functions.
2. Derive equation (5.41) for marginal cost, using the relations between output $Q_t$ and various inputs given by (5.40).
3. This is a small-scale term paper based on section 5.2. Read Long and Plosser (1983). By using the method of Lagrange multipliers, solve the dynamic optimization problem for the model of that paper and determine the prices, wages, and the interest rate in the model. Select a small number $m$ of sectors and find the optimal control functions for consumption $c_{it}$, inputs $x_{kit}$ and labor input $L_{it}$ in sector $i$, $i = 1, \ldots, m$. Choose reasonable values for the parameters. Simulate the model to derive the relevant dynamic characteristics of the time series generated by the model.
4. As a continuation of problem 3, estimate the parameters of the model formulated in problem 3 by maximum likelihood. Compare the dynamic characteristics of the time series generated by this ML estimated model with those presented in problem 3. Use the methodology discussed in section 5.4 if you like.
5. Read Kwan and Chow (1996). Using the data described in that article, estimate the model of section 5.3 and check the estimates of the economic losses due to the Great Leap Forward Movement and the Cultural Revolution in China as reported in that article.
6. Read Chow and Kwan (1997). Reproduce the estimates and the results of that article as described in section 5.4. If this project is too long, reproduce only a selected part of the results in which you are interested.
7. Comment on the differences between the method of maximum likelihood as reported in sections 5.3 and 5.4 and the generalized method of moments as discussed in section 5.5 for estimating the structural parameters of a dynamic optimization model. Which method would you prefer and why?

8. Explain how the method of maximum likelihood can be applied to estimate the model of section 5.5.
9. Explain how the generatized method of moments can be applied to estimate the model of section 5.4.

## CHAPTER SIX

# Dynamic Games

## 6.1 A Formulation of Models of Dynamic Games

In section 5.6, dynamic game theory was applied to study oligopoly pricing. This section can serve as an introduction to the subject of dynamic games. From the viewpoint of dynamic optimization, which is a main theme of this book, it is convenient to introduce a model of dynamic games by specifying two decision makers (players) each trying to solve the standard dynamic optimization problem of section 2.3 with the vector state variable $x_{t+1}$ depending on $x_t$ and the vector control variables $u_{1t}$ and $u_{2t}$ of both players; thus,

$$x_{t+1} = f(x_t, u_{1t}, u_{2t}) + \varepsilon_{t+1} \tag{6.1}$$

By using the notation of section 2.3, the Lagrangean expression of the $i$th player's optimization problem is

$$\mathcal{L}_i = \sum_{t=0}^{\infty} \mathrm{E}_t \left\{ \beta_i^t r_i(x_t, u_t) - \beta_i^{t+1} \lambda'_{i,t+1} \left[ x_{t+1} - f(x_t, u_t) - \varepsilon_{t+1} \right] \right\} \qquad (i = 1, 2) \tag{6.2}$$

in which the discount factor $\beta_i$ and the return function $r_i$ may be player specific, and in which $u_t$ is a vector of control variables consisting of $u_{1t}$ and $u_{2t}$. Each player is assumed to maximize the first part of his or her Lagrangean expression $\mathcal{L}_i$, subject to the constraint given in the second part.

Three solution concepts have found important applications, depending on the empirical problems at hand. By the Nash solution, each player solves his or her optimization problem by taking the other player's strategy or decision function as given. This is the competitive solution in a market economy when each firm, in setting its price, assumes that the prices of all other firms to be given. By the Stakleberg solution, one player is specified as the dominant player. Imagine the dominant player to play first. Given the dominant player's strategy, the other player or the follower tries to optimize by choosing his or her strategy. This being the case, the dominant player or leader will take the follower's reaction into account in choosing his or her strategy. To find the

Stakleberg solution, first solve the follower's optimization problem, which depends on the leader's strategy. Then, solve the optimization problem of the leader who recognizes that his or her strategy will influence the follower's optimal strategy. This solution can be applied to an oligopoly in which one firm is assumed to dominate. In addition, there is a cooperative solution, in which the two (or many) players jointly optimize as if they belong to the same firm. The formulation is different from equation (6.2). There is only one return function $r$ (which might be a linear combination of $r_1$ and $r_2$), and a central planner is assumed to solve one optimization problem as in section 2.3. The solution depends on the relative weights given to $r_1$ and $r_2$ in the central planner's return function. If $r_i$ denotes profit of firm $i$, the central planner may try to maximize the expected sum of discounted joint profits in future periods with $r = r_1 + r_2$. Then, a problem remains as to how the joint profits will be shared by the two firms or partners. These solution concepts will be more fully understood as I apply them in the following sections. For a more systematic treatment of game theory and its microeconomic applications, see Mas-Collel, Whinston, and Green (1995, chapters 7, 8, 9, 12, and 14).

## 6.2 Price Determination of Duopolists with no Consumer Switching

To further develop and apply the concept of Nash equilibrium, apply the method of Lagrange multipliers to solve the model of Beggs and Klemperer (1992) on price determination of duopolists that face a market with high consumer switching costs. The material in this section is based on Chow (1995).

Let $v$ be the number of new consumers entering the market in each period. The new consumers' tastes are distributed uniformly along a line segment [0,1] with duopolists A and B located at 0 and 1, respectively. If a new consumer with taste $y$ chooses A's product and is assumed not to change product in the future, he or she will have discounted life-time utility

$$r - \tau y + \sum_{t=1}^{\infty} \delta_c^t R - \sum_{t=0}^{\infty} \delta_c^t p_{At}$$

because he or she obtains utility $r - \tau y$ ($\tau$ being "transport cost" per unit distance) in the first period, and utility R in each subsequent period with discount factor $\delta_c$ and with firm A charging price $p_{At}$ in period $t$. Choosing B's product, he or she will have discounted life-time utility

$$r - \tau(1 - y) + \sum_{t=1}^{\infty} \delta_c^t R - \sum_{t=0}^{\infty} \delta_c^t p_{Bt}$$

First assume that the consumer is myopic, that is, $\delta_c = 0$, and later drop this assumption to allow for the effects of future prices on his or her choice of products. A myopic consumer will be indifferent between choosing the two products if his or her taste is

$$z = (2\tau)^{-1}\left[(-p_A + p_B) + \tau\right] \equiv \beta(-p_A + p_B) + \alpha$$

Because $y$ is distributed uniformly along [0,1], the above expression is the fraction of new customers buying A's product. The remaining fraction $\beta(-p_B + p_A) + \alpha$ will buy B's product.

The profit of firm $i$ ($i$ = A, B) at time $t$ is

$$\pi_{it} = (p_{it} - c_i)\left[x_{it} + v\beta(-p_{it} + p_{jt}) + v\alpha\right] \tag{6.3}$$

in which $c_i$ is unit cost for firm $i$, and $p_{At}$ is understood to be a function of $x_{At} = x_t$, the number of A's old customers, and $p_{Bt}$ is a function of $x_{Bt} = S - x_t$, S being the constant stock of old customers in the market. Because only a fraction ρ of all customers is assumed to remain and become old customers after one period, $x_t$ and $x_{Bt}$ evolve according to

$$x_{t+1} = \rho x_t + \rho v\left[\beta(-p_{At} + p_{Bt}) + \alpha\right]$$

$$x_{B,t+1} = \rho x_{B,t} + \rho v\left[\beta(-p_{Bt} + p_{At}) + \alpha\right] \tag{6.4}$$

Both firms are assumed to maximize expected total discounted profits in infinitely many periods with discount factor δ by choosing price $p_i(x_{it})$ and by taking the other firm's price function $p_j(x_{jt})$ as given. The problem is to find the equilibrium price functions.

Given $p_B(x_B)$, firm A's optimization problem can be solved by the method of Lagrange multipliers. To apply the method, differentiate the following Lagrangean expression (with $\lambda_t$ as Lagrange multiplier):

$$\mathscr{L}_A = \sum_{t-0}^{\infty} E_t\left\{\delta^t \pi_{At} - \delta^{t+1}\lambda_{t+1}\left[x_{t+1} - \rho x_t - \rho v\left(\beta\left(-p_{At} + p_B(S - x_t)\right) + \alpha\right)\right]\right\}$$

with respect to $p_{At}$ and $x_t$ ($t = 0, 1, 2, \ldots$), yielding the first-order conditions

$$\delta^{-t}\frac{\partial \mathscr{L}_A}{\partial p_{At}} = x_t + v\beta\left(-p_{At} + p_B(S - x_t)\right) + v\alpha - v\beta(p_{At} - c_A) - \rho v\beta\delta E_t\lambda_{t+1} = 0 \tag{6.5}$$

$$\delta^{-t}\frac{\partial \mathscr{L}_A}{\partial x_t} = -\lambda_t + (p_{At} - c_A)\left(1 + v\beta p_B'(S - x_t)\right) - \delta\left[-\rho - \rho v\beta p_B'(S - x_t)\right]E_t\lambda_{t+1} = 0 \tag{6.6}$$

Similarly, given $p_A(x) = p_A(S - x_B)$, firm B's problem can be solved by differentiating a similar Lagrangean expression $\mathscr{L}_B$ (with $\lambda_{Bt}$ as Lagrange Multiplier), with respect to $p_{Bt}$ and $x_{Bt}$, yielding first-order conditions (6.5B) and (6.6B), which are identical to (6.5) and (6.6), except with subscripts A and B interchanged. The solution by my method consists of $p_A(x)$, $\lambda(x)$, $p_B(x_B)$ and $\lambda_B(x_B)$, which satisfy the four equations (6.5), (6.6), (6.5B), and (6.6B), in which $\lambda_{t+1} = \lambda(x_{t+1})$ and $\lambda_{B,t+1} = \lambda_B(x_{B,t+1})$, with $x_{t+1}$ and $x_{B,t+1}$ given by equation (6.4). In this model, the transition equation (6.4) for the state variable $x_t$ happens to be nonstochastic. For exposition of the method that is applicable to stochastic $x_t$, keep the conditional expectation operator $E_t$ in (6.5).

To solve these equations by the method described in section 2.4, we assume λ and $\lambda_B$ to be linear.

$$\lambda = l + mx; \quad \lambda_B = l_B + m_B x_B \tag{6.7}$$

In (6.7), $l = h$ and $m = H$ in the notation of section 2.4; $l$ and $m$ agree with the notation of Beggs and Klemperer (1992), who use quadratic value functions of dynamic programming to solve this problem. To solve A's problem by using (6.5), (6.6), and (6.7), first use (6.4) to evaluate

$$\lambda_{t+1} = l + mx_{t+1} = l + m\left[\rho z_t + \rho v\left[\beta\left(-p_{At} + p_B\left(S - x_t\right)\right) + \alpha\right]\right\} \tag{6.8}$$

Assuming tentatively $l$ and $m$ to be given, substitute (6.8) for $E_t\lambda_{t+1} = \lambda_{t+1}$ in (6.5) and solve the resulting equation for $p_{At}$. Simple algebra shows that $p_{At}$ is a linear function in $x_t$ provided that $p_A(x_B)$ is also linear. Substituting the resulting function $p_{At} = p_A(x_t)$ into (6.6) and equating coefficients of $\lambda_t = l + mx_t$, we can find $l$ and $m$ ($h$ and H in the notation of section 2.4). Given $l$ and $m$, the function $p_A(x_t)$ is known. Similarly, by using (6.5B) and (6.6B), one can find $p_{Bt} = p_B(x_{Bt})$ and $\lambda_{Bt} = l_B + m_B x_{Bt}$. Note, that $p_A(\cdot)$ depends on the parameters of $p_B(\cdot)$, and $p_B(\cdot)$ depends on the parameters of $p_A(\cdot)$. Equilibrium is reached when these parameters are consistent.

To proceed with the solution, let

$$p_A\left(x\right) = d_A + e_A\left(x\right) = d_A + e_A S - e_A x_{Bt}$$

$$p_B\left(x_B\right) = d_B + e_B\left(x_B\right) = d_{BA} + e_B S - e_B x_t \tag{6.9}$$

Substituting (6.9) for $p_B(x_{Bt})$ in (6.8), one finds

$$E_t\lambda_{t+1} = l + m\rho v\left\{\beta\left(d_B + e_B S\right) + \alpha\right\} + m\rho\left(1 - v\beta e_B\right)x_t - m\rho v\beta p_{At} \tag{6.10}$$

Substituting (6.10) for $E_t\lambda_{t+1}$ in (6.5) and solving for $p_{At}$ yield

$$\begin{aligned} p_{At} = {} & \left[v\beta\left(\delta\rho^2 v\beta m - 2\right)\right]^{-1}\left[\left(1 - v\beta e_B\right)\left(\delta\rho^2 v\beta m - 1\right)\right]x_t \\ & + v\beta\left(d_B + e_B S + \alpha/\beta\right)\left(\delta\rho^2 v\beta m - 1\right) - v\alpha + \delta\rho v\beta l\Big] \end{aligned} \tag{6.11}$$

Equation (6.5) is used to solve for $E_t\lambda_{t+1}$, and the result is substituted into (6.6) to obtain

$$\begin{aligned} \lambda_t = l + mx_t &= -c_A\left(1 - v\beta e_B\right) + \left(1 - v\beta e_B\right)p_{At} + \delta\rho\left(1 - v\beta e_B\right)E_t\lambda_{t+1} \\ &= -\left[v\beta\left(\delta\rho^2 v\beta m - 2\right)\right]^{-1}\left(1 - v\beta e_B\right)\left[v\beta\left(d_B + e_B S + \delta\rho l\right) + \left(1 - v\beta e_B\right)x_t\right] \end{aligned} \tag{6.12}$$

By equating $m$ to the coefficient of $x_t$ on the last line of (6.12), one has a quadratic equation in $m$, the solution of which is

$$m = \left(\rho^2 v\beta\delta\right)^{-1}\left(1 \pm \left[1 - \rho^2\delta\left(1 - v\beta e_B\right)^2\right]^{1/2}\right) \tag{6.13}$$

Next, solve for $e_A$, which is the coefficient of $x_t$ in (6.11), simplifying by (6.12).

$$e_A = \left[\nu\beta\left(\delta\rho^2\nu\beta m - 2\right)\right]^{-1}\left[\left(1-\nu\beta e_B\right)\left(\delta\rho^2\nu\beta m - 1\right)\right]$$
$$= \left(\nu\beta\right)^{-1}\left[\left(1-\nu\beta e_B\right) - \left(1-\nu\beta e_B\right)^{-1}\nu\beta m\right] \tag{6.14}$$

Note that both $m$ and $e_A$ are functions of $e_B$. Substituting (6.13) for $m$ in (6.14), one obtains the following quadratic equation in $e_A$:

$$\left(\nu\beta\right)^2\left(1-\nu\beta e_B\right)e_A^2 - 2\nu\beta\left[1-\rho^2\delta\left(1-\nu\beta e_B\right)^2\right]e_A$$
$$+\left(1-\nu\beta e_B\right)\left[\rho^2\delta\left(1-\nu\beta e_B\right)^2 - 2\right] = 0 \tag{6.15}$$

The identical solution to firm B's problem yields equation (6.13B) for $m_B$, which is the same as (6.13), with $e_A$ replacing $e_B$, equation (6.14B) for $e_B$, which is the same as (6.14) with $e_A$ and $m_B$ replacing $e_B$ and $m$, and a quadratic equation (6.15B) in $e_B$, which is the same as (6.15) with $e_A$ and $e_B$ interchanged. Equations (6.15) and (6.15B) provide a pair of equations for $e_A$ and $e_B$.

For the remaining parameters, solve for $l$ by equating it to the intercept term of (6.12), yielding a linear function in $l$, given $m$. $d_A$ is set equal to the intercept term in (6.11), which depends on $d_B$ and $e_B$. Given $e_A$ and $e_B$, the intercepts of (6.11) and (6.11B) provide a pair of equations for $d_A$ and $d_B$. Thus, the equilibrium price functions $p_A(x) = d_A + e_A x$, and $p_A(x) = d_B + e_B x$ can be obtained.

To allow for the fact that consumers take future prices into consideration in choosing product $i$, Beggs and Klemperer (BK) assume that the sum $W_i$ of the expected discounted utilities of firm $i$'s old customers is linear in $x_i$, that is,

$$W_i\left(x_t\right) = g_i + h_i x_i \tag{6.16}$$

Hence, the marginal new consumer's distance from $i$, $Z_i(p_i, p_j, x_i)$, satisfies BK's equation (A6), with time subscript $t$ suppressed:

$$-\tau Z_i\left(p_i, p_j, x_i\right) - p_i + \rho\delta_c W_i\left(x_{i,t+1}\right)$$
$$= -\tau\left(1 - Z_i\left(p_i, p_j, x_i\right)\right) - p_j + \rho\delta_c W_j\left(S - x_{i,t+1}\right) \tag{A6}$$

and the evolution of $x_{it}$ follows:

$$x_{i,t+1} = \rho x_{it} + \rho\nu Z_i\left(p_{it}, p_{jt}, x_{it}\right) \tag{6.17}$$

Profit of firm $i$ at time $t$ is, with $Z_{it}$ denoting $Z_i(p_{it}, p_{jt}, x_{it})$,

$$\pi_{it} = \left(p_{it} - c_i\right)\left(x_{it} + \nu Z_{it}\right) \tag{6.18}$$

Assuming that firm $i$ maximizes the sum of expected discounted profits subject to the constraint (6.17), form the Lagrangean

$$\mathcal{L}_i = \sum_{t=0}^{\infty} E_t\left\{\delta^t \pi_{it} - \delta^{t+1}\lambda_{i,t+1}\left[x_{i,t+1} - \rho x_{it} - \rho\nu Z_{it}\right]\right\} \tag{6.19}$$

and obtain the first-order conditions

$$\delta^{-t}\frac{\partial \mathcal{L}_i}{\partial p_{it}} = x_{it} + vZ_{it} + (p_{it} - c_i)v\frac{\partial Z_{it}}{\partial p_{it}} + \delta\rho v\frac{\partial Z_{it}}{\partial p_{it}}E_t\lambda_{i,t+1} = 0 \tag{6.20}$$

$$\delta^{-t}\frac{\partial \mathcal{L}_i}{\partial x_{it}} = -\lambda_{it} + (p_{it} - c_i)\left(1 + v\frac{\partial Z_{it}}{\partial x_{it}}\right) + \delta\rho(1+v)\frac{\partial Z_{it}}{\partial x_{it}}E_t\lambda_{i,t+1} = 0 \tag{6.21}$$

Differentiate (A6) by using (6.16) and (6.17) to obtain

$$\frac{\partial Z_{it}}{\partial p_{it}} = \left[\rho^2\delta_c v(h_A + h_B) - 2\tau\right]^{-1} \tag{6.22}$$

In equilibrium, $x_{it} + vZ_{it} = \rho^{-1}x_{i,t+1} = \rho^{-1}(\eta_i + \mu x_{it})$, in which $\eta_i$ and $\mu$ are defined by BK's equations (A1) and (A2). As before, assume that $\lambda_i(x_i) = l_i + m_i x_i$, as given by equation (6.7). Substituting (6.7), the above equilibrium condition, and (6.22) into (6.20), we can obtain $p_{it}$ as a linear function of $x_{it}$ with parameters $e_i$ and $d_i$, as given by BK's equation (A7)—with the factor 2 in front of $\rho\delta m_i$ for both $e_i$ and $d_i$ missing. Given $e_i$ and $d_i$, substitute (6.7), the above equilibrium condition and its implication $1 + v\partial Z_{it}/\partial x_{it} = \mu/\rho$ into (6.21) and equate coefficients to obtain the parameters $l_i$ and $m_i$ of $\lambda_i(x_i)$. As compared with the method of dynamic programming (BK, p. 663), this method saves the trouble of finding the constants $k_i$ in the quadratic value functions and, having found them, the trouble of differentiating the value functions and ignoring these constants to solve for the parameters of $p_i(x_i)$ by using the first-order condition (6.20). For cases of both myopic and forward-looking consumers, this section has demonstrated the usefulness and simplicity of the method of Lagrange multipliers in solving problems of dynamic games.

### 6.3 A Characterization of Subgame Perfect Equilibrium for Infinitely Repeated Games

The previous section illustrated in a duopoly example a pair of price functions or strategies of the duopolists that form a Nash equilibrium. This equilibrium is sustained because, given that the opponent plays the prescribed strategy, each player will achieve the highest discounted profits by playing his or her prescribed strategy. In other words, there is nothing for any player to gain by deviating from the prescribed strategy at any period of play of an infinitely repeated game. Such a set of prescribed strategies is said to be a *Nash equilibrium*. It is called a *subgame perfect Nash equilibrium* when there is nothing for any player to gain by deviating at any instance *t* of play, that is, in any subgame that starts at period *t*. In this section, I characterize the set of subgame perfect equilibria as presented in the work of Abreu (1988).

Some notation is needed to describe an infinitely repeated game. The notation is adapted from Rubinstein (1979). The investment in mastering this notation is worthwhile if one wishes to understand the subject. Let $N = \{1, \ldots, n\}$ be the set of players, $S_i$ be a set of pure strategies for player $i$, and $\pi_i$ be player $i$'s payoff function, which has the strategies of all $n$ players as arguments. The one-period stage game is denoted by $G = (\{S_i\}_{i=1}^n; \{\pi_i\}_{i=1}^n)$. In elementary expositions of game theory for $n = 2$, a table of payoffs $(\pi_1, \pi_2)$ is often exhibited, with its $i$–$j$ cell showing the payoffs $(\pi_1, \pi_2)$ for players 1 and 2 when player 1 chooses his or her $i$th strategy from the set $S_1$ and player 2 chooses his or her $j$th strategy from the set $S_2$. If the game is zero-sum, $\pi_1 + \pi_2 = 0$, and only $\pi_1$ is displayed in the table of payoffs with the understanding that $\pi_2 = -\pi_1$. The elements of $S_i$ are denoted by $q_i$ and are called *actions*. Set S is the product set $S_1 \times S_2 \times \ldots \times S_n$; $q = (q_1, \ldots, q_n)$; and $\pi = (\pi_1, \ldots, \pi_n)$. G is assumed to be *simultaneous* so that all players choose their actions simultaneously in each period. (The assumption of simultaneity is important; otherwise assymmetry will be introduced if one player moves first.)

$G^\infty(\delta)$ denotes the supergame with discounting, which is constructed by repeating G infinitely and evaluating payoffs by the discount factor $\delta$, $0 \leqslant \delta \leqslant 1$. $\sigma_i$ denotes a *pure strategy* for player $i$; it is a sequence of functions $\sigma_i(1)$, $\sigma_i(2), \ldots, \sigma_i(t), \ldots$, one for each period $t$. $\sigma_i(t)$ determines player $i$'s action at $t$ as a function of the actions of all players in all previous periods. $\sigma_i(1) \in S_i$. For $t = 2, 3, \ldots, \sigma_i(t)$ is a function with domain $S^{t-1}$, that is, the product of sets S in all previous $t - 1$ periods.

Note that this definition of the strategy $\sigma_i(t)$ is different from the price function $p_i(x_i)$ defined in section 6.2, which is a strategy determining the action (price) of the $i$th duopolist. In the formulation of sections 6.1 and 6.2, a vector of state variables $x_t$ is introduced, together with a stochastic model for its dynamic evolution in which the actions of all $n$ players enter as a vector $u_t$ of control variables. Without specifying a dynamic model involving state and control variables, the formulation of this section lets the strategy $\sigma_i(t)$ of player $i$ at period $t$ depend on the actions of all players in all periods up to $t - 1$. Having such a dynamic model with $x_{t+1}$ depending on only $x_t$ and $u_t$, the formulation of sections 6.1 and 6.2 allows the action $u_{it}$ of player $i$ at time $t$ to depend only on the state $x_t$ and on the pricing functions $p_{jt}(x_t) = u_{jt}(x_t)$ of other players $j$. Recall that in the derivation of the price function $p_{At}(x_t)$ for player A by equations (6.5) and (6.6), the price function $p_B(x_B)$ is taken as given. Thus, in section 6.2, the action of the other player is taken into account except that the entire history of actions of all players up to $t$–1 is not required, because history is determined by the given dynamic model and the control or decision functions of all players. The distinction between the formulation of infinitely *repeated games* without using a dynamic model of state variables and the formulation of *dynamic games* using such a dynamic model and employing reaction or control functions as strategies will become clear as I complete the specification of repeated games in this section and reformulate the analysis for dynamic games in the next section.

Returning to the formulation of Abreu (1988), player $i$'s strategy set is denoted by $\Sigma_i$; $\Sigma \equiv \Sigma_1 \times \Sigma_2 \times \ldots \times \Sigma_n$ denotes the set of *strategy profiles*. A stream of *action profiles* $\{q(t)\}_{t=1}^{\infty}$ is referred to as a *path* and is denoted by Q. Note, that a strategy $\sigma_i(t)$ of player $i$ at time $t$ is a function that maps the past actions of all players into the space of actions of player $i$. Hence, $\sigma_i(t)$ should be distinguished from the action $q_{it}$, which is the outcome. Abreu (1988) calls the action *path* $\{q(t)\}_{t=1}^{\infty}$ or $\{q_1(t), \ldots, q_n(t)\}_{t=1}^{\infty}$ for all $n$ players a *punishment* Q to call attention to the fact that the actions of all players (the prices set by all firms in an oligopoly) at all time $t$ serve as a punishment to each player because this *path* affects the payoff (or profits) of each player. Bear in mind that Q is the action paths of all players. Because the action of each player is determined by his or her strategy, a strategy profile $\sigma \in \Sigma$ generates a path denoted by $Q(\sigma) = \{q(\sigma)(t)\}_{t=1}^{\infty}$. The path is defined inductively as: $q(\sigma)(1) = \sigma(1)$, and

$$q(\sigma)(t) = \sigma(t)\big(q(\sigma)(1), \ldots, q(\sigma)(t-1)\big)$$

The above definition is easier to read if, having understood $q(\sigma)(t)$ to depend on the strategy profile $\sigma$, suppress the argument $\sigma$ and simply write

$$q(t) = \sigma(t)\big(q(1), \ldots, q(t-1)\big)$$

In other words, the vector $q(t)$ of action paths for all $n$ players is a vector function $\sigma(t)$ of all past actions $q(1), \ldots, q(t-1)$ of all $n$ players.

Next, consider payoffs generated by the action paths. Recall that the payoff $\pi_i(q(t))$ to player $i$ in period $t$ depends on the vector $q(t)$ of actions of all players. One can define the (total) discounted payoffs of player $i$ as

$$v_i(Q) = \sum_{t=1}^{\infty} \delta^t \pi_i\big(q(t)\big) \tag{6.23}$$

and the payoff *function* of player $i$ as

$$\tilde{v}_i(\sigma) = v_i\big(Q(\sigma)\big) \tag{6.24}$$

to indicate that the total payoff of each player $i$ is a function of the set of strategies $\sigma$ of all players. Period $t$ payoffs are received at the end of period $t$, so that payoffs of period 1 are discounted by $\delta$, a discount factor assumed to be common to all players. $H = (q(1), \ldots, q(t)) \in S^t$ denotes an arbitrary $t$-period history.

To characterize a subgame perfect equilibrium Abreu (1988) introduces a *simple* strategy profile and shows that all subgame perfect equilibria can be found by such strategy profiles. A *simple strategy profile* is defined by $n + 1$ paths $(Q^0, Q^1, \ldots, Q^n)$. Recall that each path contains action paths of all $n$ players. The initial path is $Q^0 \cdot Q^i$ $(i = 1, \ldots, n)$ is a path or punishment, which all players will follow if player $i$ alone chooses to deviate from any ongoing prescribed path (including the initial path $Q^0$ and one of the $n$ punishments). That is, when player $i$ deviates from an ongoing path, all players will play $Q^i$. To be specific, we have

DEFINITION 1: *The* simple strategy profile *$\sigma(Q^0, Q^1, \ldots, Q^n)$ specifies: (i) play $Q^0$ until some player deviates singly from $Q^0$; (ii) if player* j *deviates singly from $Q^i$, $i = 0, 1, \ldots, n$, in which $Q^i$ is an ongoing previously specified path, play $Q^j$; continue with $Q^i$ if no player deviates or if two or more players deviate simultaneously (the latter case is irrelevant because the equilibrium solution discussed by Abreu is noncooperative, and it suffices to treat deterrence of uncoordinated deviations only).*

By restricting attention to simple strategy profiles, one is able to check whether an equilibrium is subgame perfect. One has to consider only $n + 1$ induced strategy profiles and check only *one-shot deviations* from each of them. The result is contained in Proposition 1. The simple strategy profile $\sigma(Q^0, Q^1, \ldots, Q^n)$ is perfect if and only if no one-shot deviation by any player $j$ from $Q^i$, $i = 1, \ldots, n$ yields him or her a higher payoff, given that he or she and all other players will conform with $Q^j$ after the deviation.

This proposition can be stated more formally. Denote the value of total payoffs to player $j$ from period $t + 1$ onward if the path Q is followed by

$$v_j\left(Q;\ t+1\right) \equiv \sum_{s=1}^{\infty} \delta^S \pi_j\left(q\left(t+s\right)\right) \tag{6.25}$$

Equation (6.25) differs from the total payoffs $\Sigma_t \beta^t r_j(x_t, u_t)$ of player $j$ in the formulation of dynamic games of equation (6.2), with the action vector now denoted by $q(t)$ instead of $u_t$, mainly by the absence of the state variables $x_t$ in the payoff function $\pi_j$ (or $r_j$ in my previous notation).

Proposition 1. *Under the assumption that $\pi(s)$, $s \in S$, is bounded the simple strategy profile $\sigma(Q^0, Q^1, \ldots, Q^n)$ is a perfect equilibrium if and only if*

$$\pi_j\left(q^i\right) + v_j\left(Q^i;\ t+1\right) \geqslant \pi_j\left(q_j^*,\ q_{\bar{j}}^i\right) + v_j\left(Q^j;\ t+1\right) \tag{6.26}$$

*for all $q_j^*$, $j \in N$, $i = 0, 1, \ldots, n$, and $t = 1, 2, \ldots$.*

On the right-hand side of (6.26) is player $j$'s life-time payoff by deviating in period $t$ from $q_j^i$ to $q_j^*$ and taking the punishment $Q^j$ from $t + 1$ on. The left-hand side is player $j$'s life-time payoff by not deviating from $Q^i$ at all. If and only if a one-period deviation yields no gain for any player $j$ for all period $t$, one has a subgame perfect equilibrium. Abreu (1988, p. 390) gives a verbal argument for Proposition 1 as follows. Consider $\sigma(Q^0, Q^1, \ldots, Q^n)$ and suppose that the assumption of Proposition 1 holds, that is, that no one-shot deviation by any player from any of the $n + 1$ path yields him or her a higher payoff. To see that a two-shot deviation will not, one knows that any deviation by player $j \in N$ results in $Q^j$ being imposed. For the second-period deviation, $Q_j$ has just been imposed and will again be imposed after the second deviation. Because one-shot deviations do not yield a higher payoff, no finite sequence of deviations by $j$ from $Q^j$ will. Given discounting and a uniform upper bound on payoffs, if an infinite sequence of deviations were profitable, a large finite sequence would be as well. The latter has been ruled out. Hence, player $j$ will confirm to $Q^i$, because no sequence of deviations can be profitable to him or her.

## 6.4 A Characterization of Subgame Perfect Equilibrium for Dynamic Games

Because Proposition 1 is based on the formulation of infinitely repeated games without a dynamic model for the state variables, I present a result similar to

Proposition 1 for dynamic games by using a dynamic model for a vector $x_t$ of state variables written as

$$x_{t+1} = f(x_t, u_t) \tag{6.27}$$

In repeated games, the action vector of $n$ players is denoted by $q_t$. In dynamic games, I also denote the outcome vector by $q_t' = (x_t', u_t')$ on which payoff $\pi_j$ (or $r_j$ in my earlier notation) depends. The difference is that the action vector $u_t$ is only a part of $q_t$. The remaining part is $x_t$, which is given when the decision on the components of $u_t$ is made. $u_t$ and $x_t$ will determine $x_{t+1}$ for the next period through the dynamic model (6.27). The action vector $u_t$ will determine the outcome $q_t$, given $x_t$.

If only *reaction function equilibria* are considered, the strategy $\sigma_i$ of the $i$th player is a sequence of functions $\sigma_{i1}, \sigma_{i2}, \ldots, \sigma_{it}, \ldots$, one for each period $t$. $\sigma_{it}$ is a function of the $t$-period history $h_t = (q_0, \ldots, q_{t-1}, x_t)$. (History H defined by Abreu begins from period 1 to $t$, not from 0 to $t - 1$.) A result on subgame perfect reaction function equilibria can be derived from Lemma 1 of Langlois and Sachs (1992). Using the notation of Abreu (1988), define a strategy $\sigma_i$ of player $i$ to be a *best response* to the $(n - 1)$-dimensional strategy vector $\sigma_{-i} = (\sigma_1, \ldots, \sigma_{i-1}, \sigma_{i+1}, \ldots, \sigma_n)$ in any subgame resulting from some $t$-period history $h_t = (q_0, \ldots, q_{t-1}, x_t)$ if for any other strategy $\sigma_i^*$ defined on $h_t$

$$\tilde{v}_i(\sigma; h_t) = \tilde{v}_i((\sigma_i, \sigma_{-i}); h_t) \geqslant \tilde{v}_i((\sigma_i^*, \sigma_{-i}); h_t), \tag{6.28}$$

in which $\tilde{v}_i(\sigma; h_t)$ is the life-time payoff to player $i$ as a function of the $n$-component strategy $\sigma$ and history $h_t$, analogous to the definition of $\tilde{v}_i(\sigma)$ in (6.24); the ~ on top of v (following Abreu) indicates that it is a function of the *strategy* $\sigma$, and not the *path* $Q$, which may be the outcome of strategy $\sigma$. If for each $i \in$ N and for any history $h_t \in S^t$, $\sigma_i$ is a best response to $\sigma_{-i}$, $\sigma$ is a *subgame perfect equilibrium.*

LEMMA 1 *A strategy vector $\sigma$ is a subgame perfect equilibrium if and only if it satisfies for any t, $h_t \in S^t$, and $h_{t+1} = \{h_t, q_t, x_{t+1}\}$ (with $q_t = \sigma(h_t)$)*

$$\tilde{v}_i(\sigma; h_t) = \sup_{q_{it} \in S_i} [\pi_i(q_{it}, q_{-i,t}) + \delta \tilde{v}_i(\sigma; h_{t+1})] \tag{6.29}$$

The right-hand side of (6.29) is the best life-time payoff of player $i$ by choosing $q_{it}$ freely in period $t$, while all other players follow their parts of the strategy $\sigma$ in period $t$ and afterwards, and player $i$ will also follow $\sigma$ from period $t + 1$ on. The two parts on the right-hand side of (6.29) are the period-$t$ payoff and the total payoffs from $t + 1$ on. Player $i$ can deviate in period $t$ by freely choosing $q_{it}$ (only its $u_{it}$ component, given $x_t$), but will adhere to the strategy $\sigma$ from $t$ + 1 on; all other players adhere to the strategy $\sigma$ from $t$ on. In other words, the right-hand side of (6.29) is the best lifetime payoff that player $i$ could achieve by a one-shot deviation. The left-hand side of (6.29) is his or her lifetime payoff if he or she adheres to the strategy $\sigma$ as all others do. By the necessary and sufficient condition (6.29), a strategy vector $\sigma$ is subgame perfect if and only if no one-shot deviation by any player $i$ at any time can improve his or her total payoff as compared with strategy $\sigma$.

Proof of Lemma 1: To prove that (6.29) is necessary, assume $\sigma$ to be subgame perfect. Because $\sigma_i$ is the best response, $q_{it} = \sigma_i(h_t)$ maximizes $[\pi_i(q_{it}, q_{-i,t}) + \delta\tilde{v}_i(\sigma; h_{t+1})]$. Thus, the supremum is reached and (6.29) must hold. Conversely, assume (6.29) to hold. Consider an alternative strategy $(\sigma_i^*, \sigma_{-i})$ and the infinite sequence of outcome vectors $(q'_t, \ldots, q'_{t+k}, \ldots)$, which it determines given some arbitrary history $h_t$. For any $k = 0, 1, 2, \ldots$, (6.29) implies by induction on $k$:

$$\begin{aligned}\tilde{v}_i(\sigma; h_t) &\geq \pi_i(q'_{it}, q'_{-i,t}) + \delta\tilde{v}_i\left((\sigma_i^*; \sigma_{-1}); h_{t+1}\right)\\ &\geq \pi_i(q'_{it}, q'_{-i,t}) + \delta\left[\pi_i(q'_{i,t+1}, q'_{-i,t+1}) + \delta\tilde{v}_i\left((\sigma_i^*; \sigma_{-1}); h_{t+2}\right)\right]\\ &\geq \pi_i(q'_t) + \delta\pi_i(q'_{t+1}) + \cdots + \delta^k\left[\pi_i(q'_{t+k}) + \delta\tilde{v}_i\left((\sigma_i^*, \sigma_{-1}); h_{t+k+1}\right)\right]\\ &= \tilde{v}_i\left((\sigma_i^*, \sigma_{-1}); h_t\right).\end{aligned}$$

Therefore, $\sigma_i$ is a best response to $\sigma_{-i}$ given some arbitrary history $h_t$. Because this holds for all players $i \in N$, $\sigma$ is a subgame perfect equilibrium.

Both Lemma 1 and Abreu's Proposition 1 state that checking possible gains from one-shot deviations is sufficient to ascertain subgame perfect equilibrium. The main difference is that Abreu introduces the notion of simple strategy profiles in the form of $\sigma(Q^0, Q^1, \ldots, Q^n)$, so that one can examine the gain or loss of a one-shot deviation from a simple strategy profile as defined by an $(n + 1)$-vector of paths $(Q^0, Q^1, \ldots, Q^n)$. Abreu's Proposition 1 can be used in the following manner. Let some equilibrium simple strategy profile $\underline{\sigma}$ yield a lower bound of the lifetime payoff $\tilde{v}_i(\underline{\sigma}; h_t)$ for all $i$ and all $t$. A strategy $\sigma$ is an equilibrium strategy if

$$\tilde{v}_i(\sigma; h_t) \geq \sup_{q_{it}\in S_i}\left[\pi_i(q_{it}, q_{-it}) + \delta\tilde{v}_i(\underline{\sigma}; h_{t+1})\right] \tag{6.30}$$

because no one can benefit by deviating in any period $t$ as he or she could be punished by the strategy $\underline{\sigma}$. The fear of punishment by the strategy $\underline{\sigma}$ makes the strategy $\sigma$ satisfying (6.30) an equilibrium strategy. This statement does not contradict (6.29) of Lemma 1 as being necessary. When player $i$ contemplates a possible deviation from $\sigma$ in period $t$, all other players are assumed by (6.29) to adhere to $\sigma$ from period $t + 1$ on, and not to contemplate a more severe punishment $\underline{\sigma}$.

To apply Lemma 1 to deal with reaction-function equilibria in the presence of a dynamic model (6.27) for the state variables $x_t$, let $\pi_i(q_t) \equiv r_i(x_t, u_t)$ be differentiable and concave and $f(x_t, u_t)$ be also differentiable and concave. The condition (6.29) becomes

$$\tilde{v}_i(\sigma; h_t) = \max_{u_{it}}\left[r_i(x_t, u_{it}, u_{-i,t}) + \delta\tilde{v}_i(\sigma; h_{t+1})\right] \tag{6.31}$$

subject to (6.27). For the $i$th player's maximization problem stated above, the Lagrangean (with the game beginning from $t = 1$) is

$$\mathcal{L}_i = \sum_{t=1}^{\infty}\left\{\delta^t r_i(x_t, u_t) - \delta^{t+1}\lambda'_{i,t+1}\left[x_{t+1} - f(x_t, u_t)\right]\right\} \tag{6.32}$$

and the associated first-order conditions are

$$\delta^{-t}\frac{\partial \mathcal{L}_i}{\partial u_{it}} = \frac{\partial r_i(x_t, u_t)}{\partial u_t} + \delta\frac{\partial f'(x_t, u_t)}{\partial u_{it}}\lambda_{i,t+1} = 0 \qquad t = 1, 2 \ldots \tag{6.33}$$

$$\delta^{-t}\frac{\partial \mathcal{L}_i}{\partial x_{it}} = -\lambda_{it} + \frac{\partial r_i(x_t, u_t)}{\partial x_t} + \delta\frac{\partial f'(x_t, u_t)}{\partial x_t}\lambda_{i,t+1} = 0 \qquad t = 1, 2 \ldots \tag{6.34}$$

When each player $i$ is deciding on his or her $u_{it}$, he or she assumes that the $u_{jt}$ of all other players $j$ to be given. Equation (6.34) can be obtained by differentiating (6.31) with respect to $x_t$ and defining $\lambda_{it}$ as $\partial\tilde{v}_i/\partial x_t$, $x_t$ being the last component of $h_t$.

One can check whether a strategy set $\sigma$ is subgame perfect or would yield a subgame perfect equilibrium. Applying Lemma 1, ask whether at any time $t$, any player $i$ can improve his or her lifetime payoff by a one-shot deviation, while all other players $j$ play their strategies in $\sigma$. Holding other players' strategies fixed, equation (6.31) compares players $i$'s lifetime payoffs when he or she adheres to $\sigma$ (on the left) and when he or she tries his or her best to deviate in choosing $u_{it}$ in period $t$ (on the right). The best choice of $u_{it}$ is mathematically accomplished by solving a dynamic programming problem in period $t$ for player $i$, while holding other payers' strategies at $\sigma$, as given by equation (6.31). Note, there is a conceptual difference between checking whether $u_{it}$ derived from the strategy $\sigma_i$ for player $i$ is subgame perfect and finding an optimum $u_{it}$ for player $i$ by dynamic programming using the same equation (6.31). In the former case, the value function $\tilde{v}_i(\sigma; h_t)$ is treated as given. Find the best $u_{it}$ to check whether the right-hand side can yield a better life-time payoff for player $i$ by possibly deviating in period $t$ than the left-hand side by not deviating. In the latter case, when player $i$ solves his or her dynamic programming problem by using the Bellman Equation (6.31) he or she has to find the optimal strategy for $u_{it}$ and the value function $\tilde{v}_i(\sigma; h_t)$ simultaneously as is usually done in dynamic optimization. In other words, the former problem treats the value function $\tilde{v}_i$ as given, and the latter treats $\tilde{v}_i$ as an unknown function. However, the two problems are mathematically equivalent in the following sense. Given $\tilde{v}_i$, if one solves the optimization problem for $u_{it}$ on the right-hand side and find both sides of (6.31) to be equal, $\tilde{v}_i$ must be a value function that satisfies the Bellman Equation of the latter dynamic optimization problem.

As is suggested in this book, I can conveniently replace the Bellman Equation (6.31) by the first-order conditions (6.33) and (6.34) derived from the Lagrangean $\mathcal{L}_i$ in (6.32), which treats as given $u_{jt}$ (for all other players $j$ and all periods $t$) or the strategies $\sigma_{-i}$ from which $u_{jt}$ can be derived. When I use the first-order conditions (6.33) and (6.34) to check whether a set of strategies $\sigma$ is subgame perfect, I conceptually take the Lagrange function $\lambda_i$ (corresponding to the value function $\tilde{v}_i$) as given. However, again if $u_{it}$ satisfies the first-order conditions (6.33) and (6.34), the associated Lagrange function $\lambda_i$ must be (or at least satisfy the first-order conditions for) an optimal solution for the dynamic optimization problem for player $i$. After all if an economically rational player $i$ wishes to achieve most gain by possibly deviating, he or she must solve a dynamic optimization problem to find the best strategy to deviate. If the best strategy happens to be the one that he or she is already practicing, he or she will not deviate.

As usual, an economic equilibrium is defined by all participants trying the best to maximize their gains and finding a situation at which they can no longer improve themselves. A subgame perfect equilibrium is no exception. In the present case, such an equilibrium can be found by solving the first-order conditions (6.33) and (6.34) for each player $i$ and each period $t$. I have thus proved that solving (6.33) and (6.34) for the functions $\lambda_i$ and $u_i$ gives a subgame perfect equilibrium for the dynamic game specified above, because equations (6.33) and (6.34) are the equations used to check for possible gain by a one-shot deviation. I have also shown that if a set of strategies $\sigma = (\sigma_1, \ldots, \sigma_n)$ are such that the action $u_{it}$ for each player $i$ at each time $t$ derived form it satisfies the first-order conditions (6.33) and (6.34), together with the associated $\lambda_i$, it is a set of subgame perfect strategies, because the condition (6.29) of Lemma 1 are both necessary and sufficient.

## 6.5 Credible Government Policy

An interesting issue in the assessment of government policy is whether the policy is *credible*. To determine whether a policy is credible, one asks whether the government has something to gain by deviating from the announced policy. If one thinks of the government as playing a repeated game with the public, the question is whether the government's policy or strategy is a subgame perfect equilibrium strategy. If it is, there is no incentive for the government to deviate from it, and the policy is credible. Such a subgame perfect equilibrium strategy is called a *time-consistent* policy in the macroeconomic literature through the work of Kydland and Prescott (1977). At an initial time 0, the government might choose an optimum decision function or strategy to maximize its objective function over time. If, at any future time $t$, the government may find it advantageous to change its policy, the policy is said to be *time-inconsistent*. In the framework of a repeated game, such a policy cannot constitute a subgame perfect equilibrium. If a policy is a subgame perfect equilibrium strategy, the government will maintain the strategy in all future time. It is time-consistent and it is credible.

Stokey (1991) applies repeated game theory to study credible government policy by using the ideas of Abreu (1988), as discussed in section 6.3, to characterize the subgame perfect equilibrium outcome paths for credible policies. The government is one player in a two-person game. The other player is the public. Because the public consists of many households, modeling the behavior of individual households is required before standard two-person repeated game theory can be applied. Let $y$ denote an action of the government chosen from a set Y and $x$ denote an action of an individual household chosen from a set X. The actions have to be feasible or satisfy certain resource and budget constraints. The utility $u(x', x, y)$ of a household choosing action $x'$ depends on the action $x$ chosen by all other households and the action $y$ chosen by the government. The utility function is assumed to be the same for all households, so that in equilibrium the strategy of each household is the same and the utility of each is $u(x, x, y)$. The government's utility is assumed to be $w(x, y) = u(x, x, y)$. Given $x$ chosen by all other households and $y$ chosen by the government, an individual household chooses $x'$ to maximize $u(x', x, y)$. If $x$ is itself a maximizing value $x'$, the pair $(x, y)$ is said to belong to the set E. A point in the set E has the following property: If the government is expected to choose $y$ and all other households are expected to choose $x$, an individual household maximizes its utility by choosing $x$ also. The definition of E restricts attention to a uniform action $x$ of all households in response to any government action $y$. It reduces the game to a standard two-person game, with the public acting as one person.

If the government is assumed to share the public's utility function, there are two important types of points $(x, y)$ in E. First, a *Ramsey outcome* $(x^r, y^r)$ maximizes government's utility $w(x, y)$. If the government moves first, it will choose $y^r$, and the households will respond by choosing $x^r$. This is a Stakleberg solution with the government as the leader. The government can achieve a maximum of $w(x, y)$ by moving first, because the maximum of a function $w(x, y)$ can be achieved in two steps: given $y$, maximize $w$ with respect to $x$ to get $\hat{x}(y)$; and maximize $w(y, \hat{x}(y))$. Second, a *no-commitment outcome* $(x^n, y^n)$ is obtained if, given any feasible $x^n$, $y^n$ maximizes $w(x^n, y)$. If the government cannot move first, it cannot commit itself first. However, its policy $y^n$ is an equilibrium policy, because it is the best action for any given action $x^n$ by the public. When the households choose $x^n$, they expect the welfare maximizing government to choose $y^n$. The pair $(x^n, y^n)$ is a Nash equilibrium.

Consider an infinitely repeated game generated by the above one-period game with bounded utility $w$. Denote by $x$ and $y$, respectively, the vectors of actions of the public and of the government from period 1 onward: $x = (x_1, x_2, \ldots)$ and $y = (y_1, y_2, \ldots)$. An outcome path of the game is a sequence $d = (x, y)$ of actions from period 1 onward. A history is a sequence $d^t = (x^t, y^t)$ of actions from period 1 to period $t$. A strategy for the households is a sequence of functions $\phi = (\phi_1, \phi_2, \ldots)$, with $x_t = \phi_t(d^{t-1})$. Similarly, a strategy for the government is denoted by $\sigma = (\sigma_1, \sigma_2, \ldots)$, with $y_t = \sigma_t(d^{t-1})$. Given a discount factor $\delta$, the present value of all future payoffs from period $t$ on is

$$v_t(x, y) = \sum_{n=0}^{\infty} w(x_{t+n}, y_{t+n})$$

When this value is expressed as a function of the strategies $\phi$ and $\sigma$ that determine the outcome path $d = (x, y)$, one writes it as $\tilde{v}_t(\phi, \sigma, d^{t-1})$. A pair of strategies $(\phi, \sigma)$ is a *credible policy* if $[\phi_t(d^{t-1}), \sigma_t(d^{t-1})] \in$ E for all $d^{t-1}$ and all $t$, and if, for every strategy $\hat{\sigma}$ of the government that makes the pair $(\phi, \hat{\sigma})$ feasible,

$$\tilde{v}_t(\phi, \sigma, d^{t-1}) \geqslant \tilde{v}_t(\phi, \hat{\sigma}, d^{t-1}). \tag{6.35}$$

Compare (6.35) with (6.28). The strategy $\sigma$ of the government is *credible* because it is the *best response* to the strategy $\phi$ of the public, that is, because the government has nothing to gain by pursuing any other feasible strategy $\hat{\sigma}$ If $(x, y)$ is an equilibrium outcome path for some credible policy, it is called a *credible outcome path.*

Assume that a no-commitment outcome $(x^n, y^n)$ exists for each period. Then, the pair of strategies that specify $\phi_t(d^{t-1}) = x^n$ and $\sigma_t(d^{t-1}) = y^n$ for all $d^{t-1}$ and all $t$ is a credible policy. The pair of strategies $(\phi_t, \sigma_t)$ is a Nash equilibrium for every period $t$. An interesting question is what other strategies are credible. Following the idea of Abreu (1988) as expressed in (6.30), define $\underline{v}$ as the greatest lower bound of the set of life-time payoffs associated with all credible policies. A simple strategy attaining the lower bound $\underline{v}$ can be used as a punishment to support a credible strategy $(\phi, \sigma)$. The idea is that a strategy $(\phi, \sigma)$ is credible, because the government cannot gain by deviating from it in any period $t$ for fear that the payoffs from period $t + 1$ on may be as low as $\underline{v}$. Stokey (1991, p. 633) provides a result in the following proposition.

PROPOSITION 1. *Given a lower bound $\underline{v}$ as defined above, necessary conditions for $(x, y)$ to be a credible outcome path are $(x_t, y_t) \in E$ for all $t$ and*

$$v_t(x, y) \geqslant w(x_t, \hat{y}_t) + \delta \underline{v}, \tag{6.36}$$

*in which $(x_t, \hat{y}_t)$ are feasible for all $t$. If there is a credible policy $(\phi, \sigma)$ that attains $\underline{v}$, then $(x_t, y_t) \in E$ for all $t$ and (6.36) are also sufficient for $(x, y)$ to be a credible outcome path.*

PROOF: To prove necessity, use the definition (6.35) for a credible outcome path $(x, y)$ associated with some credible policy $(\phi, \sigma)$, as expressed in the first line below. For any deviation $\hat{y}_t$, define the strategy $\hat{\sigma}$ by $\hat{\sigma}_t(d^{t-1}) = \hat{y}_t$,

$$\begin{aligned} v_t(x, y) &= \tilde{v}_t(\phi, \sigma, d^{t-1}) \geqslant \tilde{v}_t(\phi, \hat{\sigma}, d^{t-1}) \\ &= w(x_t, \hat{y}_t) + \delta \tilde{v}_{t+1}(\phi, \sigma, [d^{t-1}, x_t, \hat{y}_t]) \\ &\geqslant w(x_t, \hat{y}_t) + \delta \underline{\tilde{v}} \end{aligned}$$

To prove sufficiency, assume (6.36) to hold and let $(\underline{\phi}, \underline{\sigma})$ be a credible policy that attain $v$. One can construct credible strategies $(\phi, \sigma)$ as follows:

(i) Start by playing $\{x_t\}$ and $\{y_t\}$.
(ii) If the government deviates from $\{y_t\}$, start playing $(\underline{\phi}, \underline{\sigma})$, and continue these strategies forever.

Because (6.36) holds and $(\underline{\phi}, \underline{\sigma})$ is a credible policy, $(\phi, \sigma)$ will satisfy the condition (6.35) to be a credible policy; any deviation would not yield a better lifetime payoff.

Stokey (1991, pp. 636–637) has applied Proposition 1 to support a Ramsey outcome of low inflation in an example of monetary policy. In each period, the government can choose $y_H = 100\%$, $y_M = 10\%$ and $y_L = 0\%$ as growth rates of money supply. Households can take actions $x_H$, $x_M$, and $x_L$, which are appropriate for high, median, and low money growth rates, such as changing the holding of the real stock of money. The utility function $w(x_i, y_j) = u(x_i, x_i, y_j)$ is exhibited in Table 6.1. The set E of equilibrium points at which each individual household is better off by taking the same action $x_i$ in anticipation of the government's action $y_i$ is marked by asterisks.

The set E consists of three points: $(x_H, y_H)$, $(x_M, y_M)$, and $(x_L, y_L)$, because each individual household considers $x_H$ the best response to the government policy $y_H$ no matter what it expects the other households to do, and similarly for the other two points. $(x_L, y_L)$ is the Ramsey outcome because, given the household's equilibrium responses in the set E, the government maximizes $w$ by choosing $y_L$. $(x_M, y_M)$ is the no-commitment outcome because, given the household's choosing $x_M$, the government's best choice is $y_M$. Looking at the last column of Table 6.1, one finds that if the households take action $x_L$ in anticipation of the government action $y_L$, the government could do better (getting utility 30) in one period by taking action $y_M$ instead. The question is whether the Ramsey outcome for each period is credible, or whether the government has something to gain by deviating from $y_L$ in the context of an infinitely repeated game. Examine the government's possible gain by using equation (6.36), assuming the discount factor $\delta = 0.9$.

By not deviating from $y_L$, the government's life-time payoff is an infinite sum equal to $9.7/(1 - 0.9) = 97$. By deviating to $y_M$ in period $t$ and returning to $(x_L, y_L)$ from period $t + 1$ onward, the government's payoff becomes $30 + 0.9 \times 9.7/(1 - 0.9)$ or 117.3. Thus, it pays to deviate, and $y_L$ cannot be in equilibrium if $(x_L, y_L)$ is used as punishment for the deviation. Even if the no-commitment outcome $(x_M, y_M)$ is used for punishment after a one-period deviation, the

TABLE 6.1 One-period utilities

$$w(x_i, y_j) = u(x_i, x_i, y_j)$$

| | $x_H$ | $x_M$ | $x_L$ |
|---|---|---|---|
| $y_H$ | 0* | −1 | 1 |
| $y_M$ | 7 | 8* | 30 |
| $y_L$ | −1 | −1 | 9.7* |

payoff by deviating is $30 + 0.9 \times 8/(1 - 0.9)$ or 102, and is still better than staying with $y_L$. Consider a more severe punishment defined by the path $(x, y)$, with $x = (x_H, x_M, x_M, \ldots)$ and $y = (y_H, y_M, y_M, \ldots)$. This stategy is a "self-enforcing" equilibrium strategy, because returning to itself is sufficient to punish the government for deviation. The payoff from this strategy is $0 + 0.9 \times 8/(1 - 0.9) = 72$. By deviating to $y_M$ in the first period and returning to this strategy afterwards, the payoff is $7 + 0.9 \times 72 = 71.8$, which is a worse outcome. Use this path $(x, y)$ to support the Ramsey outcome by defining the strategies:

(i) Start by playing the Ramsey outcome $(x_L, y_L)$ each period.
(ii) If the government deviates from this path or any ongoing path, start the path $(x, y)$ defined above.

By deviating one period and returning to $(x, y)$, the government's payoff is $30 + 0.9 \times 72 = 94.8$. Because this is smaller than 97, which is the payoff from the Ramsey outcome $(x_L, y_L)$, the Ramsey outcome is an equilibrium supported by this strategy.

The interpretation of the punishment path $x$ is that after the government deviates for one period, households will take appropriate actions in anticipation of high money growth in the following period and moderate money growth thereafter. If high money growth does not occur in the following period as they anticipate, they will expect high money growth in the period after, to be followed by moderate money growth. Realizing this possible punishment after a one-period deviation, the government will not deviate. By changing the discount rate from 0.9 to 0.88, one finds that the above path $(x, y)$ is still "self-enforcing," because its payoff $0 + 0.88 \times 8/(1 - 0.88)$ or 58.67 is greater than the payoff from a one-period deviation $7 + 0.88 \times 58.67 = 58.63$. However, this path can no longer support the Ramsey path as an equilibrium path or a credible outcome path. The Ramsey path yields a payoff equal to $9.7/(1 - 0.88) = 80.83$. Deviation would yield a payoff $30 + 0.88 \times 58.67$ or 81.63, a better outcome than staying with the Ramsey path.

When state variables $z_t$ are introduced to the model, $(x_t, y_t)$ still denotes the actions of the households (each responding to identical actions of other households) and the government, but there is a dynamic model written as

$$z_{t+1} = f(x_t, y_t, z_t) \tag{6.37}$$

Given a path $(x, y)$ of the actions of the households and the government and given the value $z_1$ of the state variable in period 1, the model (6.37) will generate the path $z$ of the state variables. One can compute the payoff $v_t$ from period $t$ on from the action path $(x, y)$,

$$v_t(x, y, z_1) = \sum_{n=0}^{\infty} \delta^n w(x_{t+n}, y_{t+n}, z_{t+n}) \tag{6.38}$$

in which the government's utility $w$ in each period is assumed to be the households' utility with all households taking uniform action $x_t$ as before, except that the state variable $z_t$ also enters the utility function. As before, a

Ramsey path starting with an initial value $z_1$ for the state variable is an outcome path $[x^r(z_1), y^r(z_1)]$ which maximizes $v_1(x, y, z_1)$, subject to the requirement that $(x, y)$ belongs to the set $A(z_1)$ which satisfies all resource constraints and the condition of each household maximizing by taking uniform action $x_t$ in each period. A pair of strategies $(\phi, \sigma)$ for the households and the government, respectively, is defined by $\phi = (\phi_1, \phi_2, \ldots)$ and $\sigma = (\phi_1, \phi_2, \ldots)$. Each $\phi_t$ gives the action $x_t$ as a function $\phi_t(d^{t-1}, z_1)$, where $d^{t-1} = (x^{t-1}, y^{t-1})$ is the history of past actions up to $(x_{t-1}, y_{t-1})$. Similarly, each $\sigma_t$ gives the action $y_t$ as a function $\sigma_t(d^{t-1}, z_1)$.

Expressing the payoff $v_t$ given by (6.38) as a function $\tilde{v}_t$ of the pair of strategies $(\phi, \sigma)$ which, given $z_1$, determine all state variables $z_2, z_3, \ldots$ and all actions $(x_1, x_2, \ldots)$ and $(y_1, y_2, \ldots)$, I can define a *credible policy* by using an inequality analogous to (6.35). A pair of strategies $(\phi, \sigma)$ is a *credible policy* from $z_1$ if for any $t$ and any history $(x^{t-1}, y^{t-1})$ feasible from $z_1$,

$$\tilde{v}_t\left(\phi, \sigma, x^{t-1}, y^{t-1}, z_1\right) \geq \tilde{v}_t\left(\phi, \hat{\sigma}, x^{t-1}, y^{t-1}, z_1\right) \qquad (6.39)$$

in which $\hat{\sigma}$ is any strategy for the government that satisties $(\phi, \hat{\sigma})$ being feasible from $z_1$. An outcome path $(x, y)$ belongs to the set $A(z_1)$, which satisfies all resource constraints and the condition that all households maximize by choosing uniform action $x_t$ in each period, is a *credible outcome path* from $z_1$ if it is the equilibrium outcome path derived from some credible policy from $z_1$. Assume that there exists at least one credible policy from any $z_1$ and that $w$ is bounded. Let $\underline{v}(z_1)$ be the greatest lower bound on the payoff that can be attained by a credible policy starting from some $z_1$. Stokey (1991, p. 462) gives the following proposition analogous to Proposition 1 of this section, given suitable assumptions on feasibility of outcome paths and of uniform actions of utility maximizing households.

PROPOSITION 4. *Given the lower bound $\underline{v}(\cdot)$ as defined above, necessary conditions for $(x, y)$ to be a credible outcome path from $z_1$ are that $(x, y) \in A(z_1)$ and*

$$v_t\left(x, y, z_1\right) \geq w\left(x_t, \hat{y}_t, z_t\right) + \delta \underline{v}\left[f\left(x_t, \hat{y}_t, z_t\right)\right], \qquad (6.40)$$

*in which $\hat{y}_t$ satisfies all feasibility conditions and $\{z_t\}$ is defined by equation (6.37) for all t. If for each value of $z_1$, there is a credible policy that attains $\underline{v}(z_1)$, then $(x, y) \in A(z_1)$ and (6.40) are also sufficient for $(x, y)$ to be a credible outcome path from $z_1$.*

To illustrate the use of Proposition 4, consider an example of tax policy given in Stokey (1991, pp. 644–651). The government can choose a vector $y_t = (\tau_t, \theta_t)$ of tax rates on income from capital and wage income respectively, subject to an assumed balanced budget in each period to provide a fixed government consumption G. Given the beginning-of-period capital stock $K_t$, each household can choose end-of-period capital stock $K_{t+1}$, consumption $c_t$, and labor supply $l_t$ to maximize utility equal to $\alpha \ln c + (1 - \alpha)\ln(L - l)$, with $L - l$ measuring leisure. The choice of capital stock is restricted to the values

0 and 1. Substituting for $c$ by using the budget constraint equating income $(1-\tau)\mathrm{RK} + (1-\theta)l$ to consumption $c$ plus capital accumulation $\mathrm{K}_{t+1} - \mathrm{K}_t$, one can maximize utility with respect to $l$, leaving $\mathrm{K}_{t+1}$ as the only control variable. One can write the household's utility as a function of the initial capital $\mathrm{K}_t$, its remaining control variable $\mathrm{K}_{t+1}$, the corresponding $k_t$ and $k_{t+1}$ for all other households, and the government's actions $\tau$ and $\theta$. The variables $k_t$ and $k_{t+1}$ enter the utility function because they affect government tax revenue from capital and thus the tax rate $\theta$ on labor income required to raise a fixed revenue G.

$$u(\mathrm{K}_t, \mathrm{K}_{t+1}, k_t, k_{t+1}, \tau, \theta) = \max_l \left\{ \alpha \ln\left[(1-\tau)\mathrm{RK}_t + \mathrm{K}_t - \mathrm{K}_{t+1} + (1-\theta)l\right] + (1-\alpha)\ln(\mathrm{L}-l) \right\}$$

Utility $u$ as a function of the above six arguments can be calculated by using parameters values $\mathrm{G} = 3.3$, $\mathrm{R} = 1.0$, $\mathrm{L} = 16$, and $\alpha = 0.5$. The government's utility, with all households taking uniform actions, is

$$w(k_t, k_{t+1}, \tau, \theta) = u(k_t, k_{t+1}, k_t, k_{t+1}, \tau, \theta).$$

Some of the calculated utilities are exhibited in Table 6.2.

By using the calculated utilities one can find the set $\mathrm{A}(k_t)$ of actions $(k_{t+1}, \tau_t, \theta_t)$ which satisfy the condition of each household maximizing utility by taking a uniform action $k_{t+1}$ as all other households. One can also find a Ramsey policy for the government corresponding to an initial period capital stock $k_1 = 0$ and $k_1 = 1$ and a self-enforcing path for $k_1 = 0$ and $k_1 = 1$ given below, given $\delta = 0.90$.

*Ramsey policy*: (a) For $k_1 = 0$, consider paths with $k_2 = k_3 = \ldots = 1$. The calculations of utility show that if the government policy is

$$(\tau_1, \theta_1) = (1.00, 0.375) \text{ and } (\tau_t, \theta_t) = (0.80, 0.318), \quad t = 2, 3, \ldots,$$

a household choosing $k_2 = k_3 = \ldots = 1$ will obtain utility $u(0, 1, 0, 1, 1.00, 0.375) = 1.7391$ in the first period and utility $u(1, 1, 1, 1, 0.80, 0.318) = 1.9060$ from period 2 onward. With a discount factor of 0.90, the household's life-time payoff is

$$1.7391 + 0.9 \times 1.9060/(1-0.9) = 18.893.$$

If a household does not accumulate capital while others do, its life-time payoff is

TABLE 6.2 One-period utilities $u(\mathrm{K}_t, \mathrm{K}_{t+1}; k_t, k_{t+1}, \tau, \theta)$

| $k_t$ | $k_{t+1}$ | $\tau$ | $\theta$ | $u(0, 0)$ | $u(0, 1)$ | $u(1, 1)$ | $u(1, 0)$ |
|---|---|---|---|---|---|---|---|
| 0 | 0 | 1.00 | 0.412 | 1.8135* | 1.7010 | 1.8135 | 1.9146 |
| 0 | 1 | 1.00 | 0.375 | 1.8444 | 1.7391* | 1.8444 | 1.9397 |
| 1 | 1 | 0.00 | 0.467 | 1.7645 | 1.6397 | 1.8755* | 1.9753 |
| 1 | 1 | 0.80 | 0.318 | 1.8878 | 1.7917 | 1.9060 | 1.9922 |
| 1 | 1 | 1.00 | 0.287 | 1.9100 | 1.8181 | 1.9100 | 1.9940 |
| 1 | 0 | 1.00 | 0.316 | 1.8892 | 1.7933 | 1.8892 | 1.9767 |

$$u(0,\ 0,\ 0,\ 1,\ 1.00,\ 0.375) + 0.9 \times u(0,\ 0,\ 1,\ 1,\ 0.80,\ 0.318)/(1 - 0.09) = 18.835.$$

Therefore, all households will maintain capital $k_t = 1$ from period $t$ on in response to the above government policy. The calculations show that a capital tax rate of 0.80 or lower will lead to $k_t = 1$ for $t = 2, 3, \ldots$ Thus, any policy with a capital tax rate of 0.80 or lower is in the set A(0).

(b) For $k_1 = 1$, the calculations show that if the government chooses a capital tax rate of 80% or less, the households will choose to hold capital from period 2 on. For the first period, the government can choose $(\tau_1, \theta_t) = (1.00, 0.287)$, followed by $(\tau_t, \upsilon_t) = (0.80, 0.318)$, $t = 2, 3, \ldots$ The total discounted utility is

$$u(1,\ 1,\ 1,\ 1.00,\ 0.287) + 0.9 \times u(1,\ 1,\ 1,\ 1,\ 0.80,\ 0.318)/(1 - 0.9) = 19.046.$$

*A self-enforcing path*: (a) $k_1 = 0$. If the government sets $\tau = 100\%$ in every period, households' optimal response is never to have $k_t = 1$. Denote by $\alpha(0)$ the outcome path with the action $(k_{t+1}, \tau, \theta) = (0, 1.00, 0.412)$ for every period. This path yields the total discounted utility

$$v[\alpha(0),\ 0] = u(0,\ 0,\ 0,\ 0,\ 1.00,\ 0.412)/(1 - 0.9) = 1.8135/(1 - 0.9) = 18.135.$$

Because there is no capital, the government has no incentive to deviate. (b) $k_1 = 1$. A self-enforcing path is $(k_2, \tau_1, \theta_1) = (0, 1.00, 0.316)$ and the above policy (0, 1.00, 0.412) for $t = 2, 3, \ldots$. Households' optimal response is to set $k_t = 0$, $t = 2, 3, \ldots$. Again with no capital, the government has no incentive to deviate, and this policy is self-enforcing. The discounted utility is

$$v[\alpha(1),\ 1] = u(1,\ 0,\ 1,\ 0,\ 1.00,\ 0.316) + 0.9 \times 1.8135/(1 - 0.9) = 18.298.$$

The Ramsey path can be supported by the above self-enforcing path, using the strategies:

(i) Start by following the Ramsey path.
(ii) If the government deviates from any ongoing path leading to a state $\hat{k}$, start by playing $\alpha(\hat{k})$.

In period 1, there is no incentive for the government to deviate, because the capital tax rate is already 100%. If the government deviates in any period after period 2 and taxes capital by 100% instead of 80%, the corresponding tax rate on labor is 28.7% to balance the budget. The households in the first period of the government deviation are already committed to $k_{t+1} = 1$, yielding utility $u$(1, 1, 1, 1, 1.00, 0.287) = 1.9100. In the following period, both players return to $\alpha(1)$, receiving utility 18.298. The discounted utility by deviating is

$$1.9100 + 0.9 \times 18.298 = 18.378$$

and is smaller than the discounted utility of not deviating. The latter discounted utility consists of getting $u$(1, 1, 1, 1, 0.80, 0.318) = 1.9060 for all periods, beginning with the first period of conceived deviation, which equals

$$1.9060/(1 - 0.9) = 19.060$$

Hence, the above self-enforcing path can support the Ramsey path.

When state variables $z_t$ are introduced, an action path $\alpha = (x, y)$ has to be defined as a function of the initial state $z_1$. Otherwise, the analysis in checking a credible policy is similar to the case with no state variables. The discounted utility of deviation equals the first-period utility plus the discounted utility of the worse punishment.

## 6.6 Credible Taxation to Redistribute Income

One distinction between a liberal and a conservative in the United States (the latter could be called a liberal in 19th century England) is that the former believes in taxing income at a progressive rate and the latter at a flat rate. Many economists believe that, other things being equal, it would be desirable to have a more equal distribution of income. However, if income is earned by working or investing, progressive income taxation may discourage people from working and investing, thus reducing wealth and income growth in the economy. Hong Kong in 1996 has a flat tax of 17 percent of annual income above HK $158,000 (US $20,000) for a married taxpayer, and the economy seems to perform well. The problem of this section, studied by Pearce and Stacchetti (1996), is to find an optimum income tax schedule for the purpose of redistributing wage income and to study the conditions under which a redistributive tax policy is credible. A part of the discussion is concerned with policies that yield after-tax income equal to a linear function pretax income $s$, for example, $10,000, plus $0.83s$, with expected total tax receipts equal to payments. It is a flat tax (of 17 percent) with a fixed subsidy (of $10,000).

The economy consists of many workers who decide to devote an amount $a$ $(0 \leqslant a \leqslant 2)$ of effort (or number of hours) to work in a firm paying a salary $s$. The worker's utility function is

$$U(s, a) = \sqrt{s} - \mu a^n \qquad \mu > 0 \qquad n > 1 \tag{6.41}$$

in which, for expositional purposes, a particular example borrowed from the authors is given on the right-hand side, in equation (6.41), and in what follows. The firm has a production technology that produces a random output $\omega$ when the worker applies effort $a$, specified by an exponential density function in the example

$$f(\omega|a) = \mu(a)e^{-\mu(a)\omega}, \quad \omega \geqslant 0, \quad \mu(a) = \frac{1}{1+ka}, \quad k > 0 \tag{6.42}$$

The gross profit from output $\omega$ is $p(\omega)$, which, in the example, equals $\omega \geqslant 0$. The expected contribution of the worker's effort $a$ to the firm's cross profit is

$$P(a) = \int p(\omega)f(\omega|a)d\omega = \frac{1}{\mu(a)} = 1 + ka \tag{6.43}$$

If the firm pays each worker according to a salary schedule $s = s(\omega)$, its expected salary cost is

$$C(s, a) = \int s(\omega) f(\omega | a) d\omega \qquad (6.44)$$

The government has two actions. At the beginning of each period $t$, it sets a minimum salary $\underline{s}_t \leqslant 0$. After production and salary payment take place, it redistributes income by using a redistribution function $R_t$, which assigns an after-tax income $R_t(s)$ to a worker earning salary $s$. Given these two government policies, the firm-worker team is assumed to solve the following *principal-agent problem*. The firm chooses a salary schedule $s_t$, and the worker applies effort $a_t$, such that the expected utility $\Phi(s_t, a_t, R_t)$ is maximized, subject to the constraints that the firms expected profit is nonnegative and that the government's minimum wage is in effect. That is, $(s_t, a_t)$ solves the problem of maximizing expected utility

$$\max_{(s, a)} \Phi(s, a, R_t) = \int U(R(s(\omega), a) f(\omega | a) d\omega \qquad (6.45)$$

subject to

$$\Phi(s, a, R_t) \geqslant \Phi(s, \alpha, R_t); \quad \text{for all } \alpha \qquad (6.46)$$

$$P(a) - C(s, a) \geqslant 0 \qquad (6.47)$$

$$s(\omega) \geqslant \underline{s}_t \qquad (6.48)$$

This problem is solved by the worker finding an effort level $a$, given the firm's salary schedule $s$, and the government's redistribution function $R_t$. Then, the firm, realizing the effect of the salary schedule on the worker's effort, maximizes the expected utility $\Phi$ with respect to the schedule subject to the nonnegative profit constraint. We illustrate the solution of the principal-agent problem by an example. In the example, assuming $R(s) = s$ or no government taxation, the worker maximizes her expected utility $\Phi(s, a, R_t)$ by differentiating with respect to $a$ and setting the derivative to zero, with $f_a$ denoting derivative,

$$\partial\Phi(s, a, R_t)/\partial a = \int \sqrt{s(\omega)} f_a(\omega | a) d\omega - \gamma n a^{n-1} = 0, \qquad (6.46')$$

which corresponds to (6.46). Assume that the salary schedule has the form $s(\omega) = (e + b\omega)^2$, with $e$ and $b$ as parameters. Using the function $f(\omega | a)$ given by (6.42), solve (6.46) to obtain the following supply function of $a$ (see problem 9):

$$a^{n-1} = bk/(\gamma n) \qquad (6.49)$$

The constraint (6.47) for expected profit of the firm to be nonnegative is, in the example,

$$P(a) - C(s, a) = 1 + ka - \int s(\omega) f(\omega | a) d\omega \geqslant 0 \qquad (6.47')$$

The salary schedule $s = (e + b\omega)^2$ is so chosen as to maximize expected utility

$$\max_{s} \Phi(s, a, R_t) = \int \sqrt{s(\omega)} f(\omega | a) d\omega \qquad (6.45')$$

Equation (6.47′) as an equality can be solved for the parameter $e$, yielding (see problem 10)

$$e = -b(1+ka) + \sqrt{P(a) - [b(1+ka)]^2} \tag{6.50}$$

The parameter $b$ can be obtained by maximizing (6.45′) with respect to $b$. However, the authors treat (6.49) as a function for $b = \gamma n a^{n-1}/k$. Substituting this function for $b$ in (6.45′) gives the expected utility as a function $\varphi(a)$ of $a$. In other words, write the salary schedule in the example as $s = s^*(\omega, a) = [e(a) + b(a)\omega]^2$, in which

$$b(a) = \gamma n a^{n-1}/k; \quad e(a) = \frac{-b(a)}{\mu(a)} + \sqrt{P(a)\left[\frac{b(a)}{\mu(a)}\right]^2} \tag{6.51}$$

Using the contract $s^*$, the value of the objective function (6.45′) is

$$\varphi(a) = \Phi(s^*, a, R_t) = \int U\left(R_t\left(s_t^*(\omega_t)\right), a_t\right) f(\omega|a)\, d\omega$$
$$= \int \left(\sqrt{s^*(\omega)} - \mu a^n\right) f(\omega|a)\, d\omega = \sqrt{P(a)}\sqrt{1 - b(a)^2 P(a)} - \mu a^n \tag{6.52}$$

See problem 11. Given the parameter values $k = 4$, $\mu = \frac{1}{2}$, and $n = \frac{3}{2}$, the function $\varphi(a)$ has a maximum $\varphi(a^*) = 1.56727$ at $a^* = 0.774169$.

I have just shown that the government's minimum wage policy and redistribution function $R_t(s)$ (which happens to be $R_t(s) = s$ in the example) will affect the salary $s$ and the employment level $a$ in the economy. The government is assumed to have a social welfare function identical with the worker's expected utility function $\Phi(s, a, R)$. In the repeated game, the government chooses $\underline{s}_t$ and $R_t$ in each period $t$, while the public chooses $s_t$ and $a_t$. Public history up to period $t$ is denoted by $h^t = (h_0, \ldots, h_t)$, with each $h_\tau$ specifying $\underline{s}_\tau$, $R_\tau$, $s_\tau(\omega, a)$, and $a_\tau$. A symmetric strategy profile $\sigma$ specifies, for each $t$ and history $h^{t-1}$, $\underline{s}_t$, $s_t$, $a_t$, and $R_t$. A symmetric strategy profile generates a unique path $\{(\underline{s}_t, s_t, a_t, R_t)\}_{t\geq 0}$ and hence also a value to the government

$$\Psi(\sigma) = (1-\delta)\sum_{t=0}^{\infty} \delta^t \Phi(s_t, a_t, R_t) \tag{6.53}$$

A symmetric strategy profile $\sigma$ is an *equilibrium* of the dynamic economy if, after any history $h^{t-1}$, with $H_t = (\underline{s}_t, s_t, a_t, R_t)$ denoting the symmetric behavior prescribed by $\sigma$ following $h^{t-1}$, the following three conditions hold:

(1) $(s_t, a_t)$ solves the principle-agent problem specified by equations (6.45)–(6.48).

(2) For any possible deviation $\hat{\underline{s}}_t \neq \underline{s}_t$ of the government's minimum wage policy, let $\hat{H}(\hat{\underline{s}}_t, \hat{s}_t, \hat{a}_t, \hat{R}_t)$ be the symmetric behavior prescribed by $\sigma$ after $h^{t-1}$ and the deviation $\hat{\underline{s}}_t$, $\hat{h}_t = (\hat{\underline{s}}_t, \hat{s}_t, \hat{R}_{,t})$, and $\hat{h}^t = (h^{t-1}, \hat{h}_t)$. Then,

$$\Psi(\sigma|h^{t-1}) \geqslant (1-\delta)\Phi(\hat{s}_t, \hat{a}_t, \hat{R}_t) + \delta\Psi(\sigma|\hat{h}^t) \qquad (6.54)$$

that is, deviation does not pay, because the equilibrium expected sum of discounted utilities $\psi(\sigma|h^{t-1})$ from period $t$ onward is equal to or larger than the amount resulting from a deviation in period $t$, the latter yielding the sum of the two terms on the right-hand side of equation (6.54).

(3) let $h_t = (\underline{s}_t, s_t, R_t)$, $h^t = (h^{t-1}, h_t)$, and the possible deviation from the described redistribution function $R_t$ be $R \neq R_t$, with $\bar{h}_t = (\underline{s}_t, s_t, R)$ and $h^{-t} = (h^{t-1}, \bar{h}_t)$. Then

$$(1-\delta)\Phi(s_t, a_t, R_t) + \delta\Psi(\sigma|h^t) \geqslant (1-\delta)\Phi(s_t, a_t, R) + \delta\Psi(\sigma|h^{-t})$$
$$\text{all } R \neq R_t \qquad (6.55)$$

That is, changing the tax function from $R_t$ to and R gives an identical or smaller expected sum of discounted utilities given on the right-hand side of (6.55).

We are interested in studying what redistribution functions $R_t$ are equilibrium functions. As suggested by Abreu (1988), we can do this by checking whether there exists a "severest credible punishment" to make any deviation R from $R_t$ unattractive according to condition (6.55). It can be shown that there exists a severest punishment for a government deviation R, in which firms and workers always expect the government to flatten salaries completely, which leads to workers choosing $a = 0$. This path is called the "no trust equilibrium." It is an equilibrium because firms and workers that anticipate a completely egalitarian redistribution of incomes will choose $a = 0$ as the rational response. The government has no reason to change from the egalitarian redistribution because it has lost its reputation. In this equilibrium, the government has a payoff $U(P(0), 0)$. It is the worst payoff because, for any action $a$ taken under any profile, the government can flatten the distribution and obtain a payoff $U(P(a), a)$, and $U(P(a), a) \geqslant U(P(0), 0)$ by an assumption about the utility function. To investigate a possible equilibrium, consider the no trust equilibrium as the only punishment regime.

Consider first the equilibrium under a government policy of nonintervention, that is, when $\underline{s} = 0$ and $R_t = I$, the identity function. The solution of the principal-agent problem by the worker and the firm has an optimum value, for any action $a$ of the agent that maximizes expected utility under constraint (6.46) and gives the firm zero expected profit under constraint (6.47). The optimum value is

$$\varphi(a) = \max_s \Phi(s, a, I)$$
$$\text{s.t.} \quad \Phi(s, a, I) \geqslant \phi(s, \alpha, I) \qquad \text{all } \alpha \in A \text{ (set of possible actions)}$$
$$c(s, a) = P(a)$$
$$s(\omega) \geqslant 0 \qquad \text{all } \omega \in \Omega \text{ (set of possible outputs)}$$

Let $s^*(\omega, a)$, $\omega \in \Omega$, be the optimal salary schedule that implements action $a$, and $a^* > 0$ be the value of $a$ that maximizes $\varphi(a)$. This solution will be called the second-best solution; it provides the best solution under government nonintervention. Whether the government can credibly enforce this solution by setting R = I depends on the discount factor $\delta$. If $\delta$ is small, the future does not count and the government can be tempted to deviate in any period $t$, so that the $t$-period gain outweighs future loss, making it profitable to deviate from $(s^*, a^*)$ in spite of the punishment with $a = 0$. This happens if

$$\varphi(a^*) < (1-\delta)U(P(a^*), a^*) + \delta\varphi(0) \tag{6.56}$$

which can occur for small $\delta$, say for $\delta < \underline{\delta}$ for some $\underline{\delta}$.

If the government intervenes by setting $R_t \neq I$, what are the effects on $a$, $s$, and consumption? Let $\sigma(\underline{s}, s, a, R)$ be the stationary symmetric profile in which $(\underline{s}, s, a, R)$ occur on the equilibrium path and any deviation triggers the no trust equilibrium. If the nonintervention policy cannot be sustained, that is, if $\delta < \underline{\delta}$, consider a profile of the form $\sigma(\underline{s}, s, \bar{a}, R)$, in which $\bar{a}$ solves the problem

$$\max \varphi(a) \quad s.t. \quad \varphi(a) \geq (1-\delta)U(P(a), a) + \delta\varphi(0). \tag{6.55}$$

Hence, $\bar{a}$ is the best action that does not violate the equilibrium condition stated in (6.54). For a reasonable specification, as it is shown below, the action $\bar{a}$ can be supported along the equilibrium path with a stationary strategy $\sigma(\bar{\underline{s}}, \bar{s}, \bar{a}, \bar{R})$. Here $\bar{R}$ is *linear* and $\bar{s}$ makes consumption $\bar{R}(\bar{s}(\omega))$ equal to wage $s^*(\omega, \bar{a})$ for all $\omega \in \Omega$.

A *linear* redistribution function with slope $m$ is defined as

$$L(s, a; m) = ms + (1-m)P(a) \qquad \text{for } s \geq \underline{s}_m = -\left(\frac{1-m}{m}\right)P(a) \tag{6.56}$$

which reduces to the identity function when $m = 1$. When the worker's effort $a$ contributes $P(a)$ to the firm's expected profit, he or she receives a post-tax salary equal to $(1 - m)P(a)$ plus $m$ times the pre-tax salary $s$. Consider the government's best choice of a linear redistribution function L. Impose the condition that the government must break even when the workers choose action $a$ and for any contract $s$ with expected cost $P(a)$, implying

$$\int L(s(\omega), a, m) f(\omega|a) d\omega = P(a) = C(s, a) = \int s(\omega) f(\omega|a) d\omega$$

Given $a$, the linear redistribution function $L(s, a, m)$ is written as $L_m(s)$. Let $K(\alpha, a, m)$ be the minimal cost for the firm to implement action $\alpha$ and to deliver an expected utility of at least $\varphi(a)$ when the government redistribution function is $L_m$. Then

$$K(\alpha, a, m) = \int s(\omega) f(\omega|a) d\omega$$

$$s.t. \quad \Phi(s, \alpha, L_m) \geq \varphi(a)$$

$$\Phi(s, \alpha, L_m) \geq \Phi(s, \beta, L_m) \text{ for all } \beta \in A$$

$$s(\omega) \geq \underline{s}_m \text{ for all } \omega \in \Omega$$

LEMMA 1:

(i) *If $s_1$ is the optimal solution of the above problem when $m = 1$, the optimal solution $s_m(\omega)$ for any other slope $m > 0$ satisfies*

$$ms_m(\omega) + (1 - m)P(a) = s_1(\omega), \text{and}$$
$$mK(\alpha, a, m) + (1 - m)P(a) = K(\alpha, a, 1)$$

(ii) *When $\alpha = a$, $s_1(\omega) = s^*(\omega, a)$ for all $\omega \in \Omega$, and $K(a, a, 1) = P(a)$.*
(iii) *$K(a, a, m) = P(a)$ for all $m > 0$.*

PROOF: The feasible contracts in the problem defining K($\alpha$, $a$, 1) are unique linear functions of those in the problem defining K($\alpha$, $a$, $m$). $s$ is feasible for the former if and only if $\tilde{s}$, which satisfies $m\tilde{s}(\omega) + (1 - m)\text{P}(a) = s(\omega)$, is feasible for the latter. The costs of feasible contracts for the problem defining K($\alpha$, $a$, $m$) are linear transformations of the costs of feasible contracts for the problem defining K($\alpha$, $a$, 1). The optimal contract for K($\alpha$, $a$, $m$) is obtained by the linear transformation from the optimal contract for K($\alpha$, $a$, 1). This proves (i). When $\alpha = a$ and $m = 1$, i.e., when R = I, $s^*(\cdot, a)$ is feasible and from the definition of $\varphi(a)$, it must also be optimal. Substituting (ii) in the second formula of (i), one obtains (iii).

By Lemma 1, for a firm wishing to implement action $a$, a linear redistribution scheme does not affect how $a$ is implemented, and the worker's consumption schedule will be unchanged, but the firm may change the action that it wishes to implement. Under the assumptions that P is concave and K($\alpha$, $a$, 1) is convex and increasing in $\alpha$ for any budget implementable $a \in$ A, the government can choose a linear redistribution scheme to induce the firm to implement action $\bar{a}$, $\bar{a}$ being the action that maximizes $\varphi(a)$ and satisfies the trust constraint for the government given by (6.57). I omit the proof of this statement and of the following theorem.

THEOREM 1:

*Let a be a budget implementable action, and* $m = \mu(a) = \dfrac{1}{P'(a)}\dfrac{\partial K}{\partial \alpha}$ *(a, a, 1). If the government imposes the linear redistribution function $R = L(\cdot, a, m)$ and $\underline{s} = -(1 - m)P(a)/m$, the optimal choice for the firm is to implement action* a *with a wage schedule* s($\omega$) *satisfying $ms(\omega) + (1 - m)P(a) = s^*(\omega, a)$, and the resulting consumption schedule for the worker is $c(\omega) = R(s(\omega)) = s^*(\omega, a)$, with expected utility $\varphi(a)$, $\sigma(\underline{s}, s, a, R)$ is an equilibrium with discounted average payoff $\varphi(a)$ for the government, with action* a *implemented optimally in every period along the optimal path. $\sigma(\bar{\underline{s}}, \bar{s}, \bar{a}, \bar{R})$ is an optimal equilibrium with value $\varphi(\bar{a})$, in which $m = \mu(\bar{a})$, $m\bar{\underline{s}} + (1 - m)P(\bar{a}) = 0$, $m\bar{s}(\omega) + (1 - m)P(\bar{a}) =$ s$^*(\omega, \bar{a})$, and $\bar{R} = L(\cdot, \bar{a}, m)$.*

The outcome of the optimal equilibrium yields a payoff $\varphi(\bar{a})$ smaller than $\varphi(a^*)$, which is obtained if the government cannot intervene. $\varphi(a^*)$ is the best attainable expected utility when the government refrains from a redistribution of income. The government refrains because if it were to break its promise, a "punishment regime" would follow leading to a "no trust equilibrium." A question arises as to whether this "no trust equilibrium" is necessarily severe and, accordingly, may not actually be carried out following a deviation by the government. To answer this question, one seeks a set of equilibria that are renegotiation-proof in the following sense. Let an equilibrium $\sigma$ stipulate that, if the government deviates, the continuation equilibrium or credible punishment has value $x$. $\sigma$ is said to be vulnerable to renegotiation if there is another equilibrium $\gamma$ that has continuation values at least $y$ for some $y > x$. When $\sigma$ is vulnerable to renegotiation, its punishment value $x$ is unnecessarily severe, because there is another social arrangement $\gamma$ which the government can propose that never requires a punishment as severe as $x$. For a discussion of this topic as applied to income redistribution, the reader is referred to Pearce and Stacchetti (1996).

## Problems

1. Construct a numerical example of the dynamic oligopoly model of section 6.1. Solve this model assuming myopic behavior. Solve this model assuming forward-looking behavior. Comment on the differences between the solutions.
2. In a one-period oligopoly model discussed in a standard intermediate-level college economics textbook, how is a Cournot equilibrium defined? How does it compare with a Nash equilibrium?
3. Define and provide an economic example of (a) a Nash equilibrium, (b) a Stackleberg equilibrium, and (c) a cooperative equilibrium.
4. Write a college-level exposition to explain the concepts of (a) subgame-perfect equilibrium, (b) time-consistency, and (c) a credible government policy. Provide an economic example of each.
5. Explain why checking a one-period deviation is sufficient to test whether a solution of a dynamic game is a subgame-perfect equilibrium.
6. How is a test for a subgame perfect equilibrium different for a repeated game and for a dynamic game with a model for the evolution of the state variables?
7. In the discussion of Abreu (1988) presented in section 6.3, a subgame perfect equilibrium is established when there is some punishment path (set of moves) by all other players that could penalize severely any player for deviating from the equilibrium. Does the existence of such a punishment path (which might be very complicated to figure out in Ph.D. examinations) imply that it will actually be carried out if a player deviate? Does the

existence imply that a potential deviant will actually know such a path and believe that it would actually be carried out if he or she were to deviate? If the answer to either question is no, how does it affect the applicability of the solution to real-life economic problems?

8. Construct another numerical example similar to the example discussed in (a) Table 6.1 and (b) Table 6.2. Give an economic interpretation of each example.
9. Show that (6.49) is the supply function of effort $a$ by the worker who tries to maximize expected utility $E[U(\underline{s}, a)]$ given the salary schedule $s(\omega) = (e + b\omega)^2$, the utility function $\sqrt{s} - \mu a^n$, and the density function $(1 + ka)^{-1} \exp\{-\omega/(1 + ka)\}$ for output $\omega$ from effort $a$.
10. Show that the parameter $e$ in the wage schedule $s = (e + b\omega)^2$ is given by (6.50) to satisfy the zero profit constraint (6.47′), in which $f(\omega|a)$ is given by (6.42).
11. Show the last equation of (6.52).
12. In this chapter, I have discussed dynamic games with perfect information by assuming that all players know the entire history up to time $t$ when they make their decision at time $t$. Explain why the theory would be more complicated if each player cannot observe parts of history, including the actions of other players. For example, which parts of the model of section 6.1 and its solution would have to be changed?
13. Find a reference on a duopoly game with imperfect information and write an elementary introduction to its solution.

# Models in Finance

## 7.1 Stochastic Differential Equations

Most models in finance are formulated in continuous time using stochastic differential equations rather than stochastic difference equations, following the work of Merton (1969). Instead of equation (2.13) of Chapter 2, the dynamic evolution of the vector of state variables is described by a stochastic differential equation written as follows

$$dx = f(x, u)dt + S(x, u)dz, \tag{7.1}$$

in which $x(t)$ is a $p \times 1$ vector of state variables (the argument $t$ being suppressed when understood), $u(t)$ is a $q \times 1$ vector of control variables, $dx(t) = x(t + dt) - x(t)$ with $dt$ denoting a small time interval, S is a $p \times n$ matrix, and $z(t)$ is an $n \times 1$ vector *Wiener process.*

A *Wiener process* $z(t)$ has the property that a change from $t$ to $t + dt$, $dz(t) = z(t + dt) - z(t)$ is normally distributed with zero mean, independent of all past history up to $z(t)$ and has a covariance matrix proportional to $dt$. One can write the covariance matrix $\text{cov}(dz)$ of $dz(t)$ as $\Phi dt$. The assumption that, for $t > s$, the covariance matrix of $z(t) - z(s)$ is proportional to $t - s$ is implied by the assumption that at each small step going from time $s$ to time $t$, for example, $s + dt, s + 2dt, \ldots, s + ndt = t$ (the interval $t - s$ being divided into $n$ equal parts, each with length $dt$), the change in $z$ is statistically independent of the change at any other step. Given the independence assumption, the variance of $z(t) - z(s)$ is the sum $\Sigma_{k=1}^{n} \text{var}[z(s + kdt) - z(s + (k - 1)dt]$ of the variances of the changes $z(s + kdt) - z(s + (k - 1)dt)$, $k = 1, \ldots, n$. Doubling the time from $s$ to $t$ will double the variance of $z(t) - z(s)$. In this sense, think of the residual $dz$ of equation (7.1) as being serially independent. It I let $\Phi = I$, the identity matrix, $z(t)$ is said to follow a standard Wiener process. The matrix $S(x, u)$ in (7.1) makes the covariance matrix of $Sdz$, or $S\Phi S'\, dt \equiv \Sigma dt$, dependent on both the vector state variable $x$ and the vector control variable $u$.

Given that the vector $x$ of state variables follows the stochastic differential equation (7.1), let $F(x, t)$ be a function of $x$ and $t$, which is assumed to be continuously differentiable in $t$ and twice continuously differentiable in $x$. To derive a stochastic differential equation for F, expand the function F in a Taylor series with $h = dt$,

$$\begin{aligned} dF &= F\big(x(t+h),\, t+h\big) - F\big(x(t),\, t\big) \\ &= \frac{\partial F}{\partial t} dt + \left(\frac{\partial F}{\partial x}\right)' dx + \frac{1}{2}(dx)' \frac{\partial^2 F}{\partial x \partial x'} dx + o(dt) \end{aligned} \tag{7.2}$$

in which $o(dt)$ denotes terms of order smaller than $dt$. Denoting the matrix of second partial derivatives of F with respect to $x$ by $F_{xx}$, using (7.1) for $dx$, and noting that $Sdz \equiv dv$ is of order $\sqrt{dt}$, because $\text{var}(dv)$ is of order $dt$, one has

$$\begin{aligned} (dx)'F_{xx}dx &= (dv)'F_{xx}dv + o(dt) \\ &= tr\left(F_{xx}dvdv'\right) + o(dt) \end{aligned} \tag{7.3}$$

Substituting (7.1) and (7.3) into (7.2) gives

$$dF = \left[\frac{\partial F}{\partial t} + \left(\frac{\partial F}{\partial x}\right)' f\right]dt + \frac{1}{2}tr\left(F_{xx}dvdv'\right) + \left(\frac{\partial F}{\partial x}\right)' dv + o(dt) \tag{7.4}$$

implying, together with $Edvdv' = \Sigma dt$,

$$E(dF) = \left[\frac{\partial F}{\partial t} + \left(\frac{\partial F}{\partial x}\right)' f + \frac{1}{2}tr\left(F_{xx}\Sigma\right)\right]dt \tag{7.5}$$

and

$$\begin{aligned} \text{var}(dF) &= E\left[dF - E(dF)\right]^2 \\ &= E\left[\frac{1}{2}tr\left(F_{xx}dvdv'\right) - \frac{1}{2}tr\left(F_{xx}\Sigma\right)dt + \left(\frac{\partial F}{\partial x}\right)' dv + o(dt)\right]^2 \\ &= E\left[\left(\frac{\partial F}{\partial x}\right)' dv\right]^2 + o(dt) \\ &= \left(\frac{\partial F}{\partial x}\right)' \Sigma \left(\frac{\partial F}{\partial x}\right) dt + o(dt) \end{aligned} \tag{7.6}$$

Equations (7.5) and (7.6) provide a justification for *Ito's lemma* or *Ito's differentiation rule*,

$$dF = \left[\left(\frac{\partial F}{\partial t}\right) + \left(\frac{\partial F}{\partial x}\right)' f + \frac{1}{2}tr\left(F_{xx}\Sigma\right)\right]dt + \left(\frac{\partial F}{\partial x}\right)' dv \tag{7.7}$$

in which $F = F(x, t)$ and $dx$ is given by (7.1). In equation (7.1), $u$ can be viewed as a vector of parameters of the functions $f$ and $\Sigma$. It can be used as a vector of exogenous variables or control variables for the system of stochastic differential equations (7.1).

A concept related to Ito's differential $dF$ is the operation

$$\lim_{dt \to 0} \frac{1}{dt} E_t dF \equiv \mathscr{L}_x\left[F(x, t)\right] \tag{7.8}$$

in which $dF$ is defined by the first line of (7.2), and $E_t$ is the conditional expectation given $x(t)$. The result gives the expected rate of change through time of the function $F(x, t)$ as induced by the stochastic process $x$. The operation $\mathscr{L}_x$ so defined is the *differential generator* of the stochastic process $x(t)$. Formally, it can be obtained by taking the expectation of (7.7) and dividing the result by $dt$. This gives

$$\mathscr{L}_x[F] = \left\{\frac{\partial}{\partial t} + f'\frac{\partial}{\partial x} + \frac{1}{2}tr\left(\Sigma\frac{\partial^2}{\partial x \partial x'}\right)\right\}[F] \tag{7.9}$$

The stochastic differential (7.7) and the differential generator (7.9) can be applied to solve optimal control problems by the method of dynamic programming.

## 7.2 Dynamic Programming for a Continuous-Time Model

The problem is

$$\max_u E_t \int_t^\infty e^{-\beta(\tau - t)} r(x(\tau), u(\tau)) d\tau = V(x(t)) \tag{7.10}$$

subject to (7.1), in which $E_t$ is the conditional expectation operator given information at time $t$ that includes $x_t$.

By considering the problem of finding the optimal control $u(t)$ in a small time interval from $t$ to $t + dt$, one can write

$$\begin{aligned} V(x(t)) &= \max_u E_t\left[r(x(t), u(t))dt + e^{-\beta dt} V(x(t + dt))\right] \\ &= \max_u \left\{r(x(t), u(t))dt + E_t(1 - \beta dt)\left[V(x(t)) + dV(x(t))\right]\right\} \end{aligned} \tag{7.11}$$

implying

$$\beta V(x(t)) = \max_u \left\{r(x, u) + \frac{1}{dt} E_t dV(x(t))\right\} \tag{7.12}$$

in which $dV(x(t))$ is defined as $V(x(t + dt)) - V(x(t))$ and can be evaluated by Ito's lemma given the stochastic differential equation (7.1) for $dx$

$$dV(x) = \left[f'\frac{\partial V}{\partial x} + \frac{1}{2}tr\left(\frac{\partial^2 V}{\partial x \partial x'} \cdot \Sigma\right)\right]dt + \frac{\partial V}{\partial x'} S dz. \tag{7.13}$$

By using (7.13) to evaluate $E_t dV$ and substituting into (7.12), one obtains the Bellman equation

$$\beta V(x) = \max_{u}\left\{ r(x, u) + f'\frac{\partial V}{\partial x} + \frac{1}{2} tr\left(\frac{\partial^2 V}{\partial x \partial x'} \cdot \Sigma\right)\right\}. \tag{7.14}$$

A standard approach to solving this optimal control problem by using dynamic programming consists of two steps. First assume that the value function $V(x)$ is known, then find the optimum $u$ by solving the maximization problem of (7.14). For differentiable functions, one may use the first-order condition obtained by differentiation with respect to $u_i$.

$$\frac{\partial r}{\partial u_i} + \frac{\partial f'}{\partial u_i} \cdot \frac{\partial V}{\partial x} + \frac{1}{2} tr\left(\frac{\partial^2 V}{\partial x \partial x'} \cdot \frac{\partial \Sigma}{\partial u_i}\right) = 0. \quad i = 1, \ldots, q \tag{7.15}$$

Denote the solution to the $q$ equations by the vector $\hat{u}' = (\hat{u}_1, \ldots, \hat{u}_q)$. If there are side conditions $g(x, u) \leq 0$, they can be imposed at this stage by using the Kuhn-Tucker Theorem (see Section 4.2 on the Kuhn-Tucker Theorem). Second, given the solution $\hat{u}(x)$ from (7.15), solve for the value function $V(x)$ by using (7.14), namely, solve the following partial differential equation for $V(x)$:

$$\beta V(x) = r(x, \hat{u}(x)) + f'(x, \hat{u}(x))\frac{\partial V}{\partial x} + \frac{1}{2} tr\left[\frac{\partial^2 V}{\partial x \partial x'} \Sigma(x, \hat{u}(x))\right] \tag{7.16}$$

The approach suggested in this book does not seek the value function V(x) in obtaining $u(x)$. Denoting $\partial V/\partial x$ by the vector $\lambda(x)$, rewrite (7.15) as

$$\frac{\partial r}{\partial u_i} + \frac{\partial f'}{\partial u_i}\lambda + \frac{1}{2} tr\left(\frac{\partial \lambda}{\partial x'} \cdot \frac{\partial \Sigma}{\partial u_i}\right) = 0, \quad i = 1, \ldots, q \tag{7.17}$$

in which the trace term can also be written as $2tr[(\partial\lambda/\partial x')(\partial S/\partial u_i)\Phi S']$. First, obtain from (7.17) a solution $\hat{u}$, which can be considered as a function of $x$, $\lambda$ and the matrix $\partial\lambda/\partial x' = \partial\lambda'/\partial x$. Second, given $\hat{u}$ and assuming the existence of the third derivative of the value function, differentiate (7.16) with respect to $x_i$ to obtain

$$\beta\lambda_i = \frac{\partial}{\partial x_i} r(x, \hat{u}) + \left[\frac{\partial}{\partial x_i} f'(x, \hat{u})\right]\lambda + \frac{\partial \lambda'}{\partial x_i} f(x, \hat{u})$$
$$+ \frac{1}{2} tr\left[\frac{\partial}{\partial x_i}\left(\frac{\partial \lambda}{\partial x'}\right) \cdot \Sigma\right] + \frac{1}{2} tr\left[\frac{\partial \lambda}{\partial x'} \frac{\partial}{\partial x_i} \Sigma(x, \hat{u})\right] \quad i = 1, \ldots, p \tag{7.18}$$

It is suggested that equations (7.17) and (7.18) be used to obtain $\hat{u}$ without solving the partial differential equation (7.16) for the value function V.

### 7.3 Solution of a Continuous-Time Optimization Problem by Lagrange Multipliers

It is instructive to derive the first-order conditions (7.17) and (7.18) by the method of Lagrange multipliers without going through the method of dynamic programming. This derivation is important, because when we solve dynamic optimization problems in the future (in sections 7.4–7.9, 8.1–8.3 and 9.7, among others), we will be efficient in bypassing the value function and concentrating on only the first-order conditions (7.17) and (7.18). To do so, form a Lagrange expression based on the objective function (7.10) and the constraint of the stochastic differential equation (7.1) by using a p × 1 vector $\lambda(x)$ of Lagrange multipliers. Follow the method of section 2.3 for a model in discrete time, recognizing $dx(t) = x(t+dt) - x(t)$, and let $dt$ be a very small time interval. The Lagrange expression for the optimization problem of section 7.2 beginning from $t = 0$ is

$$\mathscr{L} = \int_0^\infty \mathrm{E}_t \Big\{ e^{-\beta t} r(x, u)dt - e^{-\beta(t+dt)} \lambda'(t+dt)\big[x(t+dt) - x(t) \\ - f(x, u)dt - \mathrm{S}(x, u)dz\big]\Big\}, \tag{7.19}$$

in which, following Ito, one defines a stochastic integral $\int_a^b g(t)dz(t)$ of a deterministic or stochastic function $g$ as the limit of the sum, with the interval $[a,b]$ divided into equally spaced intervals going from $t_1$ to $t_{n+1}$,

$$\int_a^b g(t)dz(t) = \lim_{n\to\infty} \sum_{j=1}^{n} g(t_j)\big[z(t_{j+1}) - z(t_j)\big]$$

The limit of a sequence of random variables $s_n$ is defined by convergence in mean square, namely,

$$\lim_{n\to\infty} s_n = s \Leftrightarrow \lim_{n\to\infty} \mathrm{E}\big[s_n - s\big]^2 = 0$$

In (7.19) the conditional expectation $\mathrm{E}_t$ is justified by the statement of the problem that when the control $u(t)$ is determined, the information at time $t$, including the value $x(t)$, is given, and, in (7.19) changing the order of integration and taking expectation is justified by Ito's definition of the stochastic integral $\int g dz$ for a stochastic function $g$. Setting to zero the derivatives of $\mathscr{L}$ with respect to $u(t)$ and $x(t)$ will yield a set of first-order conditions for the optimum if Ito's differentiation rule is applied to evaluate the vector $d\lambda$. The $i$th component of $d\lambda$ is

$$d\lambda_i = \left[\frac{\partial \lambda_i}{\partial x'} f + \frac{1}{2} tr\left(\frac{\partial^2 \lambda_i}{\partial x \partial x'} \cdot \Sigma\right)\right]dt + \frac{\partial \lambda_i}{\partial x'} \mathrm{S}(x, u)dz \qquad i = 1, \ldots, p \tag{7.20}$$

in which $\partial\lambda_i/\partial x'$ is a $1 \times p$ vector and $\partial^2\lambda_i/\partial x\partial x'$ is a $p \times p$ matrix. In equation (7.20), the function $\lambda$ is assumed to be in a steady state and therefore independent of $t$.

Differentiating (7.19) with respect to $u_i(t)$ yields

$$e^{\beta t}\frac{\partial \mathscr{L}}{\partial u_i} = \frac{\partial r}{\partial u_i} dt + e^{-\beta dt}\left[\frac{\partial f'}{\partial u_i} \mathrm{E}_t \lambda(t+dt)dt + \mathrm{E}_t dz' \frac{\partial \mathrm{S}'}{\partial u_i} \lambda(t+dt)\right]$$

$$= \frac{\partial r}{\partial u_i} dt + (1 - \beta dt)\left[\frac{\partial f'}{\partial u_i}(\lambda dt + \mathrm{E}_t d\lambda dt) + \mathrm{E}_t dz' \frac{\partial \mathrm{S}'}{\partial u_i}(\lambda + d\lambda)\right] + o(dt)$$

$$= \frac{\partial r}{\partial u_i} dt + \frac{\partial f'}{\partial u_i} \lambda dt + (1 - \beta dt) \mathrm{E}_t tr \left[ \frac{\partial \mathrm{S}'}{\partial u_i} \cdot d\lambda dz' \right] + o(dt)$$

$$= \frac{\partial r}{\partial u_i} dt + \frac{\partial f'}{\partial u_i} \lambda dt + tr \left[ \frac{\partial \mathrm{S}'}{\partial u_i} \frac{\partial \lambda}{\partial x'} \mathrm{S}\Phi \right] dt + o(dt) = 0, \quad i = 1, \ldots, q \quad (7.21)$$

in which I have noted that any product of $dt$, $d\lambda$, and $dz$ (being of order $\sqrt{dt}$) is of order smaller than $dt$ and $\mathrm{E}_t dz = 0$ and I have used the stochastic vector $(\partial\lambda/\partial x')\mathrm{S}dz$ for $d\lambda$ from (7.20), $\partial\lambda/\partial x'$ being a $p \times p$ matrix. Noting the term $e^{-\beta t} \lambda'(t)[x(t) \ldots]$ in the integrand of (7.19), one obtains

$$e^{\beta t} \frac{\partial \mathcal{L}}{\partial x_i} = \frac{\partial r}{\partial x_i} dt - \lambda_i + e^{-\beta dt} \left[ \mathrm{E}_t \lambda_i (t + dt) + \frac{\partial f'}{\partial x_i} \mathrm{E}_t \lambda(t + dt) dt + \mathrm{E}_t dz' \frac{\partial \mathrm{S}'}{\partial x_i} [\lambda(t + dt)] \right]$$

$$= \frac{\partial r}{\partial x_i} dt - \lambda_i + (1 - \beta dt) \left[ \lambda_i + \mathrm{E}_t d\lambda_i + \frac{\partial f'}{\partial x_i} \lambda dt + \mathrm{E}_t dz' \frac{\partial \mathrm{S}'}{\partial x_i} (\lambda + d\lambda) \right] + o(dt)$$

$$= \frac{\partial r}{\partial x_i} dt - \beta \lambda_i dt + \left[ \frac{\partial \lambda_i}{\partial x'} f + \frac{1}{2} tr \left( \frac{\partial^2 \lambda_i}{\partial x \partial x'} \cdot \Sigma \right) \right] dt + \frac{\partial f'}{\partial x_i} \lambda dt$$

$$+ tr \left[ \frac{\partial \mathrm{S}'}{\partial x_i} \frac{\partial \lambda}{\partial x'} \mathrm{S}\Phi \right] dt + o(dt) = 0, \quad i = 1, \ldots, p \quad (7.22)$$

Equations (7.21) and (7.22) are the conditions (7.17) and (7.18) for the optimum control $u$ and the Lagrange multiplier $\lambda$. To ensure that the solution of (7.21) and (7.22) achieves a maximum, one has to examine the second-order conditions for the method of Lagrange multipliers, which are discussed in section 2.5 for the analogous stochastic optimization problem in discrete time.

If the model is nonstochastic, S and $\Sigma = \mathrm{S}\Phi\mathrm{S}'$ are zero. All the trace terms in the last lines of (7.21) and (7.22) vanish. My solution reduces to the well-known solution of the corresponding nonstochastic optimal control problem in continuous time with the dynamics given by

$$dx = f(x, u) dt$$

In the above solution, assume $\lambda$ to be a function of $x$ only and not of $t$. If I relax this assumption, equation (7.20) for $d\lambda_i$ will have a term $\partial\lambda_i/\partial t$ inside the square brackets. The same term will appear inside the square brackets multiplying $dt$ after the last equality sign of (7.22), yielding the following partial differential equation for $\lambda$:

$$\frac{\partial \lambda}{\partial t} + \frac{\partial \lambda}{\partial x'} f + \frac{\partial f'}{\partial x} \lambda + \frac{\partial r}{\partial x} - \beta \lambda = 0 \quad (7.23)$$

Equation (7.23) and equation (7.21) with the trace terms omitted, or

$$\frac{\partial r}{\partial u} + \frac{\partial f'}{\partial u} \lambda = 0 \quad (7.24)$$

provide a pair of equations for $u$ and $\lambda$. These equations can be derived from the well-known Pontryagin's maximum principle for solving nonstochastic optimal control problems in continuous time.

To apply Pontryagin's maximum principle to this nonstochastic control problem, form the Hamiltonian

$$H = r(x, u) + e^{-\beta dt}\lambda' f(x, u) \tag{7.25}$$

and set

$$\frac{\partial H}{\partial u} = 0 \tag{7.26}$$

$$\frac{\partial(e^{-\beta dt}\lambda)}{\partial t} = -\frac{\partial H}{\partial x} \tag{7.27}$$

and

$$\frac{dx}{dt} = \frac{\partial H}{\partial(e^{-\beta dt}\lambda)} \tag{7.28}$$

Equations (7.26) and (7.27) are identical with the first-order conditions (7.24) and (7.23) respectively, and equation (7.28) gives the differential equation for the dynamics of the state variable. Note that I have written this differential equation as $dx = fdt$, rather than $dx/dt = f$ because, in the stochastic version of this problem, the derivative $dx/dt$ does not exist. $dx$ has a term $dz$, which is of order $(dt)^{1/2}$. Hence, $dz/dt$ is of order $(dt)^{-1/2}$, which approaches infinity as $dt$ approaches zero.

### 7.4 An Algebraic Method for Finding the Optimal Control Function

Using (7.17) and (7.18), the problem is to find an optimal control function $\hat{u}(x)$ and the associated $\lambda(x)$. I will find a linear approximation to $\hat{u}(x)$. To this end choose an appropriate (vector) value $x_*$ to perform the linearization. In empirical econometric research on policy analysis for a particular period, the (vector) sample mean $\bar{x}$ might be used. If the deterministic version of the optimal control problem reaches a steady state $(x_*, u_*)$ by solving equations (7.26), (7.27) and (7.28), the steady state value can be used. See section 9.8. Approximate the Lagrangean function by a linear function about $x_*$, namely,

$$\lambda(x) = Hx + h \tag{7.29}$$

with the understanding that the parameters H and $h$ depend on $x_*$, H being symmetric. Then use (7.17) and (7.18) to solve for these parameters, thus finding $u(x)$ and $\lambda(x)$.

To carry out the suggested strategy, linearize the vectors of required derivatives at $x_*$ and some initial value $u_*$ for $u$.

$$\frac{\partial r}{\partial x} = K_{11}x + K_{12}u + k_1, \quad \frac{\partial r}{\partial u} = K_{22}u + K_{21}x + k_2$$

$$\frac{1}{2}\frac{\partial tr(H\Sigma)}{\partial x} = d_1, \quad \frac{1}{2}\frac{\partial tr(H\Sigma)}{\partial u} = d_2 \tag{7.30}$$

and linearize the function f about $x_*$ and $u_*$,

$$f(x, u) = Ax + Cu + b \tag{7.31}$$

First, assuming H and $h$ to be known and using the above linear approximations, rewrite (7.17) as

$$K_{22}u + K_{21}x + k_2 + C'(Hx + h) + d_2 = 0$$

Solving this equation for $u$, one obtains

$$u(x) = Gx + g \tag{7.32}$$

in which

$$G = -K_{22}^{-1}(K_{21} + C'H) \tag{7.33}$$

$$g = -K_{22}^{-1}(k_2 + C'h + d_2) \tag{7.34}$$

Substitute these linear functions into (7.18) to yield

$$(\beta I - A')\lambda = (K_{11} + K_{12}G)x + K_{12}g + k_1 + H[(A + CG)x + Cg + b] + d_1$$

Given $\lambda = Hx + h$, the above equation implies

$$H = (\beta I - A')^{-1}[K_{11} + K_{12}G + H(A + CG)] \tag{7.35}$$

$$h = (\beta I - A')^{-1}[K_{12}g + k_1 + H(Cg + b) + d_1] \tag{7.36}$$

Starting with an initial guess for H, use (7.33) to obtain a new value for G and, employing this value for G, use (7.35) to obtain a new value for H in our iterations. Having solved (7.33) and (7.35) iteratively for G and H, we can solve (7.34) and (7.36) iteratively for g and h. The resulting $\hat{u} = Gx + g$ can be used to replace $u_*$ in the linearization of (7.30) and (7.31) until $\hat{u} = u_*$. If any $u_i$ is required to be nonnegative, the $i$th equation in (7.17) will be replaced by an inequality $<0$ for $u_i = 0$, with the equality holding for $u_i > 0$ as in standard treatment of the method of Lagrange multipliers with nonnegative decision variables (see Dixit, 1990, p. 28). In the case of $u_i = 0$, the derivative with respect to $u_i$ in the set of equations of (7.17) will be omitted.

For solving first-order conditions (7.17) and (7.18), a linear approximation for $\lambda$ may be inadequate. In the derivation of the first-order condition (7.22) for $\lambda$, the essential term $E_t\lambda(t + dt) = \lambda + E_t d\lambda$ involves $E_t d\lambda$. According to equation (7.20), $d\lambda$ requires a vector of second derivatives of $\lambda$ with its $i$th element equal to $tr[\partial^2\lambda/\partial x_i\partial x')\Sigma]$ or $tr[\partial^2\lambda_i/\partial x\partial x')\Sigma]$. Hence, to solve the first-order conditions (7.22) or (7.18) for $\lambda$, it would be prudent to approximate $\lambda$ by a quadratic function of $x$. In section 9.7, I present a numerical method for solving equations (7.17) and (7.18) by using a quadratic approximation for $\lambda$. Equation (7.18) is solved by equating the coefficients of a quadratic function on both sides as it is done for the coefficient H and $h$ of the linear approximation given by equations (7.35) and (7.36). The method is the same although the algebra is more tedious, and that discussion should be postponed. In reading the remainder of this chapter, the reader should bear in mind that numerical methods exist for solving the first-order conditions (7.17) and (7.18) derived from the method of Lagrange multipliers.

When the optimal control function $\hat{u}(x)$ can be computed, one can study the dynamics of the system under optimal control by substituting $\hat{u}(x)$ for $u$ in equation (7.1), yielding

$$dx = f\left(x,\ \hat{u}\left(x\right)dt\right) + S\left(x,\ \hat{u}\left(x\right)dw\right) \tag{7.37}$$

The dynamics of the costate variables $\lambda$ can be readily obtained by using equations (7.20) and (7.18).

To eliminate the second partials of $\lambda$ in (7.20), replace the sum of the two terms in square brackets by the four remaining terms of (7.18) to obtain

$$d\lambda_i = -\left\{\frac{\partial}{\partial x_i} r\left(x,\ \hat{u}\left(x\right)\right) + \frac{\partial}{\partial x_i} f'\left(x,\ \hat{u}\left(x\right)\right)\lambda \right.$$
$$\left. + \frac{1}{2} tr\left[\frac{\partial \lambda}{\partial x'} \frac{\partial}{\partial x_i} \Sigma\left(x,\ \hat{u}\left(x\right)\right)\right] - \beta\lambda_i \right\} dt + \frac{\partial \lambda_i}{\partial x'} S dz \quad \left(i = 1, \ldots, p\right) \tag{7.38}$$

In the literature, equations (7.18) and (7.38) are known. For example, a version of (7.18) can be found in Benveniste and Scheinkman (1979) and is referred to by Sargent (1987, p. 21). A discrete-time version of (7.18) can be found in Chow (1975, pp. 158 and 281). A version of (7.38) can be found in Malliaris and Brock (1982, p. 112). However, equation (7.18) has not been treated as an essential component in obtaining the optimal control function $\hat{u}(x)$. The standard procedure that uses dynamic programming has been to solve the partial differential equation (7.16) for the value function V($x$). This book suggests that $\hat{u}(x)$ can be obtained directly by exploiting only the first-order conditions (7.17) and (7.18), without having to solve for the value function. Those computations yield $\hat{u}(x)$, V($x$), the shadow price vector $\lambda(x)$, and the matrix of first partials of $\lambda$.

## 7.5 Optimum Consumption and Portfolio Selection Over Time

The problem of this section was studied by Merton (1969, 1971), and its discrete-time version by Samuelson (1969). At time $t$, the individual chooses his or her rate of consumption $c(t)$ per unit time during period $t$ (between $t$ and $t + dt$) and the number $N_i(t)$ of shares to be invested in asset $i$ during period $t$, given his initial wealth $W(t) = \Sigma_i^n N_i(t - dt)P_i(t)$, and the prices $P_i(t)$ per share of the assets. The problem is to maximize

$$E_0 \int_0^\infty e^{-\beta t} u(c) dt \tag{7.39}$$

To simplify exposition, assume that the prices follow a geometric Brownian motion

$$\frac{dP_i}{P_i} = \alpha_i dt + s_i dz_i \tag{7.40}$$

in which $z_i$ are components of a multivariate Wiener process, with $E(dz_i) = 0$, $var(dz_i) = 1$ and $E(dz_i dz_j) = \rho_{ij}$. If there is no wage income and all incomes are derived from capital gains (dividends being included in changes in asset prices), it can be shown that the change in wealth from $t$ to $t + dt$ satisfies the budget constraint

$$dW = \sum_1^n N_i(t) dP_i - c(t) dt \tag{7.41}$$

Let $w_i(t) = N_i(t)P_i(t)/W(t)$ be the fraction of wealth invested in asset $i$, with $\Sigma_i w_i = 1$. Substitute (7.13) for $dP_i$ in (7.14) to obtain

$$dW = \sum_1^n w_i W \alpha_i dt - cdt + \sum_1^n w_i W s_i dz_i \tag{7.42}$$

If one assumes that the $n$th asset is risk-free, that is, $s_n = 0$, and denotes the instantaneous rate of return $\alpha_n$ of this asset by $r$, one write (7.15) as, with $m = n - 1$,

$$dW = \sum_1^m w_i(\alpha_i - r) W dt + (rW - c) dt + \sum_1^m w_i W s_i dz_i \tag{7.43}$$

The state variable of this problem is W, which is governed by the stochastic differential equation (7.42). The control variables are c and $w = (w_1, \ldots, w_n)'$, with $\Sigma_1^n w_i = 1$. This model assumes that assets are traded continuously in time and that there are no transaction costs in trading.

The Lagrangean expression for this optimization problem is

$$\mathcal{L} = \int_o^\infty E_t \left\{ e^{-\beta t} u(c) dt - e^{-\beta(t+dt)} \lambda'(t+dt) \left[ dW - \left( W \sum_1^n w_i \alpha_i - c \right) dt \right. \right.$$

$$\left. \left. - W \sum_1^n w_i s_i dz_i \right] + e^{-\beta t} \mu \left[ 1 - \sum_1^n w_i \right] dt \right\} \tag{7.44}$$

Noting $f(x, u) = (W\Sigma_1^n w_i \alpha_i - c)$ in this case, with W as the state variable and c and $w' = (w_1, \ldots, w_n)$ as the control variables, one can write the first-order condition (7.17), in which the matrix S is now the row vector $W(w_1 s_1 \ldots w_n s_n)$ as

$$u'(c) - \lambda = 0 \tag{7.45}$$

$$\mathrm{W}\alpha_i\lambda + \mathrm{W}^2 tr\left\{\begin{bmatrix}0\\ \vdots\\ s_i\\ \vdots\\ 0\end{bmatrix}\lambda_w\begin{bmatrix}w_1 s_1 & \dots & w_n s_n\end{bmatrix}\begin{bmatrix}1 & \rho_{12} & \dots & \rho_{1n}\\ \rho_{21} & 1 & \dots & \rho_{2n}\\ & \dots & & \\ \rho_{n1} & \rho_{n2} & \dots & 1\end{bmatrix}\right\} - \mu$$

$$= \mathrm{W}\alpha_i\lambda + \mathrm{W}^2\lambda_w\sum_{j=1}^{n} w_j\sigma_{ij} - \mu = 0, \quad i = 1, \dots, n \tag{7.46}$$

in which I have denoted $\partial\lambda/\partial \mathrm{W}$ by $\lambda_w$ and $s_i s_j \rho_{ij}$ by $\sigma_{ij}$. The first-order condition (7.18) implies, with $\lambda_{ww}$ denoting $\partial^2\lambda/\partial \mathrm{W}^2$,

$$\beta\lambda = \left(\sum_1^n w_i\alpha_i\right)\lambda + \lambda_w\left(\mathrm{W}\sum_1^n w_i\alpha_i - c\right) + \frac{1}{2}\lambda_{ww}\cdot \mathrm{W}^2\sum_{ij} w_i w_j\sigma_{ij}$$
$$+ \lambda_w \mathrm{W}\sum_{ij} w_i w_j\sigma_{ij}. \tag{7.47}$$

Without solving for $\lambda$ using (7.47), one can define the inverse function $\mathrm{G} = [u'(c)]^{-1}$ and solve (7.45) for the optimal consumption function $\hat{c} = \mathrm{G}(\lambda)$. To obtain the optimal portfolio $w$, divide (7.46) by $\mathrm{W}^2\lambda_w$, denote $-\mu/(\mathrm{W}^2\lambda_w)$ by $\mu^*$, and write the resulting equations together with $\Sigma w_i = 1$ in matrix form as

$$\begin{bmatrix}\sigma_{11} & \sigma_{12} & \dots & \sigma_{1n} & 1\\ & & & & \vdots\\ \sigma_{n1} & \sigma_{n2} & \dots & \sigma_{nn} & 1\\ 1 & 1 & \dots & 1 & 0\end{bmatrix}\begin{bmatrix}w_1\\ w_2\\ \vdots\\ w_n\\ \mu^*\end{bmatrix} = -\frac{\lambda}{\mathrm{W}\lambda_w}\begin{bmatrix}\alpha_1\\ \alpha_2\\ \vdots\\ \alpha_n\\ 1\end{bmatrix} \tag{7.48}$$

Partitioning the coefficient matrix of (7.48) into four blocks and finding the partitioned inverse, one obtains the first $n$ rows of the inverse as

$$\left(\sigma^{ij}\right) - \gamma^{-1}\begin{bmatrix}\left(\Sigma\sigma^{1j}\right)\left(\Sigma\sigma^{1j}\right) & \left(\Sigma\sigma^{1j}\right)\left(\Sigma\sigma^{2j}\right) \dots \left(\Sigma\sigma^{1j}\right)\left(\Sigma\sigma^{nj}\right)\\ & \dots \\ \left(\Sigma\sigma^{1j}\right)\left(\Sigma\sigma^{nj}\right) & \left(\Sigma\sigma^{2j}\right)\left(\Sigma\sigma^{nj}\right) \dots \left(\Sigma\sigma^{nj}\right)\left(\Sigma\sigma^{nj}\right)\end{bmatrix}, \quad \gamma^{-1}\begin{bmatrix}\Sigma\sigma^{1j}\\ \vdots\\ \Sigma\sigma^{nj}\end{bmatrix} \tag{7.49}$$

in which $(\sigma^{ij})$ denotes the matrix inverse $(\sigma_{ij})^{-1}$ and $\gamma = \Sigma_i\Sigma_j\sigma^{ij}$. Premultiplying (7.48) by (7.49), one obtains the well-known optimal portfolio rules of Merton (1969, 1971):

$$\hat{w}_k = \sum_l\left[\sigma^{kl} - \gamma^{-1}\left(\sum_j\sigma^{kj}\right)\left(\sum_i\sigma^{li}\right)\right]\frac{-\lambda}{\mathrm{W}\lambda_w}\alpha_l + \gamma^{-1}\sum_j\sigma^{kj}$$
$$= \gamma^{-1}\sum_j\sigma^{kj} - \frac{\lambda}{\mathrm{W}\lambda_w}\left[\sum_l\sigma^{kl}\alpha_l - \gamma^{-1}\sum_j\sigma^{kj}\sum_l\sum_i\sigma^{li}\alpha_l\right]$$
$$= h_k + m(\mathrm{W}, t)\cdot g_k, \quad k = 1, \dots, n, \tag{7.50}$$

in which I have defined

$$h_k = \gamma^{-1} \sum_j \sigma^{kj} \tag{7.51}$$

$$m(\mathrm{W}, t) = \frac{-\lambda}{\mathrm{W}\lambda_w} \tag{7.52}$$

$$g_k = \sum_j \sigma^{kj} \left[ \alpha_j - \gamma^{-1} \sum_l \sum_i \sigma^{li} \alpha_l \right], \tag{7.53}$$

implying $\Sigma_1^n h_k = 1$ and $\Sigma_1^n g_k = 0$.

The first component $h_k$ of the optimal fraction $\hat{w}_k$ invested in asset $k$ is proportional to the elements $\sigma^{kj}$ in the $k$th row of the inverse of the covariance matrix of the relative rates of returns $d\mathrm{P}/\mathrm{P}_j$ stipulated by (7.40). The factor $g_k$ in the second component of $\hat{w}_k$ is a weighted average, using $\sigma^{kj}$ as weights, of the difference between the expected rate of return $\alpha_j$ for asset $j$ and the average expected rate of return $\gamma^{-1}\Sigma_l\Sigma_i\sigma^{li}\alpha_l$ for all assets. If the covariances $\sigma_{ij}$ were zero for $i \neq j$, $g_k$ would become $\sigma_{kk}^{-1}[\alpha_k - \gamma^{-1}\Sigma_l\sigma_{ll}^{-1}\alpha_l]$, thus, measuring the expected rate of return $\alpha_k$ for asset $k$ as compared with the average expected rate $\gamma^{-1}\Sigma_l\sigma_{ll}^{-1}\alpha_l$ for all assets. The first component $h_k$ recommends investment proportional to the inverses of the variances and covariances. Because $\lambda > 0$ $\lambda_w < 0$ for optimum $\lambda$, $m(\mathrm{W}, t) > 0$ by (7.52). The second component $m(\mathrm{W}, t)g_k$ recommends investment in asset $k$ proportional to the expected rate of return $\alpha_k$ for $k$ (and to the expected rates $\alpha_j$ for other assets correlated with it), as compared with the average expected rate for all assets. The factors $h_k$ and $g_k$ are determined entirely by the means, variances, and covariances of the relative rates of returns of the assets, and not by the utility function, the amount of wealth, and the time horizon. $m(\mathrm{W}, t)$ certainly depends on the wealth and the utility function of individual $i$ who makes the decision.

Because an individual's relative demand $\hat{w}_k$ for the $k$th asset has only one parameter $m(\mathrm{W}, t)$, which is affected by his or her wealth and utility function, the demand can be satisfied by selection from shares of only two "mutual funds," the first holding a fraction $\delta_k$ of its value in asset $k$ and the second a fraction $\lambda_k$, with

$$\begin{aligned} \delta_k &= h_k + (a - b)g_k \\ & \qquad\qquad\qquad k = 1, \ldots, n, \\ \lambda_k &= h_k - bg_k, \end{aligned} \tag{7.54}$$

in which $a$ and $b$ are arbitrary constants. Any value of $m(\mathrm{W}, t)$ for an individual can always be met by a suitable linear combination of $\delta_k$ and $\lambda_k$, i.e., by

$$\begin{aligned} m &= \theta(a - b) + (1 - \theta)(-b) \\ &= \theta a - b, \end{aligned}$$

or by investing a fraction $\theta = (m + b)/a$ in the first fund and the remainder $(1 - \theta)$ in the second fund. This is known as a mutual fund theorem.

If the $n$th asset is riskless, $s_n = 0$, $\alpha_n = r$, and equation (7.43) replaces (7.42). One needs only to solve for $m = n - 1$ optimal control equations for $\hat{w}_k$, $k = 1, \ldots, m$, with $\hat{w}_n = 1 - \Sigma_1^m \hat{w}_k$. The Lagrangean multiplier $\mu$ in (7.46) disappears. In these derivations, $m$ replaces $n$, $(\alpha_i - r)$ replaces $\hat{\alpha}_i$, and (7.48) becomes

$$\begin{bmatrix} \sigma_{11} & \sigma_{12} & \cdots & \sigma_{1m} \\ \vdots & \vdots & & \vdots \\ \sigma_{m1} & \sigma_{m2} & \cdots & \sigma_{mm} \end{bmatrix} \begin{bmatrix} w_1 \\ w_2 \\ \vdots \\ w_m \end{bmatrix} = \frac{-\lambda}{W\lambda_w} \begin{bmatrix} \alpha_1 - r \\ \alpha_2 - r \\ \vdots \\ \alpha_m - r \end{bmatrix} \tag{7.55}$$

the solution of which is

$$\hat{w}_k = m(W, t) g_k, \quad k = 1, \ldots, m, \tag{7.56}$$

in which

$$g_k = \sum_{j=1}^{m} \sigma^{kj} [\alpha_j - r], \quad k = 1, \ldots, m \tag{7.57}$$

To satisfy the demands $\hat{w}_k$ for any individual, there need be only two mutual funds, the first holding a fraction $\delta_k = (a - b) g_k$ of its value in asset $k$ ($k = 1, \ldots, m$), and the second holding a fraction $\lambda_k = -b g_k$. To achieve any $m(W, t) g_k$ desired, the individual again invests a fraction $\theta = (m + b)/a$ of his or her wealth in the first fund. Let $b = 0$, so that the second fund holds only the riskless assets $n$ and no risky assets. Thus, only one mutual fund that holds the risky assets by proportions $a g_k$, with $\Sigma_{k=1}^m a g_k = 1$, and a second fund that holds only the riskless asset will satisfy the demand of any individual.

Let the $n$th asset be money, with $r = 0$. The relative holdings of the risky fund are, by (7.57)

$$\delta_k = a g_k = a \sum_{j=1}^{m} \sigma^{kj} \alpha_j, \quad k = 1, \ldots, m, \tag{7.58}$$

in which, to ensure $\Sigma_{k=1}^m a g_k = 1$, $a = (\Sigma_k \Sigma_j \sigma^{kj} \alpha_j)^{-1}$. The holdings (7.58) are in agreement with the traditional Tobin-Markowitz mean-variance analysis. One finds the portfolio $\delta = (\delta_1, \ldots, \delta_m)'$ for the fund that minimizes the variance $\sigma^2 = \delta' \Sigma \delta$ of the rate of return for a given mean rate of return $m = \delta' \alpha$, with $\alpha = (\alpha_1, \ldots, \alpha_m)'$, yielding a function $\sigma(m)$. In the $(m, \sigma)$ diagram, if one draws a line going through the origin and tangential to the curve $\sigma(m)$, one will find the portfolio $\delta$ given by (7.58).

The above mutual fund theorem and generalization of the mean-variance portfolio analysis were obtained without using a specific form for the utility function and without deriving the function $\lambda$ explicitly. The reader is referred to Merton (1969) and (1971) for explicit solutions of the value function V and for further discussions of the economics of this problem, and to Rosenberg and Ohlson (1976) for a critique of the assumption that the rates of return are stationary and serially independent.

## 7.6 Capital Asset Pricing with Shifts in Investment Opportunities

One variation of the model of section 7.5 suggested by Merton (1973) is to introduce a new vector $x = (x_1, \ldots, x_N)$ of N state variables to the model. The shocks $dq_i$ to these state variables may be correlated with the shocks $dz_j$ to the prices $P_j$ of the assets given by equation (7.40). These variables may include the parameters $\alpha_i$ in equation (7.40), which will themselves be assumed to satisfy the stochastic differential equation.

$$d\alpha_i = a_i dt + b_i dq_i, \tag{7.59}$$

in which $dq_i$ are Wiener processes with unit variance. Write the stochastic differential equations for the elements of this new vector as

$$dx_i = f_i(x)dt + g_i^*(x)dq_i. \quad i = 1, \ldots, N \tag{7.60}$$

Let $E(dq_i dz_j) = \eta_{ij}$ and $E(dq_i dq_j) = v_{ij}$, $dz_j$, being defined for (7.40), with $E(dz_i dz_j) = \rho_{ji}$. Further, let the $n$th asset be "instantaneously riskless" in the sense of $s_n = 0$ and $\alpha_n = r(t)$ in (7.40), but $b_n \neq 0$ in (7.59) for $d\alpha_n = dr$.

Assume that each individual maximizes utility over time as in section 7.5. The present variation with state variable s(W, $x$) requires the following constraints in the Lagrange expression (7.44),

$$-e^{-\beta(t+dt)}\lambda_0(t+dt)\left[dW - \left(W\sum_1^n w_i\alpha_i - c\right)dt - W\sum_1^n w_i s_i dz_i\right]$$

$$-e^{-\beta(t+dt)}\sum_{i=1}^N \lambda_i(t+dt)\left[dx_i - f_i(x)dt - g_i^*(x)dq_i\right] \tag{7.61}$$

Then, in the case of the $n$th asset being riskless, that is, $s_n = 0$ and $\alpha_n = r$, the first-order condition (7.46) becomes, with $m$ denoting $n - 1$ and $\lambda_{ij}$ denoting $\partial\lambda_i/\partial x_j$,

$$W\lambda_{0w}\sum_1^m \sigma_{kj}w_j + \lambda_0(\alpha_k - r) + \sum_1^N g_j^* s_k \eta_{jk}\lambda_{jw} = 0, \quad k = 1, \ldots, m \tag{7.62}$$

The solution of this linear system of equation for $w_k$ yields

$$\hat{w}_k W = A\sum_{i=1}^m \sigma^{ki}(\alpha_i - r) + \sum_{i=1}^m\sum_{j=1}^N H_j g_j^* s_i \eta_{ji}\sigma^{ki}, \quad k = 1, \ldots, m \tag{7.63}$$

in which $A = -\lambda_0/\lambda_{0w}$ and $H_j = -\lambda_{jw}/\lambda_{0w}$. The first term of this demand function is the same as given by (7.57). To interpret the second term, note that $\lambda_0 = u_c$ by (7.45) and, hence, $\lambda_{0w} = u_{cc}(\partial c/\partial W)$ and $\lambda_{jw} = u_{cc}(\partial c/x_j)$, implying

$$H_j = -\frac{\partial c}{\partial x_j}\Big/\frac{\partial c}{\partial W} \tag{7.64}$$

If the $j$th state variable has a negative or "unfavorable" effect on consumption, that is, $\partial c/\partial x_j < 0$, $H_j$ will be positive. Because $(g_j^* s_i \eta_{ji})$ is the covariance between $dx_j$ and $dP_i$, the expression $H_j\Sigma_{i=1}^m(g_j^* s_i\eta_{ji})\sigma^{ki}$ measures the investment in asset $k$

to hedge against the unfavorable effect of state variable $j$, which acts through its correlation with $P_i$ for all $i = 1, \ldots, m$.

Consider the special case when the vector $x$ of state variables consists only of $\alpha_n = r$, which affects the mean rates of return $\alpha_i(x)$ of the assets $i = 1, \ldots, m$. Equation (7.63) becomes

$$\begin{aligned} \hat{w}_k W &= A\sum_{i=1}^{m} \sigma^{ki}(\alpha_i - r) + H_r \sum_{i=1}^{m} \text{cov}(dr,\ dP_i/P)\sigma^{ki} \\ &= Ag_k + H_r d_k, \quad k = 1, \ldots, m \end{aligned} \tag{7.65}$$

and $\hat{w}_n = 1 - \Sigma_1^m \hat{w}_k$, in which $g_k$ and $d_k$ are independent of the individual's utility function and wealth. Equation (7.65) is a generalization of the asset demand functions (7.56) and (7.57). Because there is an additional term $H_r$, which depends on the individual's utility function and wealth, any individual's demand can be satisfied by three mutual funds. Let the first fund hold a fraction $\delta_k = ag_k$ of its value in asset $k$, $k = 1, \ldots, m$. Let the second fund hold only the "instantaneously riskless" asset $n$. Let the third fund hold a fraction $cd_k$ in asset $k$. The demand function (7.65) for any individual will be satisfied by investing proportions $\theta_1$, $(1 - \theta_1 - \theta_3)$, and $\theta_3$ in the three funds respectively, in which

$$\theta_1 ag_k + \theta_3 cd_k = \frac{A}{W} g_k + \frac{H_r}{W} d_k, \quad k = 1, \ldots, m$$

or $\theta_1 = A/Wa$ and $\theta_3 = H_r/Wc$. Summing the above equation over $k$, one gets $\theta_1 + \theta_3 = \Sigma_1^m \hat{w}_k = 1 - \hat{w}_n$, which ensures that the demand $\hat{w}_n$ for the instantaneously riskless asset $n$ can be met by investing the remaining proportion $1 - \theta_1 - \theta_3$ of the individual's wealth in the second mutual fund. Comparison of (7.63) and (7.65) shows that if there are two state variables that shift the mean rates of return or investment opportunities that one would wish to hedge against, that is, $N = 2$ in the model, there will be one extra term in (7.65) and four mutual funds will be required.

This analysis provides a theory of mutual funds. The first type of funds holds a portfolio $\delta_k$ proportional to $g_k$ in the demand function (7.65). The second holds an instantaneously riskless asset like a short-term government bond. Each of the remaining funds holds a collection of capital assets to hedge against one type of contingency. If there were no transaction costs, the individual could make up the collection himself. Because there are transaction costs, each fund provides a service in offering the required collection of assets. This analysis also provides an equilibrium theory of market prices of the $m$ capital assets, interpreted as securities of $m$ firms. Let the demand functions (7.65) for asset $k$ by individual $i$ be written as

$$D_k^i = A^i \sum_{j=1}^{m} \sigma^{kj}(\alpha_j - r) + H_r^i d_k = A^i g_k + H^i d_k, \quad k = 1, \ldots, m \tag{7.66}$$

The market demand for the asset of firm $k$ is the sum of above over all individuals $i$, that is,

$$\mathrm{D}_k = \sum_i \mathrm{D}_k^i = \left(\sum_i \mathrm{A}^i\right) g_k + \left(\sum_i \mathrm{H}^i\right) d_k = \mathrm{A} g_k + \mathrm{H} d_k \tag{7.67}$$

If we redefine $w_k$ to be the ratio of the value of the assets of firm $k$ to the total market value M of the assets of all firms, in equilibrium, $\mathrm{D}_k = w_k\mathrm{M}$. Given $\mathrm{D}_k = w_k\mathrm{M}$, we use (7.67) to solve for the equilibrium expected rates of return $\alpha$ for assets $k$, noting $g_k = \Sigma_{j=1}^{m}\sigma^{kj}(\alpha_j - r)$ in (7.67). The solution of these linear equations is

$$\alpha_k - r = \left(\frac{\mathrm{M}}{\mathrm{A}}\right)\sum_{j=1}^{m} w_j \sigma_{kj} - \frac{\mathrm{H}}{\mathrm{A}}\sum_{j=1}^{m} d_j \sigma_{kj}, \quad k = 1, \ldots, m \tag{7.68}$$

which provides an explanation of the expected rate of return of an asset $k$. Because $\Sigma_j w_j \sigma_{kj}$ is the covariance of the (instantaneous) rate of return of asset $k$ and the aggregate of the rates of return of all assets in the market (i.e., the aggregate rate of the market portfolio), this covariance being known as the "beta" to the $k$th asset in the finance literature, the first term of (7.68) requires a higher expected rate of return for asset $k$, insofar as its price change varies with those of the entire collection of risky assets in the market. Recall that $d_j$ represents the portfolio of the third mutual fund that can be used to hedge against the shifts in expected return. $\Sigma_j d_j \sigma_{kj}$ is thus the covariance of the rate of return for asset $k$ and the rate for this fund. The second term of (7.68) justifies a lower expected rate of return for asset $k$, insofar as it serves the hedging function provided by the third mutual fund. For further discussion of equilibrium capital asset pricing, the reader may refer to Long (1974).

## 7.7 The Pricing of Options and Corporate Liabilities

A European call option entitles the owner to purchase a share of a given stock (or an asset) at an exercise price $c$ at a fixed maturity date T. An American call option entitles its owner to purchase a share of a given stock at an exercise price $c$ at any time up to the maturity date T. European and American put options are similarly defined with the word "sell" replacing "purchase" in the above definition. The price F of an option is a function $\mathrm{F}(\mathrm{P}, t)$ of the price P of the stock. The latter is assumed to follow

$$\frac{d\mathrm{P}}{\mathrm{P}} = \alpha(\mathrm{P}, t)dt + s(\mathrm{P}, t)dz \tag{7.69}$$

By Ito's lemma, the price $\mathrm{F}(\mathrm{P}, t)$ of the option will follow

$$\begin{aligned} d\mathrm{F} &= \left(\mathrm{F}_t + \alpha\mathrm{P}\mathrm{F}_\mathrm{P} + \frac{1}{2}\mathrm{F}_{\mathrm{PP}} s^2\mathrm{P}^2\right)dt + \mathrm{F}_\mathrm{P}\mathrm{P}s\,dz \\ &\equiv \mathrm{F}\alpha' dt + \mathrm{F}s' dz \end{aligned} \tag{7.70}$$

in which I have defined

$$\mathrm{F}\alpha' = \mathrm{F}_t + \alpha\mathrm{P}\mathrm{F}_\mathrm{P} + \frac{1}{2}\mathrm{F}_{\mathrm{PP}} s^2\mathrm{P}^2 \tag{7.71}$$

$$Fs' = F_P P s \tag{7.72}$$

If $\alpha'$ and $\alpha$ were known, (7.71) is a partial differential equation that can be solved for F.

Black and Scholes (1973) derived the function $F(P, t)$ by observing that a hedged position consisting of one option long and $\partial F/\partial P = F_P$ shares of the stock short will be riskless. When the stock price changes by $\Delta P$, the option price will change by $(F_P)\Delta P$, which is the same as the change in value of the $F_P$ shares of stock in the hedged portfolio. Such a portfolio should yield the riskless rate of interest $r$, that is,

$$\frac{dF - (F_P)dP}{F - (F_P)P} = rdt \tag{7.73}$$

which provides a condition for determining the function F. Equations (7.70) and (7.69) imply

$$dF - F_P dP = \left( F_t + \frac{1}{2} F_{PP} s^2 P^2 \right) dt \tag{7.74}$$

Equating the terms $dF - F_P dP$ in (7.74) and (7.73) yields the Black-Scholes partial differential equation for $F(P, t)$,

$$F_t = rF - rPF_P - \frac{1}{2} s^2 P^2 F_{PP} \tag{7.75}$$

The solution of (7.75) will give the function F for the pricing of options. (See problem 20 for a generalization of (7.75).) The boundary condition for a call option is $F(P, T) = P - c$ for $P \geqq c$ and $F(P, T) = 0$ for $P < c$, $c$ being the exercise price. The boundary condition for a put option is $F(P, T) = c - P$ for $c \geqq P$ and $F(P, T) = 0$ for $c < P$.

To solve (7.75) compare and identify it with the partial differential equation (7.71) for an option price F with a mean rate of return $\alpha' = r$ and with the underlying stock having a mean rate of return $\alpha = r$. The price of such an option at time $t$ will be its expected price at time T discounted back to $t$, namely

$$F(P, t) = e^{-r(T-t)} E[F(p, T)] \tag{7.76}$$

To find the expectation of F at time T, one needs the distribution of $P(T)$. Let $X = \ln P$. By using (7.69) with $\alpha = r$ and Ito's lemma, one has

$$\begin{aligned} dX &= \left( \frac{d \log P}{dP} rP + \frac{1}{2} \frac{d^2 \log P}{dP^2} s^2 P^2 \right) dt + \frac{d \log P}{dP} sP dz \\ &= \left( r - \frac{1}{2} s^2 \right) dt + s dz \end{aligned} \tag{7.77}$$

Given $X_t = \log P_t$, if $s$ is a constant, (7.77) implies that the distribution of $X_T$ is normal with mean $X_t + (r - \frac{1}{2}s^2)(T - t)$ and variance $s^2(T - t)$. The price of a call option at the T will be zero if $P_T < c$, and it will be $P_T - c$ if $P_T \geqq c$. Therefore, the expected price of a call option at T is

$$E\left[F(p,\,T)\right]=\int_{c}^{\infty}\left(P_T-c\right)pdf\left(P_T\right)dP_T \tag{7.78}$$

in which *pdf* stands for the probability density function.

Because the *pdf* of $X_T = \log P_T$ is normal with mean and variance given above, (7.78) can be written as

$$E\left[F(p,\,T)\right]=\int_{\log c}^{\infty}\left(e^{x}-c\right)\frac{1}{\sqrt{2\pi s}\sqrt{T-t}} \times\exp\left\{-\frac{1}{2}\cdot\frac{\left[x-X_t-\left(r-\frac{1}{2}s^2\right)(T-t)\right]^2}{s^2(T-t)}\right\}dx \tag{7.79}$$

Substituting (7.79) into (7.76) and simplifying, one obtains the solution for the price of a call option

$$\begin{aligned}F(P,\,t)&=e^{-r(T-t)}\int_{\log c}^{\infty}\frac{1}{\sqrt{2\pi s}\sqrt{T-t}}\\&\quad\times\exp\left\{-\frac{1}{2}\cdot\frac{\left[x-X_t-\left(r+\frac{1}{2}s^2\right)(T-t)\right]^2}{s^2(T-t)}+X_t+r(T-t)\right\}dx\\&\quad-e^{-r(T-t)}c\int_{\log c}^{\infty}\frac{1}{\sqrt{2\pi s}\sqrt{T-t}}\times\exp\left\{-\frac{1}{2}\cdot\frac{\left[x-X_t-\left(r-\frac{1}{2}s^2\right)(T-t)\right]^2}{s^2(T-t)}\right\}dx\\&=P_tN\left(\frac{\ln\left[P_t/c\right]+\left[r+\frac{1}{2}s^2\right]\left[T-t\right]}{s\sqrt{T-t}}\right)-ce^{-r(T-t)}N\left(\frac{\ln\left[P_t/c\right]+\left[r-\frac{1}{2}s^2\right]\left[T-t\right]}{s\sqrt{T-t}}\right)\end{aligned} \tag{7.80}$$

in which N stands for the cumulative unit normal distribution function. Black and Scholes (1973) have pointed out that, by considering corporate liabilities as combinations of options, the pricing formula (7.78) can be applied to corporate liabilities such as common stocks, corporate bonds, and warrants.

## 7.8 Asset Pricing and Portfolio Selection with Noise in Supply

Since the works of Merton as presented in sections 7.5 and 7.6, the theory of asset pricing has progressed in several directions. First, instead of assuming asset prices P to follow exogenously given stochastic process (7.40) or (7.40) combined with (7.59), the model may determine the pricing function in a general equilibrium framework, as it is done in sections 4.1 and 4.4. See Cox,

Ingersoll, and Ross (1985) and problems 18, 19, and 20. Second, random noise is introduced into the quantity supplied, so that in equilibrium the holding of assets can fluctuate. Without noise in supply, recall from the model in section 4.4 with money and one-period bonds, in equilibrium, the purchase or sale of bond by each economic agent equals to zero, that is, there is no trade in the economy. Third, economic agents are allowed to be heterogeneous in the information that they possess. Following the works of Grossman (1976), Hellwig (1980), Admati (1985), and Wang (1993), an article by Zhou (1995) incorporates these elements and is summarized in this and the following section, the latter dealing with asymmetric information among agents.

The model has one physical good, which can be used for consumption or investment, $n$ risky assets each paying dividend at rate $D_i$ ($i = 1, \ldots, n$) and one risk-free bond yielding a rate of interest $r$. The flow of dividend $D_i$ is affected by a state variable $F_i$ (such as earnings or profitability) as follows:

$$dF_i = -a_{iF}F_i dt + b_{iF} dz \qquad (a_{iF} \geqslant 0) \tag{7.81}$$

$$dD_i = g_i F_i dt + b_{iD} dz \qquad (g_i \geqslant 0) \tag{7.82}$$

in which $z$ is a vector of $3n$ independent Wiener processes. The first $2n$ affect the $2n$ state variables $F_i$ ($i = 1, \ldots, n$) and the dividends $D_i$, and the third $n$ affect the noise $N_i$ in the supply $X_i = 1 + N_i$ of risky asset $i$. $N_i$ follows

$$dN_i = -a_{iN}N_i dt + b_{iN} dz \qquad (a_{iN} \geqslant 0) \tag{7.83}$$

These three key equations in matrix terms are

$$dF = -A_F F dt + B_F dz \tag{7.84}$$

$$dD = GF dt + B_D dz \tag{7.85}$$

$$dN = -A_N N dt + B_N dz \tag{7.86}$$

in which F, D, and N are $n \times 1$; $A_F$, G, and $A_N$ are diagonal matrices with $a_{iF}$, $g_i$ and $a_{iN}$ along their diagonals respectively; $B_F$ and $B_D$ are $n \times 3n$, each with zeros in its third $n \times n$ submatrix, and $B_N$ is $n \times 3n$ with zeros in its first two $n \times n$ submatrices. The arrangement of zeros in $B_F$, $B_D$, and $B_N$ allows $dF$ and $dD$ to be correlated and makes $dN$ uncorrelated with $dF$ and $dD$. To motivate the specification of equation (7.84)–(7.86) for the three state variables F, D, and N, note that (vector) dividend D affects portfolio choice and has to be specified. The pair of equations (7.84) and (7.85) is exactly the setup to model some uninformed investors who can observe D but not F and wish to estimate F from D (by using the Kalman filter as described in section 7.9 below). Equation (7.84) is the *plant equation* and (7.85) is the *observation equation* in the standard setup. N has to be modeled for noise to be introduced in the supply of assets.

Assume the information set of all investors at time $t$ to be $\{P_{i\tau}, D_{i\tau}, F_{i\tau} \mid i = 1, \ldots, n; \tau \leqslant t\}$, namely the price $P_{i\tau}$ of each asset, its dividend $D_{i\tau}$, and the state variable $F_{i\tau}$ that affects the dividend of all time $\tau$ up to $t$. Given this information and given a (vector) price function P for all risky assets, each investor-consumer is assumed to maximize

$$E_t\left[\int_0^{\infty} e^{-\rho s} u(c(s))ds\right], \quad u(c) = -\exp(-\phi c), \quad \phi > 0 \tag{7.87}$$

The particular form of the utility function is assumed to yield an explicit solution for the investor-consumer's choice of assets and consumption and a price function P linear in the state variables F, D, and N. It is reasonable to expect that the price $P_i$ of asset $i$ is related to the present value of its dividends. Therefore, define the fundamental value $V_i(t)$ of asset $i$ as the expected present value of its dividend flow discounted at rate $r$,

$$V_i(t) = E_t \int_0^{\infty} e^{-rs} D_i(t+s)ds = \int_0^{\infty} e^{-rs} E_t D_i(t+s)ds$$

To evaluate $V_i(t)$, note from (7.81)

$$E_t F_i(t+s) = e^{-a_{iF}s} F_i(t)$$

and from (7.82)

$$\frac{dE_t D_i(t+s)}{ds} = g_i E_t F_i(t+s) = g_i e^{-a_{iF}s} F_i(t)$$

Solving this differential equation for $E_t D_i(t+s)$ yields

$$E_t D_i(t+s) = D_i(t) + \frac{g_i}{a_{iF}}\left[1 - e^{-a_{iF}s}\right] F_i(t)$$

Evaluating the integral defining $V_i(t)$, one obtains

$$V_i(t) = \gamma_i D_i(t) + \theta_i F_i(t); \quad \gamma_i = 1/r, \quad \theta_i = g_i/\left[r(r + a_{iF})\right] \tag{7.88}$$

In vector form, the $n \times 1$ vector $V = \Gamma D + \Theta F$, $\Gamma$ and $\Theta$ being diagonal $n \times n$ with $\gamma_i$ and $\theta_i$, respectively, as elements. By using (7.84) and (7.85), one has

$$dV = \Gamma dD + \Theta dF = A_V dt + B_V dz; \quad A_V = (\Gamma G - \Theta A_F)F,$$
$$B_V = (\Theta B_F + \Gamma B_D) \tag{7.89}$$

The problem is to find the price function P of all $n$ risky assets in market equilibrium. This problem is solved in two steps:

*Step 1*: Given a price function P to be specified in (7.92), with parameters $p^*$ and $A^*$, the consumer is assumed to maximize (7.87), subject to an appropriate wealth constraint to be given in (7.91) to form a demand function for the assets.
*Step 2*: By equating demand with the supply of assets, the parameters of the price function P is determined.

To proceed with Step 1, specify a dynamic constraint on the wealth W of an investor that consists of stocks valued at $q'P$, $q$ being an $n \times 1$ vector of his or her holdings of the $n$ risky assets, plus the value of bonds $(W - q'P)$. W changes with interest income from bonds $r(W - q'P)$, dividend income from stocks $q'D$, consumption $c$, and capital gain $q'dP$. Thus.

$$\begin{aligned} dW &= \left[r(W - q'P) + q'D - c\right]dt + q'dP \\ &= (rW - c)dt + q'\left[(D - rP)dt + dP\right] \\ &= (rW - c)dt + q'd\pi \end{aligned} \tag{7.90}$$

in which, in the second line, one separates the term $(rW - c)dt$ of certain income flow from the remaining term $q'd\pi$ of income from holding a vector $q$ of risky assets. The risky assets yield excess returns $d\pi$:

$$d\pi = (D - rP)dt + dP \tag{7.91}$$

which consists of dividend rate D in excess of the yield $rP$ from holding bonds plus capital gains $dP$. The consumer-investor is assumed to maximize (7.87) with respect to $c$ and $q$, subject to the dynamic wealth constraint (7.90) given a price function. In equilibrium, demand $q$ equals supply $X = \underline{1} + N$, $\underline{1}$ being a vector of $n$ ones. This equilibrium condition, together with the demand function for $q$, determines the price function. In this model, the equilibrium price function is linear in the state variables D, F, and N. In fact, it is linear in the variables $V = \Gamma D + \Theta F$ and N:

$$P = p^* + V + A^* N, \tag{7.92}$$

in which the vector p* and the matrix A* are parameters of the price function. To prove this proposition, solve the consumer's optimization problem assuming (7.92), and then use the equilibrium condition to determine the parameters p* and A*.

Given the price function (7.92), evaluate $dP$ by using the definition $V = \Gamma D + \Theta F$ and equations (7.84), (7.85), and (7.86) for $dF$, $dD$, and $dN$. By using the result for $dP$ and (7.92), rewrite (7.91) as

$$d\pi = e_\pi dt + B_\pi dz; \quad e_\pi = \left[-rp^* - A^*(rI + A_N)N\right], \quad B_\pi = B_V + A^* B_N, \tag{7.93}$$

in which, $e_\pi$ is the conditional expectation of the excess return vector $d\pi$. The Lagrangean of the consumer's optimization problem is

$$\begin{aligned} \mathcal{L} = \int_0^\infty E_t\Big\{ & e^{-\rho t}\left[-e^{-\phi c}\right]dt - e^{-\rho(t+dt)}\lambda(t+dt) \\ & \times\left[W(t+dt) - W - (rW - c + q'e_\pi)dt - q'B_\pi dz\right]\Big\}. \end{aligned} \tag{7.94}$$

The first-order conditions are (with $c$ and $q$ as control variables and W as the state variable subject to control):

$$e^{\rho t}\frac{\partial \mathcal{L}}{\partial c} = \phi e^{-\phi c}dt - e^{-\rho dt}E_t\lambda(t+dt)dt = 0 \Rightarrow \phi e^{-\phi c} = \lambda \tag{7.95}$$

$$e^{\rho t}\frac{\partial \mathcal{L}}{\partial q} = e^{-\rho dt}\left[e_\pi E_t\lambda(t+dt)dt + E_t\lambda(t+dt)B_\pi dz\right] = 0$$

$$\Rightarrow e_\pi \lambda dt + B_\pi E_t dz d\lambda = 0 \tag{7.96}$$

$$e^{\rho t}\frac{\partial \mathcal{L}}{\partial W} = -\lambda + e^{-\rho dt}\left[E_t\lambda(t+dt) + rE_t\lambda(t+dt)dt\right]$$

$$= (r-\rho)\lambda dt + E_t d\lambda = 0 \tag{7.97}$$

Equations (7.95), (7.96), and (7.97) are three functional equations to be solved for the control functions $c$ and $q$ and the Lagrange function $\lambda$.

If one conjectures that the consumption function is linear in W and quadratic in N,

$$c(W, N) = rW + k + h'N + \frac{1}{2}N'HN \tag{7.98}$$

with parameters $k$, $h$, and $H = H'$, (7.95) implies that $\lambda$ will take the form

$$\lambda = \phi \exp\left\{-\phi\left(rW + k + h'N + \frac{1}{2}N'HN\right)\right\} \tag{7.99}$$

By using (7.90) and (7.93) for $dW$ and (7.86) for $dN$, and by denoting partials by subscripts, use Ito's lemma to evaluate $d\lambda$ given (7.99):

$$d\lambda = \left\{\lambda_W(rW - c + q'e_\pi) - \lambda'_N A_N N + \frac{1}{2}\lambda_{WW}q'B_\pi B'_\pi q + \lambda'_{WN}B_N B'_\pi q\right.$$

$$\left. + \frac{1}{2}tr\left[\lambda_{NN'}B_N B'_N\right]\right\}dt + \left(\lambda_W q'B_\pi + \lambda'_N B_N\right)dz \tag{7.100}$$

By using the coefficient $(\lambda_W q'B_\pi + \lambda'_N B_N)$ of $dz$ in (7.100) to evaluate $E_t dz d\lambda$ in (7.96), noting $E_t dz dt = o(dt)$, solve (7.96) for $e_\pi$ to obtain

$$e_\pi = \phi\left[rB_\pi B'_\pi q + B_\pi B'_N(h + HN)\right] \tag{7.101}$$

Equation (7.101) shows that the required expected excess return for holding an optimal portfolio $q$ is, given $e_\pi$,

$$\tilde{e} \equiv q'e_\pi = \phi q'\left[rB_\pi B'_\pi q + B_\pi B'_N(h + HN)\right] \tag{7.102}$$

By applying Ito's lemma to equation (7.98) for $c$, obtain the random term of $dc$ as

$$\frac{\partial c}{\partial[W, N']}\begin{bmatrix} q'B_\pi dz \\ B_N dz \end{bmatrix} = \left[r, h' + N'H\right]\begin{bmatrix} q'B_\pi \\ B_N \end{bmatrix}dz \tag{7.103}$$

Equation (7.103) can be used to show that the covariance between wealth as given by (7.90) and consumption as given by (7.98) is

$$E\left\{q'B_\pi dz \cdot dz'\left[rB'_\pi q + B'_N(h + HN)\right]\right\} = q'\left[rB_\pi B'_\pi q + B_\pi B'_N(h + HN)\right],$$

which is the same as the required expected excess return given by (7.102) divided by $\phi$. Equation (7.103) can also be used to find the variance of consumption

$$\sigma_c^2 = \left[rq'\mathrm{B}_\pi + \left(h' + \mathrm{N}'\mathrm{H}\right)\mathrm{B}_\mathrm{N}\right]\left[r\mathrm{B}_\pi' q + \mathrm{B}_\mathrm{N}'\left(h + \mathrm{HN}\right)\right], \tag{7.104}$$

which implies that a given level of consumption variance $\sigma_c^2$ can correspond to different optimal portfolios $q$. Each portfolio corresponds to a different required excess return $\tilde{e}$ as given by (7.102). For any given $\sigma_c^2$, the portfolio with the lowest $\tilde{e}$ is determined by $\min_q \tilde{e}$ subject to the constraint (7.104). The economics of this exercise is found by doing problem 11 at the end of the chapter. The optimal portfolio $q$ can be obtained by solving equation (7.101):

$$q = \left(\phi r \mathrm{B}_\pi \mathrm{B}_\pi'\right)^{-1}\left[e_\pi - \phi \mathrm{B}_\pi \mathrm{B}_\mathrm{N}'\left(h + \mathrm{HN}\right)\right] \tag{7.105}$$

To find the unknown parameters $k$, $h$, and H of the consumption function and the Lagrange function, substitute (7.98) for $c$ and (7.101) for $e_\pi$ into the first-order condition (7.97), after evaluating $\mathrm{E}_t d\lambda$ by (7.99) and (7.100). The resulting equation is quadratic in N. Noting $q = \underline{1} + \mathrm{N}$ in equilibrium and setting the constant term, the coefficient vector of N and the matrix of the quadratic form in N to zero will yield, respectively, $k$, $h$, and H as follows (with $\underline{1}$ denoting a column of ones) (see problem 12):

$$k = \frac{-1}{r\phi}\left\{\left(r - \rho\right) - \frac{1}{2}\left(r\phi\right)^2 \underline{1}'\mathrm{B}_\pi \mathrm{B}_\pi' \underline{1} + \frac{1}{2}\phi^2 tr\left[\left(hh' - \mathrm{H}\right)\mathrm{B}_\mathrm{N}\mathrm{B}_\mathrm{N}'\right]\right\} \tag{7.106}$$

$$h = r^2\phi\left(r\mathrm{I} + \mathrm{A}_\mathrm{N}' + \phi \mathrm{HB}_\mathrm{N}\mathrm{B}_\mathrm{N}'\right)^{-1}\mathrm{B}_\pi \mathrm{B}_\pi' \underline{1} \tag{7.107}$$

$$r\mathrm{H} + \mathrm{A}_\mathrm{N}'\mathrm{H} + \mathrm{HA}_\mathrm{N} + \phi \mathrm{HB}_\mathrm{N}\mathrm{B}_\mathrm{N}'\mathrm{H} = r^2\phi \mathrm{B}_\pi \mathrm{B}_\pi' \tag{7.108}$$

Finally, to find the parameters $p^*$ and $\mathrm{A}^*$ of the price function P, use the market clearing condition $q = \underline{1} + \mathrm{N}$, and equate coefficients in the following equation derived from (7.93) and (7.101):

$$e_\pi = -\left[rp^* + \mathrm{A}^*\left(r\mathrm{I} + \mathrm{A}_\mathrm{N}\right)\mathrm{N}\right] = r\phi \mathrm{B}_\pi \mathrm{B}_\pi' q + \phi \mathrm{B}_\pi \mathrm{B}_\mathrm{N}'\left(h + \mathrm{HN}\right)$$

The results are

$$p^* = -\phi \mathrm{B}_\mathrm{V}\mathrm{B}_\mathrm{V}'\underline{1}; \quad \mathrm{A}^* = -\phi\left(r\mathrm{B}_\pi \mathrm{B}_\pi' + \mathrm{B}_\pi \mathrm{B}_\mathrm{N}'\mathrm{H}\right)\left(r\mathrm{I} + \mathrm{A}_\mathrm{N}\right)^{-1} \tag{7.109}$$

Thus, the price function

$$\mathrm{P} = p^* + \mathrm{V} + \mathrm{A}^*\mathrm{N} = p^* + \Gamma\mathrm{D} + \Theta\mathrm{F} + \mathrm{A}^*\mathrm{N}$$

is obtained by equating demand and supply of the excess returns of risky assets. For more discussion on the economic issues, the reader is referred to Zhou (1995).

## 7.9 Asset Pricing and Portfolio Selection with Asymmetric Information

In the last section, all consumer-investors are assumed to have information set $\{P_{i\tau}, D_{i\tau}, F_{i\tau} | i = 1, \ldots, n; \tau \leq t\}$ at time $t$ when the consumption and investment decisions are made. Now, suppose there are two types of investors. The informed investors have the above information set. The uninformed observe only $\mathcal{F}_t^u = \{P_{i\tau}, D_{i\tau} | i = 1, \ldots, n; \tau \leq t\}$ and not the state variable $F_{it}$. The uninformed investors are assumed to utilize the information on $P_{it}$ and $D_{it}$ to estimate other variables, which are useful for making investment decisions. Having solved this estimation problem, they will maximize to determine consumption $c^u$ and portfolio $q^u$. Market demand of both types of investors are set equal to available supply to determine the prices of assets as before. When the investors make their decisions, a price function P is assumed to be given. Market equilibrium will determine the parameters of P as in the previous section. Thus, first assume P, solve the uninformed investors' estimation or information extraction problem, solve both type of investors' optimization problems to determine market demand, and equate demand and supply to determine P.

In the previous section, price P is assumed to be a function of the state variables D, F, and N, the fundamental value V being $\Gamma D + \Theta F$. The informed investors knowing P, D, and F can infer N or at least $A^*N$ from the price function. The uninformed investors have to use information P and D to estimate N by $\hat{N}$. Let $\hat{N} = E[N | \mathcal{F}_t^u]$ denote the conditional expectation of N given the information $\mathcal{F}_t^u$ of the uninformed investors. Assume the price function to be

$$P = p + \Gamma D + \Theta F + AN + B\hat{N} = p + V + AN + B\hat{N} \tag{7.110}$$

Given this price function, information on P, D (hence $\hat{N}$), and F implies information on AN for the informed investors. For the uninformed investors, information on P and D (hence $\hat{N}$) implies information on $\Phi = \Theta F + AN$, as the latter can be solved by using (7.110); information on $\Phi$ and D (assuming $\hat{N}$ to be linear in P and D) implies information on P, as P can be solved using (7.110). Thus, information of P and D is equivalent to information on $\Phi$ and D, the latter set being more convenient to use in deriving $\hat{N} = E[N | \mathcal{F}_t^u]$.

### 7.9a The Kalman Filter in Continuous Time

An uninformed investor's information extraction problem is solved by using the Kalman filter. Let each investor have information

$$s = (D_1, \ldots, D_n, \Phi_1, \ldots, \Phi_n)' = (D', \Phi') \tag{7.111}$$

from which he or she wishes to estimate

$$y = (F_1, \ldots, F_n, N_1, \ldots, N_n)' \tag{7.112}$$

By using (7.84) for $dF$, (7.85) for $dD$, and (7.86) for $dN$, $\Phi$ being $\Theta F + AN$, write

$$ds = C_{sy} y\, dt + B_s dz \tag{7.113}$$

$$dy = C_{yy} y\, dt + B_y dz, \tag{7.114}$$

in which

$$C_{sy} = \begin{bmatrix} G & 0 \\ -\Theta A_F & -AA_N \end{bmatrix}_{2n\times 2n} \qquad C_{yy} = \begin{bmatrix} -A_F & 0 \\ 0 & -A_N \end{bmatrix}_{2n\times 2n}$$

$$B_s = \begin{bmatrix} B_D \\ \Theta B_F + AB_N \end{bmatrix} \qquad B_y = \begin{bmatrix} B_F \\ B_N \end{bmatrix} \tag{7.115}$$

Given a vector $s$ of observed signals generated by a vector $y$ of unobserved state variables according to an *observation equation* (7.113), in which $y$ itself evolves according to a *plant* equation (7.114), the problem is to find the conditional expectation $d\hat{y}$ of $dy$ given the information $\mathcal{F}_t^u$.

Because the solution of this problem for models in discrete time is well known (see, for example, Chow (1975, p. 188)), I will try to solve the problem in continuous time in the same manner, noting merely that $ds = s(t + dt) - s$ and $dy = y(t + dt) - y$, the argument $t$ of $s$ and $y$ being understood. At time $t$, we have an estimate $\hat{y} = E(y|\mathcal{F}_t^u)$. The problem is how to update this estimate to form $\hat{y}(t + dt) = E(y(t + dt)|\mathcal{F}_{t+dt}^u)$. The difference is $d\hat{y} = \hat{y}(t + dt) - \hat{y}$. First, find $\hat{y}(t + dt; t) = E(y(t + dt)|\mathcal{F}_t^u)$ and then $\hat{y}(t + dt) \equiv \hat{y}(t + dt; t + dt)$. Take the conditional expectation of (7.113) and (7.114) given $\mathcal{F}_t^u$:

$$\hat{s}(t + dt;\ t) - s = C_{sy}\hat{y}\, dt \tag{7.116}$$

$$\hat{y}(t + dt;\ t) - \hat{y} = C_{yy}\hat{y}\, dt \tag{7.117}$$

in which note, in (7.116), that $\hat{s} = E(s|\mathcal{F}_t^u) = s$, because $s$ is observed at time $t$. To estimate $y(t + dt)$, use the regression (conditional expectation) of $y(t + dt)$ on $s(t + dt)$ given $\mathcal{F}_t^u$. By the well-known theory of regression (Chow, 1975, p. 188), the regression function is

$$\hat{y}(t+dt) - \hat{y}(t+dt;\ t) = \mathrm{Cov}\left[y(t+dt) - \hat{y}(t+dt;\ t),\ s(t+dt) - \hat{s}(t+dt;\ \mathrm{t})\right]$$
$$\left[\mathrm{Cov}\left(s(t+dt) - \hat{s}(t+dt;\ t)\right)\right]^{-1}\left[s(t+dt) - \hat{s}(t+dt;\ t)\right],$$

in which both the (vector) dependent variable $y(t + dt)$ and the (vector) explanatory variable $s(t + dt)$ are measured from their conditional means $\hat{y}(t + dt;\ t)$ and $\hat{s}(t + dt;\ t)$, respectively.

The above regression formula to estimate $y(t + dt)$ by $\hat{y}(t + dt)$ is the essense of the *Kalman filter*. To write it in terms of the parameters of the model (7.113) and (7.114), simply evaluate the two covariance matrices by using (7.116) and (7.117).

$$\mathrm{Cov}\left[y(t + dt) - \hat{y}(t + dt;\ t),\ s(t + dt) - \hat{s}(t + dt;\ t)\right]$$
$$= E\left[(y - \hat{y}) + C_{yy}(y - \hat{y})dt + B_y dz\right]\left[C_{sy}(y - \hat{y})dt + B_s dz\right]'$$
$$= E_t(y - \hat{y})(y - \hat{y})'C_{sy}' dt + B_y B_s' dt$$

as any product of $dt$ and $dz$ (of order $\sqrt{dt}$) is of order $o(dt)$ and can be omitted.

$$\mathrm{Cov}\big(s(t+dt)-\hat{s}(t+dt;\ t)\big)=\mathrm{E}_t\big[\mathrm{C}_{sy}(y-\hat{y})dt+\mathrm{B}_s dz\big]\big[\mathrm{C}_{sy}(y-\hat{y})dt+\mathrm{B}_s dz\big]'=\mathrm{B}_s\mathrm{B}_s' dt$$

After substituting for these covariances, and using (7.117) for $\hat{y}(t + dt;\, t)$ and (7.113) to rewrite the explanatory variable $s(t + dt) - \hat{s}(t + dt)$, obtain the *Kalman filter*:

$$\hat{y}(t+dt)-\hat{y}\equiv d\hat{y}=\mathrm{C}_{yy}\hat{y}\,dt+\big[\mathrm{Cov}_t(y-\hat{y})\mathrm{C}_{sy}'+\mathrm{B}_y\mathrm{B}_s'\big]\big(\mathrm{B}_s\mathrm{B}_s'\big)^{-1}\big[ds-\mathrm{C}_{sy}\hat{y}\,dt\big]$$

$$\equiv \mathrm{C}_{yy}\hat{y}\,dt+\mathrm{J}\big(\mathrm{B}_s\mathrm{B}_s'\big)^{-1}\big[ds-\mathrm{C}_{sy}\hat{y}\,dt\big] \qquad (7.118)$$

To complete the derivation of the Kalman filter, one needs a formula for $\mathrm{Cov}_t(y - \hat{y}) \equiv \Omega_t$, which is a part of the matrix J defined above. This is the problem of finding the covariance matrix $\mathrm{Cov}_t(\hat{y} - y)$ of a stochastic process $\hat{y} - y$, given the differential equation for $d(\hat{y} - y) \equiv dx$. The differential equation is obtained by subtracting (7.114) from (7.118):

$$dx\equiv d\hat{y}-dy=\mathrm{C}_{yy}x\,dt-\mathrm{B}_y dz+\mathrm{J}\big(\mathrm{B}_s\mathrm{B}_s'\big)^{-1}\big[\mathrm{C}_{sy}x\,dt+\mathrm{B}_s dz\big] \qquad (7.119)$$

It is well known (see Chow 1981, pp. 269–273) that given a linear stochastic differential equation

$$dx=\mathrm{C}(t)x\,dt+dv$$

the covariance matrix $\Omega$ of $x$ satisfies the following (nonstochastic) differential equation:

$$\frac{d\Omega}{dt}=\Omega\mathrm{C}'+\mathrm{C}\Omega+\mathrm{Cov}(dv)/dt$$

Applying this result to the covariance matrix $\Omega = \mathrm{Cov}_t(y - \hat{y})$ in equation (7.118), one finds

$$\frac{d\Omega}{dt}=\Omega\Big[C_{yy}-B_yB_s'\big(B_sB_s'\big)^{-1}C_{sy}\Big]'+\Big[C_{yy}-B_yB_s'\big(B_sB_s'\big)^{-1}C_{sy}\Big]\Omega$$

$$-\Omega C_{sy}'\big(B_sB_s'\big)^{-1}C_{sy}\Omega+B_yB_y'-B_yB_s'\big(\mathrm{B}_s\mathrm{B}_s'\big)^{-1}B_sB_y' \qquad (7.120)$$

in which $\Omega C'_{sy} + B_yB_s'$ has replaced J in (7.119). Equation (7.120) is a differential equation to determine $\Omega_t = \mathrm{E}_t(y - \hat{y})(y - \hat{y})'$ in the Kalman filter (7.118). In the steady-state, $\Omega_t = \Omega$ and $d\Omega/dt = 0$ in (7.120). Here, the derivation of the Kalman filter to solve the uninformed investor's signal extraction problem to estimate $\hat{y}$ is completed.

To interpret the Kalman filter (7.118) as a stochastic differential equation for $d\hat{y}$, note that $d\hat{y} = \hat{y}(t + dt) - \hat{y}$ is the change in our estimate of $y$ from time $t$ to $t + dt$. The change comes from two sources. The first part $\mathrm{C}_{yy}\hat{y}dt$ is the same as $\mathrm{C}_{yy}y dt$ for the prediction of $dy$ itself using equation (7.114). The second part is due to the error $[ds - \mathrm{C}_{sy}\hat{y}dt]$ in predicting $ds$ at time $t$ by the conditional expectation $E_t(ds) = \mathrm{C}_{sy}\hat{y}dt$ using $\hat{y}(t)$ given by (7.116). The error in predicting $ds$ by using $\hat{y}(t)$ should induce a change in the prediction $\hat{y}(t + dt)$. In this application, the uninformed investors use dividends D (part of $s$) to predict the unobserved states F of firms issuing the dividends (part of $y$). A shock to dividends $ds$ will be interpreted as a change in the state $dy$. For a second interpretation of the Kalman filter, see problem 15.

To apply the Kalman filter to estimate dN (the second component of $dy$) we have

$$d\hat{N} = -A_N \hat{N} dt + B_N^u \left[ ds - C_{sy} \hat{y}\, dt \right] \tag{7.121}$$

in which $B_N^u$ is the lower half of the matrix $J(B_s B_s')^{-1}$, J being defined as $\text{Cov}(y - \hat{y})C_{sy}' + B_y B_s'$. Observe that the error $v = \hat{N} - N$ in estimating N satisfies a mean-reverting process

$$dv = -A_v v\, dt + B_v dz \tag{7.122}$$

in which $A_v$ is an $n \times n$ constant matrix and $B_v$ is an $n \times 3n$ matrix, being the lower half of $J(B_s B_s')^{-1} B_s - B_y$. To prove (7.122), note that $dv$ is the lower part of the vector $dx$ defined by (7.119). Rearrange the right-hand side of (7.119) into two terms involving $dt$ and $dz$. The coefficient matrix of $dz$ is $J(B_s B_s')^{-1} B_s - B_y$. Concerning the coefficient matrix $A_v$ in (7.122), because $\Phi = \Theta F + AN$ is in the information set $\mathcal{F}_t^u$, we have $\Theta\hat{F} + A\hat{N} = \Theta F + AN$, which implies

$$\hat{F} - F = -\Theta^{-1} A v; \quad x = \hat{y} - y = \begin{bmatrix} \hat{F} - F \\ \hat{N} - N \end{bmatrix} = \begin{bmatrix} -\Theta^{-1} A \\ I \end{bmatrix} v$$

When this expression for $x$ is substituted in (7.119), an expression for $A_v$ can be obtained.

Before solving the optimization problems of the informed and uninformed investors, one should derive an equation for the rates of return $d\pi$ of the risky assets. Substituting the conjectured price function (7.110) into the definition of $d\pi$ and using (7.122) for $d\hat{N} - dN$,

$$d\pi = (D - rP)dt + dP = (e_0 + E_N N + E_v v)dt + B_\pi^i dz \tag{7.123}$$

in which

$$e_0 = -rp; \quad E_N = -(A + B)(r \cdot I_n + A_N)$$

$$E_v = -B(r \cdot I_n + A_v); \quad B_\pi^i = B_v + (A + B)B_N + BB_v$$

For the uninformed investors, use (7.123) to find E $[d\pi / \mathcal{F}_t^u]$. Let $dP = (\Gamma\ I)\, ds + (0\ B) d\hat{y}$ and use (7.118) to find the coefficient $B_\pi^u$:

$$d\pi = (e_0 + E_N \hat{N})dt + B_\pi^u \left[ ds - C_{sy} \hat{y}\, dt \right] \tag{7.124}$$

in which

$$B_\pi^u = \left[ (\Gamma\ I) + (0\ B) J (B_s B_s')^{-1} \right]$$

The conditional covariance matrix of $d\pi$ from the viewpoint of the uninformed investors is, by (7.124),

$$\mathrm{Cov}\left(d\pi \middle| \mathcal{F}_t^u\right) = \mathrm{E}\mathrm{B}_\pi^u\left[ds - \mathrm{C}_{ys}\hat{y}\,dt\right]\left[ds - \mathrm{C}_{ys}\hat{y}\,dt\right]'\mathrm{B}_\pi^{u\prime} = \mathrm{B}_\pi^u\mathrm{B}_s\mathrm{B}_s'\mathrm{B}_\pi^{u\prime} \qquad (7.125)$$

The optimization problems for the informed and the uninformed can be solved in the same manner as in section 7.8. Denote their conditional expectations respectively by $\mathrm{E}_t^i = \mathrm{E}[\cdot|\mathcal{F}_t^i]$ and $\mathrm{E}_t^u = \mathrm{E}[\cdot|\mathcal{F}_t^u]$. The informed investor's Lagrangean is

$$\mathcal{L} = \int_0^\infty \mathrm{E}_t^i\Big\{e^{-\rho t}\left[-e^{-\phi c}\right]dt - e^{-\rho(t+dt)}\lambda(t+dt)\left[\mathrm{W}(t+dt) - \mathrm{W}\right.$$

$$\left. - \left(r\mathrm{W} - c - q'e_\pi\right)dt + q'\mathrm{B}_\pi dz\right]\Big\} \qquad (7.126)$$

in which $e_\pi$ is specified by (7.123), with $d\mathrm{N}$ given by (7.86) and $dv$ given by (7.122). The uninformed investors Lagrangean is the same as (7.126) except for the change from $\mathrm{E}_t^i$ to $\mathrm{E}_t^u$. Superscript $i$ or $u$ is not used for the variables $\lambda$, W, $c$, and $q$ as it is understood when we solve the optimization problem for each type of investors. For the uninformed, $e_\pi$ is specified by (7.124), with $d\hat{\mathrm{N}}$ given by (7.121).

The informed investor has $n + 1$ control variables $(c, q)$ and $2n + 1$ state variables $(\mathrm{W}, \mathrm{N}, v = \hat{\mathrm{N}} - \mathrm{N})$. Simplify the notation for the state variables N and $v$ by defining

$$\Psi^i = \begin{bmatrix} \mathrm{N} \\ v \end{bmatrix} \qquad \mathrm{A}_\Psi^i = \begin{bmatrix} \mathrm{A_N} & 0 \\ 0 & \mathrm{A}_v \end{bmatrix} \qquad \mathrm{B}_\Psi^i = \begin{bmatrix} \mathrm{B_N} \\ \mathrm{B}_v \end{bmatrix}$$

which implies

$$d\Psi^i = -\mathrm{A}_\Psi^i\Psi^i dt + \mathrm{B}_\Psi^i dz \qquad (7.127)$$

By using this notation, the informed investor's optimization problem is solved by conjecturing a Lagrange function

$$\lambda = \phi\exp\left\{-\phi\left(r\mathrm{W} + k^i + h^{i\prime}\Psi^i + \frac{1}{2}\Psi^{i\prime}\mathrm{H}^i\Psi^i\right)\right\} \qquad (7.128)$$

Setting the partials of (7.126) with respect to $c$, $q$, and W equal to zero and solving the first-order conditions (see problem 16) yield the following consumption function and optimum portfolio for the informed investors:

$$c^i = r\mathrm{W} + k^i + h^{i\prime}\Psi^i + \frac{1}{2}\Psi^{i\prime}\mathrm{H}^i\Psi^i \qquad (7.129)$$

$$q^i = g_0^i + \mathrm{G}_\Psi^i\Psi^i = g_0^i + \mathrm{G}_\mathrm{N}^i\mathrm{N} + \mathrm{G}_v^i v \qquad (7.130)$$

Conjecture a similar Lagrange function to (7.128) for the uninformed investors with $\Psi^i$ replaced by $\hat{\mathrm{N}}$. Setting to zero the partials of the Lagrangean expression for the uninformed with respect to $c$, $q$, and W and solving the first-order conditions (see problem 17) yield the following consumption and portfolio for the uninformed investors:

$$c^u = rW + k^u + h^{u\prime}\hat{N} + \frac{1}{2}\hat{N}'H^u\hat{N} \tag{7.131}$$

$$q^u = g_0^u + G_N^u\hat{N}. \tag{7.132}$$

To find the parameters ($p$, A, B) of the price function (7.110), equate demand and supply of assets, assuming a fraction $k$ of uninformed and a fraction $1 - k$ of informed investors:

$$(1-k)q^i + kq^u = \underline{1} + N \tag{7.133}$$

Using equation (7.130) and (7.132) for $q^i$ and $q^u$ in (7.133) gives

$$(1-k)\left[g_0^i + G_N^i N + G_v^i(\hat{N} - N)\right] + k\left(g_0^u + G_N^u\hat{N}\right) = \underline{1} + N$$

Equating coefficients of 1, N and $\hat{N}$, one obtains

$$(1-k)g_0^i + kg_0^u = \underline{1}$$

$$(1-k)(G_N^i - G_v^i) = I$$

$$(1-k)G_v^i + kG_N^u = 0$$

These equations determine $p$, A, and B, using the parameters of (7.130; 132):

$$g_0^i = -r^{-1}\left(B_\pi^i B_\pi^{i\prime}\right)^{-1}\left(rp/\phi + B_\pi^i B_\Psi^{i\prime} h^i\right)$$

$$\left[G_N^i \;\; G_v^i\right] = -r^{-1}\left(B_\pi^i B_\pi^{i\prime}\right)^{-1}\left\{\left[(A+B)(rI + A_N) \;\; B(rI + A_v)\right]/\phi + B_\pi^i B_\Psi^{i\prime} H^i\right\}$$

$$g_0^u = -r^{-1}\left(B_\pi^u B_s B_s' B_\pi^{u\prime}\right)^{-1}\left(rp/\phi + B_\pi^u B_s B_s' B_N^{u\prime} h^u\right)$$

$$G_N^u = -r^{-1}\left(B_\pi^u B_s B_s' B_\pi^{u\prime}\right)^{-1}\left[(A+B)(rI + A_N)/\phi + B_\pi^u B_s B_s' B_\pi^{u\prime} H^u\right].$$

For a discussion of the economics of the results of this section the reader is referred to Zhou (1995).

## Problems

1. Let $dy = fdt + sdz$, in which $y$ is a scalar and $z$ is a Wiener process, and let $F = e^y$. Find the stochastic differential equation for F.
2. Let $dy = Aydt + dv$, in which $y$ is a vector and $v$ is a vector Wiener process with incremental covariance matrix $\Sigma(t)dt$, and let $F = y'k(t)y$. Find the stochastic differential equation for F.
3. By partitioning the bordered matrix in (7.48), show that the first $n$ rows of its inverse are as given by (7.49).
4. Let $\delta = (\delta_1, \ldots, \delta_m)'$ be the fractions of a fund invested in the $m$ assets that have mean (proportional) rates of return $\alpha = (\alpha_1, \ldots, \alpha_m)'$ and covariances for the rates $\sigma_{ij}$. Find the minimum variance $\sigma^2$ of the rate of return to the

fund for a given mean rate $m$. Show that the portfolio selection $\delta$ obtained by drawing a straight line through the origin of the $(m, \sigma)$ diagram and tangential to the function $\sigma(m)$ is the one given by (7.58).

5. Let the utility function be $u(c, t) = e^{-\rho t}\gamma^{-1}c^{\gamma}$. Let there be only one risky asset with mean $\alpha$ and variance $\alpha^2$ for its rate of return and one riskless asset with rate of return $r$. The proportion of wealth W invested in the risky asset is $w$. Using the differential generator defined by (7.9), write out the partial differential equation $u(c, t) + \mathcal{L}_w[V(W, t)] = 0$. Try the solution $V(W, t) = b(t)e^{-\rho t}W^{\gamma}/\gamma$ for this partial differential equation, in which $b(t)$ is some function. Deduce a differential equation for $b(t)$. (The results of this problem and of problem 6 are found in Merton (1969).)
6. Derive the optimal control equations for $c(t)$ and $w(t)$ in problem 5 as functions of $b(t)$.
7. Assume that there exists an asset, say the $m$th, in the model of section 7.6 whose rate of return is perfectly negatively correlated with changes in $r$, which the third mutual fund serves to hedge against. In the notation for equation (7.60), this means $E(dqdz_j) = \eta_{rj} = -E(dz_m dz_j) = -\rho_{mj}$ in which, because $r$ is the only state variable $x_i$, write $dq_i$ as $dq$, $g_i^*$ as $g^*$, and $\eta_{ij}$ as $\eta_{rj}$. In (7.65), $\mathrm{Cov}(dr, dP_i/P) = g^* s_i \eta_{ri} = -g^* s_i s_m \rho_{mi}/s_m = -g^* \sigma_{mi}/s_m$. Simplify equations (7.65) and (7.68) in terms of $\sigma_{mi}$ and $s_m$. Interpret the second terms of these equations.
8. Using (7.79) and (7.76), derive the option pricing equation (7.80).
9. Show that (7.80) satisfies the differential equation (7.75).
10. Find the optimum consumption function (7.98) by solving equation (7.95) as a partial differential equation for $c$, after applying Ito's lemma to obtain $d\lambda$ and using (7.96) and (7.97) to eliminate $q$ and $\lambda$, respectively. (The solution process requires somewhat lengthy algebra and is an alternative to solving the first-order conditions (7.95)–(7.97) as provided in the text).
11. For a mean-variance efficient portfolio $q$, in the model of section 7.8, which minimizes consumption variance $\sigma_c^2$ for a given expected excess return $e^* = q'e_\pi$, show that the following relation holds:

$$\sigma_c^2 = \gamma_1 e^{*2} + 2\gamma_2(N)e^* + \gamma_3(N), \tag{1}$$

in which $\gamma_1$ is a constant and $\gamma_2$ and $\gamma_3$ are functions of the noise vector N. Show that for any consumption variance $\sigma_c^2$, the lowest required expected excess return $\tilde{e}$ satisfies

$$\tilde{e} = \left[\sigma_c^2 - r\tilde{e}/\phi + f(N)\right]^2 \left[(h+HN)' B_N B_\pi' (B_\pi B_\pi')^{-1} B_\pi B_N' (h+HN)\right]^{-1}, \tag{2}$$

in which $f(N)$ is a function of the noise vector N. This is Theorem 3 of Zhou (1995, Chapter 1). In the nonnoisy case, in the mean-variance space, equation (1) is the upper part of a parabola. Equation (2) is a quadratic curve rather than a straight line. The right-side intersection $q$ of these two curves is the investor's equilibrium portfolio holdings, as shown in Figure 1.2 of Zhou (1995, Chapter 1).

12. Derive the parameters given by (7.106)–(7.108) by substituting (7.98) and (7.101), respectively, for $c$ and $e_\pi$ in (7.97) after evaluating $E_t d\lambda$ by (7.99) and (7.100). The parameters are obtained by setting to zero the scalar constant, the vector coefficient, and the matrix of the quadratic form in N in the resulting equation.

13. Change the observation equation (7.113) and the plant equation (7.114), respectively, to

$$ds = \left(C_{sy}y + C_{ss}s + c_s\right)dt + B_s dz$$

$$dy = \left(C_{yy}y + C_{ys}s + c_y\right)dt + B_s dz$$

Derive the Kalman filter for $d\hat{y} = E_t[dy]$ corresponding to (7.118). Comment on the changes from (7.118).

14. For the model of problem 13, find the differential equation for the covariance matrix $\Omega = \text{Cov}_t(y - \hat{y})$, in which $\hat{y} = E_t y$. Compare it with equation (7.120) and comment on the differences.

15. Rearrange the right-hand side of (7.118) into two terms multiplying $dt$ and $dz$, respectively, using (7.113) to eliminate $ds$ in (7.118). Interpret these two terms as factors affecting the change of the estimate from $\hat{y}(t)$ to $\hat{y}(t + dt)$ and give an intuitive explanation of their effects.

16. Derive the informed investor's consumption function $c^i$ and optimum portfolio $q^i$ as given by (7.129) and (7.130).

17. Derive the uninformed investor's consumption function $c^u$ and optimum portfolio $q^u$ as given by (7.131) and (7.132).

18. Following Cox, Ingersoll and Ross (1985), replace equations (81)–(83) of the model of section 7.8 by their equations

$$dY = \mu\left(Y, t\right)dt + S\left(Y, t\right)dw \tag{2}$$

$$d\eta = I_\eta \alpha\left(Y, t\right)dt + I_\eta G\left(Y, t\right)dw \qquad G = \left(g_{ij}\right) \tag{1}$$

where Y is a column vector of $k$ state variables, $\mu$ is a vector function, S is a $k \times (n + k)$ matrix, $w$ is a vector of $n + k$ independent standard Wiener processes, $\eta$ is a vector of $n$ outputs $(\eta_1, \ldots, \eta_n)$ of the consumer-producer good, $I_\eta$ is a diagonal matrix with $\eta_1, \ldots, \eta_n$ along its diagonal, $\alpha$ is a vector function, G is an $n \times (n + k)$ matrix, and the state variables Y affect the $n$ production processes given by (1). Let $F^i$ $(i = 1, \ldots, k)$ be the market value of one share of contingent claim $i$. Write

$$dF^i = \left(F^i\beta_i - \delta_i\right)dt + F^i h_i dw \tag{3}$$

where $h_i$ is a $1 \times (n + k)$ vector valued function, being the ith row of a matrix H = $(h_{ij})$; $F'\beta_i$ is the mean return of the ith claim, which equals the payout rate $\delta_i$ plus the mean price change $(F'\beta - \delta_i)$.

A representative individual invests a fraction $a_i$ of his wealth W in the production process (in industry) $i$, a fraction $b_i$ in the ith contingent claim. Analogous to equation (7.43), his wealth changes according to

$$dW = \left[\sum_{i=1}^{n} a_i(\alpha_i - r) + \sum_{i=1}^{k} b_i(\beta_i - r) + rW - c\right]dt$$
$$+\sum_{i=1}^{n} a_i W \sum_{j=1}^{n+k} g_{ij} dw_j + \sum_{i=1}^{k} b_i W \sum_{j=1}^{n+k} h_{ij} dw_j$$
$$\equiv W\mu(W)dt + W\sum_{j=1}^{n+k} q_j dw_j \qquad (5)$$

where $r$ is the rate of interest for borrowing and lending and $c$ denotes consumption.

Set up the Lagrangean (with multiplier $\lambda(W, Y, t)$) for a representative consumer-investor who wishes to maximize

$$E\int_t^{t'} U[c(s), Y(s), s]ds \qquad (4)$$

by choosing consumption $c$, the vector $a$ of fractions to invest in $n$ production processes and the vector $b$ of fractions to invest in $k$ contingent claims, given $r$ and the processes (1), (2) and (3). Using the Lagrange method, show that the first-order conditions for optimum is given by

$$U_c - \lambda = 0 \qquad (11a)$$

$$[\alpha - r1]W\lambda + [GG'a + GH'b]W^2\lambda_w + GS'W\lambda_Y = 0 \qquad (11c)$$

$$[\beta - r1]W\lambda + [HG'a + HH'b]W^2\lambda_w + HS'W\lambda_Y = 0 \qquad (11e)$$

where $\beta$ is a $k \times 1$ vector with elements $\beta_i$, $\lambda_Y$ is a vector of partial derivatives of $\lambda$ with respect to the vector Y and 1 is a $(k \times 1)$ unit vector. These are equations (11) of Cox, Ingersoll and Ross (1985, p. 370), ignoring the solutions $c = 0$ and $a = 0$.

19. Continuation of Problem 18. Define an *equilibrium* in the economy by a set of stochastic processes $(a, r, \beta, c)$ satisfying the first-order conditions (11) of problem 18 and the market clearing conditions $\Sigma a_i = 1$ and $b_i = 0$ for all $i$.

Using (11c) and the equilibrium conditions $b = 0$ and $\Sigma a_i = a'1 = 1$, solve for the optimum fractions $a$ to invest in the $n$ production activities and show that the equilibrium interest rate is, with $\lambda^*$ denoting the Lagrange multiplier associated with the constraint $1'a = 1$,

$$r(\mathrm{W},\ \mathrm{Y},\ t) = \lambda^*/\mathrm{W}\lambda = a'\alpha + a'\mathrm{GG}'a\mathrm{W}(\lambda_\mathrm{W}/\lambda) + a'\mathrm{GS}'(\lambda_\mathrm{Y}/\lambda)$$
$$= a'\alpha - (-\lambda_\mathrm{W}/\lambda)(\mathrm{var}\ \mathrm{W}/\mathrm{W}) - \sum_{i=1}^{k}(-\lambda_{\mathrm{Y}_i}/\lambda)(\mathrm{cov}(\mathrm{W},\ \mathrm{Y}_i)/\mathrm{W}) \qquad (14)$$

where cov(W, $Y_i$) is the covariance of changes in optimally invested wealth with changes in the state variable $Y_i$.

Using (11e) show that the equilibrium expected return on the ith contingent claim is given by

$$(\beta_i - r)\mathrm{F}^i = [\phi_\mathrm{W}\ \phi_{\mathrm{Y}_1}\ \ldots\ \phi_{\mathrm{Y}_k}][\mathrm{F}^i_\mathrm{W}\ \mathrm{F}^i_{\mathrm{Y}_1}\ \ldots\ \mathrm{F}^i_{\mathrm{Y}_k}]' \qquad (20)$$

where

$$\phi_\mathrm{W} = \left[(-\lambda_\mathrm{W}/\lambda)\mathrm{var}(\mathrm{W}) + \sum_{i=1}^{k}(-\lambda_{\mathrm{Y}_i}/\lambda)\mathrm{cov}(\mathrm{W},\ \mathrm{Y}_i)\right]$$

$$\phi_{\mathrm{Y}_i} = \left[(-\lambda_\mathrm{W}/\lambda)\mathrm{cov}(\mathrm{W},\ \mathrm{Y}_i) + \sum_{j=1}^{k}(-\lambda_{\mathrm{Y}_j}/\lambda)\mathrm{cov}(\mathrm{Y}_i,\ \mathrm{Y}_j)\right]$$

20. Continuation of Problem 19. Show that the price F of any contingent claim satisfies the partial differential equation

$$\frac{1}{2}\mathrm{var}(\mathrm{W})\mathrm{F}_{\mathrm{WW}} + \sum_{i=1}^{k}\mathrm{cov}(\mathrm{W},\ \mathrm{Y}_i)\mathrm{F}_{\mathrm{WY}_i} + \frac{1}{2}\sum_{i=1}^{k}\sum_{j=1}^{k}\mathrm{cov}(\mathrm{Y}_i,\ \mathrm{Y}_j)\mathrm{F}_{\mathrm{Y}_i\mathrm{Y}_j}$$
$$+[r(\mathrm{W},\ \mathrm{Y},\ t)\mathrm{W} - c(\mathrm{W},\ \mathrm{Y},\ t)]\mathrm{F}_\mathrm{W}$$
$$+\sum_{i=1}^{k}\mathrm{F}_{\mathrm{Y}_i}\left[\mu_i - \left(\frac{-\lambda_\mathrm{W}}{\lambda}\right)\mathrm{cov}(\mathrm{W},\ \mathrm{Y}_i) - \sum_{j=1}^{k}\left(\frac{-\lambda_{\mathrm{Y}_j}}{\lambda}\right)\mathrm{cov}(\mathrm{Y}_i,\ \mathrm{Y}_j)\right]$$
$$+\mathrm{F}_t - r(\mathrm{W},\ \mathrm{Y},\ t)\mathrm{F} + \delta(\mathrm{W},\ \mathrm{Y},\ t) = 0 \qquad (31)$$

where $r(\mathrm{W}, \mathrm{Y}, t)$ is given by equation (14) of problem 19. Hint: Use Ito's lemma to find $\beta\mathrm{F} - \delta$, use (20) of problem 19 to evaluate $\beta\mathrm{F}$, and combine the results.

# Models of Investment

## 8.1 Investment as Exercising an Irreversible Option to Invest

Consider a model for the investment decision of a firm that treats the decision as exercising an option to invest. Once the option is taken or exercised, it cannot be reversed. Such theories of investment are surveyed and discussed in Pindyck (1991), Dixit (1992), and Dixit and Pindyck (1994). In the simplest case, assume that to exercise the option, it would cost the firm I dollars. The present value $v(t)$ of the investment project at time $t$ is assumed to vary through time according to the stochastic differential equation

$$dv = \alpha v dt + \sigma v dz \tag{8.1}$$

in which $z$ is a Wiener process with $\text{var}(dz) = dt$. The problem is to determine the optimum time T to invest or to exercise the option. When the option is exercised, the firm gains $v(\text{T}) - \text{I}$, but loses the opportunity to invest in a future time $\text{T} + s$ when $v(\text{T} + s)$ may be larger than $v(\text{T})$.

Formulate this optimization problem starting from time 0 by using the Lagrangean expression

$$\begin{aligned}\mathcal{L} = \text{E}_0 e^{-\beta \text{T}}\left(v(\text{T}) - \text{I}\right)u - \int_0^{\text{T}} \text{E}_t e^{-\beta(t+dt)}\lambda(t+dt) \\ \times\left[v(t+dt) - v(t) - \alpha v(t)(1-u)dt - \sigma v(t)(1-u)dz(t)\right].\end{aligned} \tag{8.2}$$

The state variable is $v(t)$. The control function $u(v)$ could be viewed as a step function, with $u(v) = 1$ meaning to undertake the investment when $v$ reaches $v(\text{T}) \equiv v^*$ and $u(v) = 0$ meaning not to undertake the investment when $v < v^*$. To maximize (8.2), consider the two cases $u = 0$ and $u = 1$. Keeping $u$ fixed, first find a first-order condition by differentiating the Lagrangean expression with respect to the state variable $v$. Then, find a second condition to determine $v^*$.

To find the function $\lambda(v)$, set the derivative of $e^{\beta(t+dt)}\mathcal{L}$ with respect to the state variable $v = v(t)$ equal to zero. To obtain $\partial\mathcal{L}/\partial v$, evaluate $d\lambda$ by Ito's lemma:

$$d\lambda = \left( \frac{d\lambda}{dv}\alpha v + \frac{1}{2}\frac{d^2\lambda}{dv^2}\sigma^2 v^2 \right) dt + \frac{d\lambda}{dv}\sigma v dz \tag{8.3}$$

By using (8.3), find

$$\begin{aligned} e^{\beta(t+dt)}\frac{\partial \mathcal{L}}{\partial v} &= -\mathrm{E}_t\lambda(t+dt)\left[-1-\alpha dt-\sigma dz\right]-e^{\beta dt}\lambda(t) \\ &= \mathrm{E}_t\left[\lambda(t)+d\lambda(t)\right]\left[1+\alpha dt+\sigma dz\right]-(1+\beta dt)\lambda(t)+o(dt) \\ &= \lambda(t)+\alpha\lambda(t)dt+d\lambda(t)+\mathrm{E}_t d\lambda(t)\sigma dz(t)-\lambda(t)-\beta\lambda(t)dt+o(dt) \\ &= \left\{\frac{1}{2}\sigma^2 v^2\frac{d^2\lambda}{dv^2}+(\alpha+\sigma^2)v\frac{d\lambda}{dv}+(\alpha-\beta)\lambda\right\}dt+o(dt)=0 \end{aligned} \tag{8.4}$$

Setting to zero the expression in curly brackets in (8.4) provides a second-order differential equation for $\lambda$.

A solution to this differential equation is

$$\lambda = av^{\gamma} \tag{8.5}$$

Substituting (8.5) and its first and second derivatives into the above differential equation yields a second-degree equation in the unknown parameter $\gamma$, the solution of which is

$$\gamma = -\alpha/\sigma^2 - \frac{1}{2} \pm \left\{ \left( \alpha/\sigma^2 + \frac{1}{2} \right)^2 - 2(\alpha-\beta)/\sigma^2 \right\}^{1/2} \tag{8.6}$$

Because, at time T, when the value of the option equals to $v(\mathrm{T}) - \mathrm{I}$, the rate of change of the option value $\mathcal{L}$ with respect to $v$, or $\lambda(v(t))$, equals 1. Thus, $\lambda(v^*) = av^{*\gamma} = 1$, yielding $a = v^{*-\gamma}$ and

$$\lambda = (v/v^*)^{\gamma} \tag{8.7}$$

The solution is complete once we can find $v^*$. To do so, observe that the value of the option at time T evaluated by the Lagrangean expression is $v^*$-I. Because the value of the option is $\int\lambda(v)dv$, which equals $(\gamma+1)^{-1}v^{*-\gamma}v^{\gamma+1}$ by (8.7). This value when $v = v^*$ is $(\gamma+1)^{-1}v^*$. Equating $(\gamma+1)^{-1}v^*$ to $v^* - \mathrm{I}$, we obtain

$$v^* = (\gamma+1)\mathrm{I}/\gamma \tag{8.8}$$

The decision rule is to undertake the investment project when $v(t)$ reaches $v^*$ given by (8.8). Because a negative $v^*$ cannot be the optimum, $\gamma$ cannot be negative and one takes the larger of the two roots of $\gamma$ given by (8.6).

The above example is the most basic example in the theory of investment when undertaking an investment project is considered an irreversible decision as surveyed by Pindyck (1991). Pindyck (pp. 1122 and 1145–1146) solves this problem by dynamic programming. The value function $\mathrm{F}(v)$ for the option to invest is solved by using the Bellman equation, which is a second-order differential equation in F:

$$\frac{1}{2}\sigma^2 v^2 \frac{\partial^2 F}{\partial v^2} + \alpha v \frac{\partial F}{\partial v} - \beta F = 0 \tag{8.9}$$

Note the similarity between (8.9) and equation (7.71) for option pricing. Differentiating (8.9) with respect to $v$ and setting $\partial F/\partial v = \lambda$ would yield the differential equation from (8.4). In this example, the differential equation for $\lambda = \partial F/\partial v$ is of the same form as the differential equation for F. In circumstances in which the value function is easy to find by solving the Bellman equation, one should by all means find it, because it contains much useful information. Dixit and Pindyck (1994) provide examples of such circumstances.

## 8.2 A Simple Model of Investment with Adjustment Cost

Next, consider a simple model of investment that a firm undertakes to accumulate or decumulate its capital stock, so as to maximize discounted net revenues subject to the constraint of a Cobb-Douglas production function and to uncertain future prices for its product. This model was studied by Abel (1983) and the optimum investment policy was obtained by dynamic programming. I will derive the optimum investment policy by the method of Lagrange multipliers introduced in section 7.3

A competitive firm's cash flow at time $t$ is

$$p_t L_t^{\alpha} K_t^{1-\alpha} - wL_t - \gamma I_t^{\beta} \tag{8.10}$$

in which $p_t$ is the price of its output, $L_t$ and $K_t$ are, respectively, the quantities of its labor and capital inputs, $w$ is a fixed wage rate, and $\beta > 1$ is a constant elasticity of the cost of investment. The state variables $K_t$ and $p_t$ are assumed to evolve according to

$$dK_t = \left(I_t - \delta K_t\right)dt \tag{8.11}$$

$$dp_t = p_t \sigma dz \tag{8.12}$$

in which $dz$ is a Wiener process with mean zero and unit variance.

The Lagrange expression for the firm's optimization problem beginning from time 0 is

$$\mathscr{L} = \int_0^{\infty} E_t\left\{e^{-rt}\left[p_t L_t^{\alpha} K_t^{1-\alpha} - wL_t - \gamma I_t^{\beta}\right]dt - e^{-r(t+dt)}\lambda(t+dt)\left[K(t+dt) - K(t) - (I - \delta K)dt\right]\right\} \tag{8.13}$$

in which $r$ is the rate of interest. The control variables are $L_t$ and $I_t$. Although $p_t$ is a state variable, its dynamic evolution is independent of the control variables and, hence, no Lagrange multiplier is required for its dynamic constraint. Writing the subscript $t$ as an argument to be omitted when understood, and differentiating with respect to L, I, and K, respectively, yield

$$e^{rt}\frac{\partial \mathscr{L}}{\partial L} = \left[\alpha p L^{\alpha-1} K^{1-\alpha} - w\right]dt = 0 \tag{8.14}$$

$$e^{rt}\frac{\partial \mathcal{L}}{\partial I} = \left[-\beta\gamma I^{\beta-1} + e^{-rdt}E_t\lambda(t+dt)\right]dt = 0 \tag{8.15}$$

$$e^{rt}\frac{\partial \mathcal{L}}{\partial K} = (1-\alpha)pL^{\alpha}K^{-\alpha}dt - \lambda + e^{-rdt}\left[E_t\lambda(t+dt) - \delta E_t\lambda(t+dt)dt\right] = 0 \tag{8.16}$$

Equation (8.14) can be solved to obtain a demand function for labor:

$$L = \alpha^{1/(1-\alpha)}w^{-1/(1-\alpha)}p^{1/(1-\alpha)}K \tag{8.17}$$

in which $w$ is a given constant, and $p$ and K are state variables. Solving equation (8.15) gives the investment function

$$I = (\beta\gamma)^{1/(1-\beta)}e^{rdt/(1-\beta)}\left[\lambda + E_t d\lambda\right]^{-1/(1-\beta)} \tag{8.18}$$

which is a function of $\lambda$ and $E_t d\lambda$. Equation (8.16) provides an equation for $\lambda$.

$$\begin{aligned}&(1-\alpha)pL^{\alpha}K^{-\alpha}dt - \lambda + e^{-rdt}\lambda + E_t d\lambda - \delta\lambda dt - \delta E_t d\lambda dt\\ &= (1-\alpha)\alpha^{\alpha/(1-\alpha)}w^{-\alpha/(1-\alpha)}p^{1/(1-\alpha)}dt - r\lambda dt + E_t d\lambda - \delta\lambda dt + o(dt) = 0,\end{aligned} \tag{8.19}$$

in which I have substituted (8.17) for L. To evaluate $E_t d\lambda$, treat $\lambda$ as a function of the state variables K and $p$, which follow the stochastic differential equations (8.11) and (8.12) rewritten as

$$\begin{bmatrix} dK \\ dp \end{bmatrix} = \begin{bmatrix} I - \delta K \\ 0 \end{bmatrix}dt + \begin{bmatrix} 0 \\ p\sigma \end{bmatrix}dz$$

and apply Ito's lemma, denoting $\partial\lambda/\partial K$ by $\lambda_K$, and so forth, to yield

$$\begin{aligned}E_t d\lambda &= \left[\lambda_K(I-\delta K) + \frac{1}{2}tr\left(\begin{bmatrix}\lambda_{KK} & \lambda_{Kp}\\ \lambda_{pK} & \lambda_{pp}\end{bmatrix}\cdot\begin{bmatrix}0 & 0\\ 0 & p^2\sigma^2\end{bmatrix}\right)\right]dt\\ &= \left[(I-\delta K)\lambda_K + \frac{1}{2}\sigma^2p^2\lambda_{pp}\right]dt\end{aligned} \tag{8.20}$$

Substituting (8.18) for I in (8.20) and noting $E_t d\lambda$ is of order $dt$, we obtain

$$E_t d\lambda = \left[(\beta\gamma)^{1/(1-\beta)}\lambda^{-1/(1-\beta)}\lambda_K - \delta K\lambda_K + \frac{1}{2}\sigma^2p^2\lambda_{pp}\right]dt + o(dt) \tag{8.21}$$

Substituting (8.21) into (8.19) gives the following partial differential equation for the marginal revenue product of capital $\lambda$:

$$\frac{1}{2}\sigma^2p^2\lambda_{pp} + (\beta\gamma)^{1/(1-\beta)}\lambda^{-1/(1-\beta)}\lambda_K - \delta K\lambda_K - (r+\delta)\lambda + hp^{1/(1-\alpha)} = 0 \tag{8.22}$$

in which

$$h = (1-\alpha)(\alpha/w)^{\alpha/(1-\alpha)} \tag{8.23}$$

If $\lambda_K$ is zero, (8.22) becomes an ordinary differential equation for $\lambda$ as a function of $p$. A solution of this differential equation is

$$\lambda = ap^{\theta} \tag{8.24}$$

with parameters $a$ and $\theta$ yet to be determined. Substituting (8.24) and its second derivative into (8.22) yields

$$\frac{1}{2}\sigma^2 a\theta(\theta-1)p^\theta-(r+\delta)ap^\theta+hp^{1/(1-\alpha)}=0$$

A solution to this equation is $\theta = 1/(1-\alpha)$, which gives

$$\frac{1}{2}\sigma^2\alpha a/(1-\alpha)^2-(r+\delta)a+h=0$$

or

$$a=h\Big/\left[r+\delta-\alpha\sigma^2(1-\alpha)^{-2}/2\right] \tag{8.25}$$

Having found $\lambda$, substitute into (8.18) to obtain the optimum investment function, for very small $dt$,

$$\mathrm{I}=(\beta\gamma)^{1/(1-\beta)}a^{-1/(1-\beta)}p^{1/(1-\alpha)(\beta-1)} \tag{8.26}$$

in which the parameter a is given by (8.25), with $h$ defined by (8.23). In the terminology of Abel (1983), $\mathrm{E}_t\lambda(t+dt)$ in (8.18) is called $q_t$, which is the expected marginal revenue product of capital. The investment function (8.18) can be written as

$$\mathrm{I}=(q_t/\beta r)^{1/(\beta-1)} \tag{8.27}$$

Abel (1983) obtained the solution (8.27) by solving the Bellman equation for the value function $\mathrm{V}(\mathrm{K}, p)$. This section has emphasized the marginal revenue product of capital $\lambda = \partial\mathrm{V}/\partial\mathrm{K}$, which is obtained by using the method of Lagrange multipliers.

## 8.3 Investment as Gradual Capacity Expansion with Adjustment Cost

The two ideas of irreversibility and adjustment cost introduced in the previous two sections can be combined to explain investment. A simple model combining both ideas is discussed in Dixit and Pindyck (1994, pp. 359–364) and is based on Pindyck (1988) and Bertola (1989). A firm has a monopoly right to invest in the industry. Each unit of capital costs $c$, and investment in the unit is irreversible. Output Q is produced by using the production function $\mathrm{Q} = \mathrm{G}(\mathrm{K})$, in which K is the number of units of capital in place. The industry demand function $\mathrm{P} = \mathrm{YD}(\mathrm{Q})$ is subject to a random shift Y, which follows

$$d\mathrm{Y}=\alpha\mathrm{Y}dt+\sigma\mathrm{Y}dz \tag{8.28}$$

Ignoring variable cost, profit is given by

$$\pi=\mathrm{YD}(\mathrm{G}(\mathrm{K}))\mathrm{G}(\mathrm{K})=\mathrm{YH}(\mathrm{K}) \tag{8.29}$$

in which H(K) is assumed to be concave.

If I define $\mathrm{J}(t) = \mathrm{K}(t+dt) - \mathrm{K}(t)$ as the *increment* of capital from $t$ to $t+dt$ (not the *rate* of investment I, which would make the increment $\mathrm{J} = \mathrm{I}dt$), maximization of expected future profits with discount rate $\rho$ can be accomplished by forming the Lagrangean

$$\mathcal{L} = \int_0^\infty E_t\left\{e^{-\rho t}\left[YH(K)dt - cJ\right] - e^{-\rho(t+dt)}\lambda(t+dt)\left[K(t+dt) - K(t) - J(t)\right]\right\} \tag{8.30}$$

Y and K are state variables. J is the control variable. The first-order conditions are:

$$\begin{aligned} e^{\rho t}\frac{\partial \mathcal{L}}{\partial J} &= -c + e^{-\rho dt}E_t\lambda(t+dt) = -c + (1-\rho dt)(\lambda + E_t d\lambda) + o(dt) \\ &= -c + \lambda - \rho\lambda dt + E_t d\lambda + o(dt) = 0 \end{aligned} \tag{8.31}$$

$$\begin{aligned} e^{\rho t}\frac{\partial \mathcal{L}}{\partial K} &= YH'(K)dt - \lambda + e^{-\rho t}E_t\lambda(t+dt) = YH'(K)dt - \lambda + (1-\rho dt)(\lambda + E_t d\lambda) + o(dt) \\ &= YH'(K)dt - \rho\lambda dt + E_t d\lambda + o(dt) = 0 \end{aligned} \tag{8.32}$$

Because the evolution of the state variable Y according to equation (8.28) does not depend on the control variable J, I did not introduce a Lagrange multiplier for Y. However, $\lambda$ is a function of both K and Y, and the evolution of $\lambda$ can be derived from the evolution of Y given by (8.28) using Ito's lemma, yielding

$$E_t d\lambda = \left[\alpha Y\frac{\partial\lambda}{\partial Y} + \frac{1}{2}\frac{\partial^2\lambda}{\partial Y^2}\sigma^2 Y^2\right]dt \tag{8.33}$$

When (8.33) is substituted into (8.32), we obtain the following partial differential equation for $\lambda$:

$$\frac{1}{2}\sigma^2 Y^2\frac{\partial^2\lambda}{\partial Y^2} + \alpha Y\frac{\partial\lambda}{\partial Y} + YH'(K) - \rho\lambda = 0 \tag{8.34}$$

A solution to the differential equation (8.34) is

$$\lambda(K, Y) = AY^\beta + YH'(K)/\delta \tag{8.35}$$

in which A and $\beta$ are unknown parameters yet to be determined and $\delta = \rho - \alpha$. Substituting the derivatives of (8.35)

$$\frac{\partial\lambda}{\partial Y} = A\beta Y^{\beta-1} + H'(K)/\delta; \quad \frac{\partial^2\lambda}{\partial Y^2} = A\beta(\beta-1)Y^{\beta-2}$$

into the differential equation (8.34) gives

$$\frac{1}{2}\sigma^2 A\beta(\beta-1)Y^\beta + \alpha A\beta Y^\beta - \rho AY^\beta = 0$$

implying the following quadratic equation for $\beta$:

$$\frac{1}{2}\sigma^2\beta^2 + \left(\alpha - \frac{1}{2}\sigma^2\right)\beta - \rho = 0 \tag{8.36}$$

To find A, use the first-order condition (8.31) as $dt$ becomes extremely small

$$\lambda = AY^{\beta} + YH'(K)/\delta = c \tag{8.37}$$

Differentiating (8.37) with respect to Y gives

$$\frac{\partial \lambda}{\partial Y} = A\beta Y^{\beta-1} + H'(K)/\delta = 0 \tag{8.38}$$

which is called the "smooth pasting" condition in Dixit and Pindyck (1994, p. 364, equation (8)). Solving equation (8.37) and (8.38) for Y and A yields

$$Y(K) = \frac{\beta}{\beta - 1}\frac{\delta c}{H'(K)} \tag{8.39}$$

and

$$A(K) = -\left(\frac{\beta-1}{c}\right)^{\beta-1}\left(\frac{H'(K)}{\beta\delta}\right)^{\beta} \tag{8.40}$$

Equation (8.39) gives that value of Y which makes positive investment worthwhile. If Y is smaller than that value, $\lambda - c < 0$ by (8.37) and the first-order condition (8.31) becomes an inequality with optimum investment equal to zero. Because that value is positive, choose the larger root for $\beta$ in solving the quadratic equation (8.36). To see this, let $\beta = \gamma + 1$ and rewrite (8.36) as a quadratic equation in $\gamma$. Take the positive root of this equation for $\gamma$ to make $(\gamma + 1)/\gamma$ or $\beta/(\beta - 1)$ positive, as was done for equation (8.6) in section 8.1.

A second model combining possibly irreversible investment with adjustment costs discussed in Dixit and Pindyck (1994, pp. 383–391) is based on the work of Abel and Eberly (1993). Retaining equation (8.28) for Y and rewriting the profit function as $\pi(K,Y)$, one can introduce depreciation rate $d$ into the capital accumulation equation

$$K(t + dt) = K(t) - dK(t)dt + J \tag{8.41}$$

and consider the following cost of adjustment C, depending on whether $J = Idt$ is positive of negative:

$$C(J, dt) = \begin{cases} \phi_1 dt + c_1 J + \psi(J/dt)dt & \text{if } J > 0 \\ 0 & \text{if } J = 0 \\ \phi_2 dt - c_2 J + \psi(J/dt)dt & \text{if } J < 0 \end{cases} \tag{8.42}$$

The case of irreversible investment results when $c_2 = 0$, so that a negative J or selling capital gives no cost and no revenue. If $-c_2 = c_1$, investment is completely reversible. If $-c_2 < c_1$, it is partially reversible. The first model of this section results when the first line of (8.42) contains only $c_1 J$ and the rate of depreciation $d$ in (8.41) is zero, while J is restricted to being nonnegative.

To solve the firm's problem of maximizing expected profits subject to the constraint (8.41), form the Lagrangean

$$\mathcal{L} = \int E_t\left\{e^{-\rho t}\left[\pi(K, Y)dt - C(J, dt)\right] - e^{-\rho(t+dt)}\lambda(t+dt)\left[K(t+dt) - K(t) + dKdt - J\right]\right\} \tag{8.43}$$

treating K and Y as state variables and J as the control variable. The first-order condition are:

$$e^{\rho t}\frac{\partial \mathcal{L}}{\partial J} = -\frac{dC}{dJ} + e^{-\rho dt}E_t\lambda(t+dt) = -\frac{dC}{dJ} + \lambda - \rho\lambda dt + E_t d\lambda + odt = 0 \tag{8.44}$$

$$\begin{aligned} e^{\rho t}\frac{\partial \mathcal{L}}{\partial K} &= \frac{\partial \pi}{\partial K}dt - \lambda - e^{-\rho dt}\left(-1 + d\cdot dt\right)\left(E_t d\lambda + \lambda\right) \\ &= \frac{\partial \pi}{\partial K}dt - (\rho + d)\lambda dt + E_t d\lambda + o(dt) = 0 \end{aligned} \tag{8.45}$$

in which $dC/dJ$ in (8.44) depends on whether J is positive, zero, or negative as given by (8.42). In the three cases and as $dt \to 0$, (8.44) becomes, respectively,

$$-c_1 + \psi'(J/dt) + \lambda = 0 \qquad \text{if } J > 0 \tag{8.44a}$$

$$\lambda < 0 \qquad \text{if } J = 0 \tag{8.44b}$$

$$c_2 + \psi'(J/dt) + \lambda = 0 \qquad \text{if } J < 0 \tag{8.44c}$$

Again, using equation (8.33) for $E_t d\lambda$, one can obtain from (8.45) the following partial differential equation for $\lambda$:

$$\frac{1}{2}\sigma^2 Y^2\frac{\partial^2 \lambda}{\partial Y^2} + \alpha Y\frac{\partial \lambda}{\partial Y} + \frac{\partial \pi}{\partial K} - (\rho + d)\lambda = 0 \tag{8.46}$$

which can be solved in the same way as (8.34), with the solution taking the form

$$\lambda(K, Y) = AY^{\beta} + \frac{\partial \pi}{\partial K}\Big/(\rho + d - \alpha) \tag{8.47}$$

## 8.4 Optimal Policy for Replacement Investment

This section is concerned with the optimal time to replace a piece of capital equipment when the equipment is indivisible. The indivisibility aspect of this problem is the same as in the problem studied in section 8.1, in which an investment project costs I dollars. There are two differences. The model in this section is formulated in discrete time. A random element in section 8.1 was introduced as a stochastic process for the present value of the investment. In this section, it is introduced in the rate of depreciation through random usage of the equipment and in the costs of replacing and maintaining equipment. Because both require a discrete control variable $u_t = 1$ or 0, for investing or not investing at any time $t$, the methods of solution are similar.

A simple example taken from Rust (1987) and summarized in Rust (1994, p. 3130) serves well to illustrate the problem. In the example, one wishes to find an optimum time to replace a bus engine. The state variable $x_t$ is the cumulative mileage of the bus. There is only one type of engine to replace; after the replacement, the bus is as good as new. The control variable $u_t$ takes the value 1 or zero for replacing or not replacing the engine at time $t$. The objective is to minimize the expected sum of discounted costs of maintaining the equipment. In each period $t$, if the equipment is replaced or if $u_t = 1$, there is a fixed labor and parts cost $\theta_1$ of installing the engine. There are also monthly maintenance and operating costs $c(0;\ \theta_2)$ of operating and maintaining a bus with 0 engine mileage and a random cost $\eta_t(1)$ for the new equipment. If $u_t = 0$, the operating cost is $c(x_t;\ \theta_2)$ for the old equipment of mileage $x_t$, and the random cost is $\eta_t(0)$. Thus, the return function in the objective function is

$$r(x_t,\ u_t) = \begin{cases} -\theta_1 - c(0;\ \theta_2) - \eta_t(1) & \text{if } u_t = 1 \\ -c(x_t;\ \theta_2) - \eta_t(0) & \text{if } u_t = 0 \end{cases} \tag{8.48}$$

Rewrite the function $r$ as

$$r(x,\ u) = u\left[-\theta_1 - c(0;\ \theta_2) - \eta_t(1)\right] + (1-u)\left[-c(x;\ \theta_2) - \eta_t(0)\right] \tag{8.49}$$

Let $\varepsilon_t$ be a random variable that represents the mileage added to the bus during period $t$. The evolution of the state variable $x_t$ for cumulative mileage of the engine in the bus at the beginning of period $t$ is

$$x_{t+1} = u_t\varepsilon_t + (1-u_t)\left[x_t + \varepsilon_t\right] = (1-u_t)x_t + \varepsilon_t \tag{8.50}$$

To find the optimum control function $u(x)$, form the Lagrangean

$$\mathcal{L} = \sum_{t=0}^{\infty} \beta_t \mathrm{E}_t\left\{r(x_t,\ u_t) - \beta\lambda_{t+1}\left[x_{t+1} - (1-u_t)x_t - \varepsilon_t\right]\right\} \tag{8.51}$$

Given $u_t$, which may be 0 or 1, differentiate (8.51) with respect to the state variable $x_t$ as in section 8.1, yielding

$$\beta^{-t}\mathcal{L}_x = r_1(x_t,\ u_t) - \lambda_t + \beta(1-u_t)\mathrm{E}_t\lambda_{t+1} = 0 \tag{8.52}$$

Because one cannot differentiate $\mathcal{L}$ with respect to the discrete control variable $u_t$, consider the difference $\Delta\mathcal{L}_u = \mathcal{L}(u_t = 1) - \mathcal{L}(u_t = 0)$:

$$\beta^{-t}\Delta\mathcal{L}_u = r(x_t,\ 1) - r(x_t,\ 0) - \beta x_t \mathrm{E}_t\lambda_{t+1} = 0 \tag{8.53}$$

Equation (8.53) is the change in the objective function by replacing the equipment in period $t$ as compared with not replacing it. When the equipment is fairly new or when $x_t$ is small, (8.53) is negative or it does not pay to change the equipment, provided that one formulates the function $r$ correctly. When $x_t$ increases to a certain point $x^*$ with $\Delta\mathcal{L}_u(x^*) = 0$, it will just pay to replace the equipment at $t$. $x^*$ is the cumulative mileage when the equipment should be replaced.

As in the rest of this book, (8.52) and (8.53) are two first-order conditions that, together with the dynamic model (8.50), can be used to solve for the Lagrange function $\lambda(x)$ and the optimum control function $u(x)$. As in section 8.1, $u(x)$ is a step function, taking the value 0 for $x < x^*$ and the value 1 for

$x \geq x^*$. To find $x^*$, let $u_t = 1$ and solve equation (8.52). The solution is $\lambda(x^*) = r_1(x^*, 1)$. That is, when the equipment is replaced at $t$ with $x_t = x^*$, the marginal cost of an extra mile, or the marginal value of driving the bus for one mile less, is $\partial r(x^*, 1)/\partial x$. At $x_t = x^*$, (8.52) also holds for $u_t = 0$. It then implies

$$\beta E_t \lambda_{t+1} = \lambda(x^*) - r_1(x^*, 0) = r_1(x^*, 1) - r_1(x^*, 0) \qquad (8.54)$$

Substituting the right-hand side of equation (8.54) for $\beta E_t \lambda_{t+1}$ in equation (8.53), one obtains an equation for $x^*$:

$$r(x^*, 1) - r(x^*, 0) - x^*\left[r_1(x^*, 1) - r_1(x^*, 0)\right] = 0$$

with solution

$$x^* = \frac{r(x^*, 1) - r(x^*, 0)}{r_1(x^*, 1) - r_1(x^*, 0)} \qquad (8.55)$$

The optimum policy is to replace the equipment when the cumulative mileage reaches the point $x^*$ given by (8.55). The critical mileage $x^*$ is the ratio of the period-$t$ return (saving) by replacing the equipment to the difference between the marginal returns per mile from replacing and not replacing the equipment. In other words, the critical mileage times the difference between the marginal returns per mile from replacing the equipment and from not replacing it must equal the gain in return by replacing the equipment (see problem 2).

## 8.5 Optimal Policy to Retire Human Capital

The goal of this section is to explain when a worker will decide to retire given the wage structure and the retirement benefits, and to study the effects of social security retirement benefits on retirement. It belongs to labor economics, but economists including T. W. Schultz (1961) and Gary Becker (1964) have decided to call labor human capital, thus calling labor services services from human capital. Using this terminology, consider when a piece of human capital (a laborer) should be retired in the same way as considering when a piece of physical capital equipment should be retired. The latter is the subject of the last section. The same method can be applied to solve the problem of this section.

The model reported here is due to Lumsdaine, Stock, and Wise (1992), which is partly summarized in Rust (1994, p. 3134). A worker has to decide when to retire. The decision variable $u_t = 1$ if the worker decides to continue working; $u_t = 0$ if the worker decides to retire and receive a pension. The pension plan studied empirically offers substantial incentives to remain working until age 55 and to retire before age 65. The observed state variable $x_t$ is the benefit (wage or pension) in year $t$, and the unobserved state variable $\varepsilon_t$ is assumed to be i.i.d. The worker's utility function is

$$r(x_t, \varepsilon_t, u_t) = \begin{cases} x_t^{\theta_1} + \mu_1 + \varepsilon_t(1) & \text{if } u_t = 1 \\ (\mu_2 \theta_2 x_t)^{\theta_1} + \varepsilon_t(0) & \text{if } u_t = 0 \end{cases} \qquad (8.56)$$

$(\mu_1, \mu_2)$ represent time-invariant worker-specific heterogeneity. When $\varepsilon_t$ is assumed to have an extreme value distribution, $\mu_1$ is assumed to be 0 and $\mu_2$ a log normal random variable with mean 1 and scale parameter $\theta_3$. When $\varepsilon_t$ is assumed to be normal, $\mu_2 = 1$, and $\mu_1$ is a normal random variable with mean 0 and standard deviation $\theta_4$. Concerning the wage or pension benefit $x_s$ in year $s$, a worker at age $t$ who continues to work will receive given wage $Y_s$ in subsequent years $s$. If a worker retires at age $r$, subsequent retirement benefits will be $B_s(r)$. $Y_s$ and $B_s(r)$ are institutional data taken as given by the worker. At age $t$, a worker can calculate the present value of his or her future income stream if he or she retires at age $r$, using a discount factor $\beta$,

$$V_t(r) = \sum_{s=t}^{r-1} \beta^{s-t} U_W(Y_s) + \sum_{s=r}^{T} \beta^{s-t} U_r[B_s(r)]$$

in which T is the compulsory retirement age, $U_W(Y_s)$ is given by the top half of equation (8.56) for $r(x_s, \varepsilon_s, u_s)$ when $u_s = 1$, and $U_r[B_s(r)]$ is given by the bottom half when $u_s = 0$. The worker is assumed to choose the retirement age or decide which year to retire (setting $u_s = 0$) by maximizing the expectation of $V_t(r)$ subject to an appropriate constraint on $x_s$ by using a Lagrangean expression similar to (8.51) and the associated first-order conditions similar to (8.52) and (8.53). The reader can pursue this topic by solving problem 3.

## 8.6 Some Other Literature on Investment

The organization of this chapter is motivated partly by a desire for continuity with the last chapter and partly by the uniformity in methods of analysis. It may suffer from over emphasis on what is current or fashionable at the expense of the basic contributions by earlier writers. This possible shortcoming, or virtue as some would argue, is present in selecting teaching material for second-year graduate students who are soon required to do original research. What would be more efficient than exposing them to the latest articles so that they could add something to the frontier of research? The possible drawback is that the current fashion might be forgotten two decades from now, but most doctoral students are not expected to write something to last much longer. Using this frontier strategy, I can be excused from not treating the past literature sufficiently at the beginning of this chapter. Before closing, I should at least point out the relevance of the current literature from the perspective of cumulative knowledge of investment behavior.

Keynes (1936) treats investment fluctuations as the major source of economic fluctuations and attributes fluctuations in investment to changes in the entrepreneur's expectations of future profits. Burns and Mitchell (1946), in the study of business cycles, also consider profits as an important variable explaining investment. Harrod (1948), Samuelson (1939), and Goodwin (1951) have emphasized the importance of the accelerations principle in investment fluctuations. The principle is based on a simple relationship between stock and flows, namely between the demand for total stock of capital goods and for the change in total stock (new purchase or gross investment minus depreciation).

It has been successful in explaining a large fraction of the fluctuations in the purchases of consumer durable goods, as well as aggregate investment expenditures, as repeatedly demonstrated in Chow (1957; 1960; 1967; 1968; 1985a,b; and 1993) and in Chow and Levitan (1969).

Jorgenson (1967) applies a dynamic optimization framework to derive an investment equation. The firm is assumed to maximize the expected sum of discounted future profits (revenue minus labor and capital costs) in deciding on the amount of labor and capital to hire. The mere fact of considering a multiperiod problem rather than a one-period problem does not necessarily change the demand functions for labor and capital services if expectations of relevant variables, such as wage and interest, in the future are constant and if there are no adjustment costs in hiring and reducing services from labor and capital. Jorgenson's demand for labor equation is the same as in a one-period model. The demand for capital services equation would be the same if not for time delays introduced in the construction and installation of physical capital. The time delays introduced make the model dynamic.

Keynes (1936) and Burns and Mitchell (1946) would disagree with Jorgenson's treatment of the subject, because to them investment should not be treated from the viewpoint of demand for capital services, which is the same in nature as the demand for labor services. Introduction of costs and delays in hiring a firing workers or in building and depreciating physical capital is still insufficient to explain the large fluctuations in aggregate investment expenditures. Instead, investment should be viewed as taking on new projects by existing firms or possibly by new firms. What makes it different is partly that an investment project is chunky or indivisible and irreversible, properties that are emphasized by the more recent authors as reported in sections 8.1 through 8.3.

Keynes (1936) and Schumpeter (1936) would say that even these considerations might be insufficient. Political events and the introduction of new technology might be so unpredictable and erratic in changing an entrepreneur's expectations about the profitability of investment projects as to dwarf the consideration of sections 8.1 and 8.3 when severe economic crisis or major technological innovations occur. If major political events and major technological innovations are so unpredictable as to defy the construction of time series models (which are based on the strong assumption that a certain probabilistic mechanism that an economist can specify generates these events through time), multiperiod optimization models that incorporate such time-series models for exogenous events may fail to explain economic events, including aggregate investment fluctuations.

## Problems

1. Discuss the similarities and differences between equation (8.9) for the value of an option to invest and equation (7.71) for option pricing.
2. Specify the functions $c$ and $\eta_t$ and the parameter values $\theta_1$ and $\theta_2$ in equation (8.48). Find the critical mileage $x^*$ for replacing the bus engine in the

problem discussed in section 8.4. Find $\lambda(x^*)$. Discuss the economic meanings of the formulas for $x^*$ and $\lambda(x^*)$.

3. For the choice of retirement age using the model of Lumsdaine, Stock, and Wise (1992), with the period-$t$ utility function given by equation (8.56) and the constraint on the wage or pension $x_t$ given by a description following (8.56), write down the Lagrangean for the worker's optimization problem and its associated first-order conditions. Explain how you would find the optimum retirement age. Provide an economic interpretation of your mathematic results.

4. The model of section 8.5 has a finite time horizon, whereas the model of section 8.4 has an infinite time horizon. If you solve these models numerically for the optimum policy, will you use different methods? Explain.

5. Write a model in discrete time using a discrete decision variable $u_t = 1$ or $0$ on another economic problem that is similar to the models for optimum policy on replacing physical capital and retiring human capital in section 8.4 and 8.5, respectively. Find the optimal policy and discuss its economic meaning. What economic phenomena can your model explain?

6. Is investment a function of the interest rate, or profits, or both? Explain using a relevant model.

7. Should the demand for a firm's capital be treated the same way as the demand for its labor? Why or why not?

8. Of all the models for investment discussed in this chapter, including those referred to in section 8.6, which you may have studied, which one would you choose to be the best? Why do you choose it? If you are not satisfied with the best, how would you improve it? An answer to the last question can form a part of a Ph.D. thesis.

9. Do you believe that dynamic optimization is the appropriate framework to build a model for investment of a firm? If so, cite one model that uses dynamic optimization, point out the most relevant and useful economic implications from the model, and explain why such implications cannot be derived from a one-period model.

10. This is the last chapter of this book that deals with economic modeling, the next chapter being concerned with numerical methods. Do you believe that dynamic optimization should almost always be used to derive dynamic economic theory? Explain. If your answer is "yes," think of yourself as a chief economist for the government or for a firm that seeks to produce a forecast or to study a policy issue, or even as a professor who has to find an answer to such problems. Are you willing to make some ad hoc assumptions (not derived from rigorous dynamic optimization) as Keynes did concerning wage rigidity and liquidity preference? If not, what are your alternatives?

# Numerical Methods for Solving First-Order Conditions in Dynamic Optimization Problems

## 9.1 Introduction

Hundreds of papers have been written on the numerical solution of dynamic optimization problems based on the method of dynamic programming. These papers have appeared in journals in economics, engineering and operations research, applied mathematics, and other fields of applied science. Averaging 25 papers per year since the publication of Bellman (1957) would make the total number close to 1,000. A survey of ten papers on the subject can be found in Taylor and Uhlig (1990). My approach is to bypass the value function and the associated Bellman equation and to concentrate on the first-order conditions for optimum based on the Lagrange method. In previous chapters, I have demonstrated that knowledge of the value function is unnecessary in solving dynamic optimization problems. In this chapter, I show that the Lagrange method is computationally more efficient and more accurate in many applications. It is more efficient because resources are wasted to obtain and store information about the value function, except for a vector of some of its derivatives, which is the Lagrange function. By using the same computational effort without seeking the value function, one can make the numerical result more accurate. Because I rely on first-order conditions, I must check whether the solution obtained is a maximum by using the results presented in section 2.5 in case there is any doubt.

I discuss numerical methods for solving the first-order conditions of equations (2.15) and (2.16) in discrete time, or (7.21) and (7.22) in continuous time, and ignore the value function in dynamic programming. As a numerical solution of the Bellman equation for the value function V has been an active area of research for over three decades, a numerical solution of the two first-order conditions derived by the method of Lagrange multipliers is an important area of research if one wishes to solve dynamic optimization problems by that method. In sections 2.4 and 7.4, I have provided numerical methods for solving the first-order conditions of stochastic dynamic optimization problems in discrete time and in continuous time respectively. A well-known but crude numerical method is to approximate the function $f$ in the dynamic model for the state variables by a linear function and the function $r$ in the objective function by a quadratic function and to solve the resulting linear-quadratic control problem, which yields a linear control function and a quadratic value function or a linear Lagrange function. In sections 2.4 and 7.4, I have discussed the numerical solution for $\lambda$ as a linear function. This chapter presents several approximate solutions to the optimum control function $u$ and the Lagrange function $\lambda$ based on the first-order conditions.

In section 9.2, I point out that before solving the first-order conditions for the optimal control function numerically, it is important to define the variables appropriately. One is free to transform the state and control variables in an optimal control problem. For example, one may prefer to use the logarithm of consumption rather than consumption as the control variable. The accuracy of a numerical approximation to the optimal control function depends on the transformation of variables. If the optimal control function is linear or very close to being linear in the logarithms of the state variables, failure to transform the variables into logarithms will make a linear approximation to the control function a poor approximation. In models of economic growth, if the variables contain exponential trends, it is necessary to use detrended variables if one wishes to deal with covariance-stationary time series. One may also wish to deal with logarithms of detrended variables if the dynamic model is approximately linear in the logarithms, because a linear model is often associated with optimal linear control functions. The question, what transformations will improve a linear approximation to the control function deserves our attention. Section 9.2 illustrates certain transformations useful in economics. Section 9.3 presents an algebraic shortcut to approximate the first-order conditions by linear functions in the logarithms of detrended variables.

In sections 9.4 and 9.5, I provide methods to solve the linearized first-order conditions. Section 9.4 deals with speeding up the solution of matrix Riccati equations, and section 9.5 with the method of undetermined coefficients. In section 9.6, I propose a quadratic approximation to the Lagrange function for models in discrete time, and in section 9.7 for models in continuous time. Section 9.8 presents a method which is applicable when the number of state variables is small.

## 9.2 Change of Variables

Consider an optimal control problem to maximize $\mathrm{E}\,\Sigma_t \beta^t r(x_t, u_t)$ subject to

$$x_{t+1} = f(x_t, u_t) + \varepsilon_{t+1}.$$

Forming a Lagrangean

$$\mathcal{L} = \mathrm{E}\sum_t \left\{\beta^t r(x_t, u_t) + \beta^{t+1}\lambda'_{t+1}\left[x_{t+1} - f(x_t, u_t) - \varepsilon_{t+1}\right]\right\},$$

differentiate with respect to $u_t$ and $x_t$ to obtain two first-order conditions (2.15) and (2.16). The problem is to find a numerical solution of the first-order conditions (2.15) and (2.16) together with the model (2.13), now rewritten as

$$r_2(x, u) + \beta f_2'(x, u) E(\lambda_{t+1}) = 0 \tag{9.1}$$

$$\lambda = r_1(x, u) + \beta f_1'(x, u) E(\lambda_{t+1}) \tag{9.2}$$

$$x_{t+1} = f(x, u) + \varepsilon_{t+1} \tag{9.3}$$

in which the time subscript $t$ for the vectors $x$ and $u$ of state and control variables are omitted when understood, the subscripts 1 and 2 of the functions $r$ and $f$ denote derivatives with respect to the first and second argument respectively, and $\varepsilon_{t+1}$ is i.i.d.

Before solving the first-order conditions numerically, it is important to transform the variables appropriately. The transformation of variables can affect the accuracy of a numerical approximation to the solution of the first-order conditions. In this section, I emphasize four points. First, if the original variables are nonstationary because of a deterministic or stochastic trend, a transformation to detrended variables will result in a stationary model. Detrending can improve the accuracy of a linear approximation to the optimum control function because Taylor expansions of the functions $f$, $r_1$, and $r_2$ can be performed about a stationary point. Second, taking logarithms may improve the accuracy of a linear approximation to the control function if it makes the resulting dynamic model for the state variables more nearly linear. It is easy to see that a linear control rule is effective in controlling a linear model $f$. Because $x_{t+1}$ depends on $f(x, u)$, controlling $x_{t+1}$ can be achieved by a linear function $u(x)$ if $f$ is linear. Third, there is also a choice of the set of control variables. Choosing one control variable rather than another can affect the functions $r$ and $f$, and hence the accuracy of a linear approximation to the optimum control function that satisfies the first-order conditions. Fourth, defining variables as deviations from the steady-state values of the associated deterministic control problem can save some computation because the intercepts of all linear approximations ($r_1$, $r_2$, $f$, $u$, $\lambda$) are zero. These four points are illustrated by an example.

Let there be a central economic planner maximizing an objective function

$$E \Sigma \beta^t \ln[c_t] \tag{9.4}$$

of per capita consumption $c$, subject to the constraints

$$q = Ak^{1-\alpha} \tag{9.5}$$

$$k_{t+1} = k + q - c \tag{9.6}$$

$$\ln[A_{t+1}] = \gamma + \ln[A] + \eta \tag{9.7}$$

in which (9.5) is a Cobb-Douglas production function for output $q$ per capita with capital stock $k$ per capita at the beginning of the period as argument;

output $q$ is net output so that $q - c$ is investment net of depreciation, and (9.7) assumes $\ln A$ to follow a random walk with drift $\gamma$.

Using this example, note that, given a dynamic optimization problem, one can change the state and control variables and thus change the functions $r$ and $f$. To illustrate, for the problem defined by (9.4)–(9.7), one may consider $c$ as the control variable, $\ln A$ and $k$ as the state variables, and hence $r = \ln c$ and the vector function $f$ is nonlinear:

$$f(\ln A,\ k;\ u) = \begin{bmatrix} \gamma + \ln A \\ k + Ak^{1-\alpha} - c \end{bmatrix}$$

As a first transformation of variables, one may wish to define new state and control variables to eliminate the stochastic trends in $q$ and $k$ to obtain a stationary model. For a discussion of stochastic trends, see section 5.2. Equation (9.7) defines a stochastic trend in $\ln A$. Letting $\ln z = (\ln A)/\alpha$, one obtains a stationary model by dividing equation (9.6) by $z$

$$\begin{aligned} k_{t+1}/z &= (k/z_{-1})\cdot(z_{-1}/z) + (z^{\alpha}k^{1-\alpha})/z + c/z \\ &= (k/z_{-1})(z/z_{-1})^{-1} + (k/z_{-1})^{1-\alpha}(z/z_{-1})^{\alpha-1} - c/z \end{aligned} \tag{9.8}$$

In this first transformation, one would chose $c/z$ as the control variable and $k/z_{-1}$ and $z/z_{-1}$ as state variables, but $f$ would not be linear. As a second transformation, take logarithms and change the control variable to $\ln(k_{t+1}/z)$ by choosing the following state and control variables:

$$x = (x_1,\ x_2)' = [\ln(z/z_{-1}),\ \ln(k/z_{-1})]';\quad u = x_{2,t+1}. \tag{9.9}$$

Substituting (9.8) for $c/z$ in $r = \ln(c/z) + \ln z$, one obtains the functions $r$ and $f$ in terms of the new variables

$$r = \ln\{\exp((1-\alpha)(x_2 - x_1)) - \exp(u) + \exp(x_2 - x_1)\} + \ln z \tag{9.10}$$

$$f = Ax + Cu + b \tag{9.11}$$

in which A is a 2 by 2 zero matrix, $C = (0,1)'$, and $b = (\mu,0)'$ with $\mu = \gamma/\alpha$. Thus, the variables and the functions $r$ and $f$ are changed, and $f$ is now linear. Note that the linear $f$ is achieved not merely by taking logarithms but by choosing $\ln(k_{t+1}/z)$ rather than $\ln(c/z)$ as the control variable. Using the latter control variable would yield a nonlinear $f$ that determines $k_{t+1}/z$ or $\ln(k_{t+1}/z)$ by equation (9.8). Using the former control variable, eliminate equation (9.8) as a nonlinear $f$ by substituting it in the function $r = \ln c$.

To solve the problem defined by (9.9), (9.10), and (9.11) after the second change of variables, differentiate the Lagrangean

$$\mathcal{L} = E\sum_t \{\beta^t r(x_t,\ u_t) - \beta^{t+1}\lambda_{2,t+1}[x_{2,t+1} - u_t]\}$$

with respect to $u$ and $x_2$ to yield the first-order conditions

$$\{\exp[(1-\alpha)(x_2 - x_1)] - \exp(u) + \exp(x_2 - x_1)\}^{-1}(-\exp(u)) + \beta E_t\lambda_{2,t+1} = 0 \tag{9.12}$$

$$\lambda_{2t} = \left\{\exp\left[(1-\alpha)(x_2 - x_1)\right] - \exp(u) + \exp(x_2 - x_1)\right\}^{-1}$$
$$\times\left\{(1-\alpha)\exp\left[(1-\alpha)(x_2 - x_1)\right] + \exp(x_2 - x_1)\right\} \qquad (9.13)$$

One finds an approximate solution to these first-order conditions by first linearizing $r_2$ and $r_1$:

$$r_2 = \left\{\exp\left[(1-\alpha)(x_2 - x_1)\right] - \exp(u) + \exp(x_2 - x_1)\right\}^{-1}\left(-\exp(u)\right) \simeq \mathrm{K}_{21}x + \mathrm{K}_{22}u + k_2 \qquad (9.14)$$

$$r_1 = \left\{\exp\left[(1-\alpha)(x_2 - x_1)\right] - \exp(u) + \exp(x_2 - x_1)\right\}^{-1}$$
$$\times\left\{(1-\alpha)\exp\left[(1-\alpha)(x_2 - x_1)\right] + \exp(x_2 - x_1)\right\} \simeq \mathrm{K}_{11}x + \mathrm{K}_{12}u + k_1 \qquad (9.15)$$

in which $x = (x_1\ x_2)'$; $\mathrm{K}_{21}$ and $\mathrm{K}_{11}$ are 1 by 2 matrices; and $\mathrm{K}_{22}$, $k_2$, $\mathrm{K}_{12}$, and $k_1$ are scalars. Because the state variables are detrended and stationary, linearize $r_1$ and $r_2$ by a first-order Taylor expansion about the steady-state values of the state and control variables in the deterministic version of the stationary model with $\varepsilon_{t+1}$ set equal to zero. The choice of the steady-state values for linearization will improve the accuracy of the linear approximation for solving the first-order conditions (9.1) and (9.2), because the state and control variables tend to be closer to these values than other values in the long run, making the resulting linear approximations to $r_1$, $r_2$, and $f$ more accurate for most of the planning horizon. These steady-state values are obtained by solving equations (9.12), (9.13), and (9.3) with $f$ given by (9.11) and $\varepsilon_{t+1}$ set equal to zero, and omitting the time subscripts in all three equations (see problems 1 and 2). These equations thus become algebraic equations for the variables $u$, $\lambda$, and $x$ rather than stochastic difference equations in the time series $u$, $\lambda$, and $x$. The steady state values are:

$$u = \left\{-\ln\left[\beta^{-1}\exp(\mu) - 1\right] + \ln\left[1-\alpha\right] + \gamma\right\}/\alpha; \quad x_1 = \mu; \quad x_2 = u \qquad (9.16)$$

The reader is urged to solve problems 1 and 2 at the end of this chapter to find a linearized set of equations based on the first-order conditions (9.12) and (9.13) before reading section 9.4 on numerical solution of the first-order conditions.

As a third change of variables, take the *deviations* of the state and control variables from the stationary values as the final set of variables. This transformation helps eliminate the intercepts in the functions $f$, $r_1$, $r_2$, the control function, and the Lagrange function. When $x$ and $u$ are defined as deviations from the steady-state values, the intercept $b$ in (9.11) is zero. At the steady state, the deviations $x$ and $u$ are zero, so that $f = x_{t+1} = 0$, implying $b = 0$. By the first-order conditions (9.1) and (9.2),

$$r_2 + \beta \mathrm{C}'\mathrm{E}_t\lambda_{t+1} = 0$$

$$\lambda = r_1 + \beta \mathrm{A}'\mathrm{E}_t\lambda_{t+1}$$

At the steady state for the deterministic model $E_t\lambda_{t+1} = \lambda$. The second condition implies (with A′ nonsingular because I include in the constraints only those state variables that are affected by the control variables, e.g., only $x_2$ and not $x_1$, in the first-order condition (9.13))

$$\lambda = (I - \beta A')^{-1} r_1 = (I - \beta A')^{-1}\{K_{11}x + K_{12}u + k_1\} = [I - \beta A']^{-1} k_1$$

If we define $\lambda$ also as a deviation from its stationary value, $\lambda = 0$ and $k_1 = 0$. Similarly, by the first condition $r_2 = k_2 = 0$. Thus, the intercepts $b$, $k_1$, and $k_2$ of the functions $f$, $r_1$, and $r_2$, respectively, are all zero when $x$, $u$, and $\lambda$ are defined as deviations from steady-state values. If one approximates $u$ and $\lambda$ by linear functions $Gx + g$ and $Hx + h$, respectively, at the steady state $u = 0$ and $\lambda = 0$ and, hence, the intercepts $g$ and $h$ of the linearized control and Lagrange functions $u$ and $\lambda$ are also zero. In section 9.4, I retain all intercepts for the sake of generality in developing an algorithm to solve for G, H, $g$, and $h$, realizing that all intercepts can be dropped if $x$, $u$, and $\lambda$ are defined as deviations from stationary values.

In this section, I have discussed the importance of the change of variables. First, detrending the variables in a nonstationary model is important to obtain a stationary model and to improve computational accuracy. Second, taking logarithms or using other transformations of variables may help if the resulting model $f$ is more nearly linear. Third, the choice of an appropriate control variable can also make the model $f$ more nearly linear. Fourth, it saves computations to define variables $x$, $u$, and $\lambda$ as deviations for their stationary values (of the corresponding nonstochastic model), because the intercepts of all the functions $f$, $r_1$, $r_2$, $u$, and $\lambda$ will be zero. In the next section, I present a shortcut to save algebra and differentiation in changing the variables to deviations of log detrended variables from stationary values.

## 9.3 A Short-Cut to Log-Linearize First-order Conditions

We have completed the detrending and the linearization of the first-order conditions in terms of the deviations of the logarithms of detrended variables from the stationary values. The algebraic steps involved can be simplified by using a short-cut proposed by Uhlig (1995). First, write the first-order conditions (9.12) and (9.13) in terms of detrended variables (denoted by *). The detrended variables are

$$z^* = z/z_{-1}; \quad k^* = k/z_{-1}; \quad c^* = c/z$$

and the two first-order conditions are

$$k^*(t+1)/c^* = \beta E[\lambda_{t+1}] \tag{9.17}$$

$$\lambda = \left[(1-\alpha)k^{*(1-\alpha)} z^{*(\alpha-1)} + k^* z^{*-1}\right]/c^* \tag{9.18}$$

To log linearize the first-order conditions in the detrended variables as deviations of logarithms from stationary values, Uhlig (1995) recommends using the following shortcut. Denote the steady state values by capital letters and the deviations of the log detrended variables from the log stationary values by ~, for example,

$$\tilde{k} = \log k^* - \log K$$
$$\tilde{z} = \log z^* - \log Z = e$$
$$\tilde{c} = \log c^* - \log C \tag{9.19}$$

To convert $k^*$ to $\tilde{k}$, Uhlig replaces the former by $K \exp(\tilde{k})$ or by the approximation $K(1 + \tilde{k})$

$$k^* = K \exp(\tilde{k}) \simeq K(1+\tilde{k}) \tag{9.20}$$

It is the ~ variables in which we are interested and for which we wish to write a linear system of equations to approximate the first-order conditions (9.17) and (9.18). The short-cut amounts to repeated use of the two parts on the right-hand side of (9.20) to replace each original (starred) variables.

Substituting the two parts of (9.20) for the * variables in the first-order conditions (9.17) and (9.18), respectively, one has:

$$\begin{aligned}\left[k^*/z^* + (k^*/z^*)^{(1-\alpha)} - c^*\right]/c^* &= (K/ZC)\exp(\tilde{k}-\tilde{z}-\tilde{c}) \\ &\quad + (K/Z)^{1-\alpha}C^{-1}\exp\left[(1-\alpha)(\tilde{k}-\tilde{z})-\tilde{c}\right]-1 \\ &= (K/ZC)(1+\tilde{k}-\tilde{z}-\tilde{c}) \\ &\quad + (K/Z)^{1-\alpha}C^{-1}\left[1+(1-\alpha)(\tilde{k}-\tilde{z})-\tilde{c}\right]-1 \\ &= \theta_1\tilde{c}_t + \theta_2\tilde{z}_t + \theta_3\tilde{k}_t + \theta_0 = \beta E_t\lambda_{t+1}\end{aligned} \tag{9.21}$$

in which

$$\theta_1 = -(K/ZC) - (K/Z)^{1-\alpha}C^{-1}, \quad \theta_2 = -(K/ZC) - (K/Z)^{1-\alpha}C^{-1}(1-\alpha) = -\theta_3$$
$$\theta_3 = (K/ZC) + (K/Z)^{1-\alpha}C^{-1}(1-\alpha), \quad \theta_0 = (K/ZC) + (K/Z)^{1-\alpha}C^{-1} - 1 = 0$$

and

$$\begin{aligned}\lambda &= (1-\alpha)(K/Z)^{1-\alpha}C^{-1}\left[1+(1-\alpha)(\tilde{k}-\tilde{z})-\tilde{c}\right] + (K/ZC)(1+\tilde{k}-\tilde{z}-\tilde{c}) \\ &= \gamma_1\tilde{c}_t + \gamma_2\tilde{z}_t + \gamma_3\tilde{k}_t + \gamma_0\end{aligned} \tag{9.22}$$

in which

$$\gamma_1 = -(1-\alpha)(K/Z)^{1-\alpha}C^{-1} - (K/ZC), \quad \gamma_2 = -(1-\alpha)^2(K/Z)^{1-\alpha}C^{-1} + (K/ZC)$$
$$\gamma_3 = (1-\alpha)^2(K/Z)^{1-\alpha}C^{-1} + (K/ZC), \quad \gamma_0 = (1-\alpha)(K/Z)^{1-\alpha}C^{-1} + (K/ZC) = 0$$

Note that the intercepts $\theta_0$ and $\gamma_0$ are zero as can be derived from (9.18) or inferred from the statement at the end of the previous section that the intercept of any linear approximation of a first-order condition in deviations of the variables from stationary values has zero intercept (because when the deviations are zero, the linear equation holds). Equations (9.21) and (9.22) are two linear stochastic difference equations in the control variable $\tilde{c}$, the costate variable $\lambda$, and the state variable $\tilde{k}$, with $\tilde{z}_t = e_t$ by (9.19). In addition, the stochastic equation for $\tilde{k}$ is the log-linearized version of the capital accumulation equation:

$$k_{t+1}^* = k^*/z^* + \left(k^*/z^*\right)^{1-\alpha} - c^*$$

$$\mathrm{K}\left(1+\tilde{k}_{t+1}\right) = \left(\mathrm{K}/\mathrm{Z}\right)\left(1+\tilde{k}-\tilde{z}\right) + \left(\mathrm{K}/\mathrm{Z}\right)^{1-\alpha}\left[1+\left(1-\alpha\right)\left(\tilde{k}-\tilde{z}\right)\right] - \mathrm{C}\left(1+\tilde{c}\right)$$

$$\begin{aligned}\tilde{k}_{t+1} &= \mathrm{Z}^{-1}\left(1+\tilde{k}-\tilde{z}\right) + \mathrm{K}^{-\alpha}\mathrm{Z}^{\alpha-1}\left[1+\left(1-\alpha\right)\left(\tilde{k}-\tilde{z}\right)\right] - \left(\mathrm{C}/\mathrm{K}\right)\left(1+\tilde{c}\right) - 1 \\ &= \delta_1\tilde{k}_t + \delta_2\tilde{c} + \delta_3\tilde{z}_t + \delta_0 \end{aligned} \tag{9.23}$$

in which

$$\delta_1 = \mathrm{Z}^{-1} + \mathrm{K}^{-\alpha}\mathrm{Z}^{\alpha-1}\left(1-\alpha\right) \qquad \delta_2 = -\left(\mathrm{C}/\mathrm{K}\right)$$

$$\delta_3 = -\mathrm{Z}^{-1} - \mathrm{K}^{-\alpha}\mathrm{Z}^{\alpha-1}\left(1-\alpha\right) = -\delta_1 \qquad \delta_0 = \mathrm{Z}^{-1} + \mathrm{K}^{-\alpha}\mathrm{Z}^{\alpha-1} - \mathrm{C}/\mathrm{K}^{-1} - 1 = 0$$

Section 9.5 discusses the solution of this system of three linear stochastic difference equations for $\tilde{c}$, $\tilde{\lambda}$, and $\tilde{k}$.

To appreciate the short-cut presented in this section, the reader may derive equations (9.21), (9.22), and (9.23) by applying the method of the previous section. That is, beginning with equation (9.8) but using $\ln(c/z)$ instead of $\ln(k_{t+1}/z)$ as the control variable, linearize $r_1$, $r_2$, and $f$ to form a system of linear first-order conditions as given in (9.21)–(9.23). (See problem 3.) This system differs from (9.14) and (9.15) in two respects: the control variable is different and all variables are measured as deviations from stationary values. As another exercise, change the variables in equations (9.14) and (9.15) and in the corresponding first-order conditions (9.12) and (9.13) to deviations from stationary values. Rederive the linearized first-order conditions by using the short-cut of this section (see problem 4). In summary, note that the short-cut suggested by Uhlig to use the two parts of equation (9.20) requires only algebraic substitutions of the ~ variables for the * variables to achieve log-linearization of the first-order conditions. No knowledge of calculus is required even when the process involves first-order Taylor expansions, because the expansion is done by approximating $\exp(\tilde{k})$ by $1 + \tilde{k}$. The resulting coefficients $\theta_i$, $\gamma_i$, and $\delta_i$ of the linearized first-order conditions are functions of the parameters of the return function $r$ and the dynamic equation $f$, because the steady-state values K, C, and Z are functions of these parameters.

## 9.4 Solving Matrix Riccati Equations Rapidly

To solve the first-order conditions (9.1)–(9.3) numerically, assume that the variables have been detrended. A steady state $(\bar{x}, \bar{u}, \bar{\lambda})$ exists which solves the first-order conditions with the random shock $\varepsilon_{t+1}$, the expectation operator $E_t$ and all time subscripts omitted. Linearizing the partial derivatives around the steady state we have

$$r_1(x_t, u_t) = r_1(\bar{x}, \bar{u}) + K_{11}(x - \bar{x}) + K_{12}(u - \bar{u})$$

$$r_2(x_t, u_t) = r_2(\bar{x}, \bar{u}) + K_{21}(x - \bar{x}) + K_{22}(u - \bar{u})$$

$$f(x_t, u_t) = f(\bar{x}, \bar{u}) + f_1(x - \bar{x}) + f_2(u - \bar{u}) \tag{9.24}$$

Let

$$\tilde{x} = x - \bar{x}, \quad \tilde{u} = u - \bar{u}, \quad \tilde{\lambda} = \lambda - \bar{\lambda}. \tag{9.25}$$

Substitute (9.24) into (9.1)–(9.3) and notice that the steady state solves (9.1)–(9.3) with the random shock omitted. The linearized first order conditions can be written as

$$K_{11}\tilde{x} + K_{12}\tilde{u} + \beta A' E_t \tilde{\lambda}_{t+1} = \tilde{\lambda}_t$$

$$K_{21}\tilde{x} + K_{22}\tilde{u} + \beta C' E_t \tilde{\lambda}_{t+1} = 0$$

$$\tilde{x}_{t+1} = A\tilde{x}_t + C\tilde{u}_t + \varepsilon_{t+1}. \tag{9.26}$$

Define

$$\hat{u} = \tilde{u} + K_{22}^{-1}K_{21}\tilde{x}, \quad \hat{K}_{11} = K_{11} - K_{12}K_{22}^{-1}K_{21}, \quad \hat{A} = A - CK_{22}^{-1}K_{21}. \tag{9.27}$$

The linearized first order conditions can be further simplified to

$$\hat{K}_{11}\tilde{x} + \beta\hat{A}' E_t \tilde{\lambda}_{t+1} = \tilde{\lambda}_t$$

$$K_{22}\hat{u} + \beta C' E_t \tilde{\lambda}_{t+1} = 0$$

$$\tilde{x}_{t+1} = \hat{A}\tilde{x}_t + C_t\hat{u} + \varepsilon_{t+1} \tag{9.28}$$

We solve (9.28) by the method of undetermined coefficients, assuming linear solutions of the form

$$\hat{u}_t = F\tilde{x}_t, \quad \tilde{\lambda}_t = H\tilde{x}_t.$$

Notice that

$$E_t\tilde{\lambda}_{t+1} = E_t H\tilde{x}_{t+1} = \hat{A}\tilde{x}_t + C\hat{u} + E_t\varepsilon_{t+1} = \hat{A}\tilde{x}_t + C\hat{u} \tag{9.29}$$

The second equation in (9.28) gives

$$\hat{u}_t = -\left(K_{22} + \tilde{C}'H\tilde{C}\right)^{-1}\tilde{C}'H\tilde{A}\tilde{x}_t \equiv F\tilde{x}_t \tag{9.30}$$

where

$$\tilde{C} = \sqrt{\beta}C, \qquad \tilde{A} = \sqrt{\beta}\hat{A}.$$

Substituting (9.29)–(9.30) into the first equation in (9.28) and equating coefficients, we obtain a matrix Riccati equation in H well-known in control theory, e.g., Chow (1975, p. 165):

$$\mathrm{H} = \hat{\mathrm{K}}_{11} + \tilde{\mathrm{A}}'\mathrm{H}\tilde{\mathrm{A}} - \tilde{\mathrm{A}}'\mathrm{H}\tilde{\mathrm{C}}\left(\mathrm{K}_{22} + \tilde{\mathrm{C}}'\mathrm{H}\tilde{\mathrm{C}}\right)^{-1}\tilde{\mathrm{C}}'\mathrm{H}\tilde{\mathrm{A}} \tag{9.31}$$

One way to solve the matrix Riccati equation is to iterate (9.31) directly, starting with an initial guess such as the identity matrix. Anderson and Moore (1979, p. 159) present the following doubling algorithm for iterating the matrix Riccati equation (9.31) starting from $\mathrm{H}_0 = 0$:

$$a_{k+1} = a_k\left(\mathrm{I} + b_k c_k\right)^{-1} a_k,$$

$$b_{k+1} = b_k + a_k\left(\mathrm{I} + b_k c_k\right)^{-1} b_k a_k',$$

$$c_{k+1} = c_k + a_k' c_k\left(\mathrm{I} + b_k c_k\right)^{-1} a_k,$$

$$a_0 = \tilde{\mathrm{A}}, \quad b_0 = \tilde{\mathrm{C}}\mathrm{K}_{22}^{-1}\tilde{\mathrm{C}}', \quad c_0 = \hat{\mathrm{K}}_{11}, \qquad k = 0, 1, 2, 3 \ldots$$

$$c_k \rightarrow \mathrm{H}_\infty \tag{9.32}$$

The doubling algorithm accelerates the direct iteration scheme (9.31) by skipping steps. In particular, the doubling algorithm is equivalent to iterating (9.31) for $k = 2, 4, 8, \ldots$ For example, iterating the doubling algorithm 8 times is equivalent to iterating (9.31) $2^8$ times.

When $\hat{\mathrm{K}}_{11} = 0$, the doubling algorithm described above has to be modified; otherwise the iteration will terminate at step 1 with a zero solution. Recall that $\hat{\mathrm{K}}_{11}$ from (9.27) is a function of the second derivatives of the return function $r(x, u)$ with respect to the state vector $x$; it will be zero when the return function is linear in the state variables. In this case, direct iteration of the matrix Riccati equation should be initialized with a non-zero $\mathrm{H}_0$, and the doubling algorithm will have to be augmented with one additional equation for updating $\mathrm{H}_k$:

$$\mathrm{H}_{k+1} = c_k + a_k'\mathrm{H}_k\left(\mathrm{I} + b_k\mathrm{H}_k\right)^{-1} a_k \tag{9.33}$$

In connection with the computational work of Kwan and Chow (1996), Kwan has encountered examples in which the doubling algorithm converges to a wrong solution while direct iteration of the Riccati equation gives the correct answer. The problem comes from rounding errors originating from inverting ill-conditioned matrices. Kwan has robustified the algorithm by avoiding matrix inversions. The idea is to utilize QR factorization, a numerically stable procedure. To illustrate, consider the right-hand-side of the first equation in (9.32). By the QR factorization, there exist an orthogonal matrix T (meaning $\mathrm{T}^{-1} = \mathrm{T}'$) and an upper triangular matrix U such that $(\mathrm{I} + b_k c_k) = \mathrm{TU}$. Thus

$$a_k\left(\mathrm{I} + b_k c_k\right)^{-1} a_k = a_k \mathrm{U}^{-1}\mathrm{T}^{-1} a_k \equiv \mathrm{XY} \tag{9.34}$$

Since T is orthogonal, $\mathrm{Y} = \mathrm{T}^{-1}a_k = \mathrm{T}'a_k$. Further, $\mathrm{X} = a_k\mathrm{U}^{-1}$ implies that $\mathrm{U}'\mathrm{X}' = a_k'$; and the latter is a lower triangular linear equation system in X′ which can be solved efficiently by forward substitution. In summary, Kwan's version of the doubling algorithm consists of the following steps:

*Step 1*: Factorize $(I + b_k c_k) = T_1 U_1$ and $(I + b_k H_k) = T_2 U_2$, for orthogonal matrices $T_1$, $T_2$ and upper triangular matrices $U_1$, $U_2$.
*Step 2*: Find $X_a$, $X_c$ and $X_h$ by solving the lower triangular systems $U_1' X_a' = a_k$, $U_1' X_c' = c_k$, and $U_2' X_h' = H_k$. Compute $Y_a = T_1' a_k$, $Y_b = T_1' b_k$, and $Z_a = T_2' a_k$.
*Step 3*: Update by

$$a_{k+1} = X_a Y_a,$$

$$b_{k+1} = b_k + X_a Y_b a_k',$$

$$c_{k+1} = c_k = a_k' X_c Y_a,$$

$$H_{k+1} = c_k + a_k' X_h Z_a. \tag{9.35}$$

The algorithm is initialized by setting $a_0 = \tilde{A}$, $b_0 = \tilde{C} K_{22}^{-1} \tilde{C}'$, $c_0 = \hat{K}_{11}$, $H_0 = I$.

In summary we obtain an approximate linear solution by the following steps:

1. Apply the doubling algorithm to solve (9.31) for H. This gives

$$\tilde{\lambda} = H\tilde{x},$$

or

$$\lambda = h + Hx, \qquad h = \bar{\lambda} - H\bar{x}.$$

2. Compute $F = -(K_{22} + \tilde{C}' H \tilde{C})^{-1} \tilde{C}' H \tilde{A}$. This gives

$$\tilde{u} = \hat{u} - K_{22}^{-1} K_{21} \tilde{x} = \left(F - K_{22}^{-1} K_{21}\right)\tilde{x} \equiv G\tilde{x},$$

or

$$u = g + Gx, \qquad g = \bar{u} - G\bar{x}.$$

### 9.5 Solving Linear First-Order Conditions by the Method of Undetermined Coefficients

One can illustrate the method of undetermined coefficients by solving the system of first-order conditions (9.17) and (9.18), which are log-linearized to become equations (9.21), (9.22), and (9.23). The method will be generalized later in this section. I have kept the intercepts for the general case, noting that if all variables including $\lambda$ are deviations from stationary values, the intercepts are zero. To solve equations (9.21)–(9.23) assume a linear feedback control rule

$$\tilde{c}_t = G_1 \tilde{z}_t + G_2 \tilde{k}_t + g \tag{9.36}$$

and find the coefficients $G_1$, $G_2$, and $g$ by the method of undetermined coefficients. Substituting (9.36) for $\tilde{c}_t$ in (9.21) yields

$$(\theta_2+\theta_1 G_1)\tilde{z}_t+(\theta_3+\theta_1 G_2)\tilde{k}_t+\theta_0+\theta_1 g=\beta E_t\lambda_{t+1} \tag{9.37}$$

Substituting (9.36) for $\tilde{c}_t$ in (9.22) yields

$$\lambda_t=(\gamma_2+\gamma_1 G_1)\tilde{z}_t+(\gamma_3+\gamma_1 G_2)\tilde{k}_t+\gamma_0+\gamma_1 g \tag{9.38}$$

Using (9.38) and (9.23) to evaluate $E_t\lambda_{t+1}$ for substitution in (9.37), write

$$E_t\lambda_{t+1}=E_t\{(\gamma_2+\gamma_1 G_1)\tilde{z}_{t+1}+(\gamma_3+\gamma_1 G_2)[\delta_1\tilde{k}_t+\delta_2(G_1\tilde{z}_t+G_2\tilde{k}_t+g)]+\delta_3\tilde{z}_{t+1}\}$$
$$+\gamma_0+\gamma_1 g=(\gamma_3+\gamma_1 G_2)[\delta_1+\delta_2 G_2]\tilde{k}_t+(\gamma_3+\gamma_1 G_2)\delta_2 G_1\tilde{z}_t+\gamma_0+\gamma_1 g. \tag{9.39}$$

When (9.39) is substituted for $E_t\lambda_{t+1}$ in (9.37), and the coefficients on both sides of the resulting equation are equated, the following three equations are obtained for the three unknowns, $G_1$, $G_2$, and $g$:

$$\theta_2+\theta_1 G_1=\beta(\gamma_3+\gamma_1 G_2)\delta_2 G_1$$
$$\theta_3+\theta_1 G_2=\beta(\gamma_3+\gamma_1 G_2)(\delta_1+\delta_2 G_2)$$
$$\theta_0+\theta_1 g=\beta(\gamma_0+\gamma_1 g) \tag{9.40}$$

Thus, the optimal feedback rule (9.36) for $\tilde{c}_t$ is found by linearizing the first-order conditions (9.17) and (9.18) in terms of the deviations of the logarithms of the detrended variables $k^*$, $z^*$, and $c^*$ from their stationary values and applying the method of undetermined coefficients (see problem 5).

To state the method of undetermined coefficients generally as it is applied to a set of first-order conditions (9.1), (9.2), and (9.3), assume that the variables are already detrended (if necessary) and are defined as deviations of logarithms from the steady-state values (if desirable). Note that the method can be applied to other first-order conditions than as stated in equations (9.1), (9.2), and (9.3). For example, when the number $q$ of control variables is equal to the number $p$ of state variables, one may use equation (9.2) to eliminate $\lambda$ and retain $p+q$ equations in $u$ and $x$ only. (See problem 5.) As another example, for the problem stated at the beginning of section 9.2 if $f(x, u)$ is a function of $u$ only and not of $x$, the first-order condition (9.2) will have $f_1(x, u) = 0$ and become $\lambda = r_1(x, u)$. When $\lambda_{t+1}$ is replaced by $r_1(x_{t+1}, u_{t+1})$ in equation (9.1), the result is known as a (stochastic) *Euler* equation. The first-order conditions are equations in $x$ and $u$ only after $\lambda$ is eliminated. Because this chapter is concerned with solving the first-order conditions (9.1), (9.2), and (9.3), including the (vector) Lagrangean multiplier $\lambda$ as a variable, we apply the method of underdetermined coefficients to this system of three questions.

For the system to be linear, the functions $r_1$, $r_2$, and $f$ must be linear. In equation (9.1), $r_2$ must be linearized, and $f$ must be linearized so that $f_2'$ is a constant matrix multiplying $E_t\lambda_{t+1}$. In equation (9.2), $r_1$ must be linearized and $f$ must be linearized so that $f_1'$ is a constant matrix multiplying $E_t\lambda_{t+1}$. Equation (9.3) must have a linearized $f$ also. Hence, if we apply the method of undetermined coefficients to a system of equations (9.1)–(9.3) after linearization, we are solving the same system as the one obtained in section 9.2 and solved in section 9.4. By the method of undetermined coefficients as illustrated in this section, let $u$ and $\lambda$ to be linear, say $u = \text{G}x + g$ and $\lambda = \text{H}x + h$, substitute these linear functions into the equations and equate coefficients to solve for G, H, $g$, and $h$. This yields the same set of equations for the coefficients G, H, $g$, and $h$ as solved in section 9.4. The intercepts $g$ and $h$ are zero if the variables are measured from stationary values so that the intercepts $k_1$ and $k_2$ in $r_1$ and $r_2$ and the intercept $b$ in $f$ are all zero.

## 9.6 Quadratic Approximation to λ in Discrete Time

In sections 9.2–9.5 solving the first-order conditions (9.1) and (9.2) by linear approximations to the optimal control function $u$ and the Lagrange function $\lambda$ has been suggested and implemented. In this section, I propose a quadratic approximation of $\lambda$ to illustrate the computational advantage of the Lagrange method, as compared with dynamic programming. Section 9.7 proposes a quadratic approximation of $\lambda$ for the continuous-time optimization problem of section 7.4. Becuase a quadratic approximation of V will yield only a linear approximation of $\lambda = \partial\text{V}/\partial x$, a quadratic approximation of $\lambda$ using (9.2) will improve on this linear approximation and provide a more accurate approximation of $u$ by solving equation (9.1). In other words, solving the Bellman equation by a quadratic approximation of the value function V amounts to a linear approximation of $\lambda$ and is therefore inferior to a quadratic approximation of $\lambda$ for the purpose of solving equation (9.1).

Let $x$ denote the vector of deviations of the detrended (or originally stationary) state variables from the steady state $x_0$ of the deterministic control problem. Approximate $\lambda(x)$ by a quadratic function obtained by a second-order Taylor expansion about the zero vector. Denoting $\partial^2\lambda_i/\partial x\partial x'$ or $\partial^2\lambda/\partial x_i\partial x'$ evaluated at $x = 0$ by $\text{Q}_i$, write

$$\lambda(x) = \lambda(0) + \frac{\partial\lambda}{\partial x'}x + \frac{1}{2}\begin{bmatrix} x'\text{Q}_1 x \\ \vdots \\ x'\text{Q}_p x \end{bmatrix} \equiv h + \text{H}x + \frac{1}{2}\begin{bmatrix} x'\text{Q}_1 \\ \vdots \\ x'\text{Q}_p \end{bmatrix} x \tag{9.41}$$

In view of the fact that the $i$th component $\lambda_i(x)$ of $\lambda(x)$ is the partial derivative of the value function with respect ot $x_i$, many elements of the matrices $\text{Q}_i\ (i = 1, \ldots, p)$ are equal. $\text{Q}_{ijk}$, the $j$–$k$ element of the matrix $\text{Q}_i$, is the third partial of the value function with respect to $x_i$, $x_j$, and $x_k$; it is equal to all elements with the same three subscripts regardless of order. One way to list the distinct elements of the Q matrices is to start with a symmetric $\text{Q}_1$ matrix, omit the first row of a symmetric $\text{Q}_2$ matrix, because all derivatives of the value function with respect to $x_1$ have been counted, omit the first two rows of a symmetric $\text{Q}_3$, and so on until only $\text{Q}_{ppp}$ of $\text{Q}_p$ is specified. The suggested iterative method for solving (9.1) and (9.2) consists of two steps. First, given $h$, H, $\text{Q}_i\ (i = 1, \ldots, p)$, solve (9.1) for $u$ as a linear function $g + \text{G}x$ of $x$. Second, given $g$, G, $h$, H, and $Q_i$ from Step 1, revise $h$, H, and $Q_i$ by equating coefficients on both sides of equation (9.2).

To carry out the first step, first evaluate $E_t\lambda_{t+1} = E_t\lambda(x_{t+1})$ using (9.41) for the function $\lambda$ and (9.3) for $x_{t+1}$, yielding

$$E_t\lambda_{t+1} = h + Hf + \frac{1}{2}\begin{bmatrix} f'Q_1 f + tr(Q_1\Sigma) \\ \vdots \\ f'Q_p f + tr(Q_p\Sigma) \end{bmatrix}, \tag{9.42}$$

in which arguments of the vector function $f(x, u)$ have been omitted. We further approximate $f$ by a linear function about $x = 0$ and $u = 0$, $u$ being the deviation of the control vector from the stationary value.

$$f(x, u) = Ax + Cu \tag{9.43}$$

and approximate $\partial r/\partial u$ by the following quadratic function about the same point:

$$r_2(x, u) = k_2 + K_{21}x + K_{22}u + \frac{1}{2}\begin{bmatrix} x'S_{1x}x + u'S_{1u}u \\ \vdots \\ x'S_{qx}x + u'S_{qu}u \end{bmatrix} \tag{9.44}$$

By using (9.42), (9.43), and (9.44), write the first-order condition (9.1) as

$$k_2 + K_{21}x + K_{22}u + \frac{1}{2}\begin{bmatrix} x'S_{1x}x + u'S_{1u}u \\ \vdots \\ x'S_{qx}x + u'S_{qu}u \end{bmatrix} + \beta C'h + \beta C'H(Ax + Cu)$$

$$+\frac{1}{2}\beta C'\begin{bmatrix} (Ax + Cu)'Q_1 \\ \vdots \\ (Ax + Cu)'Q_p \end{bmatrix}(Ax + Cu) + \frac{1}{2}\beta C'\begin{bmatrix} tr(Q_1\Sigma) \\ \vdots \\ tr(Q_p\Sigma) \end{bmatrix} = 0 \tag{9.45}$$

Equation (9.45) is a quadratic function of $x$ and $u$. To express $u$ as a linear function of $x$, linearize (9.45) about $x = 0$ and $u = 0$ (thus voiding the quadratic terms of (9.44)) to obtain

$$k_2 + K_{21}x + K_{22}u + \beta C'h + \beta' CHAx + \beta C'HCu + \frac{1}{2}\beta C'\begin{bmatrix} tr(Q_1\Sigma) \\ \vdots \\ tr(Q_p\Sigma) \end{bmatrix} = 0 \tag{9.46}$$

Solving (9.46) for $u$ yields

$$u = Gx + g, \tag{9.47}$$

in which

$$G = -\left(K_{22} + C'HC\right)^{-1}\left(K_{21} + \beta C'HA\right) \tag{9.48}$$

$$g = -\left(K_{22} + C'HC\right)^{-1}\left(k_2 + \beta C'h + \frac{1}{2}\beta C'\begin{bmatrix} tr(Q_1\Sigma) \\ \vdots \\ tr(Q_p\Sigma) \end{bmatrix}\right) \tag{9.49}$$

If $\lambda$ is linear, all terms involving $Q_i$ disappear. The resulting linear control function (9.47) is as given in section 9.4. Quadratic terms in $\lambda$ permit us to account for the effect of uncertainty as measured by the covariance matrix $\Sigma$ of the residual $\varepsilon_{t+1}$ on the optimal control function.

In the second step, approximate $\partial r/\partial x$ by a quadratic function about $x = 0$ and $u = 0$ and substitute $Gx + g$ for $u$,

$$r_1(x, u) = k_1 + K_{11}x + K_{12}u + \frac{1}{2}\begin{bmatrix} x'P_{1x}x + u'P_{1u}u \\ \vdots \\ x'P_{px}x + u'P_{pu}u \end{bmatrix}$$

$$= k_1 + K_{12}g + \frac{1}{2}\begin{bmatrix} g'P_{1u}g \\ \vdots \\ g'P_{pu}g \end{bmatrix} + \left\{K_{11} + K_{12}G + \begin{bmatrix} g'P_{1u} \\ \vdots \\ g'P_{pu} \end{bmatrix} G\right\}x + \frac{1}{2}\begin{bmatrix} x'P_{1x}x + u'P_{1u}u \\ \vdots \\ x'P_{px}x + u'P_{pu}u \end{bmatrix} \tag{9.50}$$

Also, reevaluate (9.42) by using (9.43) and (9.47). By denoting $Cg$ by $c$ and $A + CG$ by $R$, we obtain

$$E_t\lambda_{t+1} = h + Hc + HRx + \frac{1}{2}\begin{bmatrix} x'R'Q_1Rx \\ \vdots \\ x'R'Q_pRx \end{bmatrix} + \frac{1}{2}\begin{bmatrix} c'Q_1c + tr(Q_1\Sigma) \\ \vdots \\ c'Q_pc + tr(Q_p\Sigma) \end{bmatrix} + \begin{bmatrix} c'Q_1 \\ \vdots \\ c'Q_p \end{bmatrix} Rx \tag{9.51}$$

By using (9.41) for $\lambda$, (9.50) for $\partial r/\partial x$, and (9.51) for $E_t\lambda_{t+1}$, equate coefficients on the two sides of equation (9.2) to obtain:

$$h = k_1 + K_{12}g + \frac{1}{2}\begin{bmatrix} g'P_{1u}g \\ \vdots \\ g'P_{pu}g \end{bmatrix} + \beta A'\left(h + Hc + \frac{1}{2}\begin{bmatrix} c'Q_1c + tr(Q_1\Sigma) \\ \vdots \\ c'Q_pc + tr(Q_p\Sigma) \end{bmatrix}\right) \tag{9.52}$$

$$H = \left\{K_{11} + K_{12}G + \begin{bmatrix} g'P_{1u} \\ \vdots \\ g'P_{pu} \end{bmatrix} G\right\} + \beta A'\left(H + \begin{bmatrix} c'Q_1 \\ \vdots \\ c'Q_p \end{bmatrix}\right)R \tag{9.53}$$

$$Q_i = P_{ix} + G'P_{iu}G + \beta\sum_{j=1}^{p} a_{ji}R'Q_jR, \quad (i = 1, \ldots, p) \tag{9.54}$$

in which $a_{ji}$ denotes the $j$–$i$ element of A. Equations (9.52), (9.53), and (9.54) show how the parameters of $\lambda$ are revised by equation (9.2), using the optimal control function $Gx + g$, the parameters A and C of the linearized dynamic model ($R = A + CG$; $c = Cg$), the parameters $k_1$, $K_{11}$, $K_{12}$, $P_{ix} (i = 1, \ldots, p)$ and $P_{iu}$ ($i = 1, \ldots, q$) of the quadratic approximation of $\partial r/\partial x$, and the parameters **h**, H, and $Q_i$ ($i = 1, \ldots, p$) from step 1. These revised parameters of $\lambda$ can be used in step 1 to continue the iterations. As indicated by equation (9.54), the parameters $Q_i$ of the quadratic terms of $\lambda$ are functions of the parameters $P_{ix}$ and $P_{iu}$ of the quadratic terms of $\partial r/\partial x$. These parameters would be omitted if $r$ were assumed to be quadratic. Equation (9.52) shows the effect of uncertainty measured by the covariance matrix $\Sigma$ on the shadow price $\lambda$ of the state variables; the effect of $\Sigma$ has also appeared in the calculation of $g$ in the optimal control function (9.47).

## 9.7 Quadratic Approximation to λ in Continuous Time

An analogous problem in continuous time is

$$\max_u E_t \int_\tau^\infty e^{-\beta(\tau - t)} r(x(\tau), u(\tau)) d\tau = V(x(t)) \tag{9.55}$$

subject to

$$dx = f(x, u)dt + dw \tag{9.56}$$

in which $w(t)$ is a vector Wiener process with $dw$ equal to $S(x, u)dz$ and having covariance matrix $\text{cov}(dw)$ $S\Phi S'\, dt = \Sigma(x, u)dt$. The Lagrangean of this problem is

$$\mathcal{L} = \int_0^\infty E_t \left\{ e^{-\beta t} r(x, u)dt - e^{-\beta(t+dt)} \lambda'(t + dt)\left[x(t + dt) - x(t) - f(x, u)dt - S(x, u)dz\right]\right\} \tag{9.57}$$

Assuming $r$ and $f$ to be concave and differentiable, the first-order conditions for $u$ and $\lambda$ are given by equations (7.21) and (7.22), now rewritten as

$$\frac{\partial r}{\partial u_i} + \frac{\partial f'}{\partial u_i}\lambda + \frac{1}{2} tr\left(\frac{\partial \lambda}{\partial x'} \cdot \frac{\partial \Sigma}{\partial u_i}\right) = 0 \qquad i = 1, \ldots, q \tag{9.58}$$

and

$$\begin{aligned} \beta\lambda_i = {} & \frac{\partial}{\partial x_i} r(x, u) + \frac{\partial}{\partial x_i} f'(x, u)\lambda + \frac{\partial \lambda'}{\partial x_i} f(x, u) + \frac{1}{2} tr\left[\frac{\partial}{\partial x_i}\left(\frac{\partial \lambda}{\partial x'}\right) \cdot \Sigma\right] \\ & + \frac{1}{2} tr\left[\frac{\partial \lambda}{\partial x'} \frac{\partial}{\partial x_i} \Sigma\right] \qquad i = 1, \ldots, p \end{aligned} \tag{9.59}$$

The approximation of $\lambda(x)$ by the quadratic function (9.41) implies

$$\frac{\partial \lambda}{\partial x'} = H; \quad \frac{\partial^2 \lambda}{\partial x_i \partial x'} = Q_i \tag{9.60}$$

As in section 9.6, we further approximate

$$\frac{\partial r}{\partial x} = k_1 + \mathrm{K}_{11}x + \mathrm{K}_{12}u + \frac{1}{2}\begin{bmatrix} x'\mathrm{P}_{1x}x + u'\mathrm{P}_{1u}u \\ \vdots \\ x'\mathrm{P}_{px}x + u'\mathrm{P}_{pu}u \end{bmatrix} \tag{9.61}$$

$$\frac{\partial r}{\partial u} = k_2 + \mathrm{K}_{22}u + \mathrm{K}_{21}x + \frac{1}{2}\begin{bmatrix} x'\mathrm{S}_{1x}x + u'\mathrm{S}_{1u}u \\ \vdots \\ x'\mathrm{S}_{qx}x + u'\mathrm{S}_{qu}u \end{bmatrix} \tag{9.62}$$

$$f = \mathrm{A}x + \mathrm{C}u \tag{9.63}$$

Denote by $\mathrm{D}_2u + \mathrm{D}_{21}x + d_2$, the $q \times 1$ vector with its $i$th element equal to the trace term of (9.58) and, by $d_1$, the $p \times 1$ vector with its $i$th element equal to the sum of the two trace terms of (9.59). In the first step, substitute (9.62), (9.63), (9.41), and the above vector $\mathrm{D}_2u + \mathrm{D}_{21}x + d_2$ into (9.58) and solve for $u$:

$$k_2 + \mathrm{K}_{21}x + \mathrm{K}_{22}u + \frac{1}{2}\begin{bmatrix} x'\mathrm{S}_{1x}x + u'\mathrm{S}_{1u}u \\ \vdots \\ x'\mathrm{S}_{qx}x + u'\mathrm{S}_{qu}u \end{bmatrix} + \mathrm{C}'h + \mathrm{C}'\mathrm{H}x + \frac{1}{2}\mathrm{C}'\begin{bmatrix} x'\mathrm{Q}_1x \\ \vdots \\ x'\mathrm{Q}_px \end{bmatrix}$$
$$+ \mathrm{D}_2u + \mathrm{D}_{21}x + d_2 = 0 \tag{9.64}$$

Linearizing the quadratic terms in (9.64) about $x = 0$ and $u = 0$ and solving the resulting equation for $u$, one obtains

$$u = \mathrm{G}x + g \tag{9.65}$$

in which

$$\mathrm{G} = -(\mathrm{K}_{22} + \mathrm{D}_2)^{-1}(\mathrm{K}_{21} + \mathrm{D}_{21} + \mathrm{C}'\mathrm{H}) \tag{9.66}$$

$$g = -(\mathrm{K}_{22} + \mathrm{D}_2)^{-1}(k_2 + \mathrm{C}'h + d_2) \tag{9.67}$$

In the second step, given G and $g$, revise the parameters of $\lambda$ by substituting (9.61), (9.63), (9.41), and $d_1$ into (9.59) to yield, letting $\mathrm{A} + \mathrm{CG} = \mathrm{R}$ and $\mathrm{C}g = c$,

$$(\beta\mathrm{I} - \mathrm{A}')\left(h + \mathrm{H}x + \frac{1}{2}\begin{bmatrix} x'\mathrm{Q}_1x \\ \vdots \\ x'\mathrm{Q}_px \end{bmatrix}\right) = k_1 + \mathrm{K}_{12}g + (\mathrm{K}_{11} + \mathrm{K}_{12}\mathrm{G})x$$
$$+ \frac{1}{2}\begin{bmatrix} x'(\mathrm{P}_{1x} + \mathrm{G}'\mathrm{P}_{1u}\mathrm{G})x \\ \vdots \\ x'(\mathrm{P}_{px} + \mathrm{G}'\mathrm{P}_{pu}\mathrm{G})x \end{bmatrix} + \begin{bmatrix} g'\mathrm{P}_{1u} \\ \vdots \\ g'\mathrm{P}_{pu} \end{bmatrix}\mathrm{G}x + \frac{1}{2}\begin{bmatrix} g'\mathrm{P}_{1u}g \\ \vdots \\ g'\mathrm{P}_{pu}g \end{bmatrix}$$

$$+\left(H+\begin{bmatrix} x'Q_1 \\ \vdots \\ x'Q_p \end{bmatrix}\right)(Rx+c)+d_1+\frac{1}{2}\begin{bmatrix} tr(Q_1\Sigma) \\ \vdots \\ tr(Q_1\Sigma) \end{bmatrix} \tag{9.68}$$

Equating coefficients of (9.68), one obtains

$$h=(\beta I-A')^{-1}\left(k_1+K_{12}g+\frac{1}{2}\begin{bmatrix} g'P_{1u}g \\ \vdots \\ g'P_{pu}g \end{bmatrix}+Hc+d_1+\frac{1}{2}\begin{bmatrix} tr(Q_1\Sigma) \\ \vdots \\ tr(Q_p\Sigma) \end{bmatrix}\right) \tag{9.69}$$

$$H=(\beta I-A')^{-1}\left(K_{11}+K_{12}G+HR+\begin{bmatrix} c'Q_1 \\ \vdots \\ c'Q_p \end{bmatrix}+\begin{bmatrix} g'P_{1u} \\ \vdots \\ g'P_{pu} \end{bmatrix}G\right) \tag{9.70}$$

$$\beta Q_i=P_{ix}+G'P_{iu}G+2Q_iR+\sum_{j=1}^{p}a_{ji}Q_j \qquad (i=1,\ldots,p) \tag{9.71}$$

in which $a_{ji}$ denotes the $j$–$i$ element of $A = \partial f/\partial x'$.

The parameters of $\lambda$, as revised by (9.69)–(9.71), can be used to solve equation (9.65) for $u$ in step 1 of the iterative method. The two-step iterative procedure will continue until convergence. To start the iterations, set H, G, $h$, and $g$ equal to the optimum values for linear $\lambda$, and set all matrices $Q_i$, $P_{ix}$, $P_{iu}$, $S_{ix}$, and $S_{iu}$ equal to zero. This is the solution using the method of section 7.4. I hope to report on computational experience in future research.

## 9.8 Solving First-order Conditions by the Galerkin Method

While the quadratic approximation of $\lambda$ suggested in the last section is applicable to problems with several state variables, higher-degree approximations of $u$ and $\lambda$ are feasible by using the Galerkin method when the numbers of state and control variables are small. This is illustrated in the case when both $u$ and $x$ are univariate. The present section is drawn form the work of Kwan and Chow (1996).

In operator notation the first-order conditions (9.59) and (9.58) can be compactly written as $R(g) = 0$, where $g = (u, \lambda) \in Y$, and Y is a function space; $R: Y \to Y$ is an operator; and the zero on the right hand side is interpreted as the zero function. A standard approach to solving a functional equation is to convert the infinite dimensional problem into a sequence of finite dimensional sub-problems from which one obtains a corresponding sequence of approximate solutions that coverge to the solution of the original problem. Let $Y_n$ be a finite dimensional subspace of Y. For example if Y is the space of continuous functions, $Y_n$ may be the space of polynomials of degree $n$. Unfortunately there is in general no discrete solution $g_n \in Y_n$ that solves the functional equation exactly, but rather the discrete solution generates an error or residual, $R(g_n) \neq 0$, even though $Y_n$ may converge to Y. A general approach is to find $g_n$ that makes a *projection* of the residual vanish; and different projections lead to different methods. The *Galerkin method* is characterized by an orthogonal projection.

To describe the Galerkin method, it is necessary to introduce some notations. Let Y be a Hilbert space with inner product $\langle f, g\rangle$, and $P_n : Y \to Y_n$ be an orthogonal projection operator, i.e., $P_n P_n = P_n$ and $\langle P_n f, g\rangle = \langle f, P_n g\rangle$ (self-adjoint); also assume $\{\Phi_i, i = 1, 2, \ldots, n\}$ forms a basis in $Y_n$ so that there exists a representation $g_n = \alpha_1\Phi_1 + \alpha_2\Phi_2 + \ldots + \alpha_n\Phi_n$. The Galerkin method requires the projected residual to vanish, i.e., find $g_n$ such that $P_n R(g_n) = 0$. Taking inner product with $\Phi_j$ we may write $\langle P_n R(g_n), \Phi_j\rangle = \langle 0, \Phi_j\rangle = 0$. The left hand side can be written as

$$\begin{aligned}\left\langle P_n R(g_n), \Phi_j\right\rangle &= \left\langle R(g_n), P_n\Phi_j\right\rangle = \left\langle R(g_n), \Phi_j\right\rangle \\ &= \left\langle R\left(\sum_{i=1}^{n}\alpha_i\Phi_i\right), \Phi_j\right\rangle = 0, \quad j = 1, 2, \ldots, n. \end{aligned} \tag{9.72}$$

The last line of (9.72) gives an algebraic equation system to be solved for $\alpha_1$, $\alpha_2, \ldots, \alpha_n$ which determines the Galerkin solution.

The equation system in (9.72) is usually nonlinear and has to be solved by iterative method. It is important to have a good starting value for the nonlinear equation solver. In our application we use as starting value a linear approximate solution obtained by linearizing the first order conditions (9.59)–(9.58) around the steady state. The linear solution is obtained by assuming certainty equivalence (i.e., setting $S(x, u) = 0$) and solving a linearized version of the deterministic first order conditions. The linearization is to be performed around the steady state $(\bar{x}, \bar{u}, \bar{\lambda})$ which satisfies the first order condition

$$\begin{aligned}\beta\bar{\lambda} &= \frac{\partial r}{\partial x}(\bar{x}, \bar{u}) + \frac{\partial f'}{\partial x}.(\bar{x}, \bar{u})\bar{\lambda} + \frac{\partial \lambda'}{\partial x}(\bar{x}, \bar{u})f(\bar{x}, \bar{u}) \\ &\frac{\partial r}{\partial u}(\bar{x}, \bar{u}) + \frac{\partial f'}{\partial u}.(\bar{x}, \bar{u})\bar{\lambda} = 0. \\ &\dot{x} = f(\bar{x}, \bar{u}) = 0.\end{aligned} \tag{9.73}$$

Given the steady state we linearize $f$ and the partial derivatives as in (9.24):

$$\begin{aligned}\frac{\partial r}{\partial x} &= \frac{\partial r}{\partial x}(\bar{x}, \bar{u}) + K_{11}(x - \bar{x}) + K_{12}(u - \bar{u}) \\ \frac{\partial r}{\partial u} &= \frac{\partial r}{\partial u}(\bar{x}, \bar{u}) + K_{21}(x - \bar{x}) + K_{22}(u - \bar{u}) \\ f &= f(\bar{x}, \bar{u}) + A(x - \bar{x}) + C(u - \bar{u}).\end{aligned} \tag{9.74}$$

Let

$$\tilde{x} \equiv x - \bar{x}, \quad \tilde{u} \equiv u - \bar{u}, \quad \tilde{\lambda} \equiv \lambda - \bar{\lambda} \equiv \mathrm{H}\tilde{x} \tag{9.75}$$

(9.73)–(9.75) imply a set of linearized first order conditions:

$$\beta \mathrm{H}\tilde{x} = \mathrm{K}_{11}\tilde{x} + \mathrm{K}_{12}\tilde{u} + \mathrm{A}'\mathrm{H}\tilde{x} + \mathrm{H}\left(\mathrm{A}\tilde{x} + \mathrm{C}\tilde{u}\right)$$
$$\mathrm{K}_{21}\tilde{x} + \mathrm{K}_{22}\tilde{u} + \mathrm{C}'\mathrm{H}\tilde{x} = 0. \tag{9.76}$$

Define, as in (9.27),

$$\hat{u} = \tilde{u} + \mathrm{K}_{22}^{-1}\mathrm{K}_{21}\tilde{x}, \quad \hat{\mathrm{K}}_{11} = \mathrm{K}_{11} - \mathrm{K}_{12}\mathrm{K}_{22}^{-1}\mathrm{K}_{21}, \quad \hat{\mathrm{A}} = \mathrm{A} - \mathrm{C}\mathrm{K}_{22}^{-1}\mathrm{K}_{21}. \tag{9.77}$$

The first order conditions can be further simplified to

$$\beta \mathrm{H}\tilde{x} = \mathrm{K}_{11}\tilde{x} + \hat{\mathrm{A}}'\mathrm{H}\tilde{x} + \mathrm{H}\left(\hat{\mathrm{A}}\tilde{x} + \mathrm{C}\hat{u}\right)$$
$$\mathrm{K}_{22}\hat{u} + \mathrm{C}'\mathrm{H}\tilde{x} = 0. \tag{9.78}$$

The second equation in (9.78) gives

$$\hat{u} = -\mathrm{K}_{22}^{-1}\mathrm{C}'\mathrm{H}\tilde{x} \equiv \hat{\mathrm{G}}x. \tag{9.79}$$

Substituting (9.79) into (9.78) and equating coefficients, we obtain an algebraic Riccati equation well known in control theory (Chow, 1981, p. 290):

$$\beta \mathrm{H} = \hat{\mathrm{K}}_{11} + \hat{\mathrm{A}}'\mathrm{H} + \mathrm{H}\hat{\mathrm{A}} - \mathrm{H}\mathrm{C}\mathrm{K}_{22}^{-1}\mathrm{C}'\mathrm{H}. \tag{9.80}$$

In summary we obtain an approximate linear solution by the following steps:

1. Iterating (9.80) until convergence to obtain H. This gives

$$\tilde{\lambda} = \mathrm{H}\tilde{x}$$

or

$$\lambda = h + \mathrm{H}x, \quad h = \bar{\lambda} - \mathrm{H}\bar{x}.$$

2. Compute $\hat{\mathrm{G}} = -\mathrm{K}_{22}^{-1}\mathrm{C}'\mathrm{H}$. This gives

$$\tilde{u} = \hat{u} - \mathrm{K}_{22}^{-1}\mathrm{K}_{21}\tilde{x} = \left(\hat{\mathrm{G}} - \mathrm{K}_{22}^{-1}\mathrm{K}_{21}\right)\tilde{x} \equiv \mathrm{G}\tilde{x}$$

or

$$u = g + \mathrm{G}x, \quad g = \bar{u} - \mathrm{G}\bar{x}.$$

As an example we can obtain a numerical solution to the neo-classical growth model

$$\max_{c} \int_{0}^{\infty} e^{-\rho t}\left[\frac{c(t)^{1-\sigma} - 1}{1-\sigma}\right]dt \tag{9.81}$$

subject to

$$\dot{k} = k(t)^{\alpha} - \delta k(t) - c(t), \quad k(0) \text{ given.} \tag{9.82}$$

The state and control are (per capita) capital stock, $k(t)$, and consumption, $c(t)$, respectively. With state and control so defined, the first order conditions (9.58)–(9.59) become

$$\beta\lambda = \left(\alpha k^{\alpha-1} - \delta\right)\lambda + \lambda'\left(k^{\alpha} - \delta k - c\right)$$

$$c^{-\sigma} - \lambda = 0. \tag{9.83}$$

One can in principle apply the Galerkin method directly to find $c(k)$ and $\lambda(k)$, both represented as polynomials in $k$. In practice however it is necessary to transform variables appropriately so as to enforce sign constraints and achieve better numerical stability when solving the Galerkin projection equations. To enforce positivity on $c$ an $\lambda$ as indicated by the second equation in (9.83), and also to facilitate the use of Hermite polynomials as basis functions (to be discussed below), we transform variables as

$$x = \ln(k), \quad u(x) = \ln(c(k)) - x, \quad \phi(x) = \ln(\lambda(k)) + \sigma x \tag{9.84}$$

and thus

$$\phi'(x) = \frac{\lambda'}{\lambda}\exp(x) + \sigma. \tag{9.85}$$

The first order conditions can now be written as

$$\alpha \exp((\alpha-1)x) - (\delta+\rho) + (\phi' - \sigma)\{\exp((\alpha-1)x) - \delta - \exp(u)\} = 0 \tag{9.86}$$

$$-\sigma u - \phi = 0 \tag{9.87}$$

(9.86)–(9.87) is a functional equation system to be solved for $u(x)$ and $\phi(x)$.

To apply the Galerkin method one has to choose a family of basis functions from which a series representation of the solution can be constructed. We use the family of Hermite polynomials $\{H_k(x), k = 0, 1, 2, \ldots\}$ whose members are mutually orthogonal with respect to the inner product

$$\langle f, g\rangle = \int_{-\infty}^{+\infty} f(x)g(x)\exp(-x^2)\,dx. \tag{9.88}$$

The explicit expression for Hermite polynomial is complicated and inconvenient to use. In practice we use a three-term recurrence relation to generate the polynomial and its derivatives:

$$H_{n+1}(x) = 2xH_n(x) - 2nH_{n-1}(x); \quad H_0 = 1, \quad H_1 = 2x \tag{9.89}$$

Further numerical efficiency can be achieved by enforcing the steady state conditon on the solution. We thus write the control function and the Lagrange multiplier as

$$u(x) = a_0 + \sum_{k=1}^{n} a_k\left[H_k(x) - H_k(\bar{x})\right], \quad \phi(x) = b_0 + \sum_{k=1}^{n} b_k\left[H_k(x) - H_k(\bar{x})\right] \tag{9.90}$$

By construction the two intercept terms should be the steady state of the control and Lagrange multiplier respectively, and thus the number of unknown parameters in each expansion can be reduced by one if such restriction is imposed. One can also let the two intercepts remain free and check if they approach the corresponding steady states as the degree of polynomial goes up. This will provide a convergence check of the numerical method.

Let $R_i(a, b; x), i = 1, 2$, be the left hand side of (9.86)–(9.87) after substituting (9.90) and $a$ and $b$ denote respectively the vectors of unknown coefficients in the polynomial expansions. The Galerkin projections can be written as

$$\int_{-\infty}^{\infty} R_i(a,\ b;\ x)H_k \exp(-x)^2\, dx = 0, \quad i = 1,\ 2; \quad k = 0,\ 1,\ \ldots,\ n. \tag{9.91}$$

We use the nonlinear equation solver NLSYS in GAUSS to solve (9.91) for the $2(n + 1)$ unknowns in vectors $a$ and $b$. It is important to provide good starting value for the nonlinear equation solver. A good candidate is the linear approximate solution obtained by linearizing first order conditions as described above. Finally the integral in (9.91) admits no analytical expression and has to be evaluated numerically. We find it adequate to evaluate the integral by an 8-point Gauss-Hermite quadrature rule.

TABLE 9.1 Optimal growth model

| *linear* | *degree 1* | *degree 2* | *degree 3* | *degree 4* | *degree 5* | *degree 6* |
|---|---|---|---|---|---|---|
| | | | Panel A: Control function | | | |
| −1.817077 | −1.806086 | −1.816954 | −1.816939 | −1.817073 | −1.817074 | −1.817077 |
| −0.297350 | −0.045111 | −0.069126 | −0.069383 | −0.067861 | −0.067902 | −0.068008 |
| 0.000000 | 0.000000 | 0.002324 | 0.002377 | 0.001894 | 0.001912 | 0.001968 |
| 0.000000 | 0.000000 | 0.000000 | −0.000003 | 0.000061 | 0.000058 | 0.000042 |
| 0.000000 | 0.000000 | 0.000000 | 0.000000 | −0.000003 | −0.000003 | −0.000000 |
| 0.000000 | 0.000000 | 0.000000 | 0.000000 | 0.000000 | −0.000000 | −0.000000 |
| 0.000000 | 0.000000 | 0.000000 | 0.000000 | 0.000000 | 0.000000 | 0.000000 |
| | | | Panel B: Lagrange multiplier function | | | |
| 0.908539 | 0.903043 | 0.908477 | 0.908470 | 0.908536 | 0.908537 | 0.908539 |
| −0.168550 | 0.022555 | 0.034563 | 0.034691 | 0.033931 | 0.033951 | 0.034004 |
| 0.000000 | 0.000000 | −0.001162 | −0.001188 | −0.000947 | −0.000956 | −0.000984 |
| 0.000000 | 0.000000 | 0.000000 | 0.000002 | −0.000031 | −0.000029 | −0.000021 |
| 0.000000 | 0.000000 | 0.000000 | 0.000000 | 0.000002 | 0.000001 | 0.000000 |
| 0.000000 | 0.000000 | 0.000000 | 0.000000 | 0.000000 | 0.000000 | 0.000000 |
| 0.000000 | 0.000000 | 0.000000 | 0.000000 | 0.000000 | 0.000000 | −0.000000 |
| | | | Panel C: Residual norm | | | |
| 5.9726e-01 | 1.4619e-14 | 3.9767e-13 | 3.6723e-13 | 2.4199e-15 | 1.4878e-16 | 1.3886e-16 |
| 3.4604e-02 | 1.6873e-03 | 2.4987e-05 | 2.6517e-05 | 1.0601e-06 | 7.8021e-07 | 2.7547e-08 |

The rows in panel A and B are respectively the coefficients $(a_0, a_1, \ldots, a_6)$ and $(b_0, b_1, \ldots, b_6)$ of the polynomial expansions in (9.90).

Table 9.1 reports polynomial solutions up to degree 6 with model parameter $(\alpha, \rho, \delta, \sigma) = (0.4, 0.5, 0.025, 0.5)$. Notice that the two intercept terms indeed approach the corresponding steady states as the degree of polynomial goes up. This indicates that the discrete solution is convergent. The column labeled by "linear" is the linear approximate solution obtained by linearizing first order conditions. Panel C of the table reports the residual norms given a solution, which should be identically zero if the solution is exact. Comparing the residual norms we see that the Hermite polynomial solutions are more accurate than linear approximation. Notice that the intercept term of the linear solution is precisely the steady state. This is because we have written the linear solution in the form as in (9.90) to be compatible with other columns. This can be checked by noting that $H_1(x) = 2x$ and using the formula in step 2 before (9.81). For more details in implementation of the Galerkin method for this model and an endogenous growth model, see Kwan and Chow (1997).

## Problems

1. Verify that (9.16) is the steady state of the deterministic control problem associated with the functions $r$ and $f$ given by (9.10) and (9.11).
2. For the optimal control problem with first-order conditions (9.12) and (9.13), find the coefficients $K_{11}$, $K_{12}$, etc., of the linear approximations of $r_1$ and $r_2$ in equation (9.14) and (9.15) by performing a first-order expansion of these functions about the steady-state (9.16).
3. Derive equations (9.21), (9.22), and (9.23) using the method of section 9.2. Beginning with equation (9.8) and using $\ln(c/z)$ instead of $\ln(k_{t+1}/z)$ as the control variables, linearize $r_1$, $r_2$, and $f$ to form a system of linear first-order conditions in $u$, $\lambda$, and $x_2$.
4. Change the variables in equations (9.14) and (9.15) and in the corresponding equations (9.12) and (9.13) to deviations from stationary values. (a) Derive the linearized first-order conditions. (b) Rederive the linearized first-order conditions by using the short-cut of section 9.3.
5. Use the first-order conditions (9.17) and (9.18) to eliminate $\lambda$ and obtain an equation in the detrended variables $k^*$, $z^*$, and $c^*$. Log linearize this equation and the dynamic equation for $k^*_{t+1}$ to yield two linear equations in $\tilde{k}_{t+1}$, $\tilde{z}_t$, and $\tilde{c}_t$, which are the deviations of the logarithms of the detrended variables from their steady-state values: $\tilde{k}_{t+1} = \log(k^*_{t+1}/K)$, etc. Assuming a feedback control rule $\tilde{c}_t = G_1\tilde{z}_t + G_2\tilde{k}_t$, find the coefficients $G_1$ and $G_2$ by the method of undetermined coefficients.
6. The formulation of the continuous-time problem in section 9.7 differs from the formulation of the discrete-time problem in section 9.6 in that the covariance matrix $\Sigma$ of the random disturbance of the dynamic equation is assumed to be a function of both the (vector) state variable $x$ and the control variable $u$. How would the algorithm of section 9.6 be changed if $\Sigma$ is a function $\Sigma(x, u)$, rather than a constant matrix?

# References


Abel, Andrew B. (1983). "Optimal Investment Under Uncertainty." *American Economic Review*, **13**: 228–233.

———and Janice C. Eberly (1993). "A Unified Model of Investment Under Uncertainty." working paper, The Wharton School, University of Pennsylvania.

Abreu, D. (1988). "On the Theory of Infinitely Repeated Games with Discounting," *Econometrica*, **56**: 383–396.

Admati, A. R. (1985). "A Noisy Rational Expectations Equilibrium for Multi-asset Securities Markets," *Econometrica*, **53**: 629–657.

Allen, R. G. D. (1956). *Mathematical Economics*. London: St. Martin's Press.

Anderson, B. and J. Moore (1979). *Optimal Filtering*. Englewood Cliffs, New Jersey: Prentice Hall.

Arnold, Ludwig (1974). *Stochastic Differential Equations: Theory and Applications*. New York: John Wiley & Sons.

Arrow, Kenneth and Alain Enthoven (1961). "Quasi-concave Programming," *Econometrica*, **29**: 779–800.

Astrom, Karl J. (1970). *Introduction to Stochastic Control Theory*. New York: Academic Press.

Baumol, William J. (1951). *Economic Dynamics*. London: Macmillan.

Becker, Gary S. (1964). *Human Capital*. New York: National Bureau of Economic Research.

Becker, Gary S., Kevin M. Murphy, and Robert Tamura, Jr. (1990). "Human Capital, Fertility and Economic Growth," *Journal of Political Economy*, **98**: S12–S37.

Beggs, Alan and Paul Klemperer (1992). "Multi-period Competition with Switching Costs," *Econometrica*, **60**: 651–666.

Bellman, Richard (1957). *Dynamic Programming*. Princeton: Princeton University Press.

Benveniste, Lawrence and Jose Scheinkman (1979). "On the Differentiability of the Value Function in Dynamic Models of Economics." *Econometrica*, **47**: 727–732.

Bertola, Giuseppe (1989). "Irreversible Investment," working paper, Princeton University.

Black, Fisher and Myron Scholes (1973). "The Pricing of Options and Corporate Liabilities." *Journal of Political Economy*, **81**: 637–654.

Blanchard, Olivier J. (1983). "The Production and Inventory Behavior of the American Automobile Industry," *Journal of Political Economy*, **91**: 365–400.

Burns, A. F. and W. C. Mitchell (1946). *Measuring Business Cycles*. New York: National Bureau of Economic Research.

Chamberlin, Edward (1933). *The Theory of Monopolistic Competition*. Cambridge: Harvard University Press.

Chiang, Alpha C. (1984). *Fundamental Methods of Mathematical Economics*. New York: McGraw Hill.

Chow, Gregory C. (1957). *Demand for Automobiles in the United States: A Study in Consumer Durables*. Amsterdam: North-Holland Publishing Co.

———(1960). "Statistical Demand Functions for Automobiles and Their Use for Forecasting," in A. C. Harberger (ed.), *The Demand for Durable Goods*. Chicago: University of Chicago Press.

———(1967). "Multiplier, Accelerator, and Liquidity Preference in the Determination of National Income in the United States," *The Review of Economics and Statistics*, **XLIV**: 1–15.

———(1968). "The Acceleration Principle and the Nature of Business Cycles," *Quarterly Journal of Economics*, **LXXXII**: 403–418.

———(1970). "Optimal Stochastic Control of Linear Economic Systems," *Journal of Money, Credit and Banking*, **2**: 291–302.

———(1975). *Analysis and Control of Dynamic Economic Systems*. New York: John Wiley & Sons.

———(1979). "Optimum Control of Stochastic Differential Equation Systems." *Journal of Economic Dynamics and Control*, **1**: 143–176.

———(1981). *Econometric Analysis by Control Methods*. New York: John Wiley & Sons.

———(1983). *Econometrics*. New York: McGraw Hill.

———(1985a). *The Chinese Economy*. New York: Harper and Row.

———(1985b). "A Model of Chinese National Income Determination," *Journal of Political Economy*, **93**: 782–792.

———(1992). "Dynamic Optimization Without Dynamic Programming," *Economic Modelling*, **9**: 3–9.

———(1993a). "Optimal Control Without Solving the Bellman Equation," *Journal of Economic Dynamics and Control*, **17**: 621–630.

———(1993b). "A Two-Step Procedure for Estimating Linear Simultaneous Equations with Unit Roots," *The Review of Economics and Statistics*, **LXXV**: 107–111.

———(1993c). "Capital Formation and Economic Growth in China," *The Quarterly Journal of Economics*, **CVIII**: 809–842.

———(1993d). "Computation of Optimum Control Functions by Lagrange Multipliers," in David A. Belsley (ed.), *Computational Techniques for Econometrics and Economic Analysis*.

———(1995). "Multiperiod Competition with Switching Costs: Solution by Lagrange Multipliers," *Journal of Economic Dynamics and Control*, **19**: 51–58.

———(1996). "The Lagrange Method of Optimization with Applications to Portfolio and Investment Decisions," *Journal of Economic Dynamics and Control*, **20**: 1–18.

———and Yum K. Kwan (1996). "Economic Effects of Political Movement in China: Lower Bound Estimates," *Pacific Economic Review*, forthcoming.

———and Yum K. Kwan (1997). "Statistical Estimation and Testing of a Real Business Cycle Model," Econometric Research Program, Princeton University, mimeo.

——— and Richard E. Levitan (1969). "Nature of Business Cycles Implicit in a Linear Economic Model," *Quarterly Journal of Economics*, **LXXXIII**: 504–517.

Christiano, Lawrence J. and Martin Eickenbaum (1992). "Current Real-Business-Cycle Theories and Aggregate Labor-Market Fluctuations," *American Economic Review*, **82**: 430–450.

Cooley, Thomas F., ed. (1995). *Frontiers of Business Cycle Research*. Princeton: Princeton University Press.

——— and Gary P. Hansen (1989). "The Inflation Tax in a Real Business Cycle Model," *American Economic Review*, **79**: 733–748.

Courant, Richard (1936). *Differential and Integral Calculus*. London: Blackie & Son. Reprint, New York: Wiley-Interscience (1988).

Cox, John C., J. E. Ingersoll and S. A. Ross (1985). "An Intertemporal General Equilibrium Model of Asset Prices." *Econometrica*, **53**: 363–384.

——— and S. A. Ross (1976). "The Valuation of Options for Alternative Stochastic Processes," *Journal of Financial Economics*, **3**: 145–166.

Dixit, Avinash K. (1990). *Optimization in Economic Theory*, 2nd ed. New York: Oxford University Press.

——— (1992). "Investment and Hysteresis," *The Journal of Economic Perspectives*, **6**: 107–132.

——— and Robert Pindyck (1994). *Investment Under Uncertainty*. Princeton: Princeton University Press.

Dorfman, Robert, Paul A. Samuelson, and Robert M. Solow (1958). *Linear Programming and Economic Analysis*. New York: McGraw Hill.

Duffie D. (1992). *Dynamic Asset Pricing Theory*. Princeton: Princeton University Press.

Ehrlich, Isaac and Francis T. Lui (1992). "Corruption and Economic Growth." Hong Kong University of Science and Technology, Mimeo 1992 (paper presented at the 1993 AEA Meeting, Anaheim, CA).

Friedman, Milton (1957). *A Theory of the Consumption Function*. Princeton: Princeton University Press.

——— (1969). *The Optimum Quantity of Money and Other Essays*. Aldine Publishing Company.

Goffe, William L., Gary Ferrier, and John Rogers (1992). "Global Optimization of Statistical Function," in Hans M. Amman, D. A. Belsley, and Louis F. Pau (eds.), *Computational Economics and Econometrics*, Vol 1, Dordrecht: Kluwer.

Golub, Gene H., and Charles F. van Loan (1989). *Matrix Computations*. Baltimore: Johns Hopkins University Press.

Goodwin, R. M. (1951). "The Nonlinear Accelerator and the Persistence of Business Cycles," *Econometrica*, **19**: 1–17.

Grossman, Gene M. and Elhanan Helpman (1991a). "Quality Ladders in the Theory of Growth," *Review of Economic Studies*, **58**: 43–61.

——— (1991b). *Innovation and Growth in the Global Economy*. Cambridge: MIT Press.

Grossman, Sanford J. (1976). "On the Efficiency of Competitive Stock Markets Where Traders Have Diverse Information," *Journal of Finance*, **31**: 573–585.

Hansen, Lars and Kenneth Singleton (1982). "Generalized Instrumental Variables Estimation of Nonlinear Rational Expectations Models," *Econometrica*, **50**: 1269–1286.

Hao, Teh-Ming (1992). "Money and Interest in a Cash-In-Advance Economy: A Corrigendum," *Econometricia*, **59**: 435–440.

Harrod, F. (1948). *Toward a Dynamic Economics*. London: Macmillan.

Hellwig, M. F. (1980). "On the Aggregation of Information in Competitive Markets," *Journal of Economic Theory*, **22**: 477–498.

Henderson, James M. and Richard E. Quant (1980). Microeconomic Theory: A Mathematical Approach. New York: McGraw Hill.

Hicks, John R. (1937). "Mr. Keynes and the 'Classics': A Suggested Interpretation," *Econometrica*. Reprinted in J. R. Hicks, *Critical Essays in Monetary Theory*. New York: Oxford University Press (1967).

———(1939). *Value and Capital*. Oxford: Oxford University Press.

Ingersoll, Jr., Jonathan E. (1987). *Theory of Financial Decision Making*. Totowa, N.J.: Rowman and Littlefield.

Intriligator, Michael D. (1971). *Mathematical Optimization and Economic Theory*. Englewood Cliffs, N.J.: Prentice Hall.

Ito, K. and H. P. McKean, Jr. (1964). *Diffusion Processes and Their Sample Paths*. New York: Academic Press.

Jones, Larry E., Rodolfo E. Manuelli, and Peter E. Rossi (1993). "Optimal Taxation in Models of Endogenous Growth," *Journal of Political Economy*, **101**: 485–517.

Jorgenson, Dale W. (1967). "The Theory of Investment Behavior," in R. Farber (ed.), *The Determinants of Investment Behavior*. New York: National Bureau of Economic Research.

Judd K. (1992). "Projection Methods for Solving Aggregate Growth Models," *Journal of Economic Theory*, **58**: 410–452.

Keynes, John M. (1936). *The General Theory of Employment, Interest and Money*. Reprint, Tucson: Harbinger, Harcourt Brace and World (1964).

King, Robert G. and Mark. W. Watson (1991). "Comparing the Fit of Alternative Dynamic Models." Paper presented before the NBER Conference.

———, Charles I. Plosser and Sergio T. Rebelo (1988a). "Production, Growth, and Business Cycles: I. The Basic Neoclassical Model," *Journal of Monetary Economics*, **21**: 195–232.

———(1988b). "Production, Growth, and Business Cycles: II. New Directions," *Journal of Monetary Economics*, **21**: 309–341.

Kwan, Y. K. and Gregory C. Chow (1996). "Estimating Economic Effects of Political Movements in China," *Journal of Comparative Economics*, forthcoming.

———(1997). Chow's Method of Optimal Control: a Numerical Solution. *Journal of Economic Dynamics and Control*, forthcoming.

Kydland, Finn E. and Edward C. Prescott (1977). "Rules Rather Than Discretion: The Inconsistency of Optimal Plans," *Journal of Political Economy*, **25**: 473–491.

———and Edward C. Prescott (1982). "Time to Build and Aggregate Fluctuations," *Econometrica*, **50**: 1345–1370.

Langlois, Jean-Pierre P. and Jonathan A. Sachs (1992). "An Integrative Approach to Subgame Perfect Reaction Function Equilibria in Discounted Oligopoly Supergames," Cornell University, mimeo.

Long, John B. (1974). "Stock Prices, Inflation, and the Term Structure of Interest Rates." *Journal of Financial Economics*, **1**: 131–170.

———and Charles Plosser (1983). "Real Business Cycles," *Journal of Political Economy*, **91**: 1345–1370.

Lucas, Jr., Robert E. (1976). "Econometric Policy Evaluation: A Critique," *Journal of Monetary Economics* (*Supp.*), **1**: 19–46.

———(1978). "Asser Prices in an Exchange Economy," *Econometrica*, **46**: 1429–1445.

———and Nancy Stokey (1987). "Money and Interest in a Cash-In-Advance Economy," *Econometrica*, **555**: 491–514.

———(1992). "Money and Interest in a Cash-In-Advance Economy: A Reply," *Econometrica*, **59**: 441–442.

Lumsdaine, R., J. Stock, and D. Wise (1992). "Three Models of Retirement: Computational Complexity v. Predictive Validity," in D. Wise (ed.), *Topics in the Economics of Aging*. Chicago: University of Chicago Press.

Malliaris, A. G. and W. A. Brock (1982). *Stochastic Methods in Economics and Finance*. Rotterdam: Elsevier Science Publishers B. V.

Mankiev, N. Gregory (1989). "Real Business Cycles: A New Keynesian Perspective," *Journal of Economic Perspectives*, **3**: 79–90.

Marschak, Jacob (1953). "Econometric Measurements for Policy and Prediction," in W. C. Hood and T. C. Koopmans (eds.), *Studies in Econometric Methods*. New York: John Wiley & Sons.

Marshall, Alfred (1920). *Principles of Economics*, 8th edition. New York: MacMillan.

Mas-Collel, Andreu, M. D. Whinston and Jerry Green (1995). *Microeconomic Theory*. New York: Oxford University Press.

McKean Jr., H. P. (1969). *Stochastic Integrals*. New York: Academic Press.

Merton, Robert C. (1969). "Lifetime Portolio Selection Under Uncertainty, the Continuous-time Case," *Review of Economics and Statistics*, **51**: 247–257.

———(1970). "Optimum Consumption and Portfolio Rules in a Continuous-time Model," *Journal of Economic Theory*, **3**: 373–413.

———(1973). "An Intertemporal Capital Asset Pricing Model," *Econometrica*, **41**: 867–887.

Modigliani, Franco and Richard Blumberg (1954). "Utility Analysis and the Consumption Function: An Interpretation of Cross-Section Data," in K. Kurihara (ed.), *Post-Keynesian Economics*, New Brunswick, N.J.: Rutgers University Press.

Pearce, David and E. Stacchetti (1996). "Time Consistent Redistributive Taxation with Moral Hazard," *Journal of Economic Theory*, forthcoming.

Pindyck, R. S. (1991). "Irreversibility, Uncertainty, and Investment," *Journal of Economic Literature*, **29**: 1110–1148.

———(1988). "Irreversible Investment, Capacity Choice, and the Value of the Firm," *American Economic Review*, **79**: 969–985.

Plosser, Charles I. (1989). "Understanding Real Business Cycles," *Journal of Economic Perspectives*, **3**: 51–78.

Radner, Roy (1966). "Optimal Growth in a Linear-Logarithmic Economy," *International Economic Review*, **7**: 1–33.

Romer, Paul (1990). "Endogenous Technological Change," *Journal of Political Economy*, **98**: S71–102.

Rosenberg, Barr and J. A. Ohlson (1976). "The Stationary Distribution of Returns and Portfolio Separation in Capital Markets: A Fundamental Contradiction," *Journal of Financial and Quantitative Analysis*, **11**: 393–402.

Rotemberg, Julio and Garth Saloner (1986). "A Supergame-Theoretic Model of Price Wards During Booms," *American Economic Review*, **76**: 390–407.

———and Michael Woodford (1992). "Oligopolistic Pricing and Aggregate Demand," *Journal of Political Economy*, **100**: 1153–1207.

Rubinstein, A. (1979). Equilibrium in Supergames with the Overtaking Criterion," *Journal of Economic Theory*, **21**: 1–9.

Rust, John (1987). "Optimal Replacement of GMC Bus Engines: An Empirical Model of Harold Zurcher," *Econometrica*, **55**: 999–1033.

———(1994). "Structural Estimation of Markov Decision Processes," in Engle, Robert and D. L. McFadden, (eds.) *Handbook of Econometrics, vol. IV*. Amsterdam: North Holland Publishing Company.

Samuelson, Paul A. (1939). "Interactions Between the Multiplier Analysis and the Principle of Acceleration," *Review of Economics and Statistics*, **21**: 75–78.

———(1948). *Foundations of Economic Analysis*. Cambridge: Harvard University Press.

———(1969). "Lifetime Portfolio Selection by Dynamic Stochastic Programming," *Review of Economics and Statistics*, **51**: 239–246.

Sargent, Thomas (1987). *Dynamic Macroeconomic Theory*. Cambridge: Harvard University Press.

Schultz, T. W. (1961). "Investment in Human Capital," *American Economic Review*, **52**: 1–17.

Schumpter, J. A. (1939). *Business Cycles*. New York: McGraw Hill.

Sims, Christopher (1980). "Macroeconomics and Reality," *Econometrica*, **48**: 1–48.

Solow, Robert (1957). "Technical Change and the Aggregate Production Function," *Review of Economics and Statistics*, **39**: 312–320.

Stadler, George W. (1994). "Real Business Cycles," *Journal of Economic Literature*, **32**: 1750–1783.

Stokey, Nancy L. (1991). "Credible Public Policy," *Journal of Economic Dynamics and Control*, **15**: 627–656.

———(1995). "R & D and Economic Growth," *Review of Economic Studies*, **62**: 469–489.

———and Robert E. Lucas, Jr. (1989). *Recursive Methods in Dynamic Economics*. Cambridge: Harvard University Press.

Summers, Lawrence H. (1986). "Some Skeptical Observations on Real Business Cycle Theory," *Federal Reserve Bank Minnesota Review*, **10**: 23–27.

Taylor, J. and H. Uhlig (1990). "Solving Nonlinear Stochastic Growth Models: A Comparison of Alternative Solution Methods," *Journal of Business and Economic Statistics*, **8**: 1–19.

Uhlig, Harald (1995). "A Toolkit for Analyzing Nonlinear Dynamic Stochastic Models Easily." Discussion paper No. 9597. Center for Economic Research, Tilburg University.

Wang, J. (1993). "A Model of Intertemporal Asset Prices Under Asymmetric Information," *Review of Economic Studies*, **60**: 249–282.

Watson, Mark W. (1993). "Measures of Fit for Calibrated Models," *Journal of Political Economy*, **101**: 1011–1041.

Zhou, Chunsheng (1995). "Dynamic Portfolio Choice and Asset Pricing with Heterogeneous Information (I)," Chapter 1 of C. Zhou, *Information, Financial Markets, and Investment*. A dissertation submitted to the Department of Economics, Princeton University.

# List of Mathematical Statements

# Solutions to Selected Problems

## CHAPTER 2

Problem 2.1

(a) $r(x_t, u_t) = \ln(x_t^\alpha - u_t)$; $f(x_t, u_t) = u_t$.
(b) $r(x_t, u_t) = \ln(\exp(\alpha x_t) - \exp(u_t))$; $f(x_t, u_t) = u_t$.

## CHAPTER 3

Problem 3.5

The Lagrangean is

$$\mathscr{L} = (1-\sigma)^{-1}\sum_{t=1}^{\infty}\beta^{t-1}\Big\{\Big[1+\theta\ln\big(Q_t/Q_t^*\big)\big(\overline{H}+H_t\big)\big(1-h_t-q_t\big)\Big]^{1-\sigma}$$
$$-\beta^t\lambda_{H,t+1}\Big[H_{t+1}-A\big(\overline{H}+H_t\big)h_t\Big]-\beta^t\lambda_{Q,T+1}\Big[Q_{t+1}-B\big(\lambda\overline{H}+Q_t\big)q_t\Big]\Big\} \quad (1)$$

from which I derived the first-order conditions:

$$\beta^{-t+1}\frac{\partial\mathscr{L}}{\partial h_t} = -c_t^{-\sigma}\Big[1+\theta\ln\big(Q_t/Q_t^*\big)\Big]\big(\overline{H}+H_t\big)+\beta A\big(\overline{H}+H_t\big)\lambda_{H,t+1}=0 \quad (2)$$

$$\beta^{-t+1}\frac{\partial\mathscr{L}}{\partial q_t} = -c_t^{-\sigma}\Big[1+\theta\ln\big(Q_t/Q_t^*\big)\Big]\big(\overline{H}+H_t\big)+\beta B\big(\lambda\overline{H}+Q_t\big)\lambda_{Q,t+1}=0 \quad (3)$$

$$\beta^{-t+1}\frac{\partial\mathscr{L}}{\partial H_t} = -c_t^{-\sigma}\Big[1+\theta\ln\big(Q_t/Q_t^*\big)\Big]\big(1-h_t-q_t\big)+\lambda_{H,t}+\beta A h_t\lambda_{H,t+1}=0 \quad (4)$$

$$\beta^{-t+1}\frac{\partial\mathscr{L}}{\partial Q_t} = -c_t^{-\sigma}Q_t^{-1}\theta\big(\overline{H}+H_t\big)\big(1-h_t-q_t\big)-\lambda_{Q,t}+\beta B q_t\lambda_{Q,t+1}=0. \quad (5)$$

Substituting for $\beta A\lambda_{H,t+1}$ in (4) by the use of (2) and solving the resulting equation for $\lambda_{H,t}$, I obtain

$$\lambda_{Ht} = c_t^{-\sigma}\left[1+\theta\ln\left(Q_t/Q_t^*\right)\right]\left(1-q_t\right). \qquad (6)$$

Substituting for $\beta B\lambda_{Q,t+1}$ in (5) by the use of (3) and solving the resulting equation for $\lambda_{Q,t}$ I obtain

$$\lambda_{Qt} = c_t^{-\sigma}\left(\overline{H}+H_t\right)\left[\theta Q_t^{-1}(1-h_t-q_t)+q_t\left(1+\theta\ln\left(Q_t/Q_t^*\right)\right)\left(\lambda\overline{H}+Q_t\right)^{-1}\right]. \qquad (7)$$

Advancing the time subscripts of the above expressions for $\lambda_{Ht}$ and $\lambda_{Qt}$, respectively, by one and substituting into (2) and (3), respectively, one obtains the following relations for intertemporal substitutions between $c_t$ and $c_{t+1}$:

$$c_t^{-\sigma}\left[1+\theta\ln\left(Q_t/Q_t^*\right)\right] = \beta A c_{t+1}^{-\sigma}\left[1+\theta\ln\left(Q_{t+1}/Q_{t+1}^*\right)\right]\left(1-q_{t+1}\right) \qquad (8)$$

$$c_t^{-\sigma}\left[1+\theta\ln\left(Q_t/Q_t^*\right)\right]\left(\overline{H}+H_t\right)\left(\lambda\overline{H}+Q_t\right)^{-1} = \beta B\left(\overline{H}+H_{t+1}\right)c_{t+1}^{-\sigma}$$

$$\times\left[\theta Q_{t+1}^{-1}\left(1-h_{t+1}-q_{t+1}\right)+q_{t+1}\left(1+\theta\ln\left(Q_{t+1}/Q_{t+1}^*\right)\right)\left(\lambda\overline{H}+Q_{t+1}\right)^{-1}\right]. \qquad (9)$$

For an individual with an average value of political capital, $Q_t/Q_t^*$ equals one, and the growth of consumption by the equation for $c_t$ is

$$\left(c_{t+1}/c_t\right) = \left[\left(\overline{H}+H_{t+1}\right)\left(1-h_{t+1}-q_{t+1}\right)\right]/\left[\left(\overline{H}+H_t\right)\left(1-h_t-q_t\right)\right]. \qquad (10)$$

By equations (8) and (9), I have

$$\left(c_{t+1}/c_t\right)^{\sigma} = \beta A\left(1-q_{t+1}\right) \equiv \beta R_h \qquad (11)$$

$$\left(c_{t+1}/c_t\right)^{\sigma} = \beta\left(\theta M_t + N_t\right) \equiv \beta R_q, \qquad (12)$$

in which

$$M_t = \left[\left(\overline{H}+H_{t+1}\right)\left(1-h_{t+1}-q_{t+1}\right)\right]/\left[q_t\left(\overline{H}+H_t\right)\right]$$

$$N_t = \left[\left(\overline{H}+H_{t+1}\right)q_{t+1}Q_{t+1}\right]/\left[\left(\overline{H}+H_t\right)q_t\left(\overline{H}+Q_{t+1}\right)\right].$$

## CHAPTER 5

### Problem 5.1

Divide the dynamic constraint for $k_{t+1}$ by $z_t$, given $\ln(z_t/z_{t-1}) = \gamma + \varepsilon_t$

$$k_{t+1}/z_t = (1-\delta)\left(k_t/z_{t-1}\right)\left(z_{t-1}/z_t\right) + k_t^{1-\alpha}n_t^{\alpha}z_t^{\alpha-1}\left(z_{t-1}/z_{t-1}\right)^{1-\alpha} - c_t/z_t$$

$$\bar{k}_{t+1} = (1-\delta)\bar{k}_t\left(z_t/z_{t-1}\right)^{-1} + \bar{k}_t^{1-\alpha}n_t^{\alpha}\left(z_t/z_{t-1}\right)^{\alpha-1} - \bar{c}_t$$

Take log of this equation, and approximate the function $f(\ln(z_t/z_{t-1}), \ln \bar{k}_t, \ln \bar{c}_t, \ln n_t)$ by a linear function about the steady state $\gamma$, $\ln \bar{k}$, $\ln \bar{c}$, and $\ln n$ of the deterministic model under optimal control.

$$\begin{aligned}
\ln \bar{k}_{t+1} &= \ln\left\{(1-\delta)\bar{k}e^{-\gamma} + \bar{k}^{1-\alpha}n^{\alpha}e^{(\alpha-1)\gamma} - \bar{c}\right\} \\
&\quad + \{\ldots\}^{-1}\left[-(1-\delta)\bar{k}e^{-\gamma} + (\alpha-1)\bar{k}^{1-\alpha}n^{\alpha}e^{(\alpha-1)\gamma}\right]\left(\ln(z_t/z_{t-1}) - \gamma\right) \\
&\quad + \{\ldots\}^{-1}\left[(1-\delta)\bar{k}e^{-\gamma} + (1-\alpha)\bar{k}^{1-\alpha}n^{\alpha}e^{(\alpha-1)\gamma}\right]\left(\ln \bar{k}_t - \ln \bar{k}\right) \\
&\quad - \{\ldots\}^{-1}\bar{c}(\ln \bar{c}_t - \ln \bar{c}) + \{\ldots\}^{-1}\alpha\bar{k}^{1-\alpha}n^{\alpha}e^{(\alpha-1)\gamma}(\ln n_t - \ln n) \\
&\equiv \ln \bar{k} + a_{21}\left(\ln(z_t/z_{t-1}) - \gamma\right) + a_{22}\left(\ln \bar{k}_t - \ln \bar{k}\right) + c_{21}\left(\ln \bar{c}_t - \ln \bar{c}\right) + c_{22}(\ln n_t - \ln n).
\end{aligned}$$

The dynamic evolution of the state variables follows:

$$\begin{bmatrix} \ln(z_{t+1}/z_t) - \gamma \\ \ln \bar{k}_{t+1} - \ln \bar{k} \end{bmatrix} = \begin{bmatrix} 0 & 0 \\ a_{21} & a_{22} \end{bmatrix} \begin{bmatrix} \ln(z_t/z_{t-1}) - \gamma \\ \ln \bar{k}_t - \ln \bar{k} \end{bmatrix} + \begin{bmatrix} 0 & 0 \\ c_{21} & c_{22} \end{bmatrix} \begin{bmatrix} \ln \bar{c}_t - \ln \bar{c} \\ \ln n_t - \ln n \end{bmatrix} + \begin{bmatrix} \varepsilon_{t+1} \\ 0 \end{bmatrix},$$

in which

$$\bar{k} = (1-\delta)\bar{k}e^{-\gamma} + \bar{k}^{1-\alpha}n^{\alpha}e^{(\alpha-1)\gamma} - \bar{c} \qquad n \text{ and } \bar{c} \text{ yet to be determined}$$

$$a_{21} = -(1-\delta)e^{-\gamma} + (\alpha-1)\bar{k}^{-\alpha}n^{\alpha}e^{(\alpha-1)\gamma} \qquad c_{21} = -\bar{k}^{-1}\bar{c}$$

$$a_{22} = (1-\delta)e^{-\gamma} + (1-\alpha)\bar{k}^{-\alpha}n^{\alpha}e^{(\alpha-1)\gamma} \qquad c_{22} = \alpha\bar{k}^{-\alpha}n^{\alpha}e^{(\alpha-1)\gamma}.$$

The quadratic approximation of $r$ is:

$$\begin{aligned}
r &= \ln \bar{c}_t + \ln z_t + \theta \ln\left[\mathrm{N} - e^{\ln n_t}\right] \\
&= \ln \bar{c}_t + \theta \ln\left[\mathrm{N} - e^{\ln n}\right] - \theta\left[\mathrm{N} - n\right]^{-1} e^{\ln n}\left[\ln n_t - \ln n\right] \\
&\quad - \frac{1}{2}\theta\left[(\mathrm{N}-n)^{-2}n^2 + (\mathrm{N}-n)^{-1}n\right]\left[\ln n_t - \ln n\right]^2 + \ln z_t.
\end{aligned}$$

The term $\ln z_t$ can be ignored in optimization, because it is independent of control.

$$\frac{\partial r}{\partial \ln \bar{c}_t} = 1; \quad \frac{\partial r}{\partial \ln n_t} = -\theta\left[\mathrm{N} - n\right]^{-1} n - \theta(\mathrm{N}-n)^{-2}\mathrm{N}n\left[\ln n_t - \ln n\right].$$

The first-order conditions are, with $x_t' = (\ln(z_t/z_{t-1}) - \gamma, \ln \bar{k}_{t+1} - \ln \bar{k})$, and $u_t' = (\ln \bar{c}_t - \ln \bar{c}_1, \ln n_t - \ln n)$:

$$(1) \quad \underset{\mathrm{K}_2}{\begin{bmatrix} 0 \\ -\theta(\mathrm{N}-n)^{-2}\mathrm{N}n \end{bmatrix}} x_t + \underset{k_2}{\begin{bmatrix} 1 \\ -\theta(\mathrm{N}-n)^{-1}n \end{bmatrix}} + \beta\mathrm{C}'\mathrm{H}(\mathrm{A}x_t + \mathrm{C}u_t) + \beta\mathrm{C}'h = 0$$

$$(2) \quad \lambda_t = \mathrm{H}x_t + h = \beta\mathrm{A}'\mathrm{H}\left[(\mathrm{A} + \mathrm{CG})x_t + \mathrm{Cg}\right].$$

The optimal control function is $u_t = \mathrm{G}x_t + g$.

To obtain the parameters G, $g$ of the optimal control function and the parameters H and $h$ of $\lambda$, solve

$$G = -(K_2 + \beta C'HC)^{-1} \beta C'HA$$

$$H = \beta A'H(A + CG),$$

iteratively, and

$$g = -(K_2 + \beta C'HC)^{-1}[k_2 + \beta C'h]$$

$$h = \beta A'HCg + \beta A'h$$

iteratively.

To find the steady state $\bar{c}$ and $n$, we solve the following constrained maximization problem

$$\mathcal{L} = \sum_{t=0}^{\infty} \beta^t \left\{ \ln \bar{c} + \theta \ln n(N-n) - \beta\lambda\left[\bar{k} - (1-\delta)\bar{k}e^{-\gamma} - \bar{k}^{1-\alpha} n^{\alpha} e^{(\alpha-1)\gamma} + \bar{c}\right]\right\}.$$

The first-order conditions are:

$$(1)\quad (1-\beta)\frac{\partial \mathcal{L}}{\partial \bar{c}} = \bar{c}^{-1} - \beta\lambda = 0 \quad \beta\lambda = \bar{c}^{-1} = \bar{k}^{-1}\left[-1 + (1-\delta)\bar{e}^{\gamma} + \bar{k}^{-\alpha} n^{\alpha} e^{(\alpha-1)\gamma}\right]^{-1}$$

$$(2)\quad (1-\beta)\frac{\partial \mathcal{L}}{\partial n} = -\theta(N-n)^{-1} + \beta\lambda\alpha\bar{k}^{1-\alpha} n^{\alpha-1} e^{(\alpha-1)\gamma} = 0$$

$$(3)\quad (1-\beta)\frac{\partial \mathcal{L}}{\partial \bar{k}} = -\beta\lambda\left[1 - (1-\delta)e^{-\gamma} - (1-\alpha)\bar{k}^{-\alpha} n^{\alpha} e^{(\alpha-1)\gamma}\right] = 0.$$

$$(1) \text{ and } (2) \Rightarrow \theta(N-n)^{-1} = \bar{k}^{-1}\left[-1 + (1-\delta)e^{-\gamma} + \bar{k}^{-\alpha} n^{\alpha} e^{(\alpha-1)\gamma}\right]^{-1} \alpha\bar{k}^{1-\alpha} n^{\alpha-1} e^{(\alpha-1)\gamma}$$

$$\theta\bar{k}\left[-1 + (1-\delta)e^{-\gamma} + \bar{k}^{-\alpha} n^{\alpha} e^{(\alpha-1)\gamma}\right] = (N-n)\alpha\bar{k}^{1-\alpha} n^{\alpha-1} e^{(\alpha-1)\gamma}.$$

Using (3), left side $= \theta\bar{k}\left[\alpha\bar{k}^{-\alpha} n^{\alpha} e^{(\alpha-1)\gamma}\right] \quad \therefore \theta n = N - n$ or $n = N/(1+\theta)$.

$$(3) \Rightarrow \bar{k}^{\alpha} = \left[1 - (1-\delta)e^{-\gamma}\right]^{-1}(1-\alpha) n^{\alpha} e^{(\alpha-1)\gamma}$$

$$\bar{k} = \left[1 - (1-\delta)e^{-\gamma}\right]^{-1/\alpha}(1-\alpha)^{1/\alpha} e^{(\alpha-1)\gamma/\alpha} N/(1+\theta).$$

$$(1) \Rightarrow \bar{c} = \bar{k}\left\{-1 + (1-\delta)e^{-\gamma} + \left[1-(1-\delta)e^{-\gamma}\right](1-\alpha)^{-1} n^{-\alpha} e^{-(\alpha-1)\gamma} \cdot n^{\alpha} e^{(\alpha-1)\gamma}\right\}$$

$$= \left[1-(1-\delta)e^{-\gamma}\right]\alpha(1-\alpha)^{-1}\bar{k} = \left[1-(1-\delta)e^{-\gamma}\right]^{(\alpha-1)/\alpha}\alpha(1-\alpha)^{(1-\alpha)/\alpha} e^{(\alpha-1)\gamma/\alpha} N/(1+\theta).$$

## CHAPTER 7

Problem 7.1

$$F = e^{y} \qquad dy = f dt + s dz$$

$$dF = \left[\frac{\partial F}{\partial t} + \frac{\partial F}{\partial y}\cdot f + \frac{1}{2}Fyy\cdot s^2\right]dt + \frac{\partial F}{\partial y}sdz$$

$$= \left[e^y f + \frac{1}{2}e^y s^2\right]dt + e^{y_{sdz}} = F\left(f + \frac{1}{2}s^2\right)dt + Fsdz.$$

Problem 7.2

$$F = y'K(t)y \quad dy = Aydt + dv \quad \mathrm{Cov}(dv) = \Sigma(t)dt$$

$$dF = \left[\frac{\partial F}{\partial t} + \left(\frac{\partial F}{\partial y}\right)'\cdot Ay + \frac{1}{2}tr(Fyy\Sigma)\right]dt + \left(\frac{\partial F}{\partial y}\right)' dv$$

$$= \left[y'\frac{dK}{dt}y + 2y'K'Ay + trK\Sigma\right]dt + 2y'Kdv.$$

Problem 7.3

Using the partitioned inverse as given in the solution to problem 7.4, write

$$\begin{bmatrix} \Omega & \begin{matrix}1\\ \vdots \\ 1\end{matrix} \\ 1\ldots 1 & 0\end{bmatrix} = \begin{bmatrix} \Sigma\left\{I - \gamma^{-1}\begin{bmatrix}1\ldots 1\\ \ldots \\ 1\ldots 1\end{bmatrix}\Sigma\right\} & \gamma^{-1}\Sigma\begin{bmatrix}1\\ \vdots \\ 1\end{bmatrix} \\ (1\ldots 1)\Sigma\gamma^{-1} & -\gamma^{-1}\end{bmatrix},$$

which is identical to (7.49).

Problem 7.4

Let $\Sigma^{-1} = \Omega$

$\sigma^2 = \text{var} = \delta'\Omega\delta;\quad \text{mean} = \delta'\alpha;\quad \delta'l = 1;\quad l = \begin{bmatrix}1\\ \vdots \\ 1\end{bmatrix}$

min var. subject to mean $= m$ and $\delta'l = 1$

$$L = \delta'\Omega\delta + 2\mu_1(\delta'\alpha - m) + 2\mu_2(\delta l - 1)$$

$$\frac{\partial L}{\partial \delta} = 2\Omega\delta - 2\mu_1\alpha - 2\mu_2 l = 0$$

$\alpha'\delta = m$
$l'\delta = 1$

$$\begin{bmatrix}\Omega & \alpha & l\\ \alpha' & & \\ l' & & 0\end{bmatrix}\begin{bmatrix}\delta\\ \mu_1\\ \mu_2\end{bmatrix} = \begin{bmatrix}0\\ m\\ 1\end{bmatrix}$$

First, find the partioned inverse:

$$\begin{bmatrix} \Omega & \alpha \\ \alpha' & 0 \end{bmatrix}\begin{bmatrix} A & B \\ B' & C \end{bmatrix} = \begin{bmatrix} I & 0 \\ 0 & I \end{bmatrix}$$

$$\Omega A + \alpha B' = I$$
$$\Omega B + \alpha C = 0$$
$$\alpha' A = 0$$
$$\alpha' B = I$$
$$A = \Omega^{-1}(I - \alpha B')$$
$$B = -\Omega^{-1}\alpha C$$
$$\alpha' B = -\alpha'\Omega^{-1}\alpha C = I$$
$$\therefore C = -(\alpha'\Omega^{-1}\alpha)^{-1}$$
$$A = \Omega^{-1}\left\{I - \alpha(\alpha'\Omega^{-1}\alpha)^{-1}\alpha'\Omega^{-1}\right\}$$

$$\alpha'\Omega^{-1}l = \sum_{j=1}^{m}\sum_{i}\sigma_{ij}\cdot\alpha_i = \theta; \quad \nu = \alpha'\Omega^{-1}\alpha; \quad \gamma = l'\Omega^{-1}l$$

$$\delta = A\cdot 0 + \Omega^{-1}[\alpha l]\left[\begin{pmatrix}\alpha' \\ l'\end{pmatrix}\Omega^{-1}(\alpha \ l)\right]^{-1}\begin{bmatrix} m \\ 1 \end{bmatrix}$$

$$= \Sigma[\alpha \ l]\begin{bmatrix} \nu & \theta \\ \theta & \gamma \end{bmatrix}^{-1}\begin{bmatrix} m \\ 1 \end{bmatrix}$$

$$= \frac{1}{\nu\gamma - \theta^2}\Sigma[\alpha \ l]\begin{bmatrix} \gamma & -\theta \\ -\theta & \nu \end{bmatrix}\begin{bmatrix} m \\ 1 \end{bmatrix}$$

$$\hat{\delta} = \frac{1}{\nu\gamma - \theta^2}\Sigma\left[(\gamma m - \theta)\alpha + (\nu - \theta m)l\right]$$

$$\text{min var} = \left(\frac{1}{\nu\gamma - \theta^2}\right)^2\left[(\gamma m - \theta)\alpha' + (\nu - \theta m)l'\right]\Omega^{-1}\Omega\Sigma\left[(\gamma m - \theta)\alpha + (\nu - \theta m)l\right]$$

$$= \left(\frac{1}{\nu\gamma - \theta^2}\right)^2\left[(\gamma m - \theta)^2\nu + 2(\gamma m - \theta)(\nu - \theta m)\theta + (\nu - \theta m)^2\gamma\right]$$

(1) $\sigma^2 = (\nu\Gamma - \theta^2)^{-1}\left[\gamma m^2 - 2m\theta + \nu\right]$ after some algebra.

One wants
$$\frac{d\sigma}{dm} = \frac{\sigma}{m}$$

or
$$\frac{d\sigma^2}{dm} = 2\sigma\frac{d\sigma}{dm} = \frac{2\sigma^2}{m}$$

$$\frac{d\sigma^2}{dm} = \frac{1}{\left(\nu\gamma - \theta^2\right)}\left[2\gamma m - 2\theta\right] = \frac{2\sigma^2}{m}$$

$$\sigma^2 = m\left(\gamma m - \theta\right)/\left(\nu\gamma - \theta^2\right)$$

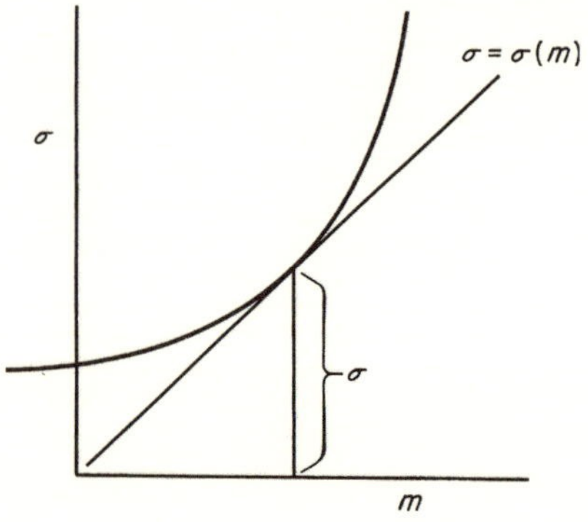


Substituting above for $\sigma^2$ in (1), one gets

$$m\left(\gamma m - \theta\right) = \gamma m^2 - 2m\theta + \nu \qquad \therefore m = \frac{\nu}{\theta}$$

$$\therefore \hat{\delta} = \frac{1}{\nu\gamma - \theta^2}\cdot\left(\gamma\frac{\nu}{\theta} - \theta\right)\Sigma\alpha = \frac{1}{\theta}\Sigma\alpha = \frac{1}{l'\Sigma\alpha}\Sigma\alpha \qquad \text{Q.E.D.}$$

Problem 7.5

$$u\left(c, t\right) = e^{-\rho t}\gamma^{-1}c^{\gamma}$$

The optimum consumption and investment are determined by (7.45) and (7.46), which become

$$e^{-\rho t}c^{\gamma-1} - V_w = 0$$

$$WV_{ww}\sigma^2 w + V_w = 0.$$

When the solutions for $c$ and $w$ are substituted back into the partial differential equation $u(c, t) + \mathcal{L}_w[V(W, t)] = 0$, one gets

$$\frac{1-\gamma}{\gamma}V_w^{\gamma/(\gamma-1)}e^{-\rho t/(1-\gamma)} + V_t + WV_w r - \frac{\left(\alpha - r\right)^2}{2\sigma^2}\frac{V_w^2}{V_{ww}} = 0$$

By assuming a convenient bequest function $V[W(T), T] = \varepsilon^{1-\gamma}e^{-\rho t}W(T)^{\gamma}/\gamma$ for small positive $\varepsilon$, one finds the solution

$$V(W, t) = b(t)e^{-\rho t}W^{\gamma}/\gamma$$

for this partial differential equation. The derivatives of V are

$$\frac{\partial V}{\partial W} = V_w = b(t)e^{-\rho t}W^{\gamma-1}$$

$$\frac{\partial^2 V}{\partial W^2} = V_{ww} = (\gamma - 1)b(t)e^{-\rho t}W^{\gamma-2}$$

$$\frac{\partial V}{\partial t} = \dot{b}(t)e^{-\rho t}\,W^{\gamma}/\gamma - \rho b(t)e^{-\rho t}\,W^{\gamma}/\gamma$$

Substituting these derivatives into the above partial differential equation and simplifying, one has

$$\dot{b}(t) = \left\{\rho - \gamma\left[\frac{(\alpha - r)^2}{2\sigma^2(1-\gamma)} + r\right]\right\}b(t) - (1-\gamma)b(t)^{-\gamma/1-\gamma}$$

The terminal condition is

$$V(W(T), T) = \frac{b(T)}{\gamma}e^{-\rho t}[W(T)]^{\gamma}, \text{ with } b(T) = \varepsilon^{1-\gamma}.$$

Therefore, $\varepsilon^{1-\gamma}e^{-\pi t}[W(T)]^{\gamma}/\gamma$ is a mathematically convenient bequest valuation function.

Problem 7.6

Using the function $V(W, t) = b(t)e^{-\rho t}W^{\gamma}/\gamma$ and the optimal control equations for $c$ and $w$, one finds

$$\hat{c}(t) = b(t)^{1/\gamma-1}W(t) \text{ and } \hat{w}(t) = \frac{\alpha - r}{\sigma^2(1-\gamma)}.$$

The solution for $b(t)$ based on its differential equation given in the solution to problem 7.5 is

$$b(t) = \left\{\frac{1}{\nu}\left[1 + (\nu\varepsilon - 1)e^{\nu(t-T)}\right]\right\}^{1-\gamma},$$

in which

$$\nu = \left\{\rho - \gamma\left[\frac{(\alpha - r)^2}{2\sigma^2(1-\gamma)} + r\right]\right\}(1-\gamma)^{-1} \equiv \frac{\mu}{1-\gamma}.$$

Problem 7.8

$$(7.79)=\int_{\log c}^{\infty}\frac{1}{\sqrt{2\pi s}\sqrt{\mathrm{T}-t}}\exp\left\{-\frac{1}{2}\cdot\frac{\left[x-x_t-\left(r-\frac{1}{2}s^2\right)(\mathrm{T}-t)\right]^2-2xs^2(\mathrm{T}-t)}{s^2(\mathrm{T}-t)}\right\}dx$$

$$-c\int_{\log c}^{\infty}\frac{1}{\sqrt{2\pi s}\sqrt{\mathrm{T}-t}}\exp\left\{-\frac{1}{2}\cdot\frac{\left[x-x_t-\left(r-\frac{1}{2}s^2\right)(\mathrm{T}-t)\right]^2}{s^2(\mathrm{T}-t)}\right\}dx.$$

Let $k=x_t+(r-\frac{1}{2}s^2)(\mathrm{T}-t)$. The exponent of the first term becomes

$$-\frac{1}{2}\cdot\frac{x^2-2kx+k^2-2xs^2(\mathrm{T}-t)}{s^2(\mathrm{T}-t)}$$

$$=-\frac{1}{2}\cdot\frac{x^2-2x\left[k+s^2(\mathrm{T}-t)\right]+\left[k+s^2(\mathrm{T}-t)\right]^2-\left[k+s^2(\mathrm{T}-t)\right]^2+k^2}{s^2(\mathrm{T}-t)}$$

$$=-\frac{1}{2}\cdot\frac{\left[x-x_t-\left(r+\frac{1}{2}s^2\right)(\mathrm{T}-t)\right]^2-\left[x_t+\left(r+\frac{1}{2}s^2\right)(\mathrm{T}-t)\right]^2+\left[x_t+\left(r-\frac{1}{2}s^2\right)(\mathrm{T}-t)\right]^2}{s^2(\mathrm{T}-t)}$$

$$=-\frac{1}{2}\cdot\frac{\left[x-x_t-\left(r+\frac{1}{2}s^2\right)(\mathrm{T}-t)\right]^2-2s^2(\mathrm{T}-t)\left[x_t+r(\mathrm{T}-t)\right]}{s^2(\mathrm{T}-t)}$$

$$=-\frac{1}{2}\cdot\frac{\left[x-x_t-\left(r+\frac{1}{2}s^2\right)(\mathrm{T}-t)\right]^2}{s^2(\mathrm{T}-t)}+\left[x_t+r(\mathrm{T}-t)\right]$$

Problem 7.10

Using (7.100) for $d\lambda$, equation (7.96) becomes

$$e_\pi\lambda dt+\mathrm{B}_\pi\left(\mathrm{B}_\pi'\lambda_{\mathrm{W}}q+\mathrm{B}_{\mathrm{N}}'\lambda_{\mathrm{N}}\right)dt=0\Rightarrow$$

$$q=-\lambda_{\mathrm{W}}^{-1}\left(\mathrm{B}_\pi\mathrm{B}_\pi'\right)^{-1}\left[\lambda e_\pi+\mathrm{B}_\pi\mathrm{B}_{\mathrm{N}}'\lambda_{\mathrm{N}}\right]. \tag{1}$$

Using (7.100) for $d\lambda$, equation (7.97) yields the following partial differential equation for $\lambda$:

$$(r-\rho)\lambda+\lambda_{\mathrm{W}}\left(r\mathrm{W}-c+q'e_\pi\right)-\lambda_{\mathrm{N}}'\mathrm{A}_{\mathrm{N}}\mathrm{N}+\frac{1}{2}\lambda_{\mathrm{WW}}q'\mathrm{B}_\pi\mathrm{B}_\pi'q+\lambda_{\mathrm{WN}}'\mathrm{B}_{\mathrm{N}}\mathrm{B}_\pi'q$$

$$+\frac{1}{2}tr\left[\lambda_{\mathrm{NN'}}\mathrm{B}_{\mathrm{N}}\mathrm{B}_{\mathrm{N}}'\right]=0 \tag{2}$$

Using (1) to eliminate $q$ in equation (2), one has only one control variable $c$ in the partial differential equation.

$$(r-\rho)\lambda + \lambda_W(rW - c) - e'_\pi(B_\pi B'_\pi)^{-1}[\lambda e_\pi + B_\pi B'_N \lambda_N] - \lambda'_N A_N N$$
$$+\frac{1}{2}\frac{\lambda_{WW}}{\lambda_W^2}[\lambda e_\pi + B_\pi B'_N\lambda_N]'(B_\pi B'_\pi)^{-1}[\lambda e_\pi + B_\pi B'_N \lambda_N]$$
$$-\frac{\lambda'_{WN}}{\lambda_w} B_N B'_\pi (B_\pi B'_\pi)^{-1}[\lambda e_\pi + B_\pi B'_N \lambda_N] + \frac{1}{2} tr[\lambda_{NN'} B_N B'_N] = 0 \quad (3)$$

Using (7.95) to replace the partial derivatives of $\lambda$ by the partial derivatives of $c$

$$\lambda_W = -\phi\lambda c_W; \quad \lambda_{WW} = \phi\lambda(\phi c_W^2 - c_{WW}); \quad \lambda_N = -\phi\lambda c_N$$

$$\lambda_{WN} = \phi\lambda(\phi c_W c_N - c_{WN}); \quad \lambda_{NN'} = \phi\lambda(\phi c_N c_{N'} - c_{NN'}); \quad \frac{\lambda}{\lambda_W} = \frac{1}{\phi c_W}$$

we have a partial differential equation in $c$:

$$(r-\rho) - \phi(rW - c)c_W - e'_\pi(B_\pi B'_\pi)^{-1}(e_\pi - \phi B_\pi B'_N c_N) + \phi N' A_N c_N$$
$$+\frac{1}{2}(e_\pi - \phi B_\pi B'_N c_N)'(B_\pi B'_\pi)^{-1}(e_\pi - \phi B_\pi B'_N c_N)[1 - c_{WW}/(\phi c_W^2)]$$
$$+(e_\pi - \phi B_\pi B'_N c_N)'(B_\pi B'_\pi)^{-1} B_\pi B'_N(\phi c_N - c_{WN}/c_W) + \frac{\phi^2}{2} c'_N B_N B'_N c_N$$
$$-\frac{\phi}{2} tr[c_{NN'} B_N B'_N] = 0. \quad (4)$$

If one assumes the solution to be linear in W and quadratic in N

$$c(W, N) = rW + k + h'N + \frac{1}{2}N'HN, \quad (5)$$

one can substitute its derivatives $c_W = r$, $c_{WW} = 0$, $c_{WN} = 0$, $c_N = h + HN$, and $c_{NN'} = H$ into the partial differential equation (4) and solve for the unknown $k$, $h$, and G:

$$(r-\rho) + \phi rk + \phi rh'N + \frac{1}{2}\phi rN'HN - e'_\pi(B_\pi B'_\pi)^{-1}[e_\pi - \phi B_\pi B'_N(h + HN)]$$
$$+\phi N' A_N h + \phi N' A_N HN + \frac{1}{2} e'_\pi (B_\pi B'_\pi)^{-1} e_\pi - \phi e'_\pi (B_\pi B'_\pi)^{-1} B_\pi B'_N (h + HN)$$
$$+\frac{1}{2}\phi^2(N'H' + h')(B_N B'_\pi)(B_\pi B'_\pi)^{-1}(B_\pi B'_N)(HN + h) + \phi e'_\pi (B_\pi B'_\pi)^{-1} B_\pi B'_N h$$
$$+\phi e'_\pi (B_\pi B'_\pi)^{-1} B_\pi B'_N HN - \phi^2(h' + N'H')B_N B'_\pi (B_\pi B'_\pi)^{-1}[B_\pi B'_N(h + HN) - e_\pi/\phi]$$
$$+\frac{\phi^2}{2}(h + HN)' B_N B'_N (h + HN) - \frac{\phi}{2} tr[HB_N B'_N]$$

This equation is quadratic in N. Setting the matrix of the quadratic form, the coefficient vector and the scalar constant equal to zero will yield solutions to the parameters H, $h$, and $k$ of the consumption function, respectively.

## CHAPTER 8

Problem 8.3

$$\mathcal{L} = \sum_{s=t}^{T} \beta^{s-t}\Big\{u_s\left[x_s^{\theta_1} + \mu_1 + \varepsilon_s(1)\right] + (1-u_s)\left[(\mu_2\theta_2 x_s)^{\theta_1} + \varepsilon_s(0)\right]$$
$$- \beta\lambda_{s+1}\left[x_{s+1} - u_s \mathrm{Y}_{s+1} - (1-u_s)\mathrm{B}_{s+1}(r)\right]\Big\}$$

The first-order conditions are obtained by setting $\partial\mathcal{L}/\partial x_s = 0$ and $\Delta\mathcal{L}_u = \mathcal{L}(u_s = 1) - \mathcal{L}(u_s = 0)$. Read Lumsdaine, Stock and Wise (1992).

## CHAPTER 9

Problem 9.5

Combining equations (9.17) and (9.18) yields:

$$1 = \beta \mathrm{E}_t\left\{c_t^*\left[(1-\alpha)z_{t+1}^{*\,(\alpha-1)} k_{t+1}^{*-\alpha} + z_{t+1}^{*-1}\right]\Big/ c_{t+1}^*\right\}. \tag{1}$$

When $c^*$ is replaced by C $\exp(\tilde{c})$ and/or $\mathrm{C}(1 + \tilde{c})$, etc.:

$$0 = \mathrm{E}\left\{\tilde{c}_t - \tilde{c}_{t+1} - \tilde{z}_{t+1} + \left[(\mathrm{Z/K})^\alpha(1-\alpha)\alpha(\tilde{z}_{t+1} - \tilde{k}_{t+1})\right]\Big/\left[(\mathrm{Z/K})^\alpha(1-\alpha)+1\right]\right\}$$
$$\equiv \mathrm{E}\left\{\tilde{c}_t - \tilde{c}_{t+1} - \tilde{z}_{t+1} + \delta_3\left[\tilde{z}_{t+1} - \tilde{k}_{t+1}\right]\right\}$$

or

$$\tilde{c}_t = \mathrm{E}_t\left[\tilde{c}_{t+1} + \delta_3\tilde{k}_{t+1}\right];\quad \delta_3(\mathrm{Z/K})^\alpha(1-\alpha)\alpha\Big/\left[(\mathrm{Z/K})^\alpha(1-\alpha)+1\right]. \tag{2}$$

Assume a feedback control equation

$$\tilde{c}_t = \mathrm{G}_1\tilde{z}_t + \mathrm{G}_2\tilde{k}_t \tag{3}$$

and substitute for $\tilde{c}_{t+1}$ in (2):

$$\tilde{c}_t = \mathrm{E}_t\left[\mathrm{G}_1\tilde{z}_{t+1} + \mathrm{G}_2\tilde{k}_{t+1} + \delta_3\tilde{k}_{t+1}\right] = \mathrm{E}_t\left[(\mathrm{G}_2 + \delta_3)\tilde{k}_{t+1}\right]. \tag{4}$$

The capital accumulation equation (9.8) can be combined with equation (3) to give

$$\tilde{k}_{t+1} = \delta_1\tilde{k}_t - \delta_1\tilde{z}_t + \delta_2\tilde{c}_t = (\delta_1 + \delta_2\mathrm{G}_2)\tilde{k}_t + (-\delta_1 + \delta_2\mathrm{G}_1)\tilde{z}_t. \tag{5}$$

When (5) is used to replace $\tilde{k}_{t+1}$ in (4), one obtains

$$\tilde{c}_t = \mathrm{E}_t\left[(\mathrm{G}_2 + \delta_3)(\delta_1 + \delta_2\mathrm{G}_2)\tilde{k}_t + (\mathrm{G}_2 + \delta_3)(-\delta_1 + \delta_2\mathrm{G}_1)\tilde{z}_t\right]. \tag{6}$$

Equating coefficients of (3) and (6) gives

$$G_2 = \left(G_2 + \delta_3\right)\left(\delta_1 + \delta_2 G_2\right) \tag{7}$$

$$G_1 = \left(G_2 + \delta_3\right)\left(-\delta_1 + \delta_2 G_1\right). \tag{8}$$

Equation (7) is a quadratic equation in $G_2$. Given $G_2$, (8) is a linear equation in $G_1$.

# Index

Department of Agricultural Economics
and Rural Sociology
The Pennsylvania State University
103 Armsby Building
University Park, PA 16802-5600